Cognitive Superiority

Dean S. Hartley III • Kenneth O. Jobson

Cognitive Superiority

Information to Power

Springer

Dean S. Hartley III
Hartley Consulting
Oak Ridge, TN, USA

Kenneth O. Jobson
Psychiatry And Psychopharmacology
Knoxville, TN, USA

ISBN 978-3-030-60183-6 ISBN 978-3-030-60184-3 (eBook)
https://doi.org/10.1007/978-3-030-60184-3

This Springer imprint is published by the registered company Springer Nature Switzerland AG
The registered company address is: Gewerbestrasse 11, 6330 Cham, Switzerland

Foreword

This book represents a certain amount of work in its compilation; however, for us, it was a most challenging pleasure, not a chore. We are indebted to many for their guidance, correction, and polish. The wise Dr. Steve A. Martin was one of the first to help in our journey, R.I.P.

We thank Professor George Schweitzer for his excellent advice, particularly with regard to education, connectivity, and complex adaptive systems. Professor Paul Ashdown provided valued guidance on journalism and education. We thank COL Andrew Hall for his review, particularly with regard to cyber war and the current military thinking and approaches to cyber war, information war, and related topics. Dr. Chuck Jones gave us editorial comments and insights. We thank Ms. Marci Willison for her encouragement concerning the accessibility of the material to a general audience. We also thank Dr. David Penniman and Dr. John D. G. Rather for their reviews and suggestions.

Further, we thank our wives, Eileen Hartley and Harriet Jobson, for their help and forbearance.

The opinions expressed in this book should not be attributed to any part of the U.S. government. All errors and omissions are our own.

Praise for *Cognitive Superiority*

There have been increasing recent developments in many small intellectual centers of the world of the potential for cybercontrol of the basic thought processes (including even fundamental presuppositions) of large segments of the general population of the world. Hartley and Jobson have provided us with an unprecedented detailed introduction to this activity and its threat: what it is, what its basic components are, how it works, how it can be used (for weal and for woe), and particularly, how it can be counteracted. The relevance of these considerations to the future of the planet is of utmost import. They cannot and must not be ignored, especially with regard to international relations, including cyberterrorism and cyberwarfare. Its message is to all of us, and it is saying "Take heed!"

—George K. Schweitzer, Professor of Chemistry, University of Tennessee

Leadership is as much art as it is skill no matter what your area of expertise may be. Jobson and Hartley have done a remarkable job capturing what it takes to be a good leader by honing in on the powers of persuasion, effective communication and collaboration. They shine a bright light on how best to motivate people, individually and collectively. For me, this was a must read.

—Kenneth W. Lowe, Founder of HGTV and Retired Chairman, President and CEO of Scripps Networks Interactive, Inc.

Hartley and Jobson's *Cognitive Superiority: Information to Power* is an urgent call for clearer thinking about a new kind of information war that threatens our security, both national and personal. Drawing on the wisdom of the ancients as well as breaking news in science and technology that usually gets lost in the disinformation miasma, the authors provide a propulsive, comprehensive analysis with a plan of action. Failure to engage will wreak havoc as enemies, both foreign and domestic, break through the fissures in the lotus-eater culture and seize the narrative advantage. Most of the knowledge necessary to achieve cognitive superiority over the exigent threat is hidden in plain sight but has remained unassembled until this book.

—Paul Ashdown, PhD, Professor Emeritus, College of Communication and Information, University of Tennessee, Knoxville

In *Cognitive Superiority: Information to Power,* Hartley and Jobson provide a comprehensive exposition of the new battleground composed of the complex interactions of information, cyber, technology. This rapidly changing domain not only affects the security of nations in the classical sense, but also that of businesses, individuals, and the very conduct of government. In order to be successful in this domain, leaders must understand its components and phenomenology. This book goes long way in facilitating that understanding, and provides a framework for analysis that promotes sound decision-making.

—Andrew G. Loerch, PhD, Colonel, US Army (ret), Professor and Associate Chair, Department of Systems Engineering and Operations Research, George Mason University

Understanding the emerging bloodless battlefields of the twenty-first century: This is a detailed and well-structured exploration of the emerging bloodless battlefield where nations will strive for dominance. We are already aware of the power that social media can wield. Hartley and Jobson have described the larger context in which that power exists. This is a complicated context and their book tackles that complexity fearlessly and comprehensively.

—W. David Penniman, Former President, Association for Information Science and Technology (ASIS&T), Fellow of The American Association for the Advancement of Science (AAAS), retired informatician

This is fascinating and frightening at the same time!

—Curtis Blais, Research Faculty, Modeling Virtual Environments and Simulation (MOVES) Institute, Naval Postgraduate School (NPS), Monterey, California

Prologue to Warfare in a Cyber Age

The central axis of our time is unending accelerating change (Kelly 2016). The motif of the universe is connectivity (Schweitzer 2019). It is so at the quantum level, in physics, in chemistry, biology, sociology, and in our traditional and digital networks. As part of this motif, there have always been battles of contending ideas up and down the human scale from dyadic relationships to the highest levels of national and international politics, policy, and statecraft. We are ever the persuader, ever the persuadee. Information has become a commodity. "The struggle for control over information and knowledge looms large (Aspesi & Brand 2020)."

These conflicts span the yawning gap across time, that most difficult dimension, from the nanosecond before the electron arrives in fast war, to the physiologic seconds before we physically behave, through the dynamics of the kill chain (Brose 2020b), to *shi*, the Oriental diachronic strategy of the present to create influence in the future that can be measured in decades or centuries.

The Conflict Domains

Information warfare and cyber warfare are too narrow as descriptions of the unfolding conflicts. The term "warfare" limits the discussion to the most intense levels of conflict. The protagonists of these conflicts will certainly engage in warfare if necessary; however, if they can achieve their goals by less obvious, more indirect means, they will.

The traditional military conflict domains were land, sea, and air. Recently, the U.S. Department of Defense has added a fourth domain, space, and the cyber domain, which is the fifth domain. When we examined the cyber domain, we realized that it was a major but not final step in addressing a larger contest for power, a contest for cognitive superiority. This cognitive domain involves a complementarity as it is both part of each of the current five domains but importantly also an emergent (more than the sum of the parts) separate sixth domain. It addresses the new forms of cognition, the unending exponential increase in the sum of human knowledge, new communities of knowledge, and information access. It is intertwined with competing world views, grand strategies and metanarratives of power, diplomacy, commerce, education, science, metascience, and the necessity for lifelong learning. It molds trust, social membership, meaning, identity, and power.

The Combatants

The combatants are many in name and form, nuanced and adaptive, from nation states and their proxies—whose goal is total domination—to attention merchants seeking profits or ideologic conversion. The internet and particularly social media allow individuals or swarms to attack at scale or to target the individual. Associative and dissociative forces, traditional and digital, swirl about us.

We are facing today multi-pronged, multi-faceted attacks on our civilization.

- There are multiple national opponents, using multiple modes of attack on multiple facets of our national life.
- There are also multiple non-nation-state opponents, both external to our country and within it, who are doing the same.
- There are also individuals or small groups of individuals, motivated by ideological or economic goals, doing the same.
- Additionally, our social media, that were assumed to be associative, have created dissociative environments that foster attacks on individuals and at scale.
- Further, there are the corporate entities that seek to advance their own ends through influence operations.
- These actors are armed with AI augmented metrics from surveillance, experimentation and favored information access. Collectively they are creating an environment of perilous conflicts.
- Finally, the barriers to entry are lower, scale is easier to obtain, and attribution is potentially problematic in the cyber domain, in the biological domain, and more broadly in the cognitive domain, thus more adversaries.

The Conflict Matrix

These multiple conflicts are not taking place in a secure and stable matrix. The central axis of our time is accelerating unending change (Kelly 2016).

- The sum of human knowledge is increasing exponentially, as its access and infrastructure changes. We use the word "noosphere" to refer to the total information available to humanity.

- We use the word "technium" to refer to technology as a whole system (Kelly 2010). The accelerating change in the technium is obvious. New technologies arise before we have mastered the old ones. Dangerous exploits are simpler because of increasingly enabled machines and reductions in the barriers between expert knowledge and end users.
- We are even witnessing the emergence of new forms of cognition. We have made advances in understanding and augmenting human cognition. We now must add the impact of artificial intelligence (AI) and cognified objects, processes and environments. New psychoactive pharmaceuticals can modify human behavior.

The world is made up of connected complex adaptive systems within complex adaptive systems. In our hyper-connected matrix, changes do not affect just one thing; their effects pervade the technium, the noosphere, and humanity. Some effects are predictable and some are emergent, known only upon their discovery. The rise of artificial intelligence/machine learning (AI/ML), ubiquitous surveillance, big data analytics, and the Internet has furthered academic research into persuasion that can be converted into actionable behavior-change. The nascent mass connectivity of the internet of things (IoT) is forecast to deliver innumerable benefits. While these benefits are evident, the increase in surfaces of vulnerability to cyberattacks is a given. The barriers to entry into cognitive warfare writ large are lowering, including in the cyberwar and bio-war domains. The ability to scale is becoming easier and attribution is often problematic. Similarly, the promise of quantum computing is for untold scientific advances, but it will certainly mean that stolen encrypted information that is currently of little value will have great value in the future because it can then be retrospectively decrypted.

Access to and use of information allows humans to group together and cooperate well enough to survive and even prosper. It also can empower polarization dynamics. Much of human thought and communication is for affiliation and affirmation, not truth-seeking. We develop cognitive and technological artifacts such as AI, the internet, and extended reality (xR) and yet we still use stories, speeches, ceremonies, symbols, and collective learning. According to Jeremy Kahn, AI "will be the most important technological development in human history (Kahn 2020)." Information has become an asset category; persuasion is the new oil and knowledge dominance the new power. Persuasion science is ever more powerful and has been weaponized to make information and cyber warfare effective. Where advertisers in the past spoke of delivering "eyeballs" or "impressions" as measures of effectiveness, now they can promise probabilistic changed opinions and behavior. Unfortunately, it is not just advertisers who are influencing us in the cognitive domain. In our surveillance-saturated world, the new science of persuasion, armed with biometrics, sociometrics, experimentation, and big data analytics, using new knowledge of human irrationalities, allows directed attention for this probabilistic persuasive control at scale with a low bar of entry for participation. The resolute can be made sequacious.

The conflicts exploit the changes in the matrix and may induce, dampen, or exacerbate those changes. While the technium and the noosphere are the means, media, and immediate targets, the cognitive domain is the overarching domain of conflict.

The Inevitable Effects

The changes are affecting communication, education, transportation, infrastructure, commerce, industry, and agriculture. Old technologies will be replaced by new ones and old business models and industries will topple. These changes will cause massive societal changes. However, there will be more important social changes because of changes in research methods, documentation, knowledge management and access, changes in education (perhaps the most significant revolution since the printing press), changes in health, changes in our understanding of man, his vulnerabilities and potentials, and changes in mechanisms of trust, social membership, human networks, and the construction of identity. Together, the inevitable effects are leading to changes in power and its distribution, warfare (how it is waged and by whom), and how peace and prosperity can be achieved. These changes can and must be successfully addressed. A twenty-first century fundamental shift of mind, a metanoia, is required (Senge, 2006).

The Claim

Global power is shifting and kinetic warfare superiority alone is no longer a guarantor of safety. Military AI superiority is positioned to be more and more central to the defense of freedom. In an interview with CNBC at Davos in 2020, Alex Karp, the CEO of Palantir, said that within five years, the country with the superior military AI will determine the rules of the future [paraphrase] (Karp, 2020). We have multiple near peers and the conflicts are morphing. The sum of human knowledge is increasing exponentially. We must integrate knowledge and access. "The ability to learn faster than your competitors may be the only sustainable competitive advantage (Anderson, 2019)." These conflicts will affect more people, more severely, more quickly, and more certainly than climate change.

Since the 1648 Treaty of Westphalia, the Westphalian Order has defined nation-states as the principal units of the geopolitical system (Kello, 2017; McFate, 2019). In practical terms, that meant that discussions of warfare and large conflict began at the national level. The list of combatants, described above, includes nations, but also includes many non-national entities. In today's environment, we may have to begin at the individual level. The spectrum of influence, persuasion, manipulation, coercion, and control contains the drivers of individual, group, corporate, and national behaviors. The global accommodations between freedom and authority will likely be settled by information, writ large and combined well. The accelerating ascension of information as power brings an urgent imperative for cognitive superiority. We propose means toward gaining that superiority.

The Audience

This book is written for those who lead, aspire to leadership, and those who teach or persuade. It is particularly relevant to the National Security and Policy communities and those in commerce or who for personal reasons wish to understand or ride the winds of change.

References

Anderson, E. (2019). Learning to learn. Havard Business Review special issue: How to learn faster and better (pp. 15–18).

Aspesi, C., & Brand, A. (2020). In pursuit of open science, open access is not enough. Science, 368, 574–577.

Brose, C. (2020b). The kill chain: Defending America in the future of high-tech warfare. New York: Hachette Books.

Kahn, J. (2020). The quest for human-level A.I. Fortune (pp. 62–67).

Karp, A. (2020). Watch CNBC's full Interview with Palantir CEO Alex Karp at Davos. Retrieved February 24, 2020, from YouTube: https://www.youtube.com/watch?v=MeL4BWVk5-k

Kello, L. (2017). The virtual weapon and international order. New Haven: Yale University Press.

Kelly, K. (2010). What technology wants. New York: Penguin Books.

Kelly, K. (2016). The inevitable. New York: Viking Press

McFate, S. (2019). The new rules of war: Victory in the age of disorder. New York: William Morrow.

Schweitzer, G. (2019). Personal communication with Professor of Nuclear Chemistry at University of Tennessee (K. Jobson, Interviewer).

Senge, P. M. (2006). The fifth discipline: The art and practice of the learning organization. New York: Doubleday.

Contents

List of Figures

List of Tables

About the Authors

Dean S. Hartley III has spent decades advising organizations on improving their operations. This advice has included technical improvements in industry and government and in understanding and modeling military operations, particularly those with large components of political, economic, social, infrastructure, and information interactions.

Dean Hartley is the Principal of Hartley Consulting. Previously he was a Senior Member of the Research Staff at the Department of Energy Oak Ridge Facilities (Oak Ridge National Laboratory, Y12 Site and East Tennessee Technology Park). He received his Ph.D. in piecewise linear topology from the University of Georgia in 1973. Hartley is a Director of the Military Operations Research Society (MORS), past Vice President of the Institute for Operations Research and Management Science (INFORMS), and past President of the Military Applications Society (MAS). He is the author of *Predicting Combat Effects*, *Unconventional Conflict: A Modeling Perspective*, *An Ontology for Unconventional Conflict*, and *An Ontology of Modern Conflict: Including Conventional Combat and Unconventional Conflict*. Hartley's interests include modeling of irregular warfare (IW), verification and validation of models, psychopharmacology modeling, and simulation. His website is http://DrDeanHartley.com/.

Kenneth O. Jobson, M.D. has had years of experience in the science and art of persuasion, and experience in improving the structure and access to information via collecting, winnowing down, bringing around and making convenient the salient and essential at the time of need for individuals, physician groups, academic communities of knowledge, and large corporate entities.

Ken Jobson founded and developed the National Psychopharmacology Laboratory (NPL), a biotechnology laboratory that was purchased by a NASDAQ listed company. He has retired from a clinical practice in psychiatry and psychopharmacology. He served as a consultant to senior management of a national digital media company and has chaired psychiatric conferences around the world. He is the founder and chairman of the board of the International Psychopharmacology

Algorithm Project (www.ipap.org), which has been recognized by the World Health Organization (WHO). He was on the clinical faculty at the University of Tennessee, Department of Psychiatry, and co-edited the textbook, *Treatment Algorithms in Psychopharmacology*. He has facilitated the establishment of algorithm projects in the United States, Europe, and Asia.

Chapter 1
Introduction: Humans and Their Matrix

Why do others have behavioral influence on you? Who are they? How did they get that power? How do they exercise it and how does it work? Why do they want power over you? What can you do about it? How does this go beyond the personal to important national security issues? The answers involve the changes in information infrastructure, access, and use. The fog over the complex ecology of information and persuasion is lifting.

The motif of the universe is connectivity. It is so at the quantum level, in physics, in chemistry, biology, sociology, and in our traditional and digital networks (Schweitzer 2019). As part of this motif, there have always been battles of contending ideas up and down the human scale from dyadic relationships to the highest levels of national and international politics, policy and statecraft. The ascendant morphing of information as power neither negates the wisdom of Sun-Tsu nor the strategy of von Clausewitz. It does not obviate moving, shooting, and killing. What it does do is reframe them in a more complex matrix where the only restrictions are the laws of physics, access to information, and the boundaries of cognition.

No sire, it's not a revolt, it is a revolution,"

was the response of the Duke of Rochefoucauld to Louis XVI, following the storming of the Bastille (Walton 2016). What we are experiencing is a revolution in information, not a revolt. The distinction is that a change—paradigmatic, transformative and accelerating—in the entire world-order is taking place. Just as events in history must be understood in the matrix (conditions) of their age, today's information conflicts must be understood in today's matrix.

A "Revolt" implies a single action; whereas, "revolution" connotes a broader set of actions and changes. Our matrix is one of accelerating change within our surrounding complex adaptive systems and the accelerating change in the very nature of man as an emergent biological, psychological, sociological, technological, and information being. The revolution is in the ***technium*** (technology as a whole system), in the ***noosphere*** (the totality of information available to humanity), in man

D. S. Hartley III, K. O. Jobson, *Cognitive Superiority*,
https://doi.org/10.1007/978-3-030-60184-3_1

and in our knowledge of man, including our "predictably, systematically irrational" aspects (Ariely 2009). As we experience these unrelenting paradigmatic, accelerating changes, it behooves us to detect them as soon as possible so that we have a hope of surviving them. First, our vision must encompass the enlarging arc of the cognitive contests. Secondly, with foresight and insight, we must navigate the novelty, produce best-in-class adaptations, and further our own new creations. Part of the future is already here; it's just unevenly distributed (Gibson 2003). We must avoid being part of the past that is still here but not uniformly receding.

The U.S. Department of Defense has an acronym that is relevant: DIME. DIME refers to the levers of power: diplomacy, **information**, military, and economics (Hillson 2009). Information has always been one of the means to gain and use power. Unsurprisingly, in the "information age" the importance, manifestations, and strength of information have greatly increased.

The technium is involved; the noosphere is the medium; but humans are the target!

Information Warfare is a generic term. It is part of both conventional warfare and unconventional conflict (Hartley 2017, 2018). It is also a stand-alone operation (Kello 2017). However, we found many discussions to be incomplete, concentrating solely on the computer aspects. Further, the term "warfare" limits the discussion to the most violent levels of conflict. Certainly computer technology provides a major method for engaging in the conflict and information stored on computers is an important part of the conflict; however, because humans are the ultimate target, all information (including information stored in human brains and our augmentations) is at risk and the engagement modes include the Internet and other technologies, such as television, and non-technological modes, such as verbal communication.

We live in polarized times. Not only are there opinion sets that divide us, but we seem to get our information from separate sources, leading to disagreements about what seem to be the facts of many situations. We describe this as living in only partially overlapping bounded realities. There are many concepts that are connected to information conflict, such as cyber warfare and persuasion science. Persuasion has been weaponized to make information and cyber warfare effective. Cognitive superiority, controlling the cognitive or sixth domain, is the topic.

The Technium

The ***technium*** is technology as a whole system. It is inextricably intertwined with the noosphere. Kevin Kelly coined this work in his book, *What Technology Wants*. He needed a word to express his vision that technology not only extends beyond the physical machines of civilization to intellectual creations of all types, but it also includes systemic interconnections in which each technology depends on other technologies for its production and generative forces that encourage more technology creation. Further, as he saw it, this system has emergent properties, including internal needs with external expressions as it interacts with the rest of the world. He was envisioning a system for which no word existed (Kelly 2010).

Technology is humanity's accelerant (Kelly 2016). Our technium is different from the technium during World War II and different from that of the Middle Ages and still more different from that of ancient Greece and Rome. However, our technium did not spring full-blown from nothing; it evolved from the technium of the recent past, which evolved from the previous technium, and so forth. The technium of a time and place supports the noosphere of the time and place and is modified by that noosphere: they are interdependent. With regard to the conflict in the noosphere, the technium provides the computation, storage and transmission mechanisms for the conflict taking place in the minds of humans. When movable type supporting cheap printing entered the technium of the time, the conflict of the noosphere gained another mechanism to add to human conversation and penned letters. Martin Luther's thoughts were spread throughout Europe in a new way. The technium includes hardware such as the printing press; however, it also includes conceptual mechanisms, such as the technical tools of persuasion.

The Noosphere

The ***noosphere***, the total information available to humanity, is expanding exponentially. In today's technological world, the noosphere is inextricably intertwined with the technium. The infrastructure of the noosphere is rapidly changing. Favored information access with analytics is critical (Aspesi & Brand 2020).

Teilhard de Chardin envisioned the noosphere as collective human consciousness, the next evolutionary step (Ockham 2013). Kevin Kelly reintroduced this concept in his book, *The Inevitable*, and even used it to refer to a possible future world brain (Kelly 2016). We will leave out the speculation. Thus, we restrict the concept to refer to the sum of human knowledge.

Epistemology, the theory of knowledge, its methods, validity, and scope, can no longer be relegated to abstract philosophy. The prevalence and power of fake news and related suspect information artifacts has made it salient to everyday life. Normally, we think of information as pertaining to facts—true things. However, when you think about it, *this* concept of information has never been accurate. The ancients accepted many things that we now know to be false: for example, the sun does not revolve around the earth. In scientific domains, we accept that our data have measurement errors, at best, and that our scientific theories are subject to modification, even paradigm shifts, as our understanding improves. Such things belong in the noosphere. We regard the scientific conflicts of information validity as benign conflicts in the noosphere. There are also malign conflicts in the noosphere. During World War II, the Allies sought to convince the Germans that the invasion that was to be in Normandy would occur elsewhere. They thus sought to corrupt the part of the noosphere perceived by the Germans, a malign act. Today, there is "fake news," both real and falsely asserted (the assertion itself being the "fake news"). All of this is in the noosphere. And this is part of the conflict in the noosphere. The noosphere provides the medium in which the conflict takes place.

An ***ontology*** is a tool for organizing what is known about a domain. It generally contains the elements of interest in the domain and relations among those elements. It may also contain multiple types of relations and other defining information. When particulars are added to the ontology, it is often termed a ***knowledge base***. For example, *bridge* might be an element in an ontology about infrastructure, indicating that this is one class of infrastructure, and "London Bridge" might be a particular instantiation in a knowledge base. In a book that described an ontology for modern conflict, Hartley included several elements that are relevant to information conflict (Hartley 2020). This particular ontology covers much more than just information conflict and thus has a larger granularity than would be required for a complete description of information conflict. Upon occasion, we will describe parts of the noosphere and the technium in ontological terms.

The Target: Humans

Every facet of our complex humanness is measurable and targetable. There is a hierarchy of targets that extends from our plume and trail at the chemical level, through our psycho-social needs and drives, via our irrational aspects, to our educated, augmented optimal state. As the sum of human knowledge increases exponentially, it is not surprising that information ascends in power with *Homo* "*Sapiens*." In his book, *The Virtual Weapon*, Lucas Kello said, "This then is the chief transforming feature of security in our time: Information has become a weapon in the purest sense (Kello 2017)." We address information conflict (which includes information war and the internal issues of conflicting information, "fake news", etc.) and bounded reality (both human and AI seeing only part of the world) and possible solutions. Thus, "Intentional Conflict in the Noosphere" refers to actions taken by significant individual actors, states, state-sponsored proxies or other non-state-group actors, to disrupt or modify the information available to humanity. In our case, we are concerned with the impacts on the U.S. and its allies.

Figure 1.1 shows **one** view of the relationships among the noosphere, the technium and humanity. The noosphere contains knowledge of the physical world and the mental world.

Some parts of the noosphere are false and are shown in the mental world because they do not represent reality. The technium also consists of things in the physical world, including things that intertwine with the mental world. It is shown as mostly contained in the noosphere; however, there are tools and techniques that we use but don't fully understand, so a part of the technium is shown to be outside of the noosphere. Humanity is shown as partly in the physical world and partly in the mental world. It is shown as intersecting the noosphere, the technium and false knowledge. It can be argued that since the noosphere is the total knowledge of humanity, the noosphere should be contained in the representation of humanity. However, we have

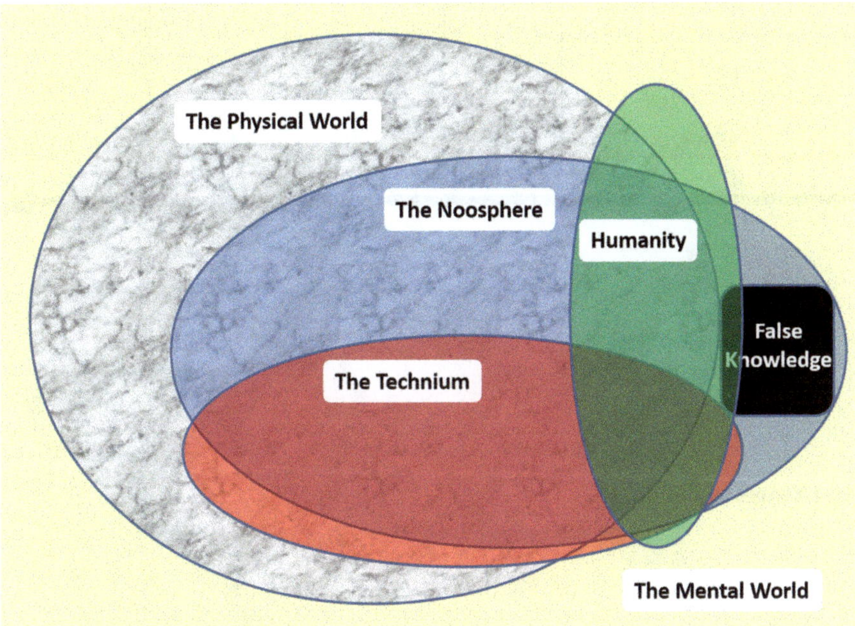

Fig. 1.1 The noosphere, the technium and humanity

chosen this representation to emphasize that the noosphere is the total information **available** to humanity and that no human knows it all and each person knows a very small portion of it. It is harder to argue that the technium should be contained in the representation of humanity, since so much of the technium consists of physical objects that are clearly not intrinsic to, but rather tools of, humanity.

This figure also suffers from this graphic's dimensionality and the "apples" and "oranges" comparison. For example, the noosphere contains knowledge **about** the physical world and the technium contains objects **in** the physical world. This difference in the meaning of the intersections is the reason for the inclusion of the word "one" and its emphasis in the first sentence of this paragraph. Figure 1.1 is meant to help in the understanding of these important concepts, but does not show all possible relationships among them.

Change

Throughout human evolution, change was generally slow, driven by climate, culture and biology. Most of the time the rate of change would have been perceived as essentially zero (omitting daily and seasonal cycles. With the advent of human society, that has changed. The inventions of tools, agriculture, writing, money, and the formation of cities in prehistoric times caused humanly observable changes. The

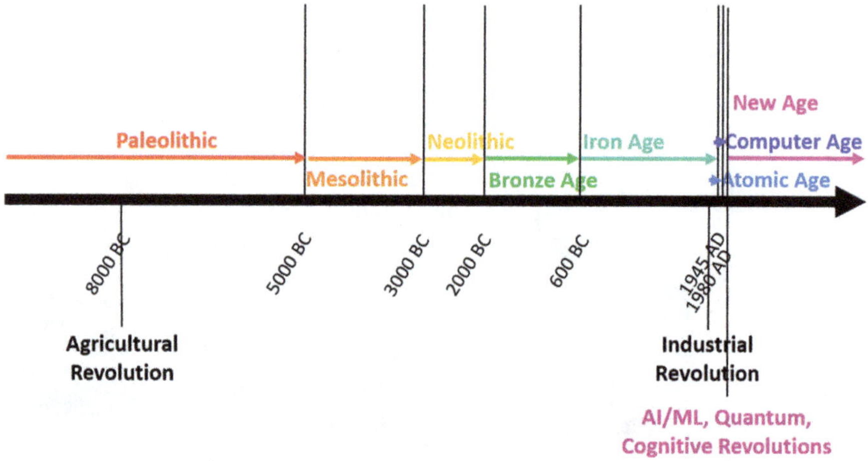

Fig. 1.2 Ages and revolutions

rate of change, while positive, was almost certainly episodic and on average slow. By the time of the industrial revolution, changes were more rapid (the rise and fall of empires, etc.); however, the average rate was still relatively low. The industrial revolution is called a revolution, because the rate of change was observably more rapid. Since then, change has been accelerating. The information revolution has further accelerated observable changes (Jobson, Hartley, & Martin 2011). The nascent AI paradigmatic revolution is upon us.

The accelerating rate of change in the technium, the noosphere, and even humanity is the central transformation of our time. Knowledge is expanding exponentially. Figure 1.2 sketches some of the changes in human history. Historians and anthropologists have named revolutions and ages in human experience. We are in the computer age now and beginning to experience artificial intelligence, quantum, and other cognitive revolutions. The chapters on the technium, the noosphere and humanity each include a section on the observed trends.

The recent past has seen fundamentally important changes. Scientific advances, aided by experimentation and big data analytics, have converted persuasion from an art to a combination of art and science. Computer technology has yielded increased processing speed and capacity, increased memory both local and remote, and increasingly powerful software applications. Total computational power is increasing by a factor of ten each year (Seabrook 2019). The Internet has connected the world. Artificial intelligence and machine learning have begun a process of restructuring many of the processes of civilization. Together, these four changes are making surveillance and control technologies ubiquitous.

These accelerating, paradigmatic, AI/ML changes have the effects shown in Table 1.1.

Table 1.1 Changes due to AI/ML

Many businesses and even industries are becoming obsolete;
Hardware and software are becoming outdated more rapidly—before we have a chance to become expert or even competent on something, it is replaced and we are beginners again;
Machines, processes and environments are becoming cognified—computer enabled and connected;
On the other hand, some things no longer require excessive levels of expertise or vast financial backing, enabling malicious use by more individuals, rather than just by governments and their proxies.

Table 1.2 Effects of AI/ML, quantum, and other technologies

Power and its distribution, warfare and how and by whom it is waged, how peace and prosperity can be achieved;
Commerce, industry, education, and research;
Our understanding of man, his vulnerabilities and potentials;
Trust, finding truth, social membership, human networks, the construction of identity, and
Emergent new forms in the system of complex adaptive systems we call cognition.

The rise of artificial intelligence/machine learning (AI/ML) and quantum technologies, sensing, computation, and communication will upend even more. These changes will affect things shown in Table 1.2.

Information conflict can extend from individual interactions to the apex of international political power, framing the structure and meaning of information across digital and traditional media to individual computers and personal contact. This national security threat disrupts or modifies the noosphere through communication and computation, from fake news through cyber war to control of metanarratives, and is initiated by nation-states, non-state-groups, and individuals. Addressing our physical vulnerabilities is not sufficient. Because humans have predictably, systemically irrational traits and operate within bounded realities, we are vulnerable and our institutions are vulnerable. We discuss the character of the conflict, the nature of the battleground, and topics for preparation and prevailing in the conflict.

The force of natural evolutionary change is anentropic toward complexity, diversity and energy density (the opposite of entropic change, which is toward increasing disorder). Many changes that we see in society are anentropic. The motif in both is connectivity. The change in the noosphere (total information available to humans) and technium (technology as a whole system) is accelerating to a point that quantity brings change in quality, of the technium, culture and man.

Accompanying the changes will be changes in scale, connectivity, complexity, and the impact of randomness. As the changes grow, multiple paradigm shifts are extant and more can be expected.

Defining Revolutions

Lucas Kello said, "The revolutionary potential of technology resides not in the invention itself but in its political and social effects (Kello 2017)." In looking at the type of revolution that computers and the Internet might induce, Kello started with a description of the current international relations theory, which describes a nation-state system, derived from the 1648 Treaty of Westphalia. This Conventional Model, also known as the Westphalian Order, consists of three sets of assumptions.

The first set of assumptions concern the organizing principle of the system. The units of the system are defined as the possible actors, such as nation-states, citizens, and an imperial hegemon. Each unit has its possible goals and capabilities defined in these assumptions. In the Conventional Model, states are the main units.

The second set of assumptions concern the structure, that is the relationships among the units. For example, the assumption that the units share a basic interest in survival and maintenance of order leads to a moderation of the rivalries among the units.

The third set of assumptions concern procedures, the laws, norms and institutions that the units have set up to govern their interactions.

Kello used these sets of assumptions to define a conceptual framework of varieties of revolutions. He described three varieties, from a third-order revolution, the least wide-ranging, to a first-order revolution, the most comprehensive.

A ***third-order revolution*** involves systemic disruption. In this type revolution, the structure is not affected. The conduct of the units may be disrupted, perhaps disastrously for some; however, the type of units that are the main units (here states) remain the main units. Kello described two types of change that fit into this type of revolution. The first type has to do with "material ingredients of power." This can lead to changes in the relative dominance of particular states. The second type has to do with changes in the procedures. For example, changes in what is considered to be moral warfare or competition fall into this category. Thus, a third-order revolution can be extremely disruptive to certain states, but leaves the nature of the system basically unchanged.

A ***second-order revolution*** involves systemic revision. In this type of revolution, the structure is not affected; however, the procedures are profoundly affected. Kello described the Soviet Union's actions to change the nature of internal workings of other states as an example of this type of revolution. He also described the project of creating the European Union, in which the procedures of interactions of the states in the European Union were radically changed, as an example of a second-order revolution.

A ***first-order revolution*** involves systems change. In this type of revolution, the nature of the units is changed. The structure of the system is affected. The existence of states may be challenged or their dominance in the system may be eliminated or greatly reduced. For example, the creation of an effective world government would constitute this type of revolution. Alternatively, the replacement of states by international corporations as the dominant actors would constitute a first-order revolution.

Kello described this as the replacement of the Conventional Model with some other model.

The meaning of the word "revolution" in Kello's work differs somewhat from that of Fig. 1.2. Kello focused on the international world order; whereas the revolutions in the figure are of a larger significance, changes in the social order of mankind as a whole. Conceivably, one of these larger significance revolutions could leave the Conventional Model intact, just irrelevant.

The Cyber Revolution

Kello evaluated the existence of cyber capabilities and actions against his definitions of third and second-order revolutions and concludes that there are situations in which these capabilities and actions might be instrumental in causing revolutions of these orders. However, it is in the evaluation of the possibilities of a first-order revolution that the danger seems highest.

Kello argued that we already have a "*partial* but still notable force of systems change." That is, we are undergoing a first-order revolution. He said, "This trend is evident in three ways. First, states are not the sole relevant source of threats to national security; nontraditional players such as political activists, criminal syndicates, and religious extremist groups can also cause significant harm against governmental, financial, even military interests. Second, states are not the only, or in some cases even the primary, providers of national-security. In some areas of national security, such as the operation of vital computer infrastructures or the collection and encryption or decryption (in forensic investigations, for instance) of personal data, the private sector is more important. Third, the traditional units are no longer able to maintain full control over the dynamics of conflict [against and] among them. Civilian culprits can disturb—sometimes gravely—the fragile political framework of interstate affairs (Kello 2017)."

More than Cyber

The conflict matrix of our age of accelerating paradigmatic change, including new forms of cognition, requires polythetic, multiordinal strategies, talent from new and transdisciplinary communities of knowledge, and minds prepared to meet the unexpected. The advances in persuasion science can use captology (computer assisted persuasion) and narratology on time scales ranging from the "always-on" news feeds to *shi*. Lifelong learning for all must address the exponential growth in the sum of human knowledge, the rapidly changing infrastructure of knowledge access, and new understanding of man's vulnerabilities and augmented potentials.

Kello's revolution is based on what may now be considered traditional computer issues: computers, networks, cognified machines, and malware. Other than malware, these issues ignore the growing capabilities of computers. Artificial Intelligence (AI) was originally envisioned as creating general, flexible human level intelligence (or better) in a computer. We have not (yet) done that; however, we have created extremely powerful tools that are conventionally called AI and the methodologies of machine learning (ML). Kai-Fu Lee described his view of the coming AI/ML revolution in his book *AI Super-Powers* (Lee 2018). This vision is one of a "larger significance" revolution that begins where Kello's first-order revolution leaves off and achieves a revolution in the sense of Fig. 1.2.

Additionally, quantum computing, communication and sensing are here in their embryonic stages. As they mature, we can expect major disruptions in digital security. The current security processes are expected to be easily defeated by quantum decryption. This is not just a "future problem." Encrypted files and communications that are stolen today will be decrypted (retrograde decryption) in the future. The full scope of its coming impact is unknown. If Lee's revolution is not as vast as he expects, quantum computing may provide the substitute. All of this is coincident and merging with the new persuasion science. The conflict is more complex, multi-domain, trans-domain, polythetic, multiordinal, more rapidly adaptive, and more patient than any previous conflict in history. We face adversaries who engage in unrestricted, rule-less means. Revolutions in the form of paradigm shifts are extant. The exponential increase in the sum of human knowledge and its applications in the technium have brought emergent forms of the complex adaptive systems that we call cognition. (For example, we now discuss cognition in machines, where its quality, not its existence, is the topic.)

Sensing—the Surveilled World (the Panopticon)

In the Acknowledgements to his book, *Out of the Mountains*, David Kilcullen talked about leaving off of thinking about conflict in urban areas close to the sea to concentrate on the immediate wars following the attacks on 9/11 in 2001. He then said that when we return to thinking about them,

> "... we'll find that the same old challenges of the urbanized littoral remain, but that much of what we thought we understood has changed. Not only have enormous advances been made over the last decade in cloud computing, complex systems theory, big data analysis, remote observation, and crowd-sourced analytics—allowing new insights into old problems—but vast amounts of real-time data are now available to inform our thinking. Most important, the environment itself has changed. The level of connectivity and networked interaction (among populations all over the planet, and between and within coastal cities) has exploded in the last decade ... (Kilcullen 2013)"

From a sensing point of view, the technology to sense and the technology to be sensed are different in capacities and in kind (for example, nuclear forensics). Not only can (by comparison) almost everything said or done be sensed, it can be attached to a person, analyzed, (more or less) "understood" automatically, curated, and recorded. These potentials can be realized for financial gain, political influence, ideological conversion, and, in certain nation-states are being used to control populations. We are approaching the Panopticon where all is seen, and much is known and acted upon. The age of experimentation (on digital site users) is improving the vision of Panopticus.

Complexity Science and Network Dynamics

The first page of each Springer Complexity series book says, "***Complex Systems*** are systems that comprise many interacting parts with the ability to generate a new quality of macroscopic collective behavior the manifestations of which are the spontaneous formation of distinctive temporal, spatial or functional structures" [emphasis added] (Fellman, Bar-Yam, & Minai 2015). The macroscopic collective behavior referred to is also called an "***emergent property***." Because there may be complex systems that are not adaptive systems and do not exhibit emergence, we prefer to use the phrase "complex adaptive systems (CAS)." The simple truth is that a system for which a comprehensive description cannot be derived from a complete description of its parts is a CAS. It is more and different from the sum of its parts.

There are several organizations that study complexity science, such as the New England Complex Systems Institute, of which Yaneer Bar-Yam is President (New England Complex Systems Institute, n.d.). Perhaps the most famous is the Santa Fe Institute, founded by Murray Gell-Mann (Santa Fe Institute 2016).

A 2004 report by the Oak Ridge National Laboratory (ORNL) (Hartley, Loebl, Rigdon, Leeuwen, & Harrigan 2004) stated, "that without explicit treatment of commonality, undesirable and wholly unexpected performance will emerge to compromise the predictability, reliability, and consistency of complex systems and systems of systems (SoS)." [A version of this was presented at an international conference in 2005 (Loebl & Hartley III 2005).] The word "commonality" referred to functions in the parts of a system that should have the same representation and to the need for these functions to correspond to external reality. A 2018 review of the book *Meltdown: Why Our Systems Fail and What We Can Do About It* described the message of the book with the caption, "Thanks to dense networks and the complacency of groupthink, small glitches can cascade into catastrophic failures (Shaywitz 2018)."

The information battleground is not a simple, deterministic, Newtonian system. It is not just the sum of the individuals and the hardware/software objects that comprise it; but it also includes the interactions among them. It is complex and adaptive.

The Six Domains of Conflict

The US Department of Defense (DoD) currently lists five domains of military conflict: land, sea, air, space, and cyberspace (Chairman of the Joint Chiefs of Staff 2017). The land, sea and air domains are familiar, having been involved in conflicts

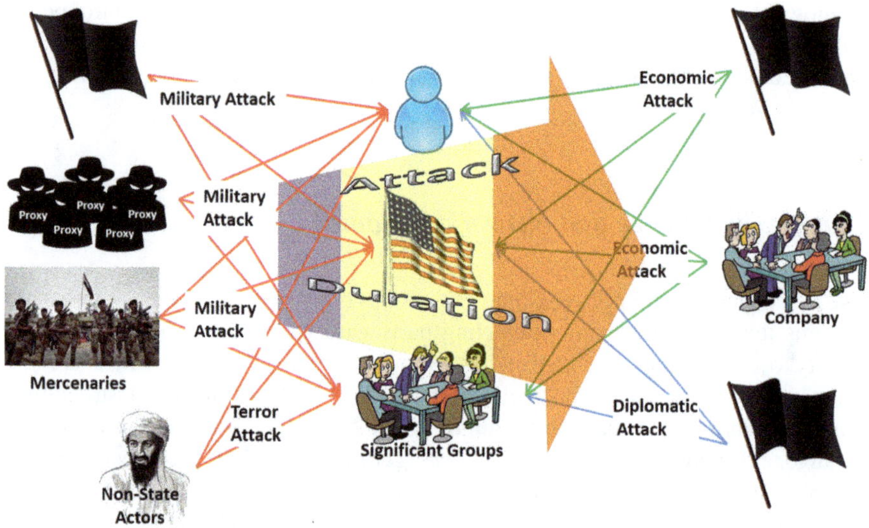

Fig. 1.3 Familiar attacks: diplomatic, military, economic

for a century in the case of the air domain, for all recorded history for the sea domain, and from pre-historical times for the land domain. The sixth domain, cognition, is extant but only now being recognized.

Figure 1.3 illustrates the "familiar" attacks: military attacks by a nation or proxies, which affect individuals, companies and our nation; terror attacks by non-state actors; economic attacks by nations or companies; and diplomatic "attacks" by nations. The U.S. is undergoing or threatened by all of these types of attacks from various opponents.

The Fourth Domain: Space

The space domain has not yet been involved in direct conflict and the extent of its possible involvement is not well-defined; however, there have been plenty of science fiction stories written about conflict in space to provide ideas of what might be possible. The U.S. has invested considerable resources in space over the last 60+ years. More than the investment, however, the value of space assets in terms of utility is large and growing. Satellites provide standard voice and television communications, location data through GPS systems, and internet connectivity.

The National Aeronautics and Space Administration (NASA) has announced its plan for a return to the Moon and human missions to Mars. A critical part of this plan is the Lunar Gateway—a spaceship in orbit around the Moon. The Gateway will provide access to the lunar surface, but also may become the hub of a cis-lunar economy (NASA 2020).

These assets are all vulnerable to both kinetic and cyberattacks. Julia Curlee, in a National Defense University capstone project, said, "An examination of potential scenarios for a war in space with China across the conflict spectrum suggests that Chinese attacks on US communications and Global Positioning Satellites (GPS) would likely feature early in a conflict (Curlee 2020)." The U.S. Space Force was created on December 20, 2019 to address these vulnerabilities and threats (Military.com 2020). Part of its mission is "to protect U.S. and allied interests in space and to provide space capabilities to the joint force (US Space Force 2019)," thus including defensive and offensive operations with an implied need for space superiority.

The Fifth Domain: Cyber

The cyber domain is so new that much of the applicable terminology is either unfamiliar to many or has varying definitions, depending on the source. We will use the following definitions when writing in our voice; however, when writing in the voice of a source, we will use that source's definitions. Our definitions are provided by Lucas Kello, who approached the problem from an international relations perspective as opposed to a military perspective (Kello 2017).

Cyberspace is all of the computers and networks in existence, including computers that are isolated from networks (air-gapped). Note that this includes embedded computers, such as those in cars (at least one in each modern car, with some having more than 30 computers). Cyberspace is manipulable through code (and on/off switches).

The term "cyberspace" conjures a picture of an amorphous continuum; however, the reality is different. Figure 1.4 is a cartoon of the Internet. It is based on a backbone of links and nodes, illustrated with fat lines and large red circles. The backbone nodes are connected to major nodes (medium-sized red circles) with major links (medium-width lines). Ultimately, the major nodes are connected to various computers (red dots) by links (thin lines). (This is a cartoon, so there can be many intermediate sized links and nodes.) Some of these computers are server

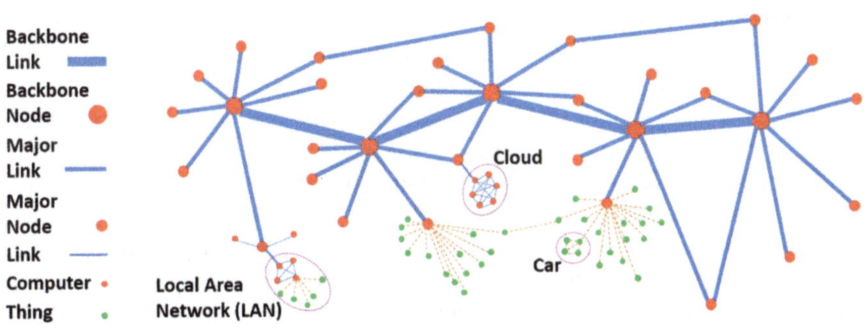

Fig. 1.4 Cyberspace

farms that comprise various "Clouds." Some of these computers are parts of local area networks (LANs), such as are found in many homes with multiple computers. (Most computers are actually connected to wide area networks (WANs), rather than directly to the Internet. Adding WANs to the cartoon would have made the drawing too cluttered.) The internet of things (IoT) is extant and rapidly growing. Some of these things are shown as green dots, connected (often wirelessly) to the Internet. One small group in the figure represents a few of the microprocessors in a car. The cyberspace is definitely not amorphous, just so complex that it is hard to grasp in its totality. Rothrock estimates that as of 2018, the number of nodes was about one trillion (Rothrock 2018).

The ***Cyber domain*** includes cyberspace and all of the human and institutional actors who operate and control cyberspace. The cyber domain also includes machinery that is controlled by cyberspace. The cyber domain affects and is affected by cyberspace and the human part is responsive to human inputs of a psychological, social and political nature.

"***Cybersecurity*** consists of measures to protect cyberspace from hostile action." It also includes measures to "protect the cyber domain from threats emanating from" cyberspace. When cybersecurity involves the military, it is called ***cyber defense***.

Information security is used to describe the control of information flows. This can be the suppression of subversive information in an autocratic state or efforts to control the exchange of child-pornography. Information security is often conflated with cybersecurity.

"***Malware*** denotes software designed to interfere with the function of a computer or degrade the integrity of its data." Malware may directly affect cyberspace or may do so indirectly by affecting human operators who then install malware into cyberspace (usually inadvertently, although conceivably the threat of harm to the operator might lead to the operator knowingly installing the malware).

The term ***cyberweapon*** is restricted to malware that is capable of and intended to do sufficient damage that the effects would be classified as the effects of a weapon in the realm of international relations.

"***Cybercrime*** entails the use of a computer for an illicit purpose under the existing penal code of a nation."

"***Cyberattack*** refers to the use of code to interfere with the functionality of a computer system for a political or strategic purpose." "Neither the goal nor the effects of a cyberattack need to be contained in cyberspace." "If the effects of a cyberattack produce significant physical destruction or loss of life, the action can be labelled ***cyberwar***, a term that should be used sparingly."

"***Cyber exploitation*** refers to the penetration of an adversary's computer system for the purpose of exfiltrating (but not defiling) data." When the goal is to steal military or industrial secrets, the exploitation is known as ***cyber espionage***. If the goal is to obtain sensitive information about a public official or organization to be released at an opportune influence government actions or undermine public confidence, then the exploitation is known as [***cyber***] ***kompromat***.

Rothrock discussed the 2013–2014 Target attack, the 2014 Sony attack, and the 2016 Democratic National Committee (DNC) attack. He discussed three commonalities: all were network attacks; all had remote origins; and although all were cyberspace attacks, all had serious consequences in the real world (Rothrock 2018).

Cognition, the Sixth Domain

When we examined the cyber domain, we realized that it was a major but not final step in addressing a larger contest for power, a contest for cognitive superiority. New warfare confronts three emergent foci within technology writ large: (1) AI and other new forms of cognition; (2) advanced gene editing and synthetic biology; and (3) and the subset of technologies labeled immersive technologies—extended reality (xR) (virtual reality (VR), augmented reality (AR), 360° video, and mixed reality). These foci are within the cognitive or sixth domain.

This cognitive domain involves a complementarity as it is both a power augmenting part of each of the current five domains but importantly also an emergent (more than the sum of the parts) separate sixth domain. It addresses the new forms of cognition, the unending exponential increase in the sum of human knowledge, and new communities of knowledge. It is intertwined with competing world views, grand strategies and metanarratives of power, diplomacy, science, metascience, and lifelong learning. It molds trust, social membership, meaning, identity, and power. The ultimate target of all conflict is the human mind, individually and collectively. This ultimate conflict domain is the Sixth Domain, the cognitive domain. The cognitive domain is both part of the other five domains and an emergent entity unto itself.

The cognitive domain entails a broad view of today's accelerating change in man in his matrix—discrete accelerating changes in cognition, in the technium (particularly, but not limited to, AI/ML) and the noosphere, in connectivity and complexity, and in our understanding of man's vulnerabilities and potentials. The DoD recognized that today's conflicts involve more than just the military (Hillson 2009). The DIME paradigm represents this realization. Four "levers" of national power were identified: diplomatic, informational, military, and economic, as shown in Fig. 1.5.

The DIME paradigm was a description of the *national* levers of power. However, today we have to contend with non-nation-state actors, including individuals, who have the power of terrorism, asymmetric warfare, biological warfare, and cyber warfare to act against nation-states (or other organizations and individuals) as only nation-states could in the past. Accordingly, we have changed the label to be just "levers of power."

As the figure shows, the conflict domains for diplomatic, informational and economic power are not usefully divided into land, sea, air, and space domains; however, they have their own traditional conflict domain divisions and they operate in their own part of the cyber domain. The inclusion of cyber within the diplomatic lever is arguable: the discovery and publication (or threat thereof) of politically damaging materials through cyber exploits could be contained in the informational lever; how-

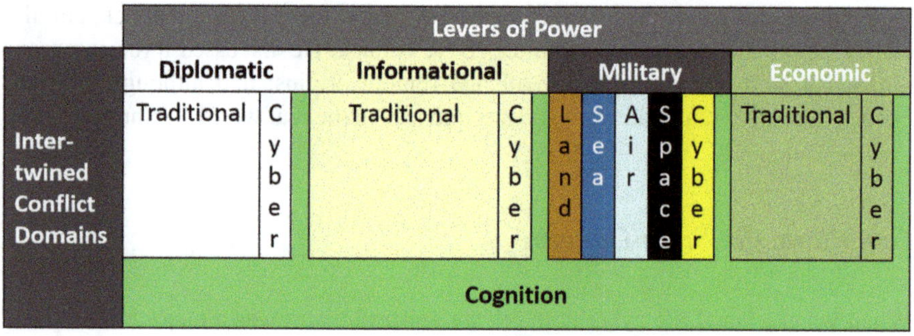

Fig. 1.5 Cognition, the sixth domain

ever, the particular impact of such an exploit and the potential for others leads us to include cyber. Similarly, the inclusion of cyber within the economic lever is based on the impacts of economic cyber exploits.

The informational lever of power is of particular interest in this book. Information conflict takes place among nation-states, group-entities and individuals. It took place before the advent of computers and continues after their creation. The informational lever of power originally could be characterized as spying (obtaining information from the enemy or competitor), deception (ensuring the incorrectness of the information that the other obtains), and counterintelligence (thwarting the attempts of the other to obtain information). The addition of the cyberspace domain has not removed these operations, but added to them. The technium can aid in the spying, deception and counterintelligence and can be used to corrupt the computers and cognified systems of the other side.

We have called the cognition domain the "sixth domain" (counting among the military domains) because we now have the ability to affect the cognitive abilities of humans (and augmented humans). We have practiced the art of persuasion (or rhetoric) since before the time of Sun-Tsu and Aristotle, but only recently have been creating an additional science of persuasion, which vastly improves the effectiveness of persuasive actions. We have developed new learning science interventions that affect cognition. In addition, we have developed tailored pharmaceuticals that affect cognition (beyond the unfocussed effects of naturally occurring drugs such as peyote, opium and the volcanic gases of the Greek oracles).

We are familiar with the need for air, land, and sea superiority. The corresponding need for space and cyber superiority is obvious, as is the need for diplomatic, economic and information superiority. However, over all we must achieve and maintain cognitive superiority. J. R. R. Tolkien's saga, *The Lord of the Rings*, contains an *apropos* poem:

Three Rings for the Elven-kings under the sky,
Seven for the Dwarf-lords in their halls of stone,
Nine for Mortal Men doomed to die,
One for the Dark Lord on his dark throne
In the Land of Mordor where the Shadows lie.

One Ring to rule them all, One Ring to find them,
One Ring to bring them all and in the darkness bind them
In the Land of Mordor where the Shadows lie (Tolkien 1965).

Cognitive superiority is the "*One Ring to rule them all.*"

The Time Frames and Battlefields

The time frame of war is now multiordinal, from "Fast wars … something that we haven't really understood yet (O'Neill 2019)", that move at the speed of the electron, to the Hundred Year Marathon (Pillsbury 2015) using *shi* (Qiao & Wang 1999; Chinese Academy of Military Science 2018).

There is and always has been a battle of ideas at the highest level of politics, policy and statecraft using speeches, stories, ceremonies, and symbols. In the West, we had Aristotle (384—322 B.C.). In his book, *Rhetoric*, Aristotle defined his subject matter, "as the faculty of observing in any given case the available means of persuasion (Aristotle 2004)." ***Rhetoric*** is persuasion through verbal means. Aristotle emphasized *ethos* (credibility), *logos* (logic), *pathos* (emotion) and *kairos* (propitious timing). Now we have TV, the Internet, and cognified objects—all trying to persuade/sell us something. Persuasion is not just verbal-aural; it includes visual perception, still and motion, real and fake; and will include remote touch, taste, and scent in immersive technologies. Persuasion science continues to transform the art of persuasion, armed as it is with new methods and metrics of sensing and experimentation and targeting human hybrid (augmented-human) cognition. Utilizing these methods together with addictive technology, persuasion is ever more central to attaining power for statecraft, computational propaganda, marketing, lobbying, public relations, and narrative and memetic warfare using "slogans, images and video on social media (Donovan 2019)." This is also part of the beyond-limits battlefield of the Chinese (Qiao & Wang 1999).

Persuasion is ubiquitous across all circumstances of human endeavor. It varies in combinatorial complexity, can be apparent or hidden, and is constructed for immediate use and delivered with urgency or with patience for the long game. Overlapping waveforms of influence come at all scales of time from the momentary to the long game and can be wrapped in disparate packages, truth, deception, perfidy, serendipity with discernment of opportunity to *shi*. *Shi* is a deception involving influencing the present as part of a larger or grand strategy to influence the future at a propitious moment, often for a long-term, zero-sum game (Pillsbury 2015).

As the battle moves from low intensity conflict toward warfare, the tactics of influence move from persuasion to coercion to control. This is true whether the lever being used is diplomatic, informational, economic, or military. As Carl von Clausewitz said, "*war is only a branch of political activity; that it is in no sense autonomous* (Clausewitz 1993)." [The emphasis is contained in the source.] In Fig. 1.6, we take a step back and derive all actions from the cognitive domain, with

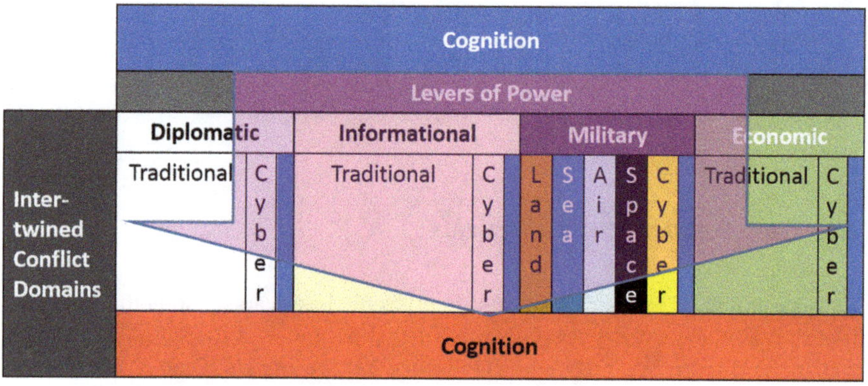

Fig. 1.6 Cognition as the key domain

the purpose of the actions being to impact the cognitive domain of the opponents. Naturally, the opponents are doing likewise, with the positions reversed. Achieving cognitive superiority is required for winning.

What is the nature of the battleground? While the cognified objects, hardware and software, are certainly part of the battleground, the most significant part is the wetware—human cognition. It is people who are affected by compromised objects and by their own exploitation. The nature of computers (at least non-quantum computers), ***cognified*** objects (objects with some level of cognition abilities), and their connection through the Internet are fairly well known and we will comment on them and their attributes without dwelling on them. However, recent advances in understanding neuro-cognition, dynamical systems theory, control theory, and human-computer interface optimization are not so widely known. These areas require a more extensive discussion. Winning on the information battleground requires an understanding of all facets of the battleground and time frames, most especially including an understanding of man and his matrix.

The imminent expansion of the digital battleground into extended reality (xR) as augmented reality (AR), virtual reality (VR) and multiple immersive technologies is *terra incognita* for persuasion and conflict. Research knows little of how AR will influence social interaction. What will be the effect of having a networked augmented avatar as a companion? Consider the work of the Stanford Virtual Human Interaction Lab, described on its website (Stanford University VHIL 2019).

Biosecurity (the Essential Tool Is Information)

A recently more obviously important, arguably under-addressed area in the sixth domain is biosecurity, in which there is "an expanding range of concerns (Evans et al. 2020)." Germs entering unprotected populations have repeatedly transformed history on an international scale (Diamond 2020). Whether the biological agents are

(1) feral diseases, (2) come from unintended releases, or (3) purposefully released, they can produce massive health and economic effects, as evidenced by the COVID-19 pandemic of 2020. N. b., although highly contagious, the lethality of COVID-19 is much lower than other biologic agents such as Ebola and Smallpox.

A low barrier to entry into the bio-war domain, the ability to scale an attack, and potentially problematic attribution make this an area of essential focus, needing best-in-class expertise and ability. Genomic science, advanced genetic engineering, synthetic biology, knowledge of network spread dynamics, augmented computational biology, and high-throughput experimentation (HTE) with automation and robotization contribute to the problem (Peplow 2019). All of these, together with big data analytics, network science, persuasion science, logistical and communication expertise, must be coordinated for security and defense (Desai 2020). Further, no knowledgeable adversary will miss the opportunity to superimpose an "infodemic (World Health Organization (WHO) 2020)" on an epidemic.

Synthetic biology can now create or modify—weaponize—a germ. The organism might be selected for high infectivity, high lethality and a low observed mutation rate. A vaccine could be produced, giving vigorous long-term immunity to the group (or country's citizens) who receive the vaccination. The vaccination program could be presented with a false narrative or be clandestinely incorporated as part of a polyvalent established vaccination program. The secret development, selective vaccination program, and release of such an organism under attributional cover and coordinated dissociative "infodemic" would likely produce a catastrophic effect on the target. The unassembled modules of such a scenario are in *forme fruste*, but extant. With purposeful biosecurity threats we must consider multiple releases (vectors) in form, location and timing, in parallel with infodemics and complex, multi-domain orchestrated attacks.

The United States must develop "global readiness" with an international "shared understanding and shared vocabulary for pandemic preparedness with an early warning system that tracks global disease trends and distributes accurate real-time information." Recommendations include: (1) Full support of the U.S. Pandemic Response Team within the National Security Council, including equipment surge capacity. (2) Expand public health capacity including surveillance structure, education and vigorous extant and more scalable vaccination capacity. (3) Innovation accelerators such as Coalition for Epidemic Preparedness Innovation (CEPI), which can develop a platform or platforms for technology innovation for rapid vaccination development (Desmond-Hellmann 2020), (4) "experimentation in biosecurity governance" with "sharing of case studies." "At present no capability for systemic learning about the effectiveness and limitations of current biosecurity governance exists (Evans et al. 2020)."

The Combatants

We are facing today multi-agent, multi-pronged, multi-faceted attacks on our civilization. There are multiple national opponents, who are acting individually or through proxies, using multiple modes of attack on multiple facets of our national life. There are also multiple non-nation-state opponents, both external to our country and within it, who are doing the same. There are also individuals or small groups of individuals, acting on economic motives, doing the same. Additionally, our social media have created an environment that fosters individual attacks on other individuals. Further, there are the traditional corporate activities that seek to advance their own ends through influence operations. Moreover, our networked system creates cognitive demands that most users are not equipped to handle. When the computer was represented by large machines, tended by acolytes in white lab coats, users could safely remain ignorant of the demands of the technology. Now, each personal computer, smart phone, smart TV, or other device requires configuration and tending by its owner, who has not been supplied with a white lab coat or the knowledge and experience to service its demands (Rothrock 2018). Together, these actors are creating an environment of constant conflict, as illustrated in Fig. 1.7.

This constant conflict does not replace the familiar attacks illustrated in Fig. 1.3; rather these multi-agent, multi-pronged attacks are added to the familiar attacks. The individual conflicts comprising the constant conflict involve the individual, countless groups, and nations, using and exacerbating the changes already described. All of the conflict is not instantaneous. While some attacks, such as a particular phishing email, may be handled with a brief moment of attention, others are "persistent enduring attacks" (Rothrock 2018). In addition, the number of attacks continues to grow. CrowdStrike reported the number of events globally was 90 billion

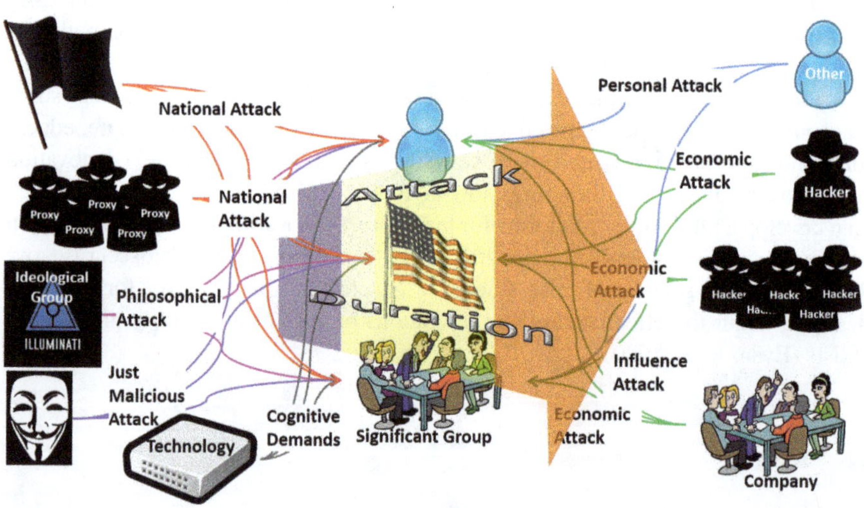

Fig. 1.7 Multi-agent, multi-pronged attacks

in 2017 and 240 billion in 2018—**per day** (Crowdstrike 2019)! While the technium and the noosphere are the means, media, and immediate targets, the cognitive domain is the actual domain of conflict.

Winning in the Sixth Domain

We have a limited history to draw from because of the brevity of experience with the digital world, its accelerating rate of change, and the preference for secrecy concerning adverse experiences with the digital world. We have repeatedly been unprepared when facing wars that threatened our survival and only after significant delays did we adapt to defend and defeat the enemy. The digital "attack" may be at the speed of light over our fiberoptic networks. Our fate may be determined in nanoseconds after a clandestine polythetic prologue. We do not have the luxury of being unprepared.

The Cognitive Battleground

Computer systems are not human-level cognitive systems (yet) and the cyber domain is but part of the cognitive domain. However, the cyber domain is closer to the cognitive domain than are the physical domains of land, sea, air, and space. Therefore, the cyber conflict produces an understandable introduction to the larger cognitive conflict.

According to Rothrock, 76% of the respondents of one study reported a computer system compromise in 2016, up from 71% in 2015 and 62% in 2014 (Rothrock 2018). That means that every system should expect to be compromised—*successfully attacked*—despite having good defenses. We certainly need defenses of various types; however, we also require resilience to bounce back from successful attacks. Rothrock ascribed the following definition of resilience to Andrew Zolli and Ann Marie Healy. ***Resilience*** is "the capacity of a system, enterprise, or a person to maintain its core purpose and integrity in the face of dramatically changed circumstances (Rothrock 2018)." The U.S. demonstrated resilience after the attack on Pearl Harbor on December 7, 1941. We will need systems resilience at all levels. Simultaneously, we must successfully engage the Hundred-Year Marathon—the long game. Rather than a win-win game, others play a zero-sum game.

Kinetic superiority is no longer a certain guarantor. Now with multiple weapons and layers hidden by method and their "local habitation and name," we must have cognitive superiority.

The goals and assumptions of humans, their differences, and perceptions and misperceptions about them are part of the cognitive domain. Samuel Visner, the Director of the National Cybersecurity FFRDC at MITRE, said the battleground is the "exercise of influence in cyberspace—as an instrument of national power (Visner

Table 1.3 Visner's views of cybersecurity

Safeguarding information;
Safeguarding information, information systems, and information technology (IT)-intensive information infrastructures;
Gaining the outcome in cyberspace that you desire, not what someone else tries to impose; or
Safeguarding a portion of sovereign space—cyberspace.

2018)." Significantly, he said that cybersecurity is viewed differently by different people, as shown in Table 1.3.

This last point of view is a critical difference between us and some adversaries. He said we regard cyberspace in much the way we regard the seas, as a global commons, whereas some countries look to claim portions of it as "territorial waters." If the goal is cognitive superiority, it is critical to understand the opponent's cognitive domain, from world-view to tactical view.

The battleground for cognitive superiority involves complex adaptive systems and systems of systems (SoS), with intelligent nodes, links, signals, and boundaries, digital, hybrid and human.

Cognitive Superiority (Condensed)

The elements of cognitive superiority (listed here) will be discussed in the body of the book. In the conclusion (Chap. 8) we will present an expanded description of cognitive superiority.

Cognitive superiority is a relative attribute—sustained better thinking, more rapid learning, and superior information access than that of the opponents. Fortunately, it does not require that we are individually smarter than each of our opponents. It does require that collectively we are smarter. Achieving cognitive superiority will require an expanded understanding of the conflict, as shown in Table 1.4.

Organization of the Book

Our questions about the complex adaptive systems of information as power require investigation into numerous domains of knowledge, covering many disparate, multiply interconnected topics. Some topics will be principally addressed in a single chapter and only mentioned peripherally elsewhere. Several themes are threads that weave through the whole book, not existing solely in one chapter. Therefore, some repetition is necessary so that the reader isn't required to continually search back for earlier parts of the thread. More importantly, the complexity is best apprehended and appreciated from multiple points of view. The topics are artificial intelligence

Table 1.4 Essentials for cognitive superiority

Vision and grand strategy for the enlarging arc of the cognitive conflict, with a national Manhattan Project-level commitment to cognitive superiority, including military AI/ML—quantum superiority,
Talent, the best and brightest,
Lifelong education developing minds prepared to meet the unexpected,
Favored access to the frontier of science and technology (an Eratosthenes affiliation),
Personalized adult adaptive learning systems, utilizing digital and traditional pedagogy with superior information access,
Persuasion science superiority as part of the new knowledge of man's vulnerabilities and potentials,
Cyber security with resilience (defensive and offensive),
Cognification of humans, objects, processes and environments to deal with emergent new forms of cognition, and
All of the above "combined well."

(AI) and machine learning (ML), atoms and bits, biosecurity, change, cognitive superiority, communication and connectivity, complex adaptive systems (CAS), education, intelligence amplification (IA), network structure and dynamics, new knowledge of man, persuasion, profiles, quantum technologies, social membership, surveillance with experimentation, and trust. These are highlighted in the descriptions of the chapters below.

A note on terminology: the terminology within the domain of discourse of this book is fluid. The U.S. government has its own terminology, as do foreign governments, corporations, and individual writers. For example, Lt. Gen. Stephen Fogarty, commander of the U.S. Army Cyber Command, says that his command may change its name to something like the "Army Information Warfare Operations Command or Army Information Warfare Dominance Command (Seffers 2018)." There are two points, first that there are discussions about the relative advisability of the terms "information operations" and "information warfare" and second that there is support for broadening the domain from just cyber to cognition. Throughout this book we will use terms that may or may not match the exact terms used by others; however, we are not aiming to define usage, but describe concepts. We have tried to make the meanings clear and will leave it to others to decide just what will be the best terminology.

Chapter 1 is this introduction, providing a statement of the problem: the multi-pronged, multi-agent, multi-mode, polythetic conflict in which we are immersed. It introduces the technium, the noosphere, the humans as the target, and the revolutionary, accelerating changes that are part of our matrix. The chapter discusses the five classical domains of conflict, land, sea, air, space, and cyber, and introduces the sixth domain, cognition. It also provides a brief statement of the *cognitive superiority* solution.

Chapter 2 describes the technium, our technological environment that contains the attack tools, digital, cognitive, and biological, and many targets of conflict. It discusses *communication* from a technical point of view, *persuasion* as a method of attack, *surveillance* as a support to attacks, and *trust* as a defense. This chapter discusses the tools for gaining power over people and how they are used. It concludes with *change* trends in the technium.

Chapter 3 discusses the noosphere, the total information available to humanity, and our bounded reality. This chapter discusses the nature of information, how we think—and limit that thinking, and how we communicate. It discusses *atoms and bits*, *education*, *communication* and *trust* as parts of cognition, which is a prerequisite for *cognitive superiority*. It concludes with *change* trends in the noosphere.

Chapter 4 describes the target of the intentional conflict: humans. This chapter discusses how and why the attack tools work on humans. It includes salient features of human nature and our individual natures, such as irrationality, biases, and human communication—the *new knowledge of man*. The chapter also discusses the nature and centrality of *persuasion* in human *communications* with respect to attacks. It discusses *surveillance* as a means of building *profiles* of people. Finally, *change* trends in our understanding of humanity are described.

Chapter 5 discusses several selected sciences and technologies to provide a deeper look at some of the transformative influences of our environment. The topics include *CAS*, *novelty*, *AI/ML* and the human brain, human and computer *networks*, *quantum technologies*, immersive technologies, and *biosecurity*. It also includes new technologies that may influence the future: superconductivity, nuclear thermal propulsion, and 3D printing. It discusses *communication and connectivity* as part of network science.

Chapter 6 describes the adversarial environment. Adversaries include individuals, groups, companies, non-state actors, nation-states, and digital adversaries. Their goals and intents include personal enmity, influence, surveillance, economic gain, philosophical and ideological causes, maliciousness, control, and war. The chapter concludes with a discussion of why this is important, now, more than ever before. It discusses *persuasion* as part of influence, a goal of many types of adversaries, and *surveillance* as an intermediate goal of many types of adversaries.

Chapter 7 describes the engagement. It is divided into two parts. The first part describes the strategy for winning the conflict: *education*, information access, *communications*, and organizational principles. The second part describes how to address the ongoing conflict during the implementation of the strategy. It describes past, present and proposed organizations, commercial, governmental and hybrid. It includes an action portfolio, potential changes to the conflict environment, and ideas on operating in the conflict as it evolves.

Chapter 8 recapitulates the situation: the accelerating *changes*, *atoms and bits*, and humanity in the matrix. It concludes with a prescription for achieving *cognitive superiority* in detail, including a proposed organizational structure, and a rationale for a Manhattan-Project-scale effort.

An appendix with two parts, discussions of the salient contents of selected sources, organized by topic, and definitions of selected is included.

A wide-ranging bibliography and an extensive index are provided at the end of the book.

Chapter 2
The Technium: Tools and Targets of the Conflicts

Why might others have inordinate influence over you? In this chapter, we look at one of the subordinate questions: How do they exercise that power? What are the tools and targets in this influence conflict? How do the tools work and what are the target vulnerabilities?

The technium is multiordinal

The ***technium*** is technology as a whole system. "Technology is humanity's accelerant (Kelly 2016)." Our technium is different from the technium of that during World War II and different from that of the Middle Ages and still more different from that of ancient Greece and Rome. However, our technium evolved from those of the past. The current technium supports our lives. The technium ranges from hardware tools and targets to specific computer applications to methods of personal contact to the framing of the structure and taxonomy of corporate information technologies and beyond. As Lucas Kello said, "The revolutionary potential of technology resides not in the invention itself but in its political and social effects (Kello 2017)." Multiordinal coordination may be the most difficult and the most important part of the desiderata for surviving and prospering in a changing world.

The technium contains both technology for offense and defense and the objects of society that are targets of attack. Tools consist of tangible tools, such as hardware, intangible but explicit tools, such as software, and intangible and variable cognitive artifacts from the noosphere.

In this chapter, we describe the targets of information conflict in the technium, the tools used in that conflict, and the trends of change to the technium.

D. S. Hartley III, K. O. Jobson, *Cognitive Superiority*,
https://doi.org/10.1007/978-3-030-60184-3_2

The Targets in the Technium

The technium provides the medium for most of our cognitive artifacts. When our technology is attacked, our lives are affected. In some situations, the effects are immediate and personal. In other situations, the effects start in the larger society and affect us by damaging our society. In *Mobile Persuasion*, Fogg said, "I believe mobile phones will soon become the most important platform for changing human behavior (Fogg & Eckles 2014)."

Basic Technium Components

The technium includes the hardware and software of our lives, serving the components shown in Table 2.1.

The technium also includes the software that controls many of these services. The technium intersects with the noosphere in the area of tactics, techniques and procedures for operating the services and creating new parts of the technium.

Cognified Objects (Toward the Internet of Things)

Cognified objects are the nodes in the extant and growing internet of things. Some of the current objects in the technium differ from the corresponding objects in the technium of the past. When is a refrigerator not just a refrigerator? The answer is, "when it *knows* what its contents are and is connected to the Internet." This refrigerator has become a cognified object. We have become familiar with computers being vulnerable to attacks; however, they are now not the only objects that are vulnerable.

Table 2.1 Patrons of the technium

Transportation services, such as automobiles, trains, and planes;
Communications services, such as phones, radios, televisions, and computers;
Energy services, such as power plants, transmission lines, and refineries;
Healthcare services, such as doctors' offices, hospitals, and clinics;
Educational services, such as schools, universities, and libraries;
Utility services, such as water, sewage, and power;
Governmental services, such as local, state, and national governments;
Military Services, such as air, ground, naval, and space services, including their cyber commands;
Personal devices, such as tools, books, and computers; and
The infrastructure that supports each of these.

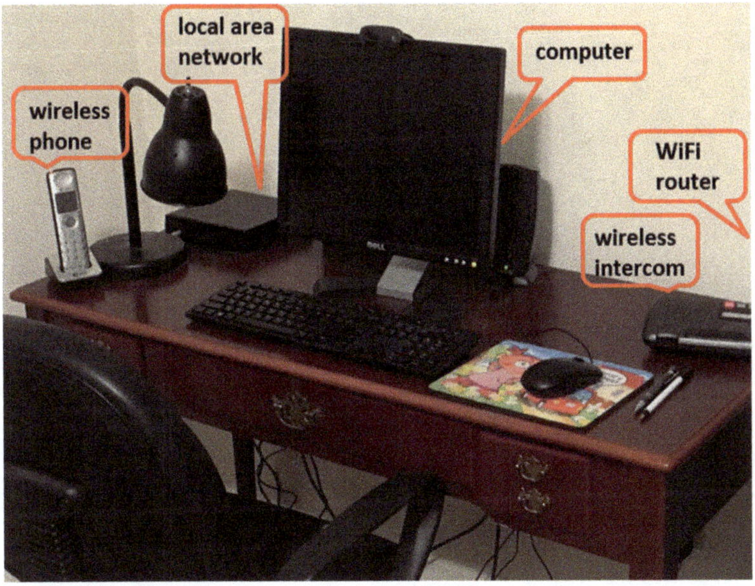

Fig. 2.1 The cognified office

Direct attacks can come through the computer, directed against that computer. However, with the advent of multiply connected and cognified devices, the vulnerabilities increase. Figure 2.1 illustrates some of the vulnerable surfaces in the home office. In addition to the attack points in the computer, there are attack points in the Wi-Fi router and the local area network (LAN). Wireless phones and wireless intercoms also have attack points.

Do you have a smart TV with a voice activated remote? It is listening to you. Do you know that it is not watching you? Digital cameras are small. The bedroom shown in Fig. 2.2 also has vulnerable surfaces. A smart TV and a voice-activated remote control provide attack points. A smart phone in the bedroom also provides attack points.

Who actually designs and builds the hardware and software of these TVs? We can imagine that the Pentagon war room has a large number of big monitors for displaying information. Who built them? What capabilities are hidden in them for monitoring the watchers and capturing the information presented on the monitors? Can any of this be tunneled out of "secure" facilities? What is your level of cyber-resilience when your systems are penetrated?

The kitchen of the future (or the current kitchen for early adopters) will also have vulnerable surfaces. Figure 2.3 shows a kitchen with an Amazon Echo Alexa device and an Internet connected refrigerator. There are lots of objects that contain or can obtain valuable information. Is your refrigerator watching you? When it orders food that is getting low, who does it tell? The figure also indicates the presence of a wireless home security system, which also has attack points.

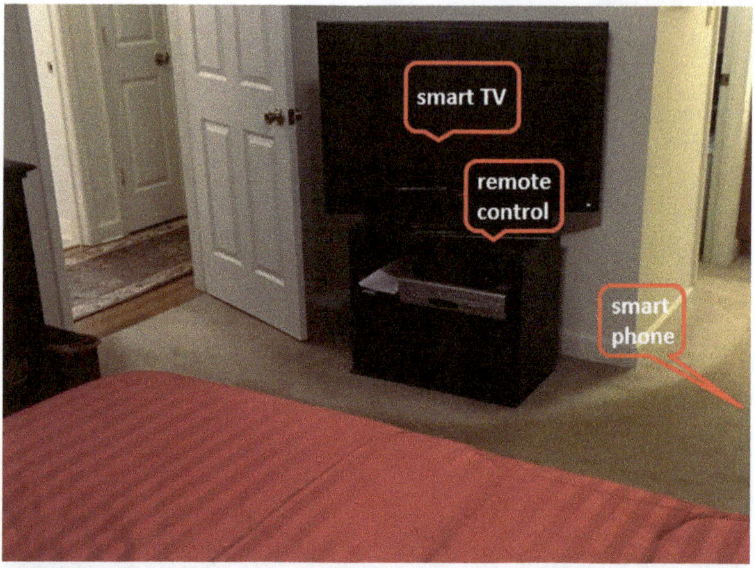

Fig. 2.2 The cognified bedroom

Fig. 2.3 The cognified kitchen

There is also your smart phone—it is always with you and it "knows" where you are and sends that information to various places. Depending on the apps you have on the phone, it passes an amazing amount of information to the apps' home servers and also to third parties—whose identity is generally undisclosed. Some of this information is sent in real-time and some is uploaded at night. Geoffrey Fowler's iPhone had 5400 hidden app trackers and sent "out 1.5 gigabytes of data over the span of a month. That's half of an entire basic wireless service plan from AT&T (Fowler 2019b)."

The individual is responsible for defending against attacks at all of these points of vulnerability. Currently, each has its own password and encryption system; however, when they are linked, the linkage can bypass the individual device security systems, a situation that may not be obvious to the individual. Even a fairly sophisticated individual may be unaware of a problem or unable to figure out how to rectify it.

These familiar cognified objects are part of the civilian world. However, cognified weapons have also been proposed. Naturally, there are worries about autonomy and control of such weapons. There are also worries about the availability of bandwidth on the battlefield for operations (Tucker 2019b). Of course, there is also the worry about the weapons being hacked.

*Communication (*Apropos *the Technium)*

Communication spans social signals (Matsumoto, Frank, & Hwang 2013), spoken language, written language, mathematical, musical and choreographic notation, and bits and bytes of the digital world, as well as all sorts of other signs and symbols. Stories, speeches, ceremonies, and symbols continue as central to communication, even as new presentations, such as video, are becoming more and more common. Video has become central in communications and with extended reality (xR) brings immersion and mixing of new communications technologies. Each hierarchical, structural level of language carries information from word choice and turn of phrase to narratives, metanarratives, and memes; language shapes thought; but stories are primal.

Physical networks are part of the technium. The telegraph was an early physical network (the "Victorian Internet" (Rothrock 2018)). It was a manual network, with telegraph operators sending messages to other telegraph operators. The telephone allowed private individuals to talk to others, originally via a manual switchboard, now through automated switching systems. Radios originally were strictly broadcast systems, providing one-way communications. (Two-way communication was accomplished by two broadcasts on the same frequency with each party taking turns broadcasting.) Later, radio networks were established to provide the same broadcasts from multiple locations. Television evolved similarly; however, it has recently added cable and satellite transmission media. Most recently, limited two-way communication was established to permit the selection of content by users ("on-demand" content). The Internet has evolved into an enormous communication system, mediated by complicated software and hardware, which serves up email, messaging, image transmission, voice-over-internet, video, and a wide variety of social media.

Figure 2.4 illustrates Claude Shannon's simple communication model (Shannon 1948a, 1948b). The mathematical formulation is germane here. Some concepts are of interest. First, information is defined by novelty: if the contents are known to the receiver before the transmission, **no** "information" was transmitted. That leads to a definition based on the number of possible states of a system. For example, a coin toss has two possible results or states. Thus, information about a single coin toss is represented by a single bit of information. Passing N bits of information requires 2^N states. (For those familiar with binary representation of decimal numbers, a byte consists of 8 bits [each represented by a '0' or a '1'] and can have 2^8 or 256 states or values.) The information we acquire may be flawed by noise in the transmission. If we add intentional distortion to the noise factor, the information fidelity problem only gets worse.

Although Shannon was describing the nature of electrical transmission of information, his theory is applicable to all communications, including speech. Figure 2.5 modifies Fig. 2.4 by adding the feedback from the receiver to the sender to illustrate two-way communication (Shannon & Weaver 1963).

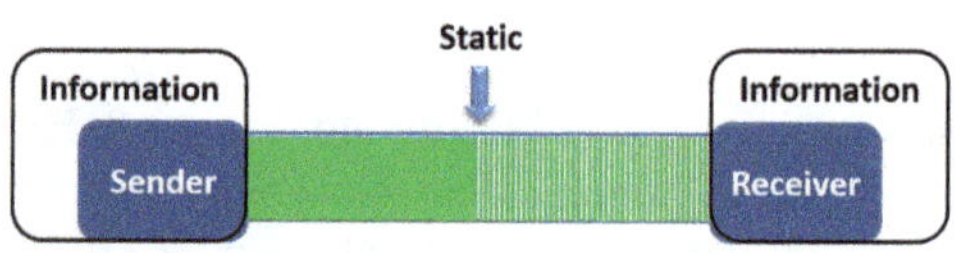

Fig. 2.4 Shannon's information flow

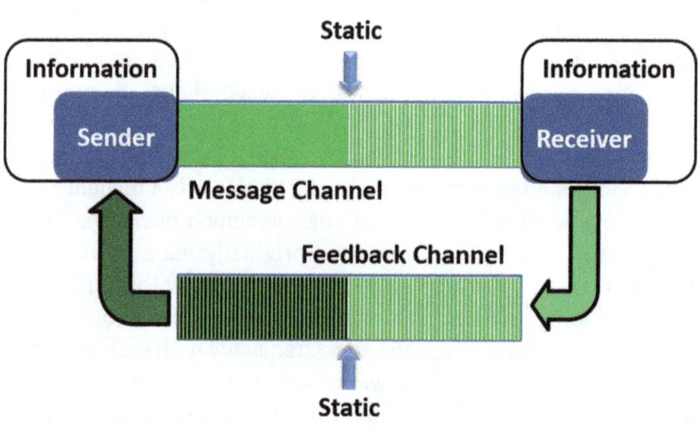

Fig. 2.5 Shannon's communication loop

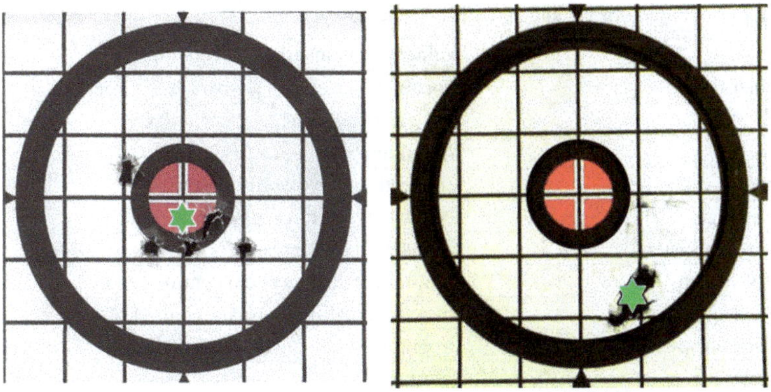

Fig. 2.6 Accuracy and precision

Shannon, after writing the formula for binary information transfer, cautioned that *technical accuracy and semantic precision do not equate to effectiveness.*

Figure 2.6 illustrates the difference between accuracy and precision. The target on the left has five bullet holes, with average strike point shown by the green six-pointed star. The target on the right also has five bullet holes, with average strike point shown by the star. The target on the left displays greater accuracy (but lower precision)—on average the bullets are hitting very close to the aim point (but are dispersed). The target on the right displays greater precision (but lower accuracy)—on average the bullets are hitting in the same spot (but further from the aim point). In shooting at paper targets, having both greater accuracy and greater precision will yield greater effectiveness. Shannon's point is that in transferring information, there is another factor at work. It you have great accuracy and precision, but the target is made of metal, the bullet may not penetrate. Similarly, in communications, having a great communications system does not guarantee the recipient will act on it as desired or even understand it.

All signals are context dependent. Signal-to-noise ratio is a part of context. With a Niagara Falls of incoming information, it is hard to distinguish the salient or even the relevant from the noise (indigestion from apocalypse).

The Internet has changed the way information is transferred and often even created. It has also brought manifold changes in languages. Internet communication "is making our language change faster, in more interesting ways, than ever before (McCulloch 2019)." The Internet is the backbone of the digital matrix bringing the network diffusion dynamics to the fore. Multiple genres from text, email, blogs, to podcasts, with new abbreviations, emojis and keysmashes that convey markers of social membership. The "always on," mobile, ubiquitous nature of this phenomenon exponentially increases communication volume, copying, accessing, sharing, filtering, remixing, and questioning. AI/ML will likely change this even more.

The dynamics of network communications are addressed in in the Network Science section in Chap. 5.

Table 2.2 Cognified objects and surfaces of attack

Object	Vulnerable items (data and controls)
Computer	Documents, pictures, passwords, connections
Router	Device connections
Printer	Stored images
Cell phone	Connections, passwords, data
Cloud storage	Documents, pictures, passwords, data
Social media system	Connections, pictures, information
Security system	Real-time visuals, system controls, entry
Cognified appliances	Inventory, real-time visuals, controls
Cognified infrastructure	Programmable industrial controls
Database	Information
Computer networks	Access to cognified objects
Internet of Things (IoT)	Control of objects, connections to networks
General infrastructure	Operations, when connected to cognified objects

Vulnerabilities in the Technium (Surfaces of Attack)

Rothrock quoted a French philosopher as saying that the existence of ships implies shipwrecks and the existence of planes implies plane crashes. He quoted the consultant Joshua Ramos as extending this to networks: the existence of networks implies network crashes (Rothrock 2018).

Attack surfaces, the span of different points where an attacker can try to enter, change or extract data, are generally considered when discussing a single computer program or system. The concept applies to your organization and your networked matrix (e.g., suppliers and customers) and easily generalizes to the technium as a whole because these cognified objects are generally connected to the Internet and, thus, connected to each other (the internet of things (IoT)) and to the whole supply chain. Attack surfaces are increasing in number and form as the technium involves the Internet. Each of the objects in Table 2.2 has its attack surfaces and each is part of the attack surface of the larger system we use in everyday life.

The internet of things forcefully exports the point of attack from a local problem to a global surface of attack, as the IoT embodies an exponential surge in the general increase in digital connectivity.

Attack-Tools of the Technium

Before computers, the noosphere consisted of the contents of people's brains and their written records. The most permanent parts were in books and the most evanescent written records were in newspapers. Today there are still brains, books and newspapers, but the technium has grown and there are also computer stores of knowledge, both localized on your own computer and indeterminate, in the "cloud," stored on someone else's computers elsewhere.

Malware and Defenses

Malware is computer software that interferes with the correct processing of information or corrupts that information. Malware is used to attack the part of the technium that is based on or connected to computers (computers themselves and machinery that uses computers, such as automobiles, the electrical grid, and centrifuge controllers). Clarke and Knake said, "66 percent of malware was delivered in email attachments (Clarke & Knake 2019)." The direct action of malware is on the technium; however, it also can act as an indirect attack on the noosphere, corrupting knowledge and inserting fake news. An article in the Journal of Cybersecurity provided a taxonomy of these "cyber-harms" (Agrafiotis, Nurse, Goldsmith, Creese, & Upton 2018).

An opinion article in The Wall Street Journal described a new type of malware—hardware malware. The article described the possibility of creating a Trojan horse in the hardware logic of a computer chip. Each chip that is manufactured and employed in a device would then come preloaded with the Trojan horse that looks legitimate, but is not. Its actual purpose may be to allow external control or exfiltrate information or simply to turn off the chip, that purpose to be activated at will by its designer. The point of the article is that most chips used in the U.S. are designed in the U.S., but manufactured in foreign countries. One such country could modify the design to include the Trojan horse and the complexity of the chip design would hide the modification (Scher & Levin 2020).

Malware

In cataloging malware, it is important to realize that the brains (cognition) behind the creation and use of the malware is more significant than the malware itself. With the exception of the unintended kind, such as the Morris worm, malware is used by humans to create ill effects. (The Morris worm was created to demonstrate vulnerabilities, but ended up infecting 10% of the computers connected to the internet in the late 1980s, causing massive denial of service by accident (Rothrock 2018).) The most sophisticated and dedicated malware users are called advanced persistent threats (APTs) (Clarke & Knake 2019).

Malware (software) is relatively cheap and easy to produce, purchase, scale, and deploy and can produce effects at almost any scale. Some of the earliest malware examples were simple "worms" that propagated through the early computer networks, produced by eager novices. Because of these and later examples, protection software and principles were created, requiring modern malware to be more sophisticated. Still, malware must be much smaller than some of the million-line programs in use today, so in relative terms, "cheap" and "easy" remain accurate descriptors. The "ease of entry" in obtaining malware is profound; there are even websites from which pre-built malware can be obtained for prices ranging from $1 to $3500 (Paganinin 2018). Naturally, there is a commercial market for anti-malware systems; however, as a result malware is evolving extremely rapidly. Currently, the advantage goes to the attacker in malware. However, Rothrock said that advances in digital resistance are eroding this advantage (Rothrock 2018).

Our ontology includes a section on malware, derived in part from a Carnegie Mellon University ontology (Costa et al. 2016). ***Malware Tool***: "A malicious piece of software," implanted in a computer for immediate or delayed activation. Figure 2.7 illustrates some types of malware.

The definitions of some of the types of malware are shown in Table 2.3.

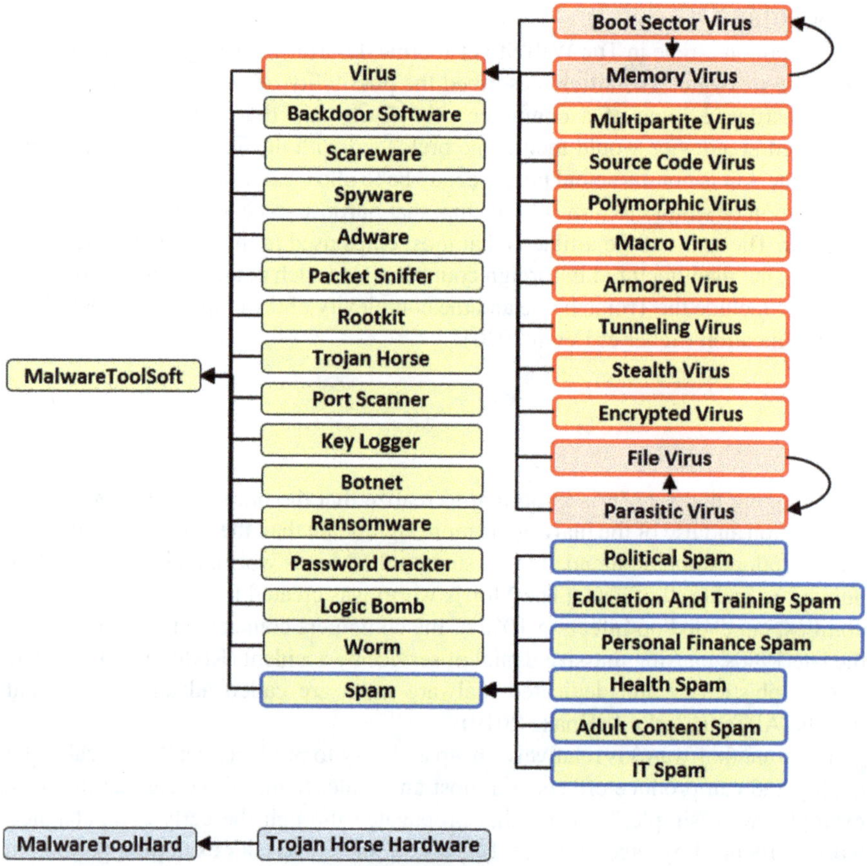

Fig. 2.7 Malware examples—software and hardware

Table 2.3 Definitions of selected malware types

Virus: "A program that is capable of replicating itself and has malicious purposes." There a number of types of virus tools shown in the figure. (The tools in orange with the "is-a" arrows going in both directions are different names for the same tool.)
Backdoor Software: "A computer program designed to allow an unauthorized path into the network or a system."
Logic Bomb: "A malicious program that is coded to execute when a certain set of requirements are met." That is, the code is implanted in the computer to be executed later.
Password Cracker: "A program that is used to identify an unknown or forgotten password to a computer or network resource."
Port Scanner: "A software program which scans a network for systems with open ports."
Key Logger: "A type of surveillance software that has the capability to record every keystroke made to a log file, usually encrypted."
Spam: "Unsolicited e-mail. May send harmful links, malware or deceptive content. Goal may be to obtain sensitive information."
Trojan Horse: Malware that looks legitimate, but is not.

Bots

Bots are "software agents used to generate simple messages and 'conversations' on social media." They range in sophistication from the very crude to extremely credible replications of humans. In 2014 a bot passed the Turing test for the first time. After a five-minute "conversation," a third of the judges believed there was a human on the other end of the conversation. This was one of the original goals of AI (Woolley & Howard 2019).

Typically, bots are hosted on a computer, whether legitimately (as with most service bots) or by infesting target computers. However, Rothrock discussed a 2016 exploit that largely used internet of things devices, rather than computers to host bots. This botnet was created by the Mirai botnet tool and consisted of around 100,000 nodes (Rothrock 2018).

Social bots or ***chat bots*** are built to respond like humans with pauses and other human cues. Some are clearly labeled as chat bots on web sites and provide a help function, releasing human help personnel to handle more difficult queries. Other social bots have more nefarious functions. For example, a set of bots can boost the apparent popularity of a product by posting positive statements from numerous "users" of the product. Sophisticated bots can maintain simultaneous presence on several social media sites, producing cross-feeds of supporting "opinions." Sophisticated bots respond to posts from other social media users (real or bot), supporting or contradicting these posts. Because they are software, bot usage is easily scaled to a very large presence (Woolley & Howard 2019).

Dubois and McKelvey investigated the use of bots in Canada. They identified several types. Political bots are social bots with an agenda of political manipulation. Dampener bots can suppress or dampen contrary political opinions by crowding out or reducing the accessibility to the public of the contrary opinions. Amplifier bots work to amplify supported political opinions by adding additional posts and reposting the supporting opinions (of real users or other bots). Transparency bots attempt to draw attention to the actions of public officials by posting those actions (generally of one given type of action per bot). Servant bots consist of bots such as the chat bots that serve help functions; however, to the extent that they collect personal information about the user chatting with them, their overall use may be problematical (Dubois & McKelvey 2019).

Singer and Brooking discussed the activities of bots. "For example, the day after Angee Dixson was outed [as a bot] in an analysis by the nonprofit organization ProPublica, a new account was spun to life named 'Lizynia Zikur.' She immediately decried ProPublica as an 'alt-left #HateGroup and #FakeNews Site.' Zikur was clearly another fake—but one with plenty of friends. The bot's message was almost instantly retweeted 24,000 times, exceeding the reach of ProPublica's original analysis. In terms of virality, the fake voices far surpassed the reports of their fakeness (Singer & Brooking 2018)."

"As businesses whose fortunes rise or fall depending on the size of their user base, social media firms are reluctant to delete accounts—even fake ones. On Twitter, for instance, roughly 15 percent of its user base is thought to be fake. For a company under pressure to demonstrate user growth with each quarterly report, this is a valuable boost (Singer & Brooking 2018)."

"Moreover, it's not always easy to determine whether an account is a bot or not. As the case of Angee Dixson shows, multiple factors, such as time of activity, links, network connections, and even speech patterns must be evaluated. Researchers then take all of these clues and marry them up to connect the dots (Singer & Brooking 2018)."

Memes

The science fiction author, David Gerrold wrote about the importance and power of memes. "Humans live and breed for their beliefs: often they sacrifice everything for the thoughts they carry. History is a chronicle of human beings dying for their convictions, as if the continuance of the idea is more important than the continuance of the person (Gerrold 2003)."

"The memetic warfare envisioned by Singer and Brooking in their book, *LikeWar*, recognizes the power of virality—the need to produce and propel viral content through the online system. But it also recognizes that the content that *goes* viral—the meme—can be quite easily hijacked. And whoever does that best determines what reality looks like (Singer & Brooking 2018)."

Wells and Horowitz described meme factories and some of the problems they cause in a Wall Street Journal article. They described how 421 Media records videos of stunts and searches for other posts that it can re-post for Instagram followers. The problem, as described, is that the volume of such posts by 421 Media and other meme factories endanger the "stylish and intimate aesthetic" of Instagram (Wells & Horowitz 2019).

Malicious Actions

Figure 2.8 illustrates some of the many malicious actions that can be performed to attack cognified systems. These include various forms of phishing, which rely on convincing a human operator to do something he or she shouldn't (like install malware) and various types of denial of service attacks that prevent the legitimate operation of the computer.

For example, suppose that Ralph (the leader), John, Sue, and Joe have invaded a system and copied a document, as shown in Fig. 2.9. Further, these individuals are linked to an instantiation (groupZeta) of the social faction class. This ontological view supports analysis at a higher level of aggregation than supported by the individual names.

Suppose it is determined that the theft was accomplished through the use of a phishing attack that allowed planting a backdoor into the system, followed by copying the document. These actions are shown in Fig. 2.10. These actions are linked to an aggregated action called *stealDocumentA*.

Two object instances are involved in this cyberattack, the document to be stolen and the malware tool used in the theft. These objects are shown in Fig. 2.11.

This example illustrates a purposeful attack with a unique goal, theft of the contents of a particular document. The cybersecurity firm Crowdstrike reported on the

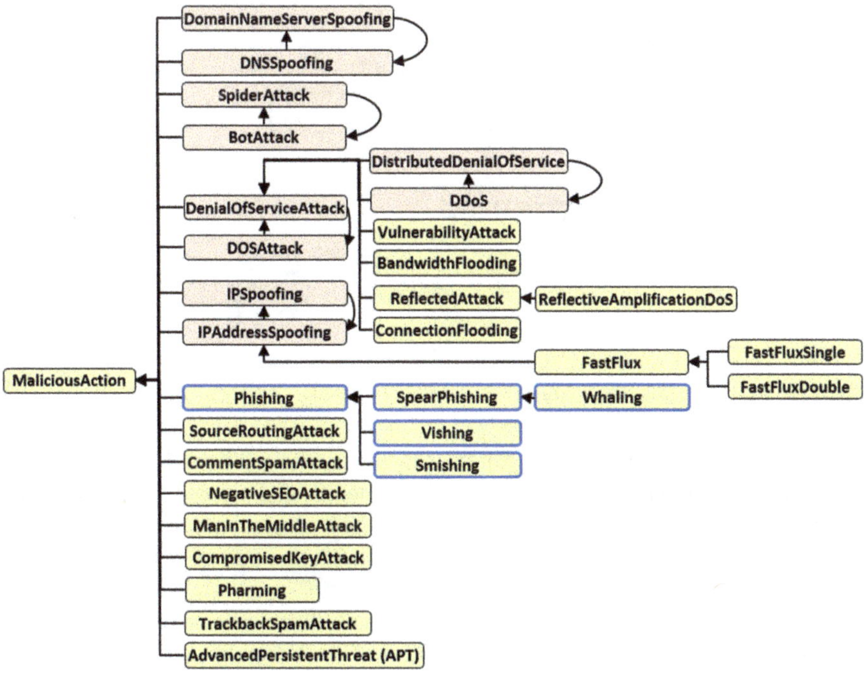

Fig. 2.8 Malicious (cyber) actions

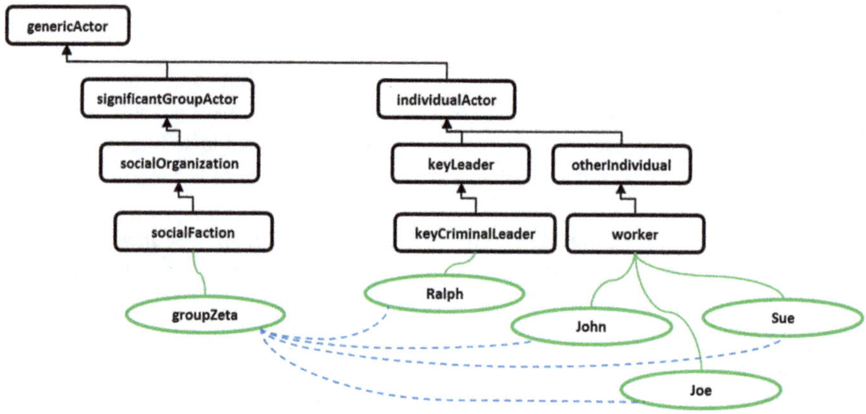

Fig. 2.9 Example cyberattack actors

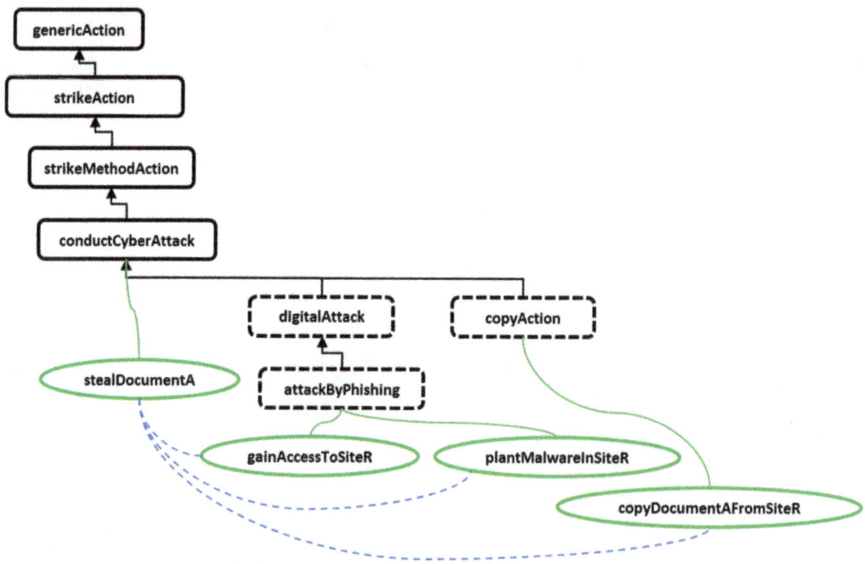

Fig. 2.10 Example cyberattack actions

2015 hacking of the Democratic National Committee computers. Russian hackers infiltrated the computers (through unspecified means) and prepared documents for exfiltration. Comparative digital footprints of these documents matched those of documents that were released, indicating that they were successfully stolen (The United States House of Representatives 2017).

However, many attacks have a general goal, with success measured in high probabilities of success, not any individual success. "The lesson for BuzzFeed, and for all aspiring social media warriors, was to make many small bets, knowing that some of them would pay off big." "Recall that ISIS could generate over a thousand official

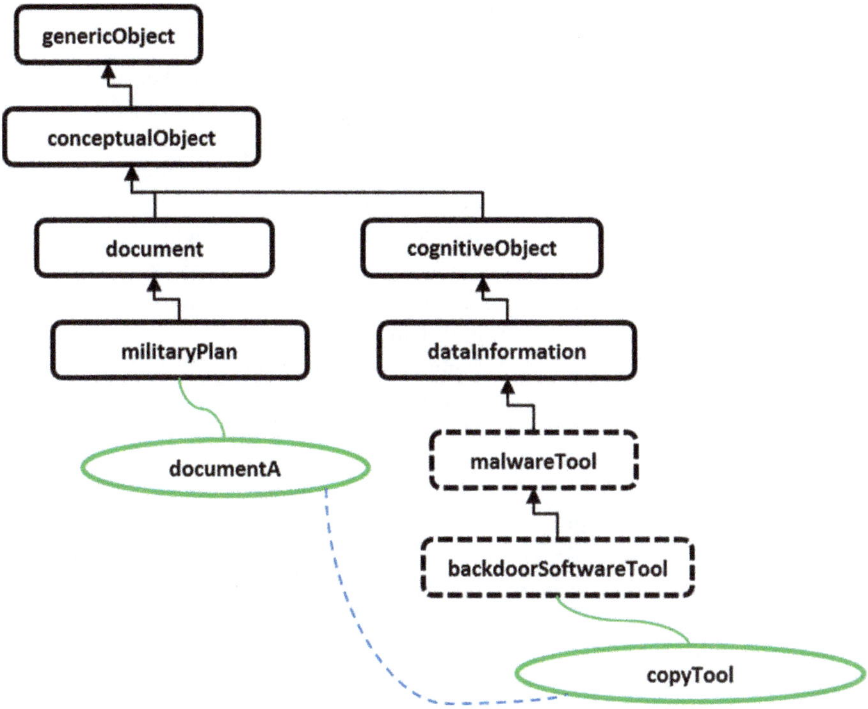

Fig. 2.11 Example cyberattack objects

propaganda releases each month. In each case, this continuous cascade allowed these savvy marketers to learn what worked for the next round (Singer & Brooking 2018)."

Computational Propaganda

Woolley and Howard defined the technical component of ***computational propaganda*** "as the assemblage of social media platforms, autonomous agents, algorithms, and big data tasked with the manipulation of public opinion." The social component is the propaganda, "communications that deliberately subvert symbols, appealing to our baser emotions and prejudices and bypassing rational thought, to achieve the specific goals of its promoters." As they explained it, "computational propaganda typically involves one or more of the following ingredients: bots that automate content delivery; fake social media accounts that require some (limited) human curation; and junk news (Woolley & Howard 2019)."

Time Duration of Successful Attacks

A denial of service attack takes milliseconds for the first set of packets to bombard a system. The technical success of the attack is apparent almost immediately. For the attack to be pragmatically successful, it must last long enough to disrupt the services of the target. Depending on the resources of the attacker and its goal, the duration can extend from hours to days.

Other types of attacks take time to develop. For example, it might take months of phishing to induce a person to click on a link or open an attachment that lets the attacker into a system. After that, it can take minutes to days for the attacker to explore the system and find the desired data. More malware may be required to actually exfiltrate the data out of the system into the hands of the attacker. Very large amounts of data may take days or weeks to exfiltrate (partially to avoid notice caused by abnormal data flows.) Ray Rothrock estimated that the Target data theft of 2013 that involved data records of 70 million customers took about two weeks, most in the exfiltration phase (Rothrock 2018). CrowdStrike defined "breakout time" as the time between the initial compromise and successful lateral movement in the victim environment. Breakout time represents the best window for stopping the attack. In 2018, the average breakout times for four major (attacker) nations and a crime group ranged from under 19 min to more than 9 h (Crowdstrike 2019).

Rothrock said, "an entire category of breach is categorized as an 'Advanced Persistent Threat' (APT), a network attack in which the intruder not only gains access to the network but remains active in it for a long period of time." (Note that here APT refers an action type, shown at the bottom of Fig. 2.8, whereas earlier it referred to a type of actor.) Rothrock referred to the "most spectacular documented APT," which is believed to be a Chinese attack. That attack maintained access to various networks for an average of 356 days, with the longest duration for one network being 1764 days (Rothrock 2018).

Defensive Tools and Actions

Protection tools and actions are relatively inexpensive; however, they must be used to be effective. ***Protection Tool***: "A piece of software that serves as protection against malware." Figure 2.12 illustrates some protection tools.

Table 2.4 defines some protection tools.

Figure 2.13 illustrates some of the actions that can be performed to prevent and mitigate malicious attacks on cognified systems and provide other protective services. Some are standard preventive security actions, such as replicating data, installing patches, and updating software regularly. Some are protection against particular types of attacks, such as authenticating sessions, limiting query types and blocking redundant queries. Reciprocal information sharing, including sharing attack profiles and attack code, can cause institutional problems, but is necessary (Falco et al. 2019). The final protection action is holistic in nature, aimed at creating and maintaining a resilient system. Modeling the network refers to more than just a

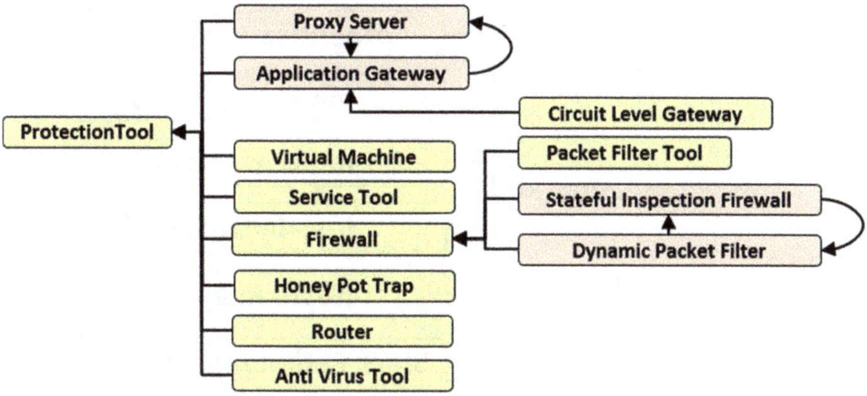

Fig. 2.12 Protection tool examples

Table 2.4 Definitions of selected protection tools

Firewall: "A system designed to prevent unauthorized connections to or from a private network." Types of firewalls are shown in the figure. (The tools in orange with the "is-a" arrows going in both directions are different names for the same tool.)
Service Tool: "A piece of software that runs in the background on a computer"
Virtual Machine: "A software implementation of a computing environment in which an operating system (OS) or program can be installed and run."
Proxy Server: "Serves as an intermediary between the user and a remote host to create the connection. May ask for password and other authentication."
Honey Pot Trap: A honey pot trap can be as simple as a dummy account or as complex as specifically created server systems, which are separated from the actual systems. Misleading documents or messages are loaded into the honey pot to induce a break in. The adversary is then identified. This is also called cyber blurring.
Router: A piece of hardware that connects multiple devices to the external internet. It provides a layer of protection for the devices.
Anti-virus Tool: A piece of software that looks for malware.

map of connections among the components, but includes methods for checking on the effects of modifying the system (Rothrock 2018). The mitigation actions support resilience. They include digital and organizational resilience, sharing of strategies and decoupling. Decoupling refers to the segmentation of data into access classes to prevent unauthorized access.

Trust Technologies

While trust is a human belief, there are technologies to support its application. You trust that when you put your money in a bank you will be able to retrieve it as needed. There was a time when this trust was sorely tested; banks failed; and people lost their money. In the U.S., the Federal Deposit Insurance Corporation (FDIC)

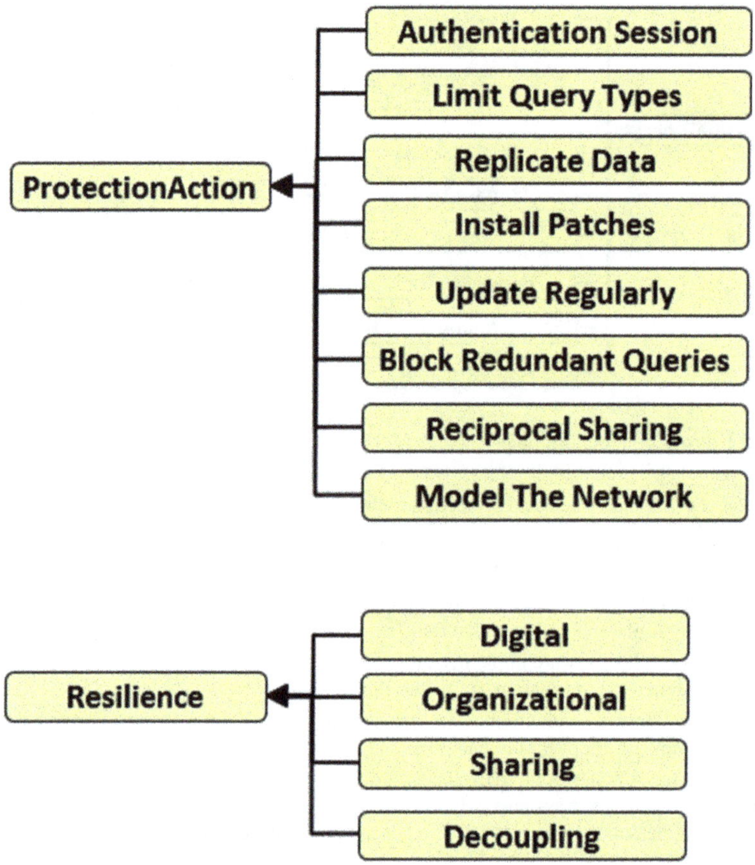

Fig. 2.13 Protection and mitigation actions

was created to restore trust in banks. The blockchain technology allows "secure" transactions outside of the traditional banking businesses (Henderson 2019). These are economic technologies. In a time when identity theft is common, we have a problem of trust—trust that our identities won't be stolen and trust that the identity proffered by someone else is valid.

A group from MIT has done extensive thinking about the subject, made presentations to various groups including the White House Commission on Cybersecurity, and published a book entitled, *Trust::Data: A New Framework for Identity and Data Sharing* (Hardjono, Shrier, & Pentland 2016). They began with the point that the systems that we use in daily life were not created with same fears about trust that we now have. Our banking systems started with personal visits to the bank: there was no need to validate electronic identities because they didn't exist. We were asked to supply our social security number when making a purchase at many places—and didn't worry about doing that. We often had it printed on our checks along with name and address! The authors remarked on the pervasive sensing that now exists: smart phones collect and share location data and people share incredible amounts (and scarcely credible [to the authors, at least] types) of data on the Internet. The authors called for reinventing societal systems to remedy the current situation—to ensure trust. Further, they described, in a fair amount of detail, proposals to do that.

Influence, Persuasion, Manipulation, Coercion, Control

Influence, persuasion, manipulation, coercion, and control are intrinsic to man, citizen of the noosphere and the technium, utterly intertwined. Malware is aimed at the objects in the technium. Thus, it acts indirectly on humans. However, there are tools in the technium that act directly on humans. This section introduces these tools. Table 2.5 lists fundamentals of persuasion. As always, consider context, timing, meta-structure, access to information, simplicity, ease of used, and repetition. The Persuasion section in the chapter on humans (Chap. 4) will define each item and discuss why and how they work.

There is and always has been a battle of ideas at the highest level of politics, policy and statecraft using speeches, stories, ceremonies, and symbols. Lies have been part of human culture since records have been kept. They are assaults on the noosphere (the total information available to humanity). However, our current (seeming) insistence on euphemisms, such as counterknowledge, half-truths, extreme views, alt truth, conspiracy theories, and fake news, in place of the word "lies" and the deterioration of our education with respect to critical thinking has lowered the bar for lies to be weaponized (Levitin 2016). The ammunition consists of stories, words, memes, numbers, pictures and statistics. Salient topics include deepfakes (artificial intelligence (AI)-augmented false news, pictures, sound and video clips putting words into the mouths of others), associative decoding (inserting false memories (Ramirez et al. 2013)), meaning platforms, serenics, knowledge of the spread dynamics of information versus spread of behavior or spread of violence, in traditional and digital systems (Centola 2018b). Weaponized lies purposefully undermine our ability to make good decisions (Levitin 2016).

Influence, as it operates in the continuum of persuasion, coercion and control, can take many forms. Default rules can eliminate choices from search engines to traditionally offered choice lists. There is power in perfidy. Trust is central and offers a target of influence. Merchants of doubt are often used. With the fragile and stringent markers of social membership and humans' powerful bias toward membership, affiliative and dissociative forces can be marshalled. Mis-directions such as bait-and-switch are seen frequently. Influencing the decision time frame can work. Denial, obfuscation, reframing, redefining, relabeling, and repositioning are methods of influence. Quantitative propaganda has manifold forms. Changes in signal-to-noise ratios are powerful: haystacks of misinformation can hide a needle of truth or confuse indigestion with apocalypse. Fake news can use bot armies and hide innumerable human biases, fears and needs.

Table 2.5 Persuasion fundamentals

Persuasion

The Panopticon:

In our surveilled world, sensing (as surveillance), when fused with computation and communication, enables the garnering and direction of attention, can influence default rules, provide biometrics and sociometrics, and fashion persuasion science strategies, all in an iteratively adaptive propitious manner. The massive data sets of the panopticon provide the raw material for the future of AI/ML, armed with experimentation.

Central Forms	Aristotle	Cicero	Cialdini	Sharot	Fogg	Thaler & Sundstein	Pink	Berger	Martin & Marks	Centola/ Jackson	Digital Attention Merchants
Personal Contact	*Ethos*	Knowledge of Audience	Liking	Priors	Motivation	Incentives	Carrots	Reduce Reactance	Messenger Bias	Network Structure	Garnering attention
Stories	*Logos*	Understand-ing the Case	Reciprocity	Emotion	Ability	Understand-ing mapping	Sticks	Ease Endowment	Hard Messenger	Network Dynamics	Addictive technology
Speeches	*Pathos*	Arranging the Argument	Authority	Incentives	Prompts /Triggers	Structure complex choices	Autonomy	Shrink Distance	Soft Messenger	Diffusion: Information Behavior	Persuasion profiles
Ceremonies	*Kairos*	Emotions	Social Proof	Agency	Captology	Defaults	Mastery	Alleviate Uncertainty		Human & Digital	Always On
Symbols		Eloquent Delivery	Consistency	Curiosity	MIP	Give feedback	Meaning	Corroborat-ing Evidence		Fulcrum of connectivity	Micro-targeting
Social Signals		Practice	Scarcity	State		Expect error				Centrality	Swarms
			Unity	Others						Virality	Global scale
			Pre-suasion								

Technology's New Ecology, Mix and Match: Adaptive, Combinatorial, AI/ML Augmented, Synchronic or Diachronic, nascent xR

Assessment of Credibility, Character and Ability underlies Trust (trust technologies are nascent)

Diachronic (occurring over time or for future effect, as opposed to synchronic or contemporaneous effect)

- ***Shi***: A central ancient Chinese stratagem of warfare, a deception involving influencing the present as part of a larger or grand strategy to influence the future at a propitious moment, often for a long-term, zero-sum game.
- **Apple of Discord**: Sowing a small disagreement to create growth to a major conflict, e.g., election interference for trust, polarization & outcomes.
- **Sleeper software**: Implanted malware to be activated at a later time.
- **Parable of the seed in the Bible**: The seed is sown in various environments with different effects at a later time.

With research, surveillance and analysis, messages can be personalized (micro-targeted) for the optimal density of learning moments. Surveillance and rhetoric are informed by new advances in multiple disciplines. Gargan personalized these concepts, discussing using new forums of cognition (social media) and new features of arrangement (attention catching, non-boring introductions and follow-through) (Gargan 2017).

Computerized Persuasion

Maurits Kaptein calculated the effect of the Internet on sales. The simple formula he used was that the effect should be proportional to the reach (the number of people touched) times the impact (effectiveness of the message). The reach has increased dramatically over time: consider pre-printing press reach, post-printing press reach, radio and television reach, and Internet reach (almost the whole world). The Facebook social network has 2.9 **billion** users (Forbes 2020). Certainly, different salesmen have different levels of competency and thus impact; however, they should average out at some level. Projecting the increased reach multiplied by impact should yield enormous increases in sales. Sales have increased; however, dividing actual sales by reach shows that impact has declined as reach has increased. The Internet has not been delivering the expected dividends! Kaptein concluded that, on average, the Internet "touches" were less effective than live salesmen. Kaptein's research showed that to have greater impact, the Internet influence efforts would need to employ the persuasion techniques described by such as Cialdini (listed in (Cialdini 2009)) and take advantage of the research of Fogg (below) (Kaptein 2015).

Captology is the study of computers as persuasive technologies (Fogg, Home, n.d.). This includes the design, research, ethics and analysis of interactive computing products (computers, mobile phones, websites, wireless technologies, mobile applications, video games, etc.) created for the purpose of changing people's attitudes or behaviors. In his book, *Persuasive Technology*, Fogg discussed the elements of captology (Fogg 2003). Clearly, the potential target of persuasion (person) is not interacting with a human being in a face-to-face encounter. However, the target is not interacting with a "computer" (think machine with blinking lights and spinning magnetic tapes), but with a computer interface—typically a computer monitor, a cell phone screen, or a speaking "personality," such as Alexa or Siri. The large amount of human interaction that occurs through these same devices reduces the perceptible difference between face-to-face persuasive encounters and computer persuasive encounters.

Fogg pointed out several advantages that computers have over human persuaders. Computers are persistent; they allow anonymity; they can access large stores of data; they can vary their presentations; they can expand the numbers of simultaneous targets; and they can be everywhere. These advantages are actually just the beginning. Humans can also vary their persuasive presentations. However, this variation is based on the skill of the particular human at reading the situation and making modifications. Computer adaptations can be based on scientific research, using those large data stores, to choose the variation that is most likely to succeed based on the situation.

Fogg's Stanford Persuasive Tech Lab website contains discussions on human behavior and techniques for changing it using technology (Fogg, Home, n.d.). This includes both individual persuasion and changing attitudes and behaviors on a mass scale—***Mass Interpersonal Persuasion (MIP)***. He also included some warnings about computer persuasion. The first warning relates to source trust: just because a website exists, does not mean its contents are true. The topic of "website credibility" has developed a large body of knowledge. Even videos can be faked or contain faked parts. The second warning concerns "seduction via video games." In all video games, the cause and effect relations that underlie the action may or may not reflect real-world cause and effect. However, as part of our human learning process we internalize our notions of cause and effect by observation, not through school courses. Where simulations lead to errors in learning, we encounter what the military calls "negative training (Hartley 1995)." Fogg said it is bad enough to have negative training just to make the video game fun; however, video games can be engineered to influence gamers' social and political views without allowing for conscious consideration of arguments concerning the influence. Finally, he warned of individualized or micro-targeted persuasion profiling. Advertisements are selectively placed on our web search results based on previously collected information on our activities. There are even more subtle strategies in which our decision-making is analyzed to create an iteratively adaptive personalized profile of our susceptibility to particular persuasion techniques. This profile can then be used later to more accurately persuade us to buy, vote, or act as desired by the site owner. Computational social science has arrived.

In 2005, Zappen surveyed the literature of digital rhetoric. He said it "encompasses a wide range of issues, including novel strategies of self-expression and collaboration, the characteristics, affordances, and constraints of the new digital media, and the formation of identities and communities in digital spaces (Zappen 2005)."

Persuasion Through Search Engines

Dr. Robert Epstein, past editor-in-chief of *Psychology Today* and currently Senior Research Psychologist at the American Institute for Behavioral Research and Technology, testified before the Senate Judiciary Subcommittee on Constitution that between 2.6 and 10.4 million votes were manipulated in the 2016 election by Google. He testified that through bias (picking one candidate over the other) and the search engine manipulation effect (SEME), the search suggestion effect, the answer-bot effect, and other techniques Google increased the votes of one candidate. In 2020, 15 million votes could be shifted (Senate Judiciary Subcommittee on Constitution 2016). Epstein's research on SEME was published in the Proceedings of the National Academy of Sciences (PNAS) (Epstein & Robertson 2015).

Persuasion in the xR World

xR refers to extended reality technology and experience. It is immersive and includes virtual reality (VR), augmented reality (AR), 360° video, and mixtures of these (MR). The use of xR is rapidly expanding, including commerce, education, entertainment, and warfare.

The new virtual reality (VR) world has been *terra incognita* of social interaction metric and analytics. This is changing with the new Stanford University Virtual Human Interactions Lab (Stanford University VHIL 2019). New persuasion forces are expected from virtual reality and companion avatars. We have seen hints of this where simulations lead to errors in learning, encountering what the military calls "negative training (Hartley 1995)."

Persuasion in the AI World

In an age of both massive and personalized surveillance, digital social networks can be personalized and "optimized for engagement," using "glimmers" of novelty, attention channeling messages of affirmation and belonging, and messages of outrage toward preconceived enemies, for affiliative or dissociative ends. AI-empowered suggestion engines, armed with conditional probabilities (driven by machine learning) are powerful persuaders (Polson & Scott 2018).

"But it doesn't take an authoritarian state to turn a neural network toward evil ends. Anyone can build and train one using free, open-source tools. An explosion of interest in these systems has led to thousands of new applications. Some might be described as 'helpful,' others 'strange.' And a few—though developed with the best of intentions—are rightly described as nothing less than 'mind-bendingly terrifying (Singer & Brooking 2018).'" "Just as they can study recorded speech to infer meaning, these networks can also study a database of words and sounds to infer the *components* of speech—pitch, cadence, intonation—and learn to mimic a speaker's voice almost perfectly. Moreover, the network can use its mastery of a voice to approximate words and phrases that it's never heard. With a minute's worth of audio, these systems might make a good approximation of someone's speech patterns. With a few hours, they are essentially perfect (Singer & Brooking 2018)."

The largest digital platforms can gather and dispense attention on a world-wide scale. Recent advances in combinatorial persuasion, armed with AI, augmented with personal and group metrics can make many individuals and the masses more prone more to follow suggestions. The resolute can become sequacious.

The technium can accelerate the decision process and thus alter the probability of an outcome.

Fake News and Disinformation (the Power of Perfidy)

A fundamental humans bias is our default to truth or initial assumption of truthfulness (Gladwell 2019). This default bias can aid in adaptive affiliation but leaves us vulnerable as described in *The Misinformation Age* (O'Connor & Weatherall 2019), *Weaponized Lies* (Levitin 2016), and the newer methods of false memory insertion (Ramirez et al. 2013). We also have a countervailing "open vigilance" or "reactance" that must be overcome for us to move from our initial opinion or be persuaded. Most efforts at mass persuasion fail (Mercier 2020).

Whereas malware is a tool in the information conflict; fake news is both a product of the information conflict and a tool in the conflict. An article in *Science* defines "'***fake news***' to be fabricated information that mimics news media content in form but not in organizational process or intent." According to the authors, this distinction is important because it plays on the trust gained by standard news media. "Failures of the U.S. news media in the early 20th century led to the rise of journalistic norms and practices that, although imperfect, generally served us well by striving to provide objective, credible information (Lazer et al. 2018)."

In a chapter titled "Fake News and Information Warfare," Guadagno and Guttieri discussed fake news in detail. They concluded that "there are many personal, political, and psychological factors" that relate to answering the questions of who spreads fake news, who falls for fake news, and what makes fake news effective. Historically, fake news has existed for a long time. Social media has made the spread of fake news easier. The allure of conspiracy theories supports some forms of fake news. Motivated belief (confirmation bias), emotional contagion, and delusions support the acceptance of fake news. The existence of political filter bubbles also supports fake news (Guadagno & Guttieri 2019).

Having been used to accepting information from news media, people are likely to be relatively uncritical in accepting fake news. Where there is conflicting information, "people prefer information that confirms their preexisting attitudes (selective exposure), view information consistent with their preexisting beliefs [their preconceptions] as more persuasive than dissonant information (confirmation bias), and are inclined to accept information that pleases them (desirability bias) (Lazer et al. 2018)." As illustrated in Figure 2.14, the aphorism "garbage in, garbage out" holds true for people as well as for computers.

In *Weaponized Lies*, Daniel Levitin said, "We have three ways to acquire information: We can discover it ourselves, we can absorb it implicitly, or we can be told it explicitly (Levitin 2016)." Figure 2.15 shows how each means of acquiring knowledge can be corrupted.

We have a bounded reality (see Chap. 3); our discovery of new knowledge is limited by our own preconceptions. When we play computer games, we follow the rules of the game, whether they are valid representations of reality or not. The more realistic the game seems, the more likely that we will absorb lessons that we will apply to reality. This means that we are vulnerable to someone engineering the rules to fit their desires. [This is true for books, also. If the books always present stereotypes of humans, whether racial stereotypes or sex-based stereotypes, we are likely

Fig. 2.14 Garbage in → garbage out

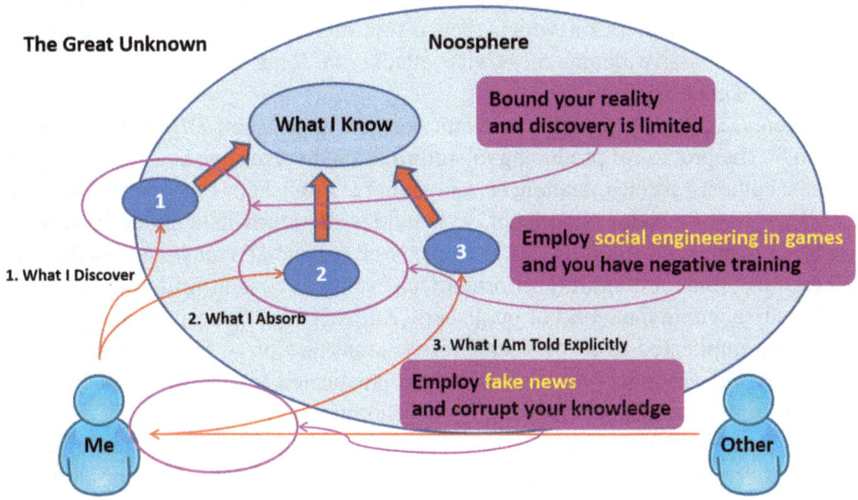

Fig. 2.15 Corrupting the acquisition of knowledge

to absorb these stereotypes into our own thinking.] When we are told something explicitly, we do have the opportunity to believe or disbelieve it. However, the alleged authority of the source can affect our choice. Creators of fake news can subvert our choice by mimicking or discrediting authoritative sources.

Within the numberless diversities and manifold singularity and forms of false information, we have selected exemplars of types and corrective responses (not to be confused with a *summa summarum*). The scale and frequency are evinced by the estimate that more than half of web traffic (legitimate and illegitimate (Neudert 2019)) and a third of Twitter users are bots (Woolley & Howard 2019). "Twitter falsehoods spread faster than the truth (Temming 2018)." This danger led the 2014 World Economic Forum to identify the rapid spread of misinformation among the 10 perils to society (Woolley & Howard 2019).

Search engines, filtering and ranking algorithms, social media platforms, blogs, Twitter threads, feckless celebrity posts, journalist reporting trending false stories, bad science, graphical bias, bad statistics, the absence of critical thinking, perfidy and computational propaganda abound. Deepfake technologies to manipulate images, including video, are extant and rapidly improving in sophistication. Among disinformation bots we find *sleeper bots*—a variety of implanted impact bots that establish a following at scale; *amplifying bots* that use liking or sharing and producing complaints to send requests for social media platforms to ban entities; *tracking bots* to detect and drive attention; and *service bots* to help automate other functions. All are among the numberless streams of misinformation (Dubois & McKelvey 2019; Wooley & Howard 2019b). Further, some bots do not act individually, but form ***botnets*** that communicate with each other and their owner. These bots have co-opted the computers on which they reside and can perform such actions as engaging in massive denial of service attacks on some other computer system (Clarke & Knake 2019).

Preference profiles "used by the giant search engines skew efforts at exhaustive search." "The process of producing misinformation involves five key elements: publishers, authors, articles, audiences and rumors. Publishers run distributive platforms which have codes of conduct, style guides and journalistic guidelines. Some are more formal and rigorous (for example, well respected mainstream media publishers) and some are entirely informal (for example, content mills for clickbait). Authors live within the world of publishers (Ruths 2019)." "Social media platforms have been implicated as a key vector for the transmission of Fake News ... using human hybrid accounts and increasingly sophisticated tools embedded in social media (Grinberg, Joseph, Friedland, Swire-Thompson, & Lazer 2019)."

This is not a theoretical problem. Tufekci discussed the increasing use of media platforms for active disinformation campaigns (Tufekci 2018). Current claims of accurate identification of fake news on the Internet using structured vocabulary and spread dynamics generally vary from 69% to 84%. Optimal identification is still unsettled, with a potential for the unintended consequence of labeling a true story as fake (Temming 2018). Further, we now have the capability to use competing AI programs, called generative adversarial networks (GAN), to produce fake news (Giles 2018).

Singer and Brooking described the propagation of fake news. "Modest lies and grand conspiracy theories have been weapons in the political arsenal for millennia. But social media has made them more powerful and more pervasive than ever before. In the most comprehensive study of its kind, MIT data scientists charted the life cycles of 126,000 Twitter 'rumor cascades'—the first hints of stories before they could be verified as true or false. The researchers found that the fake stories spread about six times faster than the real ones. 'Falsehood diffused significantly farther, faster, deeper, and more broadly than the truth in all categories of information,' they wrote (Singer & Brooking 2018)."

Singer and Brooking reported on fake news resulting in real threats of war, which did not escalate when the fake news was debunked. They continued, "Sadly, not all false online reports have been stopped before they've sparked real wars. In mide-2016, the rival armies of South Sudan's president and vice president had settled into an uneasy truce after years of civil war. But when the vice president paid a visit to the presidential palace, his spokesperson published a false Facebook update that he had been arrested. Reading the post, the vice president's men paid an angry (and heavily armed) visit to the palace to rescue him. The president's bodyguards in turn opened fire—igniting a series of battles that would leave over 300 dead and plunge the nation back into conflict (Singer & Brooking 2018)."

AI is contributing to the alteration of the perception of reality. A small note in Forbes (Bosilkovski 2018) said, "In November 2016, Adobe introduced Sensei (Japanese for "teacher"), artificial-intelligence and machine learning software that can, for instance, recognize facial features in a Photoshop file and allow a person's expression to be changed without making the image look unnatural."

Detecting Fake News and Disinformation

"If there is no truth, there can be no trust" "with the attendant corrosion of group identity and national unity (Snyder 2018)." Deepfakes must be unmasked using image verification technology.

"Information overload and the average web surfer's limited attention span aren't exactly conducive to fact checking." "People will likely choose something that conforms to their own thinking, even if that information is false (Temming 2018)." The computer programs designed to detect fake news are now in their infancy and give rough conditional probabilities. Substance, style, structure, word choice and social network structures are guides in this imperfect art/science of fake news detection. "False articles tended to be shorter and more repetitive with more adverbs. Fake news stories also had fewer quotes, technical words and nouns." "Fake news like a virus can evolve and update itself (Temming 2018)."

There is a nascent, expanding understanding of the skills of correcting misinformation. Of course, it is preferable to get the facts and incorporate the facts before the misinformation to take advantage of the anchoring bias of initial opinion.

Narrative Warfare

As Ajit Maan put it, "[narrative warfare] is not information warfare; it is warfare over the *meaning* of the information (Maan 2018)." Narratives tell the meaning of the facts. Narratives have always been central to persuasion. The tools of persuasion are manifold and powerful. Persuasion is undergoing an accelerating growth in complexity and change in the morphology of its causal chains and systems of power at multiple scales. Persuasion operates at all levels of power: political, diplomatic, commercial, military, financial, educational, and personal.

Narrative warfare consists of a coherent strategy that uses honest or fake news as a tactic. "The currency of the narrative isn't truth, it is meaning (like poetry) (Maan 2018)." The idea is to create a **story** that leads to the desired conclusion. The story need not be "true," but it must resonate with the audience. It is effective because it bypasses critical thinking and shapes the identity of the receptive audience, and thus its beliefs and actions (Maan 2018). The relationship between the persuader and persuadee is central (Martin & Marks 2019). Knowledge of the audience is critical from their orienting, metanarratives from world view to politics, personality and local matrix of relationships and identity (see section on Persuasion in Chap. 4). It is essential to understand the distinctive features of efforts to correct misinformation versus having a clean slate of a neutral recipient.

"Narratives are the building blocks that explain both how humans see the world and how they exist in large groups. They provide the lens through which we perceive ourselves, others, and the environment around us. They are the stories that bind the small to the large, connecting personal experience to some bigger notion of how the world works. The stronger the narrative is, the more likely it is to be retained and remembered (Singer & Brooking 2018)."

"[C]ognitive science has demonstrated countering lies by repeating them with the word 'no' (or some other negative) actually has the opposite effect. That strengthens the false statement in the mind of the audience (Maan 2018)." To counter the false or the established opinion, we must understand the audiences' assumptions, preconceptions, social memberships, and identity as currently constructed. It is often best to avoid a direct counter narrative and instead use a larger metanarrative to reframe or encompass the opposition. Generally, it is important to actively engage the listener. Offer a bigger, better, stronger, smarter alternative way of understanding, of identifying, of acting (Maan 2018). If the persuader is seen as an "authority," "them," or not one of "us" by the persuadee, it may be useful to begin with a faint denouncement of oneself to be sure you are on eye level with the audience as a step toward common ground (Berger 2020).

Surveillance and the Panopticon (Our Surveilled World)

Surveillance is the fusing of sensing (both outward and inward), communication and computation. Ubiquitous surveillance is inevitable. "We are on our way to manufacture 54 billion sensors every year by 2020 (Kelly 2016)." Panopticus was the mythical Greek Giant who saw all with his many eyes. Now by extension, the ***Panopticon*** refers to the surveillance state, where the state sees all and knows much. The Internet is the world's largest and fastest sensing machine. Early awareness of discovery and emergence within the noosphere and technium is critical, as surveillance technologies from satellite imagery to single photon detection are rapidly increasing in power and scope.

Sensing and Communication

The domain (what is sensed), matrix (the environment within which the sensing takes place), and technology of sensing are morphing. The domain now must include awareness (traditional sensing), emergence and reification in the noosphere and technium, as well as traditional spying. A critical example of change in both domain and matrix of sensing is "quantum inspired computational imaging (Altmann et al. 2018)." With quantum-inspired computational imaging and "fusing of high temporal resolution (a trillion frames a second) together with single photon sensitivity (Hadfield 2009; Migdall, Polyakov, Fan, & Bienfang 2013) and advanced computational analysis techniques, a new generation of imaging devices is emerging." The 3D images can be taken of a scene that is hidden behind a wall or through fog.

Our digital society is approaching the Panopticon, in which everything is observed, recorded, analyzed, and (potentially) acted upon. Currently, almost anything that can be tracked is being tracked. Everything means all communications, whether audio, video or text, location and movement, activity types, and computer data. Data on our click streams, our online activities, and our on-and-off-line human networks are available. New technologies are permitting the addition of social signals (non-verbal clues to thinking and feeling) to this mix (Pentland 2008). Pentland described using monitoring and analysis to design "better" city environments and to design better, smarter, more effective teams and larger social groups. Utilizing sociometric badges for collecting data and sociometrics for analysis resulted in findings of improved collective cognition (Pentland 2014). Human senses can be augmented with multiple points of view from satellite to microscopic views. For example, the Mojo Lens replaces AR headsets with a contact lens that displays context-related information on the retina using "invisible computing (Mojo Vision Inc 2019)." The surveilled data is quantified, producing biometrics (physiologic and behavioral), psychometrics, neurometrics, and sociometrics. Use of GPS, voice and facial recognition is widespread. More and more often, sensing data is processed using AI/ML to infer new patterns and produce data about data (metadata). Multimodal sentiment analysis and other new disciplines of knowledge are upending traditional surveillance modalities and changing cognition (Poria, Hussain, & Cambria 2018). Continuous sensing allows experimental design and implementation for iterative additive influence (Luca & Bazerman 2020).

The future may hold additional surveillance threats. Single photon detection is nascent and will extend surveillance into the dark and through selected walls and barriers (Hadfield 2009; Migdall et al. 2013). Commercial, hand-held digital olfaction tools are in use (Bombgardner 2020). Each person is enveloped in a genomic, epigenomic, proteomic, and microbiomic plume and leaves a trail when moving. (Did you think bloodhounds track people by magic?) Automated methods of location, tracking and contact tracing (for marketing, surveillance, and public health) of individuals are extant (Stern 2020). Neuralink seeks to directly connect the individual brain to the silicon computer world (Neuralink Corp 2018; Hernandez & Mack 2019). There are current DOD efforts to effect a direct brain/computer interface, the place where silicon and carbon meet (Tullis 2019). Consider the possibility of hacking our brains through such a link.

Meanwhile, wide-area surveillance technology continues to advance. "Over a period of three months in 2016, a small aircraft circled above the same parts of West Baltimore that so recently drew the ire of President Trump. Operated by a company called Persistent Surveillance Systems, the plane was equipped with 12 cameras which, at 8000 feet, could take in 32 square miles of city in minute detail (Mims 2019a)." Christopher Mims reported that this and other similar systems permit tracking suspects from a crime scene to getaway cars. Other systems can then identify the cars' license plates as they pass by closed-circuit cameras. He reported that some multi-camera systems used to cost a half million dollars, but now cost between $82,000 and $140,000 and will cost half that for their next versions. He continued, "But as the technology rolls out—and roll out it will—it's likely to stoke considerable debates about a new definition of privacy." In the new age of experimentation, the vision of the Panopticon is extended by designed experiments on the users of digital platforms (Luca & Bazerman 2020).

Computation

There is new data science and technology to gather and analyze big data to discover individual identity and social signals. The data are enhanced with experimentation and data-driven predictive analytics. Data are gathered from our monitored world and from social media use and directly from smart phone use. We are subject to hacking into our home security system, cars and even baby monitors. We regularly are subject to phishing, attempts to induce us to reveal information, such as passwords and credit card numbers through false, but ostensibly valid, emails. Hackers, corporations, digital social media platforms, nation-states, and data brokers are pervasive in the world of surveillance.

Profiling and targeting for influence will soon use much finer granularity and quantities of information from an ever widening variety of sources, such as persuasion science (utilizing AI/ML to claim the propitious moment (see Humu, below)) and information from man's genomic, epigenetic, proteomic, and microbiomic plumes and trails.

An exemplar of the nascent emergence of the Orwellian power to influence (control) man is seen in Humu (Humu, Inc. 2018). Here the potential of the confluence of learning science, persuasion science, motivational science and network science arrives with statements of beneficence. Humu advertises that it will "Transform your organization." It has a Nudge Engine® to deliver personal suggestions. Traditionally, the manifold forms and forces of persuasion were found in stories, speeches, ceremonies, and symbols. Now to these can be added algorithms that can drive systems of persuasion. The new ability can be embedded in AR, VR, xR, cognified objects and the software that enwraps our wetware (*a persuasion matrix*).

Workplace or human analytics sounds benign and possibly beneficial. However, the analyses require data and that data are being collected from the workers—and not always "anonymized"—the data are tied to each worker to allow improvement efforts. The data can include recipient and timing of emails, contents of texts and phone calls, appointment calendars and actual meetings, duration data on time spent on various activities at work and at home, tonal analysis of conversations in meetings, behavior patterns such as talking over others, speech speed and volume, stress levels, network connections within and outside of the company, movement within the office, keystrokes and screens viewed on the computer, even videos of the worker taken from the computer. Companies such as TrustSphere, Microsoft, Teramind, and Humanyse provide software, hardware and services to capture and analyze these data (Krouse 2019). Cutter and Feintzeig describe companies who market and companies who use software to monitor employees' happiness and general mental states (Cutter & Feintzeig 2020). China is expanding the requirement that digital communication device owners download an aggregating surveillance app (Li & Wen 2019b).

Status

The U.S. has a history of antipathy toward spying and the military in general. Henry Stimson shut down the State Department's cryptanalytic office in 1929 saying, "Gentlemen don't read each other's mail (Stubblebine 2018)." During the Vietnam War, ROTC was kicked off many college campuses (Cohen 2010). Recently more than 100 students, many from Stanford University, signed a petition to boycott Google until it quits defense work. And 4000 Google staffers signed a petition for Google to withdraw from a defense contract analyzing military drone data (Baron 2018). In the United States, public opinion limits the government. Our intelligence agencies have the capabilities to create a Panopticon, but are restricted by law from doing so—although there are recent reports of using driver licenses to create a database of faces for facial recognition (Harwell 2019).

However, Google, Facebook, Amazon, and perhaps other corporations are closing in on their own versions of the panopticon (McNamee 2019). In other countries, such as China, the state is not so restricted and is rapidly approaching their own Panopticon. China even has access to almost all individual purchase information (Lee 2018). Facebook has set about creating its own crypto-currency (similar to Bitcoin), called Libra (BBC 2019). One fear is that this will give it access to similar data on purchases external to the Internet-world. The surveillance state and the major corporate Internet platforms have bio-behavioral personalized metrics to target for maximum influence; thus, we are more easily persuaded, influenced and potentially controlled.

The COVID-19 pandemic has provided a justification for some surveillance. For example, hospitals are installing automated, face-recognition thermal cameras for detecting the temperatures of people entering the building. Similar systems have been discussed for sporting events, casinos, theme parks, airline terminals, and businesses (Taylor 2020). The concept is that someone with a fever may have the virus and can be excluded. This type of surveillance and other surveillance systems that have been added in response to the pandemic cost money. When the pandemic is over, will these surveillance systems be dismantled—or retained and repurposed?

The relevant fields, beyond governance, include cognitive science, information science, and psychology, and are delivering results such as our new understanding of man's predictably, systematically irrational aspects. Artificial Intelligence / Machine Learning (AI/ML) armed with big data analytics from the Panopticon (surveillance state) can micro-target or sway a group.

Biological Tools

In the twentieth century man began to develop biological tools to cure diseases, influence mood and optimize cognition. More recently, partial control at the fundamental information/genetic level has become extant.

Biosecurity and Biological Attacks

Whether biological agents (1) are feral diseases, (2) come from unintended releases, or (3) are purposefully released, they can produce massive health and economic effects. A low barrier to entry into the bio-war domain, the ability to scale an attack, and the potential of problematic attribution make this an area of urgent concern. Genomic science, advanced genetic engineering, synthetic biology, and augmented computational biology with high-throughput manufacturing could contribute to a biological attack. Further, the World Health Organization (WHO) coined the word "infodemic" to refer to the deluge of discussions, including misinformation, that the COVID-19 pandemic engendered (World Health Organization (WHO) 2020). In the future, no knowledgeable adversary will miss the opportunity to superimpose an infodemic on an epidemic.

Directed Human Modification

Up to this point, we have considered human nature and even a given person's nature as relatively static, i.e., changes took place in slowly in the past. The techno/info parts of the model of humanity permit new ways for a person to change or be changed (Hartley & Jobson 2014). This model will be discussed in Chap. 4.

Operant conditioning is learning brought about by reinforcements or punishments. Classical conditioning arises from repeatedly pairing a stimulus with a response. Conditioning by modeling (moving the subject through an action) is observational learning—a form of human modification.

Pharmaceuticals supply an avenue for changing psychology. Treatments of many general medical, neurologic and psychiatric conditions influence cognitive capital. Illness or intentional new forces can produce mild cognitive decline, attentional deficits, and mood and anxiety disorders, modify impulsivity or conflict aversion, influencing cognitive capital. The basic use of digital enhancement, exercise, chronotherapeutic optimization, the current, even if temporary, influence of affect, positive expectation and the field of nootropics, are areas of interest (Turner et al. 2003; Sahakian & Morein-Zamir 2007; Mohammed & Sahakian 2011). Biologic cognitive enhancement effects are (currently) largely experimental. Cognitive enhancement effects range from genetic considerations to Sahakian's recent selected use of modafinil at the Cambridge Brain Institute (Seife 2014) and by extension the prospect of the use of D-cycloserine to promote neuro-plasticity (new learning) for fear extinction (Kuriyama, Honma, Koyama, & Kim 2011). The possibility that PTSD might be detected through blood tests (Kesling 2019), expands the possibility of understanding it biochemically or using it as a surface of attack.

Neurotoxicants are substances capable of causing adverse effects on the nervous system and sense organs. The huge number and variety of potentially neurotoxic substances include metals, inorganic ions, botanical toxins, and other organic matter and their sources include solvents, pesticides, fine particle air pollution, agricultural soil contamination, and inappropriate pharmaceutical use. Entry can occur via absorption, ingestion, or injection and can be active from *in-utero* to current.

The integrated stress response (ISR) is a complex cellular physiologic system to coordinate difficult adaptive optimization. Its allocation of brain protein synthesis makes it relevant to cognitive capital maintenance and optimization. Where possible, we should optimize our ISR (Costa-Mattioli & Walter 2020).

Advanced genetic engineering and synthetic biology are extant. The modified and "very fast" CRISPR plus gene-drive technology cuts and splices large segments of the genome, not just short contiguous segments, and spreads them rapidly (Service 2019; Liu et al. 2020). The 'prime' gene-editing system could surpass CRISPR. David Liu, a chemist at the Broad Institute in Cambridge, Massachusetts, said "Prime editors offer more targeting flexibility and greater editing precision (Champer, Bushman, & Akbari 2016; Cohen 2019)." Synthetic biology is at hand.

A "direct" brain-computer interface is an obvious objective. It is in the laboratory but not yet realized in the field, but the race is on (Tullis 2019). Both wire and electromagnetic wave crude connections are extant. Companion VR teaching avatars are coming (Stanford University VHIL 2019).

Trends in the Technium

Kevin Kelly's central thesis in *The Inevitable* is that there are technological forces that are emerging and can be expected to exert increasing influence as time progresses (Kelly 2016). Kelly made the following points, each of which is accompanied by a comment on its relevance to national security. (The authors have inserted the text in square brackets and the comments in italics.)

1. We can expect to be perpetual novices: not only will our computers develop new functions that we will always be behind in mastering, but so will our phones, our cars, our refrigerators, everything! *We know that our military hardware is no longer driving newness, but cannot keep up with civilian applications. Will this continue or will national defense hardware and software require this rapid change? What are the training implications?*
2. Kelly cited three breakthroughs in producing real AI applications: a. cheap parallel computation, b. big data [and analytics], and c. better algorithms. He was not worrying about "the computer comes alive and takes over the world." He started with the things we can see happening: specific machine skills, such as winning at chess; more general skills, such as Alexa understanding what you ask for and finding it and then doing it; and the implications. He called these machines "robots," for simplicity. He categorized their future jobs as, (1) jobs humans can do but robots can do even better, (2) jobs humans can't do but robots can, (3) jobs we didn't know we wanted done, and d. jobs only humans can do—at first. *What national defense jobs will robots be doing and which ones do we definitely not want them doing? Just think of the implications of a self-driving tank—it cuts the crew by 25%. We've already considered an automated loader—that means the crew is down to 2. Who or what makes targeting decisions? Can the tank be hacked?*
3. Virtual reality [(VR), augmented reality (AR), 360° presentation, and mixed reality (MR), together called extended reality (xR)] technology is rapidly improving. *The military training applications are already here. The military uses mixes of live simulations (sometimes called wargames), virtual simulations (using VR of various types), and constructive simulations (computer-driven simulations). Some of the VR simulations are 360° presentations. The mixed simulations are essentially AR simulations.*
4. There is increasing surveillance and tracking of almost everything. An amazing number of things are tracked already, including your (modern) car's position, speeds, accelerations, etc. We don't have "Big Brother," we have lots of "big brothers." *Suppose we don't want our national defense organizations to access, compile and integrate all of this information. How do we prevent adversaries from doing so?*

Kelly re-emphasized that all of these technological forces are just beginning to operate and show no signs of slowing or stopping. So, this is just the beginning. (During the research for this book, the authors kept finding new technologies that had only recently been developed. As you are reading this, you may know of even newer technologies, developed since the book went to press.)

Samuel Visner, the Director of the National Cybersecurity FFRDC at MITRE, saw a coming change in the technium that will radically change the world. Internet Protocol version 4 (IPv4) defines slightly more than four billion addresses (2^{32}). The new version of the protocol, IPv6, will have 2^{128} addresses, approximately 3.4×10^{38} addresses. That is a factor of more than a billion billion billion larger—not a billion billion billion more addresses, but a billion billion billion times as many addresses.

This huge number of addresses will allow almost everything to be connected—an internet of things. The new fifth generations (5G) networks will, of course, provide higher speed connections. However, it will also allow for direct connections between all of those (almost) innumerable things in the internet of things. The implications are still being pondered. Any emergent properties are likely to be unforeseen.

Kai-Fu Lee concentrated on the trends in the coming AI revolution (Lee 2018). Lee divided technological changes of the past into two kinds of disruptors: simple (change to a single task such as typewriters, elimination of a kind of labor such as (human) calculators, and a single industry disruption such as the cotton gin) and general purpose technology (GPT) disruptors. He identified only three GPT events in recent history: the steam engine, electricity, and information and communication technology. Lee identified the AI revolution as a fourth GPT. And he said this GPT will cause massive job displacements.

Within **physical labor**, Lee classified jobs by two dimensions: highly social versus asocial interactions and low dexterity/highly structured environment versus high dexterity/unstructured environment. These dimensions divide physical labor into four quadrants:

1. **Danger Zone**: high risk of replacement. Jobs in the danger zone are in the low dexterity/highly structured environment, asocial interactions quadrant. These include such jobs as teller/cashier, truck driver, assembly line inspector, and fast food preparer. AI systems will be able to do all of these within the near future.
2. **Safe Zone**: very low risk of replacement. Jobs in this zone require high levels of social interaction and high dexterity in an unstructured environment. These include such jobs as hair stylist and physical therapist.
3. **Human Veneer**: job enhancement. Jobs in this zone require high levels of social interaction and low dexterity/highly structured environment. Jobs in this zone will require humans as the interface with customers with AI support systems. These include such jobs as bartender and café waiter.
4. **Slow Creep**: job reduction over time. Jobs in this zone will gradually be replaced by AI systems as the AI systems improve in capability. These include such jobs as taxi driver and night-watch security.

Within **cognitive labor**, Lee also classified jobs by two dimensions: highly social versus asocial interactions and optimization-based versus creativity or strategy-based. These dimensions divide cognitive labor into four quadrants:

5. **Danger Zone**: high risk of replacement. Jobs in the danger zone are in the optimization-based, asocial interactions quadrant. These include such jobs as telemarketer, basic translator, personal tax preparer, and radiologist. AI systems will be able to do all of these within the near future.
6. **Safe Zone**: very low risk of replacement. Jobs in this zone require high levels of social interaction and are creativity or strategy-based. These include such jobs as psychiatrist, CEO, and social worker.
7. **Human Veneer**: job enhancement. Jobs in this zone require high levels of social interaction and are optimization-based. Jobs in this zone will require humans as

the interface with customers with AI support systems. These include such jobs as wedding planner, teacher, doctor (GP), and financial planner.

8. **Slow Creep**: job reduction over time. Jobs in this zone will gradually be replaced by AI systems as the AI systems improve in capability. These include such jobs as graphic designer, financial analyst, medical researcher, and scientist.

Lee then discussed the scale of job losses to be expected. He estimated that between 40 and 50% of the jobs in the U.S. can be automated within 10–20 years. He went on to say that there will be forces that reduce the rate of job losses, such as social friction, regulations and "plain old inertia." Further, there will be new jobs that are created. Still, he estimated net unemployment increases in the 10–25% range.

In an article in the Wall Street Journal, Eric Morath provided support for some of Lee's thesis. Morath described how AI targets higher-paying jobs, such as radiologists, financial advisers, market research analysts (Morath 2020).

Finally, it should be noted that the cognification of objects brings new opportunities and vulnerabilities.

Learning science, motivation and persuasion science are now in play. From augmented reality to single photon detection to the psychopharmacology of cognition, impulsivity and aggression in man can be changed.

Academic discussions of such potentialities exist. However, the authors can certainly envision those who might want to reduce the will to fight or induce group violence in others. The cyber and psychosocial surfaces of attack are part of our continuous change.

The vulnerable points, dynamics, and other complexities of the battlefield are morphing with increasing speed. The internet of things brings new connectivity and vulnerabilities. New understanding of the multitude of human biases and irrational aspects opens ways to connect to affiliative and dissociative opportunities. A conspicuous example of morphing of the dynamics is the new learning about propagation dynamics in social systems. Here we find the difference in moving information (simple contagions) across the system versus complex contagions of behavior beliefs and attitude (Centola 2018a, 2018b).

Chapter 3
The Noosphere

How might others have power over you? In this chapter, we look at information, particularly persuasive information. If information is transformed into that power, just what is that information and how is it deployed?

As our knowledge increases, we know "less."

That is, as we learn more, we discover how much more we don't know. *The acceleration of the expansion of the technium and noosphere is outpacing our ability to be aware of the newest science and technology.* As the radius of human knowledge increases, the circumference of our ignorance increases sixfold (Fig. 3.1).

The ***noosphere***, the total information available to humanity, is expanding exponentially. Normally, we think of information as pertaining to true things. However, "fake news," is also part of the noosphere. Information is intangible; however, it is often expressed in tangible form, such as books and libraries. One of the themes of this book is "***atoms*** and ***bits***." The "atoms" symbolize matter and the "bits" (from computer representations) are a metaphor for information.

The noosphere provides the medium in which information conflicts take place.

Not only do we not know everything—an obvious statement—but we are more and more provincial in the noosphere, more provincial in the Johari Window (Fig. 3.2). We exist in a ***bounded reality***. Part of this is imposed on us by our senses, both natural and the extension of our senses through instruments. However, part of this resides in human nature, in our limited memory and computational capacity. Our view of our limits follows.

Any one individual's knowledge is a small percent of the human noosphere; our individual bounded reality is provincial. Figure 3.2 illustrates the Johari Window (Wikipedia 2018c). The changes that increase surveillance create less privacy. The vast increase in the noosphere increases our blind spot.

If we consider the set of things, known and unknown, there are known knowns—things we know that we know. The things that we know and others know we know

D. S. Hartley III, K. O. Jobson, *Cognitive Superiority*,
https://doi.org/10.1007/978-3-030-60184-3_3

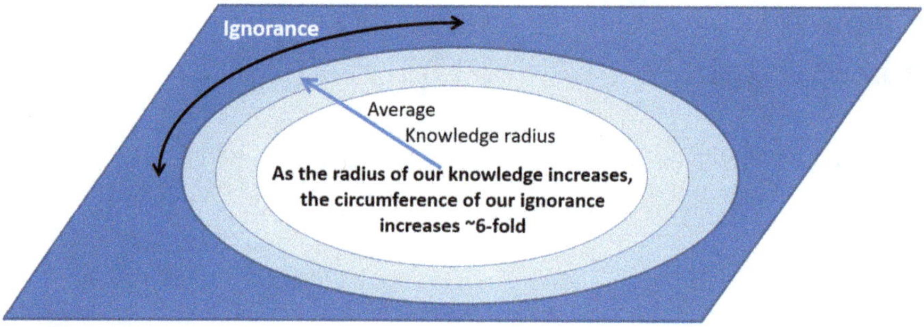

Fig. 3.1 Knowledge in a sea of ignorance

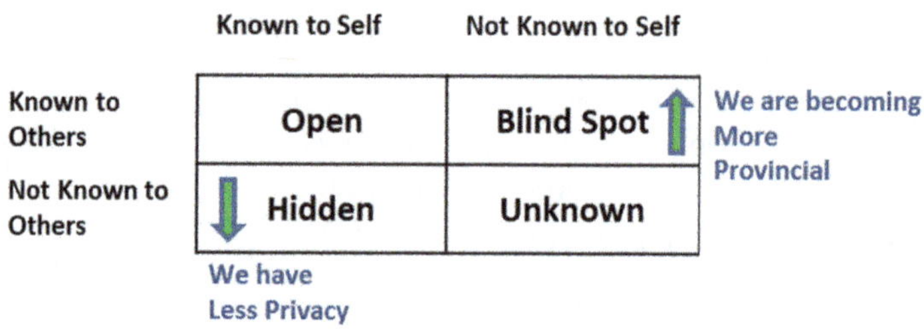

Fig. 3.2 Johari window

go in the "Open" part of the window and things we know that others don't know we know go in the "Hidden" part of the window. Our known unknowns—things we know we don't know, but that others know, go in the "Blind Spot." The "Unknown" part of the window contains the unknown unknowns—things we don't know that we don't know. Daniel Levitin adds another category, the things we know that aren't so (Levitin 2016). As the size of the noosphere grows, our position in this Johari Window is more provincial (Jobson, Hartley, & Martin 2011).

In this matrix, understanding the changes in surveillance and persuasion is relevant. Further, optimizing information access individually and at a systems level from the frontiers of science and technology and superior learning speed and ability are necessary. Useful understanding and response will have to be more complex, engaging more disciplines, more connected and more predictive, more iteratively inductive (concluded from evidence) and abductive (pulled out, compare to Sherlock Holmes' process of abducing the simplest and most likely explanation or model to fit the data).

Bounded Reality

According to Sloman and Fernbach, we believe that we know things when we don't and often think we knew them (in the past) when we didn't (Sloman & Fernbach 2017). We have the *illusion* of knowing things. In the first case, something falls down the drain of a sink. We know there is a trap in the drain, see the fittings for taking the trap off and believe we know how to solve the problem. After successfully removing the trap, we discover that we don't know as much as we thought because we fail to get the trap back on and water-tight. Sloman and Fernbach also describe several examples of the second case, for example, after looking up something on the web, we may forget the search and believe we always knew the result.

We also know less than we could because of self-imposed boundaries. We know that we cannot see all of reality. Part of the goal of a classical liberal education is to enlarge our horizons so that we are aware of a greater part of reality than is apparent in our daily lives. Even when this is "successful," we still live in a bounded reality, albeit with larger horizons than before.

Filter Bubbles

We may now be entering into a time of self-created straight-jackets, which limit our bounds. Some bounds involve our choices and others are systemic, algorithmic defaults. For example, Facebook allows us to see what our friends see—the things that interest them and the things they believe. Further, the Facebook algorithms reinforce a bounded reality by filtering out those things that mesh poorly with these interests and beliefs. This is not done for any reason other than to deliver us to the advertisers who are most likely to be able to sell things the group wants to buy. Similarly, Google records our searches and generates results that match most closely the things we have searched for before. When there are thousands or hundreds of thousands of possible results for a search, we want to see those things that are most relevant at the top of our list of search results. The more successful these filters are at producing what we think we are looking for, the tighter the straight-jacket becomes. Indiana University professor Filippo Menczer and colleagues looked at this homogeneity bias and found it in search engines. However, Facebook was worse than the search engines; Twitter was worse than Facebook; and YouTube was the very worst (Mims 2018).

Currently, we see the results as a polarizing of society. The people of one political persuasion mostly see, and want to see, only those things that agree with their beliefs and the people of another political persuasion have their beliefs similarly reinforced (Fig. 3.3). Horwitz and Seetharaman reported in The Wall Street Journal that an internal Facebook presentation in 2018 said, "Our algorithms exploit the human brain's attraction to divisiveness (Horwitz & Seetharaman 2020)."

However, there is a possibility for even darker results. The increasing use of media platforms for active disinformation campaigns can exacerbate the situation (Tufekci 2018). Countering such campaigns is difficult for several reasons. First, humans default to truth (assume truthfulness) (Gladwell 2019), with many exceptions (Mercier 2020). The next problem lies in discovering the existence of the campaign: if you are not in the target group, you may never see the traffic. Then we must deliver the counter messages. How do you get past the filters if your

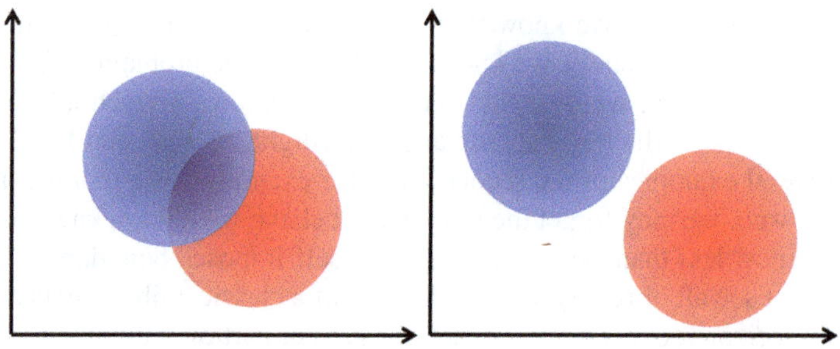

Fig. 3.3 Disjoint bounded spaces

counter-message doesn't match the self-imposed restrictions? The final problem lies in designing an effective counter-message (see the section on Confronting the Established in Chap. 4): how do you determine the cultural nature of the target audience when you don't really know who they are?

It seems that humans have an affinity for thinking like their neighbors, sometimes to the exclusion of what is fact. The power of the crowd, utilizing man's primal desire for affiliation (membership) and affirmation, can be harnessed to change an individual's initial view to that of the crowd (Edelson, Sharot, Dolan, & Dudai 2011). "The markers of social membership are stringent and fragile (Moffett 2018)." They can provide surfaces for influence.

AI systems also suffer from bounded reality. This will be discussed in Chap. 5.

Advantages of Bounds

We have described some disadvantages to disjoint bounded spaces; however, there are also advantages. Figure 3.3, above, illustrated two unlabeled bounded spaces that are disjoint in some space with unlabeled axes. Consider the blue space to the left as IBM PC computers and the red space to the right as Apple computers. For a long time, there were few or no viruses for Apple computers, not because they couldn't be written, but because Apple viruses would require different code and Apple computers were not around in sufficient numbers to be worth the trouble.

Now suppose the bounded spaces represent disjoint political viewpoints in social media space. By disjoint in this space, we mean that the recommended new material for each contains almost nothing of the other and searches by a person in one space are unlikely to result in material from the other space because of variant information flows such as media algorithms. An attack has to be tailored to be found in the recommended material or in the search space, which means the flowed versions are required to be relevant to multiple viewpoints.

Cognition

Before we had invented computers, we were only concerned with humans when we discussed cognition. It is now more complex and is changing in the direction of increased complexity.

Figure 3.4 presents a reductionistic graphic of the complex adaptive systems known as cognition. The level at the bottom represents individual human cognition. The top level represents human group cognition. These two levels comprise standard cognition.

The individual level contains basic "algorithmic" circuits (feedback and feedforward for regulatory actions and "reflexes"), microstate cognition, and conscious cognition.

Reflexes are essentially programmed responses to stimuli. Some of these are built-in, such as the knee jerk reflex that doctors test. Others are learned, such as the automobile breaking reflex in which a driver slams on the brakes of the car.

A ***microstate*** is a temporary confluence that informs the larger state (Jobson et al. 2011). They abound in complex adaptive systems, from social organizations to the brain. They are an integrative part of cognition at all levels, part of the motif of connectivity. In the brain microstates are brief, semi-stable neurophysiologic patterns

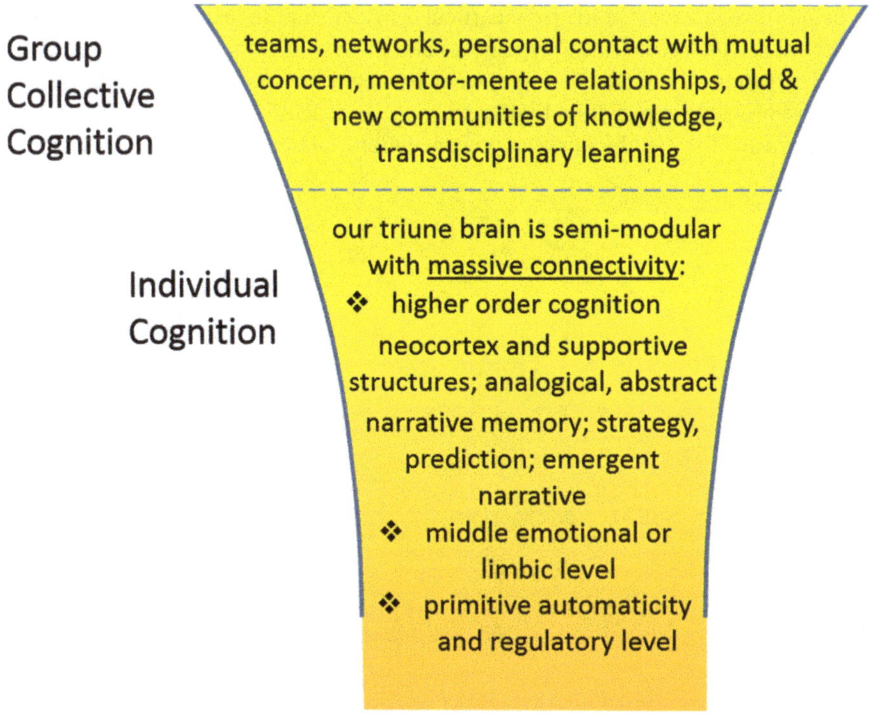

Fig. 3.4 Standard cognition

(Fig. 3.5). A current hypothesis is that microstates are atomistic cognition steps. Using functional imaging, one can see the brain approach a problem; it arrays temporary connected patterns (microstates) across its semipermeable, semi-modular structure. Each array is unique to the problem and may, with its multiple channels of communication, construct and connect to other microstates, internal and external.

Microstates are Mother Nature's temporary confluences that inform. They are a basic affordance of complex adaptive systems, including social groups. In an organizational setting, a cross-departmental meeting is a microstate, a temporary confluence of selected people suited for the need that may influence future events.

Microstate cognition in the human brain involves specifically conformal, time-limited neural circuit activation, appropriate to the need from disparate neuronal modules and locations. In an organization, microstate cognition consists of time-limited, specifically salient conformal team formations for consideration of issues and decisions. Both are temporary confluences that inform.

Learning

Table 3.1 lists some considerations with respect to cognition and learning. First, we use several types of logic. In deductive logic, we begin with a general premise and conclude, prove, that it holds for a particular instance. In inductive logic, we make observations and create rules, hypotheses and theories that incorporate and explain the observations. In abductive logic, we gather evidence and create a model that is our most probable explanation for the evidence. In seductive logic, we are led astray by arguments distorted by our own preconceptions, biases and limits.

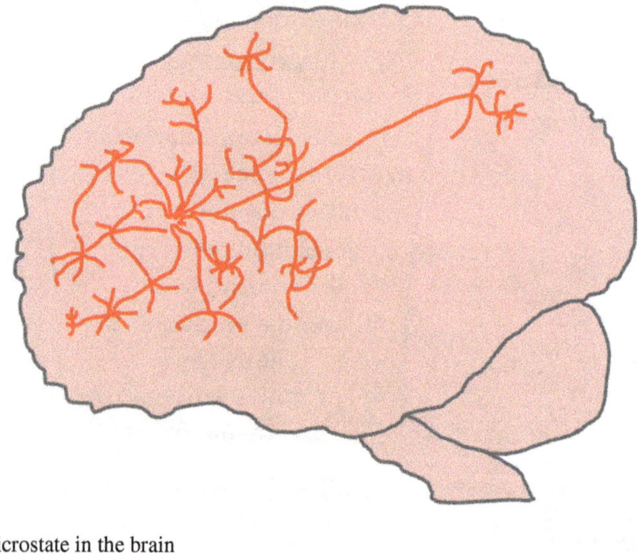

Fig. 3.5 Microstate in the brain

We face complexity of various types and have different methods for dealing with it. Abstraction is the process of reducing complexity by keeping certain parts (presumably the important parts) and discarding the rest. Creating a flexible hierarchy (up and down the scales of abstraction and time and across the domains of interest and ranges of effects) emphasizes certain relationships. Heuristic searches reduce search times (compared to an exhaustive search). Cognitive artifacts, such as words, the Internet and AI support more sophisticated cognition.

Collective learning consists of multiple types of learning in groups, traditional and digital. The many forms of collective learning are intrinsic to man's adaptation and social nature and include dyads, small teams, larger organizations, multiple variations of microstates (temporary confluences that inform), the use of consultants, and outsourcing connections, wikis and crowdsourcing.

Humans use these modes of cognition separately and in combinations. For each there are concerns or facets, such as the available (or lack of availability) of evidence, the point of view of the interested party or a contending party, the features of arrangement of the situation, questions about alternatives, and questions of salience. We should avoid mitigated speech, invite and give feedback, and realize how uncomfortable, by necessary for excellence, these open interchanges can be. It pays

Table 3.1 Selected elements of cognition and learning

Types of Logic	Human Approach to Complexity	Facets	Awareness of our	The Prepared Mind to Address the Unexpected
Deductive	Abstraction	Evidence	Systematic, Predictable, Irrational Aspects	Trans-domain knowledge
Inductive	Hierarchy	Point of View		Open-mindedness—lateral thinking
Abductive	Heuristic Search	Features of Arrangement		Error tolerant
"Seductive"	Construction of Cognitive Artifacts	What If?	Limited Knowledge Base, Perception & Intelligence	Passionate effort
	Collective Learning	So What? (Salience)		Tolerance of the shattering of the established model
		Mistake tolerant		Sagacity for engaging the opportunity for discovery or invention
		Openness to "I might be wrong."	Network Forces	
		Knowing best in class, then exceeding it		Heuristics, habits of mind—Polya
				Fostering originality
				Dilemma flipping
				Personalized Adult Adaptive Learning Systems (PAALS)
	Lifelong learning: Know, Do, Teach—Always a student, Always a teacher			

to be tolerant of mistakes, because they are endemic to the human condition. This includes the mistakes of others and our own. It also pays to know what methodology is considered "best in class," toward a goal of exceeding it or, if necessary, be willing to adopt it.

Each of these modes of thought is being augmented, changed by the unending accelerating change in the technium and noosphere. We must be lifelong learners, always a student, always a teacher, and recognize that we are forever newbies in the expanding noosphere and technium.

Creativity and Problem Solving

Human attributes have, at base, genetic, epigenetic and environmental roots. Assessment tools are available to discern intellectual capital, emotional capital and social capital and to measure analytic intelligence, creative intelligence, and practical intelligence. It is centrally important that problem solving (Polya 1945), originality (Grant 2017) and creativity **can** be taught and augmented to great advantage. Learning science, cognitive science and business schools, design laboratories and all excellent teachers are among the sources attempting to create people with inspired originality, inventiveness, prepared to provide new solutions to problems. Their methods, which bring into play the inventive facilities, involve personal contact with mutual concern, light the fires of Steiner's "demanding festival" (Steiner 1997), provide mentors with passion, have commitment to practice new forms of individual and collective learning, and teach how to learn.

The habits of mind listed by Polya are shown in Table 3.2. Polya connected with the students and modeled curiosity and sagacity. He evinced and asked for the polythetic and the multiordinal (Polya 1945).

Adam Grant in his book, *Originals*, emphasized that one can learn to be original. He found a larger volume of ideas correlated with producing important original discoveries and inventions, emphasizing effort and time. He recommended using other original thinkers as role models. Edison produced 1100 patents to achieve six major breakthroughs. The prolific are generally original. Further, he emphasized the need to take risks (Grant 2017).

Table 3.2 Polya's habits of mind

Focusing on understanding the problem, the unknowns, the data, and the conditions;
Drawing a picture, even if the problem is not geometric and separating the parts of the condition;
In devising a plan, consider if there are similar, if slightly different, forms of a related problem; look at the unknowns to see if the related problems had the same unknowns; see if the problem can be restated—"change your point of view;" make the problem interesting;
Viewing the problem both forward and backward; and
Using abduction and induction.

Much cognitive content, including originality, resides in the group with diverse experiences, spread across a number of communities of knowledge. Optimizing the many forms of collective learning and discovery includes avoiding mitigated speech and sometimes using the Delphi method. In groups and individuals, it is important to ask questions: What if? So what? etc. Giving and inviting feedback requires sufficient emotional and social capital and, in certain cases, flexible hierarchy, with sufficient distributed authority. Trans-domain knowledge within the individual and the group is foundational. The capacity to use abstraction to produce generalization and see similar problems cuts across much of originality

Occasionally the "original" is not solving a problem, but sees it as a dilemma, unsolvable, but flipping it to become a benefit by changing the frame, process, goal, or time orientation (Johansen 2007). (The classic computer system statement, "That's not a bug; it's a feature," is an attempt to flip a problem.) To have a mind prepared to address the unexpected and hold complexity in one's mind, one must tolerate the shattering of one's preconceptions or current paradigms and foster sagacity for new discovery. One must be willing to "Get in that lab and make a lot of mistakes [attributed to Linus Pauling, twice Nobel Laureate]." "Smart creatives" empowered by the right management metrics can produce revolutionary power (Schmidt & Rosenberg 2017).

Reasoning

Sloman and Fernbach discussed reasoning. Forward reasoning is thinking about how causes have produced effects. Prediction is a kind of forward reasoning. Backward reasoning is thinking about what causes might produce an effect. Medical diagnoses are examples of backward reasoning (Sloman & Fernbach 2017).

We may make a statement about the probability of an Action (or set of Actions) taking place, given an agenda; however, we want to know what the probability is that an agenda is held, given the occurrence of an Action (or set of Actions). They are not the same. Bayes' theorem gives the connection (where *P(X)* means the probability of *X* and *P(X|Y)* means the (conditional) probability of *X* given *Y*):

$$P(\text{Agenda}|\text{Action}) = \left[P(\text{Action}|\text{Agenda}) / P(\text{Action})\right] * P(\text{Agenda}).$$

This can be read as updating our initial estimate of the probability of the agenda (to the probability of the agenda given the action) by a factor that represents new knowledge.

The necessity for and utility of prediction is continuous. "We never make perfectly objective predictions…along the way we are tainted by our own subjective point of view." We constantly face branching streams of conditional probabilities. Further AI/ML centrally depends on conditional probabilities. Probabilistic think-

Table 3.3 Silver's cognitive characteristics of those best at predicting

They are multidisciplinary in their scope.
They are adaptable and open to change and trying multiple approaches.
They are self-critical and willing to acknowledge mistakes.
They are tolerant of complexity and see that some fundamental problems are inherently unpredictable or insoluble.
They are empirical, relying more on observation than theory.

ing requires that you accept that your subjective perceptions of the world are likely approximations of the truth (Silver 2012).

The dimensionality of the systems of complex adaptive systems in which we live counsels a certain attitude of humility and an awareness of uncertainty. Beyond this attitude of humility and probabilistic thinking, we must be armed with statistical literacy.

The best human predictors of future conditions are the ones who have the cognitive characteristics shown in Table 3.3 (Silver 2012). They are algorithmically armed, not algorithmically ridden.

Sloman and Fernbach also discussed the fast and slow thinking of Kahneman (also known as associative versus rule-based thinking and System 1 versus System 2). They refer to it as the distinction between intuition and deliberation. In any case, humans use both types of thinking, the choice depending on the situation. Fast thinking is cheap in terms of brain power and time, although it can easily be wrong. Slow thinking is expensive in terms of brain power and time. It can also be wrong, but does allow the possibility of rational consideration of multiple factors (Sloman & Fernbach 2017).

Defining a Problem

Josh Kerbel said "metaphors are key to our thinking in that they are nothing less than linguistic manifestations of mental models (Kerbel 2018)." He posited that many of the metaphors in common use are borrowed from Newtonian mechanics (or based on a similar world-view of deterministic cause and effect) and bias our thinking, inappropriately, in the current situation. He argued for the replacement of these "linear" metaphors with "nonlinear" metaphors that are more biologically based. He displayed a list of legacy metaphors (Table 3.4) and a list of suggested new metaphors (Table 3.5).

Kerbel said there is a temptation to look for a new term that can be simply swapped out for the old term; however, this needs to be resisted. The idea is to find new concepts to replace the old ones and determine the appropriate metaphors for the new concepts.

Table 3.4 Kerbel's common linear/mechanical metaphors

Trajectory	*Leverage/levers*	*Recoil*
Tension	*Backlash*	*Shape*
Inertia	*Linchpin*	*(Security) Vacuum*
Momentum	*Pivot*	*Stability*
Uni/Bi/Multi-polar	*Center of gravity*	*Balance (of power)*

Table 3.5 Kerbel's examples of nonlinear metaphors

Risk factors	*Vulnerability*	*Virulence*
Acute/chronic	*Diagnosis/prognosis*	*Toxicity*
Side effects	*Immunity*	*Fog*
Ripeness	*Contagion*	*Dormant*
Susceptibility	*Symptomatic*	*Evolutionary*

Serendipity and Sagacity

We confront the unexpected and it is the road to discovery and invention. When we confront the unexpected, by accident or chance, we have a bias to see it from our current pattern of thought even if it doesn't fit and has disorder or elements of chaos. This is our bias toward pattern completion, our mad dash for order. Much of discovery and/or invention is made by those possessing broad trans-domain knowledge, with a prepared and open mind, with passion to learn, capacity for lateral thinking and the ability to temporarily tolerate the recognition of this challenge to our established pattern of thought and possessing the sagacity or discernment, to capture or create the discovery or invention. The maximum density of discovery and invention is located in where we meet the unexpected.

Vadim Kotelnikov divided accidental discoveries into two types: "***by-product***: occurred while inventors were trying to discover something else" and "***serendipitous***: were stumbled upon by chance (Kotelnikov 2019)." Kotelnikov pictured serendipity as coming in the intersection of an attitude of open-mindedness, a creative chaos environment, and having cross-functional knowledge and systems thinking skills. He saw four elements as necessary for converting accidental discoveries into a habit: having an open mind, broad knowledge, lateral thinking, and passion.

Decision-Making

When decisions are made sufficiently rapidly, humans use automatic default responses of multiple types or ***frugal heuristics*** (simple "rules of thumb," easily "computable" algorithms). These are examples of the fast thinking discussed above. Generally, the options are pre-selected or obvious.

When the options need to be identified and the optimal one selected, a search is needed. Frugal heuristics are distinct from ***heuristic search***, which is a search through options based on a function (heuristic) that is not mathematically guaranteed as optimal and which is not an exhaustive search through all options. However, the quality of the heuristic is based on its likelihood of approaching the optimal solution. For some problems, there are techniques that are guaranteed to yield the optimal solution. For some problems, the option set is finite and small enough that an exhaustive search can be performed, one that checks each possibility. These are examples of slow thinking.

Group and Augmented Problem Solving

Brainstorming is a technique used in group problem solving to elicit ideas from the participants that may be useful in solving a problem. The typical approach involves asking for possible solutions. In an article by Hal Gregersen (Gregersen 2018), the author introduced the concept of asking for "new questions that we could be asking about this problem." He said, "Brainstorming for questions rather than answers makes it easier to push past biases and venture into uncharted territory." Table 3.6 shows his principles regarding the types of questions to consider.

Crowdsourcing is a deliberate blend of a bottom-up, open, creative process with top-down organizational goals. It is generally online. "In crowdsourcing, the locus of control, regarding the creative production of goods and ideas exists *between* the organization and the public, a shared process of bottom-up, open creation by the crowd and top-down management by those charged with serving an organization's strategic interests (Brabham 2013)." Wikis, such as "Wikipedia and open-source software projects are not technically crowdsourcing because the commons is organized and produced from the bottom-up and its locus of control is in the community (Brabham 2013)." Simply soliciting opinions from outside the organization does not strictly qualify as crowdsourcing for in the process the locus of control is within the organization. "The four dominant crowdsourcing types, based on the kind of problem being

Table 3.6 Gregersen's types of question

Traditional divergent-thinking techniques (for example, making random associations or taking on an alternative persona) can help unlock new questions, and, ultimately, new territory.
Questions are most productive when they are open versus closed, short versus long, and simple versus complex.
Descriptive questions (what's working? what's not? why?) best precede speculative ones (what if? what might be? why not?).
Shifting from simple questions that require only recall to more cognitively complex ones that demand creative synthesis produces better breakthrough thinking.
Questions are annoying and distracting when they don't spring from deeply held conviction about what the group wants to achieve.
Questions are toxic when they are posed aggressively, putting people on the spot, casting unwarranted doubt on their ideas, or cultivating a culture of fear.

solved, are the knowledge-discovery and management approach, the broadcast-search approach, the peer-vetted creative-production approach, and the distributed-human-intelligence tasking approach (Brabham 2013)."

The OODA Loop

One considered level of decision-making is described by Boyd's ***Observe-Orient-Decide-Act (OODA) loop*** (Wikipedia 2018e), depicted in Fig. 3.6. The idea is that certain steps are required for making decisions and acting on them (originally conceived for fighter pilots acting in a dogfight. This was important in recognizing that two opponents had to engage in this process and the one that could execute the cycle fastest had an advantage. The loop starts with observing—determining what comprises the situation. The second step is orienting—comparing the situation to other known factors, including goals and capabilities. The third step is deciding—choosing what to do. The fourth step is acting—implementing the decision. After acting, the loop is continued, as necessary.

Depending on the situation, the OODA loop may be implemented as structured fast thinking or as structured slow thinking.

The "kill chain" is a variant of the OODA loop. The kill chain has only three steps: "gaining understanding about what is happening," collapsing the first two steps of the OODA loop; "making a decision about what to do;" and "taking action that creates an effect to achieve an objective (Brose 2020b)."

In Fig. 3.4, the upper level represents human group cognition. The OODA loop process, first applied to individual decision-making was later applied to military

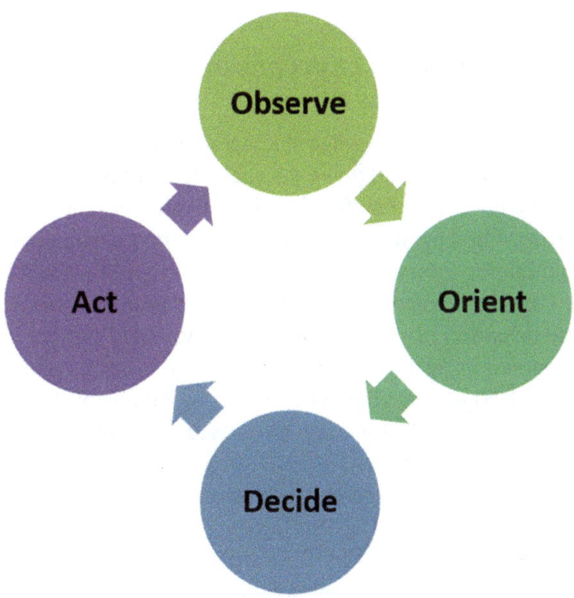

Fig. 3.6 Boyd's OODA Loop

decision-making and then to non-military structured group decision-making. Larger groups will tend to have slower cycle processing capabilities than smaller groups. Unstructured groups, such as committees and an entire democracy, generally use unstructured cognitive processes on more complex cognition problems, with mixed results. Group cognition can also be improved through education and training.

Metrics

Many decisions are made using metrics. In its simplest form, something is measured regularly. If the measurement falls above (or below) a particular value, the user does something. The measured value and the target value are called metrics. Using metrics in this fashion is a standard and valuable practice in manufacturing. An entire science, called analytics, has been created to discover useful metrics for novel things, such as structuring a baseball team (Lewis 2003).

Metrics are also used in corporate (and other enterprise) strategies to convert narrative goals into measurable targets and programs. A problem arises in the "convert" action. If the conversion is not 100 percent valid, surrogation can occur. Surrogation is the replacement of the actual goal with the achievement of the surrogate metric goal (Harris & Tayler 2019). A classic example was the "body count" metric of the Vietnam War. Not only was the metric a flawed measure of winning, but it also suffered from counting all the dead, as opposed to enemy deaths, and from pure inflation. It also may have influenced choices of operations, favoring those that produced high body counts rather than some that might have been more effective for winning the war (Wikipedia 2019d).

Communication (Apropos *the Noosphere)*

George Schweitzer, noted nuclear chemist, stated that the motif of the universe is connectivity, up and down the scale, from quantum to sociology (Schweitzer 2019).

We have said that the noosphere is growing; however, it does not grow as a plant grows—having its own agency for growth. Humans add to the noosphere (and sometimes subtract from it, as with the loss of information in the destruction of the library at Alexandria in 48 BC or other improper storage in giant data sets). Before the invention of writing, knowledge was held only in human memories. Now it can be stored in various formats; however, to be used by humans (at least until the invention of cognified objects) it has to be taught by humans and learned by humans. Over our long history, we have used the word, the book, and now the screen to convey information.

Human knowledge can be characterized by the ease of conveyance, as shown in Table 3.7 (Jobson et al. 2011).

These divisions (Fig. 3.7) are partially personal in nature, rather than totally dependent on the information content. That is, it depends on the expertise of the

Table 3.7 Explicit, implicit and tacit knowledge

Explicit knowledge is codified or can be codified into documents. It is easy to convey.
Implicit knowledge is the practical application of explicit knowledge and contains meta-knowledge. (*Meta-knowledge* is knowledge about explicit knowledge.) Implicit knowledge is more difficult to convey.
Tacit knowledge (expert or contextualized knowledge) is the most difficult to convey (Polanyi 1958, 2009). It is gained from human experience and embedded in human minds. Tacit knowledge is traditionally transferred from a mentor to a mentee, an example of ongoing personal contact with mutual concern. Expert contextualized (tacit) knowledge requires not only observing and knowing, but also doing and ideally teaching that knowledge. In teaching, we find our limits, consolidate our gains and often find better questions. (We should always be lifelong students as well as lifelong teachers.)

Fig. 3.7 Explicit, implicit and tacit knowledge overlaps

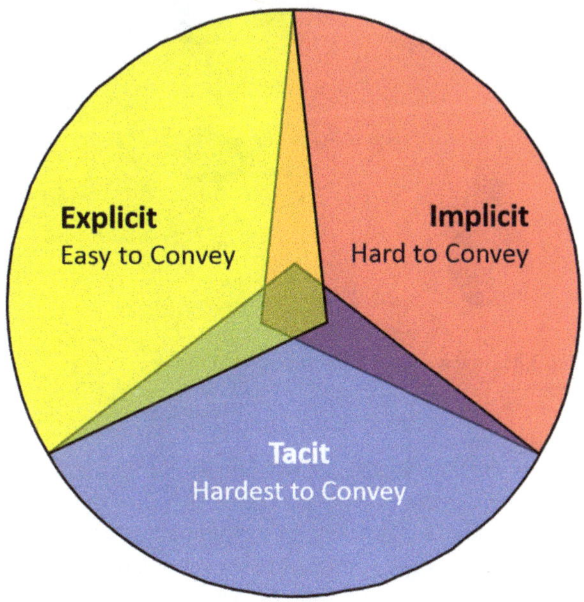

person. An expert may be able to codify information that is tacit for another person into explicit knowledge. This variability is illustrated by the overlaps in the figure.

In *Weaponized Lies*, Daniel Levitin said, "We have three ways to acquire information," shown in Table 3.8.

These methods are illustrated in Fig. 3.8. Method 1, discovery, includes individual observation of something in its context and observation through participation with a mentor. However, some of the information gained through participation with a mentor will be absorbed implicitly, using Levitin's methods. Levitin included reading something in a book as being told it explicitly. There is an unfortunate dual use of the words "explicit" and "implicit." We just defined three types of knowledge: explicit, implicit and tacit. These characterize the content of the noosphere

Table 3.8 Levitin's three ways of acquiring information

1.	"We can discover it ourselves,
2.	we can absorb it implicitly, or
3.	we can be told it explicitly."

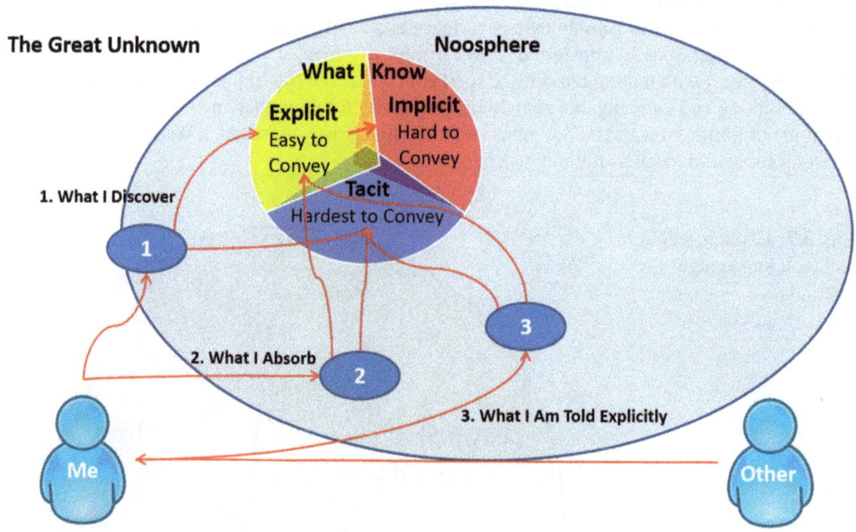

Fig. 3.8 How we acquire information

ellipse and the "What I Know" ellipse in Fig. 3.8, whereas, Levitin's words characterize the way the content gets there. Some of the information acquired through any of the methods may reside in the explicit category of "What I Know." Most of the implicit knowledge results from conversion of explicit knowledge, rather than being acquired from external sources. The tacit knowledge comes from experience, discovery, observation, working in an apprenticeship, or learning from and with a mentor. Some of what an expert knows he cannot convey verbally; it must be observed in context.

Our reality is not static. We can sense—perform individual, original research—collect seashells or plants or observe the stars—and create knowledge, expanding our reality. However, most of the change to our own personal noosphere comes through communication with others.

Compare Shannon's simple communication (Fig. 2.4) to method 3 of acquiring information in Fig. 3.8, in which someone tells us something, even explicitly. The information we acquire may be flawed by noise in the transmission. If we add intentional distortion to the noise factor, the information fidelity problem only gets worse.

Claude Shannon, after writing the formula for binary information transfer, cautioned that technical accuracy and semantic precision do not equate to effectiveness. Figure 2.6 illustrated the difference between accuracy and precision. Accuracy

Table 3.9 Future forces creating cognitive emergence

Launchbury's third AI wave moves beyond "handcrafted knowledge and statistical learning" to approach contextualized abstraction and reasoning (Launchbury 2017);
Increasingly cognitively enabled machines with a drop in the barrier between expert knowledge and the end user (Susskind & Susskind 2017);
The exponential increase in the sum of human knowledge (Schweitzer 2019);
The tools of cognitive optimization and augmentation of man;
The cognification of objects (IoT, the internet of things), processes and environments (ambient intelligence) and immersive technologies;
The fusion of sensing, computation and communication;
Learning science and modern forms of pedagogy including personalized augmented (human hybrid), adaptive, collective and immersive features (e.g., xR) with methods to develop the prepared mind to deal with the unexpected for discovery or invention;
Expanded adult education for lifelong learning;
The panopticon's experimentation augmented input with exponentially increased connectivity (the delocalized mind);
Improved meta science; and
New forms of collaborative and hybrid cognition.

refers to hitting the aim-point, while precision refers to repeatability. In shooting at paper targets, having both greater accuracy and greater precision will yield greater effectiveness. Shannon's point is that in transferring information, there is another factor at work. It is as if you have great accuracy and precision; however, if the target is made of metal, the bullet may not penetrate. Similarly, in communications, having a great communications system does not guarantee the recipient will act on it as desired.

New Forms of Cognition

There is a paradigmatic emergence in the complex adaptive systems of cognition. AI/ML is involved in the merging streams of influence creating this emergence, shown in Table 3.9.

The premise is that there is a progressive importance/necessity of cognitive superiority for homeland security and military superiority. The accelerating expansion of the frontier of knowledge and technology "overtakes existing military concepts and capabilities and necessitates a rethinking of how, with what, and by whom war is waged (Brose 2019)."

In the individual, cognition starts with algorithmic feedback and feedforward regulatory systems and reflexes, adds microstate cognition, and *where necessary*, adds conscious cognition. Structured groups *may* use Observe, Orient, Decide, Act (OODA) loop procedures (the larger the group, the slower the loop). Unstructured groups at best have unstructured cognition. Figure 3.9 adds a new layer to the standard cognition shown in Fig. 3.4. Human optimization and augmentation include

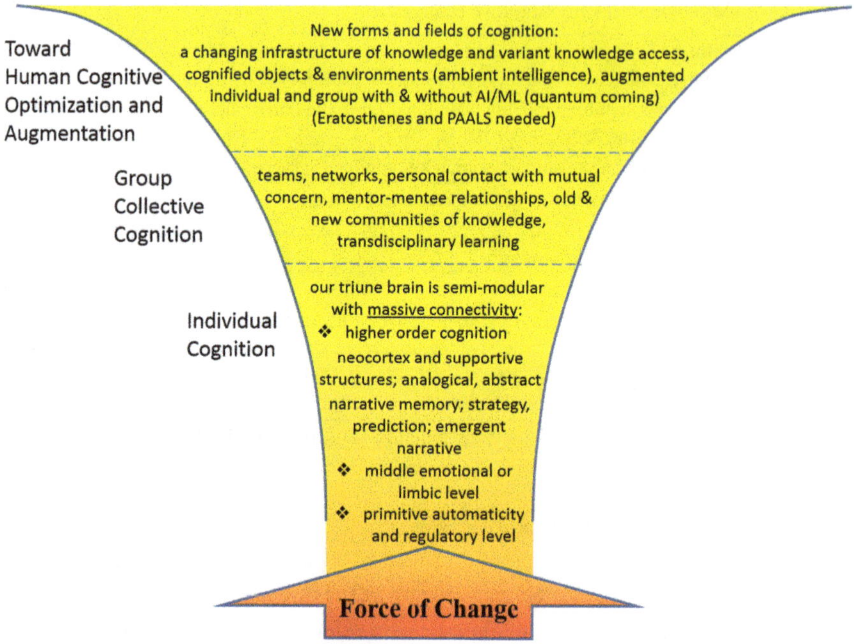

Fig. 3.9 Accelerating changes in cognition

nootropics (medications to enhance cognition), software (including AI/ML), and hardware, both external and integrated.

The central axis is accelerating change; the motif is of increased connectivity and complexity. Temporary confluences that inform (microstates) abound at every level. The scaffolding is a semi-permeable modularity. Note: the limits of visual representations of structures and computational procedures of cognition arise from cognition's dimensionality far exceeding Euclidean three-dimensional space.

Trust and Doubt

Humans default to truth (assume truthfulness) (Gladwell 2019), with many exceptions (Mercier 2020). However, the concept has been extended from trust in a person to trust in information sources and conclusions based on information. Humans have built institutions to certify the authenticity and trustworthiness of transactions. For example, money is deposited in banks, based on trust and banks lend money based on trust. Government regulations have been created to attest to the trustworthiness of companies. For example, taxicabs are licensed by governments and regulated to ensure their trustworthiness. Brokers created the New York Stock Exchange to prevent misbehavior by its members. The ride-sharing companies, Lyft and Uber, have created customer rating systems to allow users to trust their drivers. The blockchain technology allows "secure" transactions outside of the traditional banking businesses (Henderson 2019).

Misinformation in endless forms is extant beyond direct prevarication. The mechanism may be in frame or context, messenger bias, in salience (escalation, minimization or a change in the numerator or denominator of a ratio). Then it comes in manifold forms of perfidy, distortions, and flavors of *ad-hominem* diversionary attack (including false accusation, satire and parody). All are now armed with persuasion science.

Truth detection is problematic. We have a limited default to truth and can have an illusion of transparency, believing that our interpersonal interactions and reading of social signals provide a valid understanding of character and honesty (Gladwell 2019). Truth detection is currently widely studied and now aided by training and technology. However, it continues to be imperfect and is still often accompanied by the illusion of knowledge.

Influence of Information on Perceived Reality

Suppose one were made a prisoner, placed in a cell with no windows into the wider world. If one were to have meals presented three times a day, with appropriate lighting changes for day and night, the cycles would establish the rhythm of life. We are absorbing information implicitly. Suppose the intervals were gradually reduced and the meal portions were also reduced. The reductions in portion size would be attributed to an effort to intensify the effects of imprisonment, masking the true reason of supporting the fiction that the "day/night" cycles were of normal length. Eventually, the captors would control the rhythm of life by controlling the information one was presented.

This is a modern version of Plato's allegory of the cave (Plato 2016). Figure 3.10 provides a brief illustration. (Plato did not use a kangaroo.) Captives from an early age were imprisoned in a cave, chained so that they could only see shadows of objects on a wall in front of them, not the actual objects. Even after being freed, they temporarily continued to believe that the shadows were the real things (the anchoring bias of initial opinion). Our perceptions are often based on incomplete information and open to multiple forms of misinterpretation and manipulation.

The first extreme example and Plato's allegory illustrate the power of information on our perception of reality. We perceive reality through our senses, which report information to us. Normally, we process information from many sources, allowing the detection of contradictory information and the subsequent search for a resolution of the contradiction. Pervasive internal propaganda within a regime is meant to control the regime's populace through managing the bulk of the information available to the populace so that the resolution of any perceived contradictions is made in the favor of the regime. External propaganda may first create contradictions within the populace external to the regime, unsettling that populace. Second, external propaganda is meant to support those segments of the external populace

Fig. 3.10 Plato's allegory of the cave

who were most affected by the original propaganda in believing the regime's injected information. Third, targeted external propaganda is meant to motivate individuals with influence in the affected populace to support the foreign regime's purposes. This is the case whether the propaganda is true or false. Thus, we see why there is an "I" in the DIME (diplomatic, information, military, and economic) paradigm of levers of power. People can be influenced by propaganda and marketing efforts.

Knowledge access, with or without analytics, is a fulcrum for much of today's and tomorrow's enlightenment, prosperity and power. We live amidst a vast array of information brokers in commerce, politics and defense offering a hierarchy of raw and processed information, profiles and ontologies.

Of course, much of the information we absorb implicitly or are explicitly told is correct. However, our final defense against acquiring false information through these means is to search, think critically, and discover the truth ourselves (Levitin 2016).

"Perception, misperception, and deception remain critical elements of success—and failure—in conflict (Mateski, Mazzuchi, & Sarkani 2010)." By now, game theory is well known as a way of describing simple conflicts and for calculating optimal strategies. Less well known is the concept of hypergames in which perception, misperception, and deception are important parts. In a hypergame, players may be playing different games and imperfectly perceiving the other players' games. This is an essential part of actual unconventional conflicts (Hartley 2017, 2018). Hypergame analysis is similar to game theory in supporting analyses of possible results; however, it is much more complicated. Mateski, Mazzuchi and Sarkani describe a diagrammatic approach to modeling the perception in hypergames.

Data

A datum by itself is uninteresting and insignificant. The number '5' is a datum. It conveys almost no information. However, in context a datum can be both interesting and significant. If the number '5' refers to the speed of a top-secret missile in thousands of miles per hour, obtaining it could be very valuable. Generally, data in sets are more valuable than any individual datum. A dataset of all of the speeds of all missiles allows comparisons. Call this a horizontal data set. A vertical data set of all of the pertinent data for a particular missile is generally more valuable than any one of the individual values. We will consider both personal data and more general categories of data.

"We humans are reasonably good at defining rules that check one, two, or even three attributes (also commonly referred to as *features* or *variables*), but when we go higher than three attributes, we can struggle to handle the interactions between them (Kelleher & Tierney 2018)." "Data science encompasses a set of principles, problem definitions, algorithms, and processes for extracting non-obvious and useful patterns from large data sets (Kelleher & Tierney 2018)." These data sets can be structured or unstructured. Actionable insights from big data analytics may involve clustering to identify membership, association-rule mining to detect patterns of correspondence, and anomaly detection or outlier analysis to detect items requiring investigation (Kelleher & Tierney 2018).

Personal Data

Your personal data consists of measurements of physical things, such as height, weight, hair color, cholesterol numbers, and the sequence of bases in your DNA and descriptions of more abstract qualities, such as your name, credit score, bank account numbers and contents, intelligence, Social Security Number, preferences for foods, favorite color, first girl/boyfriend, and name of high school attended. Your personal data also includes inferences that are drawn from the primary data. You will recognize some of these as data you would consider private and some of these as data used as security questions to access online websites.

Almost all of your data is known in part by someone other than you. In fact, some of your data is not known by you, but is known to someone else. When you send off a sample for DNA testing to some company, after they test it and before they return the results, they know more about it than you do. Probably, after they return the results, they still know more about it than you do. When you interact with a website, such as Google or Facebook, they build profiles of you based on the data you enter and the actions you take on the website. You do not know the contents of these profiles, including your persuasion profile. You also do not know the implications of the contents. They do.

People are advocating for the individual ownership of the individual's data (Hardjono, Shrier, & Pentland 2016). Currently, the *de facto* ownership and control resides with the collectors, whether your doctor, Google, or the government. The ownership question is unresolved. Even if the ownership issue were resolved today, the control issue will remain unresolved. What would you do with all that data? If someone asked permission to access some part of it, how would you know what your response should be?

General Data

The questions about general data are both easier and more difficult. Consider the (non-personal) data created, collected, and held by a corporation. The information that corporations believe to be most important are generally stored in databases, where it is codified, annotated and protected. However, a corporation generally consists of numbers of people, not all of whom need access to all of the data. Some should definitely not have access to some of the data. Data segmentation (decoupling) and access restrictions are part of ensuring data security and system resilience (Rothrock 2018). Government (non-personal) data can be considered a special case of corporate data. Even the non-classified/classified data considerations in the government have analogs in corporate data. In both cases, the data often includes personnel data, which is personal to each individual described in that data. Which data ought to be considered owned by the individuals and which should not be even shared with the individual concerned. (The authors remember when colleges administered IQ tests to students and specifically withheld those results from the students. The justifications may have varied, but the results were the same.)

The authors of *Trust::Data* described a proposal originated by one of the authors (Pentland) called the New Deal on Data. They described it saying, "individual ownership of personal data must be balanced with the need of corporations and governments to use certain data—account activity, billing information, and so on—to run their day-to-day operations. The proposed New Deal on Data therefore gives individuals the right to possess, control, and dispose of these data as well as all the other incidental data collected about you (Hardjono et al. 2016)." To enforce this proposal, they advocated for decentralized trust networks.

Storage and Retrieval

In Fig. 8.6 (Chap. 8), there is an icon for "curated data." In one sense, this is central to a successful team with an Eratosthenes connection. The team can do nothing if it knows nothing. Part of its functioning will be collecting data and part will be using data. The data that are collected must be stored in a fashion that supports retrieval and use. This is curated data.

Validation and Accessibility

The noosphere contains the total knowledge available to humanity. Some of this knowledge is true, some is provisionally true—subject to amendment as our understanding of the world increases, and some is false. To the extent possible, data should be labeled with its estimated validity. Such data about data is termed metadata.

There is a chronic and addressable delay in harvesting advances from the frontier of science and technology for storage, retrieval, deployment, and use. The period of delay is less, but present, even when there is obvious advantage to those with vast financial resources, such as when the advance is deemed essential for national defense or very lucrative commerce. There is a yawning gap of delay outside these two areas. Where something is currently not judged as salient, the discovery may still eventually yield emergent manifold national advantages, including to defense or commerce.

Part of the delay in knowledge transfer from the frontier is because of an accepted practice by even the most prestigious academic journals of allowing publication without sufficient transparency of procedures, data collection, and description of metrics to be readily reproduced for validation. Examples of this can be seen in the short, discovery-announcing articles found in the journals *Science* and *Nature*. This can be remedied by a policy of not publishing without transparency and detail commensurable with reproducibility. (The publisher Wiley and the software firm Scite are teaming up to use the software Scite.ai to use AI to help determine which articles are reproducible (Brainard 2020). This may be a step in the right direction.) This could be strengthened by an independent certifying body attesting that the article provided sufficient information for reproducibility. Successful pressure for journal article method transparency would speed the path from print to use. Pre-registration of hypothesis *(ex ante predictum)* would also improve the advancement of science (DellaVigna, Pope, & Vivalt 2019).

Remedies are shown in Table 3.10.

These five meta-scientific normative and structural changes can speed the path from frontier to usage and bring great cognitive advantage to those that employ the resulting bounty.

The scientific community has revealed a new problem in the age of digital technologies: maintaining the integrity of data. In 2007, the U.S. National Academy of Sciences was informed about the problem of the manipulation of digital images in scientific manuscripts. This resulted in a committee charged with examining the "impact on acquiring, sharing, and storing data across scientific disciplines (Kleppner & Sharp 2009)." Daniel Kleppner and Phillip Sharp chaired the committee and wrote an editorial in *Science*, discussing the report. The conclusions included the statement: "legitimate reasons may exist for keeping some data private or delaying their release, the default assumption must be that research data and the information needed to interpret them will be publicly accessible in a timely manner to allow verification of findings and facilitate future discoveries (Kleppner & Sharp 2009)." They also discussed storage, "The questions of who is responsible for storing

Table 3.10 Remedies for delay in knowledge transfer

A medium such as arXiv for publishing preliminary results (Cornell University 2019);
A policy of not publishing without transparency and detail that allows commensurable reproducibility;
Certification by an independent body attesting that the article provided sufficient information for reproducibility testing; and
A public-private alliance (see Eratosthenes affiliation) to identify, increase connectivity, winnow down and make convenient for use, information from the vast frontier of science and technology for defense and security.
Individual understanding the importance and mechanisms for developing a personalized adult adaptive learning system (see PAALS section in Chap. 8)

research data and who pays for maintaining the archive are urgent (Kleppner & Sharp 2009)."

Document Storage and Retrieval

The U.S. Central Intelligence Agency (CIA) experience is relevant. The CIA and its predecessors spent years searching for good document indexing strategy (Burke 2018). At one point it used a semi-Dewey Decimal hierarchical system. Categories, subcategories, sub-subcategories, etc., were defined. The top-level categories and their numbers in Table 3.11 provide a flavor of the system:

After defining the system, documents had to be tied (manually) to the system and stored. The CIA also spent years searching for mechanized ways to retrieve the information once it had been stored. It tried microfilm, edge-notched cards, punched cards, and (once sufficiently powerful computers were available) computers.

A purely hierarchical system has flaws. For instance, not all categories of knowledge have obvious (preferably unique) decompositions. This means that retrieval requires knowledge of the decomposition actually being used. Further, there are items that could reasonably be classified in two different places. Other systems were considered in the CIA's search, including term-based systems, in which the terms used in the document provide the index keys. These other systems also had flaws. For example, the principle term for a scientific paper might be omitted because it was published within a journal or collection of papers with that principle term as a common factor and hence understood by a reader to be extant.

A document storage and retrieval system is an ontology. A library card catalog system is an ontology. The part of the card catalog system dedicated to fiction uses three or more cards (records for each book). Each record must have subject, title, and author information, just sorted differently, as shown in Table 3.12.

An additional record type can be added to deal with series of books. For example, Robert B. Parker wrote more than 50 books, many in the crime fiction genre (sub-subject). More than half revolved around Spenser, a private investigator (PI) in Boston. However, he also created a series around Jesse Stone, chief of police of a

Table 3.11 CIA Dewey decimal type system

100.000 Government, Politics, and International Activities and Institutes;
200.000 Social and Cultural Structure and Institutions;
300.000 Science and Technology, Engineering;
400.000 Commerce, Industry, Finance;
500.000 Transportation and Communications Systems;
600.000 Resources, Commodities, Weapons; and
700.000 Armed Forces.

Table 3.12 Minimal card catalog system for fiction

Subject index (can have a hierarchy of sub-subjects) records—there are expected to be many records for each subject value;
Title index records—there may be multiple records for a title, as different authors may have come up with the same title; and
Author index records—there will be multiple records for each author, as authors try to have multiple books published.

small New England town, and one around Sunny Randall, a female PI in Boston. Each book needs a series identification and a sequence number within its series. This information could simply be contained in the three records already mentioned; however, as with several popular authors, after Parker's death, other authors took up his series. To date there are two other authors who have written Jesse Stone books, an additional author who has written Spenser books, and an additional author who has written a Sunny Randall book. To find all the books in a series, a Series index record is required. (Complicating matters further, some series intersect. Thus, Sunny Randall appears in Jesse Stone books and Jesse Stone appears in Sunny Randall books.)

A typical card catalog system will also provide for non-fiction storage and retrieval using the Dewey Decimal hierarchical system (or some variant). The structure is similar to that described in the CIA effort above, although the categories are different.

Note that the card catalog *system* is the ontology. Each record is an instantiation of a part of the ontology. The *card catalog* is a populated ontology or knowledge base. The books in the library are not part of the ontology or the direct knowledge base. The direct knowledge base points to the books. The library itself can be considered an extended knowledge base.

Prior to the wide-spread availability of the Internet and the development of search technologies to access it, some sort of ontology was the only practical storage and retrieval system for documents. The documents were all physical entities that used enormous amounts of physical space to store. Once the number of documents exceeded the quantity that the owner could remember, some sort of system was required. (Consider the items you have on your desk or piled on the floor or shelves around you. You can probably remember where each item is when you only have a dozen or two to keep track of (random access ontology). However, eventually, you will have to make piles of similar items and remember which pile each thing is in (primitive subject/list ontology). If you reach numbers of items in the hundreds or thousands, you will need a more formal system.)

Modern Document Storage and Retrieval

When you search the Internet for something, you have no idea how it is stored. You just type in some terms, possibly with Boolean "and," "or," and "not" operators, and hit the search button. Depending on the storage mechanisms actually used (on a great many systems), you may find just titles or authors, or subjects, or series information. Or you may find your terms in the body of a paper or book or website. The search engine could be doing an exhaustive search of every item on the web or an indexed search or using some unknown algorithm. (For example, some searches find "book" and "books" when you search for "book." Clearly, there is more than just a pure match of characters that is going on.) You don't know and you probably don't care. Often your search yields thousands of results. However, many results that you would like for your search to have retrieved are not retrieved. They are on the web, but are behind walls that require passwords to get through. For casual searches, this situation is bearable; however, for the curated data of a dedicated team, this situation is not adequate.

The curated data must be stored so that it can be retrieved. Structured datasets range from lists with fixed sequences of elements (think of a single sheet in a spreadsheet file, with headers for each column identifying the contents of the column) to elaborate databases. The commonality is that there is a schematic model that identifies each piece of information. The existence of the schematic model means that each piece of information can be retrieved and connected to its environment, even if the retrieval is somewhat complex. Unstructured data, however, is just that—unstructured. A block of text contains information, but its structure (if any) cannot be assumed to match that of some other block of text (Kelleher & Tierney 2018). (There are semi-structured datasets, such as emails, which have structured headers and unstructured bodies.)

In non-modern document storage systems, unstructured data had to be stored as a block. For instance, a book had to be stored in one location. Citations to the book could be created. In fact, citations to parts of the book could be created; however, they depended on the particular print version of the book, citing page numbers. In any case, these citations required manual operations **prior** to the necessity for retrieval. In modern document storage systems, unstructured data can be searched **at retrieval time** for words, symbols, parts of words, or variants of words.

Documents can be tagged or indexed using various schemes, such as subject matter, author, location, type of document, use of terms from a fixed term-set, and so forth. Attaching these tags generally requires prior manual operations. Now, they also can be searched based on words and phrases in the text. However, context can still be lost using these methods. Burke described a method created by Eugene Garfield that associated a context with a document (Burke 2018). The sources cited in a document constitute an implicit description of the context for the document. Shared citations imply some connection of the contents.

Visual and auditory data, such as pictures, maps, voice recordings, and music tracks, present another problem. They belong in the unstructured data category and required prior citations for retrieval. Modern systems can use AI/ML image recognition and speech recognition to support ad hoc retrieval, with good results for some of these types of unstructured data (Lee 2018).

Storage and Retrieval of Activities-Data

Besides a need for a document storage and retrieval system a dedicated team will need to store and retrieve other types of information. Activities must be captured, recorded and analyzed.

For example, suppose that Ralph (the leader), John, Sue, and Joe have invaded a system and copied a document (Fig. 2.9 in Chap. 2). The Modern Conflict Ontology (MCO) provides the Actor classes to instantiate with this information. Further, the ontology provides the means to link these individuals to an instantiation (groupZeta) of the social faction class. This supports analysis at a higher level of aggregation than provided by just the individuals' names.

Suppose it is determined that the theft was accomplished through the use of a phishing attack that allowed planting a backdoor into the system, followed by copying the document (Fig. 2.10 in Chap. 2). These actions are linked to an aggregated action called *stealDocumentA*. Two object instances are involved in this cyberattack, the document to be stolen and the malware tool used in the theft (Fig. 2.11 in Chap. 2).

The MCO also supports a structure called the Actor-Action-Results Set, which connects the actors, the actions, the resources needed, the environment (here the site containing the document and the attacking site), and the results (here the successfully stolen document).

The Modern Conflict Ontology (MCO) is start, but not sufficient. Some of the classes in this example are of too fine a level of granularity for the purposes of the MCO. However, they are needed here and can be represented in an extension of the MCO.

Technology Identification, Storage and Retrieval

In Chap. 2 we discussed the technium and introduced the concept of technology readiness levels (TRLs). Clearly, not every technology is relevant to our topic of cognitive superiority; however, many that may not appear relevant at first glance, will prove to be so after sufficient consideration. The most immediately useful will be those with TRLs of 8 or 9. Certainly a dedicated team should work to identify and classify the germane technologies. However, the existence of the Valley of Death funding gap means that some promising technologies with TRLs around 4 may die before they can be developed into useful and salient products. The team should also work to identify, classify and promote the funding of any of these technologies that appear very promising.

The team will need to develop an ontology for the storage and retrieval of technologies. This ontology will need to identify standard data, such as name, place, and scientific category of each technology. It will also need to include tags for potential uses and salience levels for each technology. Because this is a new category of information, part of the storage system can be structured. However, other parts, such as patent claims, journal articles, and so forth, will be unstructured data.

Storage and Retrieval Enterprises

Not all information requires new solutions for storage and retrieval. Burke describes several enterprises that store and retrieve documents (Burke 2018). JSTOR (Journal Storage) is a large enterprise that stores full text academic journal articles, books, and primary sources and sells subscriptions to allow search and retrieval of the contents (JSTOR 2019). SPARC (Scholarly Publishing and Academic Resources Coalition) provides access to academic research articles and data at no cost, although it does ask for donations (SPARC 2019). The arXiv enterprise is operated by Cornell University and provides free access to preprints of scientific papers (Cornell University 2019). There are also specialized enterprises, concentrating on such fields as medicine and the law.

Combined Storage and Retrieval Systems

We have described storage and retrieval for structured data, unstructured data (both text and visual/auditory types), and activities data. Clearly, a plan is required to support the storage and retrieval of multiple types of data, each requiring its own technologies. Creating a good plan will require careful thought. The description of the problems the CIA had should serve as a warning (Burke 2018).

However, there is an additional problem that only seemed to be an administrative problem at the time of the CIA's technical document problems. This problem is one of volume of data. In the CIA's case, this arose as a constraint on floor space for files (Burke 2018). With digital data, the problem presents as a practical computation problem. Even with the speed of modern computers, very large data sets (big data) are too large to process on a single computer. Gangs of computers with distributed storage, working in parallel are required to access and process retrievals. There are various techniques that have been developed to do this type of work. The one with the largest name recognition is Hadoop, developed by the Apache Software

Foundation (Kelleher & Tierney 2018). Whatever the choice may be, the storage and retrieval plan must also take data volume into account.

Resilience in Data Storage

Any data stored in a computer is subject to loss: the computer may be attacked or the computer may simply crash. Storing the data in the cloud is simply storing the data on someone else's computers. However, duplication of the data does provide resilience to loss on one site.

Data can also be stored on off-line media, such as on compact discs (CDs) or DVDs or flash drives. This provides protection against many dangers and thus improves resilience. There are two different problems with off-line media storage for long-term retention. The examples of magnetic tape and magnetic floppy disks as early off-line media are salutary.

The first problem concerns the internal storage format and the medium itself. Data storage requires format definitions and these have changed over the years. Current computers may not be able to interpret the data. For many years, WordPerfect was the dominant word-processing program, but today Word is dominant. A document in WordPerfect format is generally not readable in Word. Further, floppy disks themselves are generally not readable on current computers because the hardware does not include a floppy disk reader. Many computers today do not have CD or DVD hardware.

The second problem concerns the life expectancy of the media. Magnetic media, such as tapes and floppy disks, lose their reliability after 10–30 years. Flash drives have an expected life of about 75 years. CDs and DVDs are reliable for storage up to 100 years (Krum 2019).

The hundred-year span may seem impressive; however, good paper data storage is truly impressive. There are paper records that have survived for millennia! For maximum resilience, paper storage provides the longest life. Paper storage is inconvenient for retrieval and takes lots of space. However, modern optical character recognition (OCR) programs are very good at recovering data from paper storage and will certainly get better. For truly long-term storage, a plan of paper storage and reconstitution as electronic records cannot be beat.

Institutional Noosphere

We have institutions that deal almost exclusively with the noosphere. Three of these are science, education and news reporting.

Science (Is Provisional)

The business of science is to increase the noosphere and to increase its truth value. Scientist in all fields work to increase our store of knowledge. They also attempt to ensure that what we think we know is as correct as we can make it. Even our paradigms shift. The ancients accepted many things that we now know to be false: for example, the sun does not revolve around the earth. In scientific domains, we accept that our data have measurement errors, at best, and that our scientific theories are subject to modification as our understanding improves. However, the aim is to decrease measurement errors and improve the validity of our theories. Scientists also aim to increase the breadth of our knowledge. Where the natural world was the principal domain of scientific research (such as physics, chemistry and biology), we have added research that impinges on art and literature. We have techniques for identifying the underlying brush-strokes in a painting and drawing inferences on the identity of the artist. We have techniques for textual analysis of literature, supporting the identification of multiple authors for a given work.

Scientific findings belong in the noosphere. There will be inconsistencies, errors and fraud. There will be arguments and retractions. We regard the scientific conflicts of information validity as generally benign conflicts in the noosphere.

Meta-knowledge is knowledge about knowledge. Meta-science is knowledge about science. The epigram,

> It ain't what you don't know that gets you into trouble. It's what you know for sure that just ain't so,

is attributed to Mark Twain. (Daniel Levitin asserted that it isn't clear who said this. Twain, Josh Billings and Will Rogers were considered. Each could have said this or something similar; but the research was inconclusive (Levitin 2016).) Regardless of the author, the sentiment is valid in general and also applies to science.

Independent replication is key to meta-science—and thus to science. Brian Nosek and a team of researchers set out to replicate 100 high-profile psychology experiments that had been performed in 2008. They reported their findings in the 28 August 2015 issue of *Science*. Only about a third of the original findings were replicated and even for these, the effect size was much smaller than in the original report (Klein 2017).

Education

"Education" is what we call the process of introducing the noosphere to a person and teaching him how to learn. (The second part is what distinguishes education from training.) Part of the goal of a classical liberal education is to enlarge our horizons so that we are aware of a greater part of reality than is apparent in our daily lives. Education includes transmission of both the facts and the methods in the noosphere.

We must understanding that expert knowledge, contextualized knowledge, is transferred differently from the transfer of explicit knowledge and implicit knowledge. Expert knowledge is generally transferred from mentor to mentee with sufficient observations, engagement and doing, teaching how, not just what. Again, we find personal contact with mutual concern and modeling, not just operant and classical conditioning.

News Reporting

Before there were newspapers, there were people who carried tales of events from one place to another. Reporters have been rewarded for their efforts and undoubtedly punished for them. (The old saying, "don't kill the messenger," did not become an old saying from lack of referents.)

During the lead-up to the U.S. Revolutionary War, the press (pamphleteers and newspapers) was very active in pointing out problems with the status quo and its members were activists in supporting change. One of the ideas promulgated was the value of a **free press** (unencumbered by governmental restrictions) to the liberty of the people. The period following the war and lasting until the Civil War is known as the "party-press era." During this time most newspapers openly aligned themselves with a particular political party. Journalistic "standards" allowed slanted news, gossip, innuendo, and *ad hominem* attacks. In 1897, the *New York Times* created the slogan, "All the News That's Fit to Print," which it continues to use. The clear intent was to declare a standard, with the implication of objectivity. The unstated problem is that someone chooses what is "fit to print" and what is not (Levin 2019). Journalism, obviously critical to freedom, can, if perfidious, be malignant.

Journalists are not credentialed or licensed. With the advent of the Internet and the ability for anyone to become a "journalist," the legal definition is in flux. Though they may be brilliant, knowledgeable, evince *caritas* and courageous *civitas*, they are basically storytellers. They give us not only the what, who, how, when, and where, but also their view / report of meaning (why) through the lens of their integrity, worldview, preconceptions, limits, and biases.

"Failures of the U.S. news media in the early 20th century led to the rise of journalistic norms and practices that, although imperfect, generally served us well by striving to provide objective, credible information (Lazer et al. 2018)." These norms and practices govern reporting the facts using the mantra of the four W's and an H (who, what, when, where, and how) and require two independent sources. Editorial opinion was legitimate, but needed to be clearly labeled and kept separate from the news. We (the authors) grew up assuming that these norms and practices defined journalism (with the exception of "tabloid" newspapers that printed anything they thought they could get away with respect to the libel laws).

The traditional business model of the newspaper and, to a lesser extent, the electronic news by appointment (e.g., the 6:30 PM television video news) has been broken by the Internet and its attendant, but flawed, drop in the barrier between "expert" or authoritative knowledge and the end user.

Journalism's new emphasis is more relevant to persuasion. It seeks to create "networks of persuasion," to garner trusted attention, to be more interpretive, more generative, not just informative, more about meaning and identity as evinced in its stories and interpretation (Wihbey 2019). Professor of Journalism Mitchell Stephens of New York University advocated "wisdom journalism" that is "filled with knowledge of what is best for us as a society (Stephens 2014)." This is persuasion. This new view of journalism is disturbing, as Tufekci said, "the most effective forms of censorship today involve meddling with trust and attention, not muzzling speech itself (Tufekci 2018)."

This overview of American news reporting shows that the standards of journalism have not been constant and remain in flux. It is not surprising that non-American standards can differ from American standards.

Today we also have radio and TV (both "broadcast" networks and "cable") and streaming news reporting. In addition, there are multitudinous Internet services that report news. Some of these services act as "clipping services," taking pieces from several reporting originators. Others, ranging from formal organizations to individual "bloggers," originate stories.

News reporting adds to the noosphere. Some of what is added is fact; some is opinion; and some is false. Sean McFate discussed the Russian RT news network: "RT is not a media company but an intelligence operation, and its purpose is not information—it's disinformation. It offers 'alternative facts' to seed doubt and change minds. … One reason why RT is effective is that it blends legitimate experts and journalists with crackpots, offering a plausible version of events that is nested within a larger global disinformation campaign (McFate 2019)."

The new field of "computational journalism" (Stanford Computational Journalism Lab, n.d.) is using AI-augmentation and "may change how stories are discovered, composed, distributed, and evaluated (BéChard 2019)."

Trends in the Noosphere

It is obvious that the total amount of knowledge, the size of the noosphere, is increasing exponentially. The growth rate in peer-reviewed articles is estimated to be more than 3% per year, with 1.5 million in 2010 (Jinha 2010) and 2.5 million in 2017 (Boon 2017). However, there are also new categories of knowledge in the noosphere and the prospect is that there will be many more.

The cuneiform writing (circa 3000 BC to 200 AD) in Mesopotamia recorded business and legal documents, maps, medical manuals, and religious stories (Wikipedia 2018a). In other words, the categories of business, government, pictorial representations, science, and religious knowledge were established very early.

Through the 19th century, we added categories and subdivided categories, changed languages, scripts and media types (e.g., papyrus, vellum, and paper); however, the concept of human readable media remained a constant. The advent of computers added non-human readable media to the mix, along with creating new categories of knowledge.

Personal medical records were created prior to the invention of computers; however, they are now (sometimes) accessible to researchers and subject to theft. X-ray images, CT scans, PET scans and other medical imaging technologies created a new sub-category of medical knowledge. Several companies provide DNA analysis for individuals, creating another new sub-category of medical records.

Social media have exploded over the last few years, allowing sociometrics and psychometrics at scale, a vast new data content on human social life, likes and dislikes, relationships, and opinions, expanding the previous category supplied by the likes of biographies and commentaries (McNamee 2019). Web-based shopping has created enormous troves of information on purchasing habits and derived information on the effectiveness of persuasion techniques (both generally and personally). GPS, computerized maps and direction-providing software have generated a new category of personal position-tracking knowledge. As people move, they also leave behind a trail of sociometric and biometric markers that may be collected for analysis of location and such things as emotional state (Powers 2018). Cognified refrigerators may generate knowledge on eating habits. The old Nielsen TV set-top boxes for tracking television watching habits have morphed into almost ubiquitous tracking and analysis of digital consumption habits. Companies are also investigating linking hardware and software to human brains, generating new categories of knowledge (Neuralink Corp 2018).

Kevin Kelly's central thesis in *The Inevitable* is that there are technological forces that are emerging and can be expected to exert increasing influence as time progresses (Kelly 2016). Kelly made the following points, each of which is accompanied by a comment on its relevance to national security. (The authors have inserted the text in square brackets and the comments in italics.)

1. The properties of media are changing. Examples include the change in music from hard copies to computer files and then the breaking up "albums" to individual songs. *There are implications for data storage and possible fragmentation of its metadata. Classified documents prefigure this change, with their classification labels on each paragraph.* Human information consumption is changing from reading a book to viewing a screen. For example, a book can have citations and footnotes; a screen can have hyperlinks. *There are definite implications for information consumption and use. New versions of manuals can be produced more easily; however, version control becomes much more complex. How do you access the "original" version—or the version you saw first?* Increasingly small pieces of information are being used to create new things. *Intelligence processing will become finer and more computationally intensive.*
2. Ownership is changing. Why own a song or a movie when you can access it whenever you want? Why own a car when you can Uber? Why own and store a

copy of Microsoft Excel when it is in the cloud? *The implications for national defense may be negative, rather than positive. When everything is held in common, how do you justify separate ownership of tanks and ships? More difficult is the problem of spare parts. If our software is all in the cloud, who controls it? The accessed things are shared. When Microsoft quits selling separate copies and develops things only for a sharing environment, what happens to security? Is the defense world stuck in the 2020 world because it can't take advantage of the new technologies that are developed in the commercial world?*

3. The immense increase in information being produced and its growth each year means there is a requirement to filter out the things you don't want to see to find the things you want to see. The AI applications (see 2, above) are required and are in existence to do this. When you Google something, your past Googling (and other activities) are used to customize what you see. If you Google your name, what you see is not the same thing someone else may see! *These techniques are of immense importance for intelligence, both in looking at classified information and in obtaining useful information in the general world. However, the problem of bounded reality arises.*
4. Information creation is changing. Kelly started with the impossibility of Wikipedia working: how do you expect a bunch of amateurs to put together a real encyclopedia? He then proceeds to calculate the value of answering a question. *The national defense implications may be extremely large. How do you safeguard classified information when open-source clues abound? How do you employ this technology to ferret out information on adversaries?*

Kelly re-emphasized that all of these technological forces are just beginning to operate and show no signs of slowing or stopping. So, this is just the beginning.

Additional points are also pertinent.

5. By enhancing the scale of the total comments and contributions, you can either imply that the topic is important or hide the salient point (control the numerator) in a massive haystack (denominator of "facts").
6. The very infrastructure of knowledge is changing. There is "bundling of access [to information] and analytics" with markets of "augmented discovery services through artificial intelligence (AI) toward mining analysis of full text," "robot disciplinary portals," and "new information arbitrage markets (Aspesi & Brand 2020)."

Chapter 4
The Target: Humans

Why can others have undue influence over you? In this chapter, we look at some of the subordinate questions: How do they exercise that power and why does it work? What are the human susceptibilities that permit this?

The technium is involved; the noosphere is the medium; but humans are the target.

Understanding the technium and the noosphere—and changes therein—is critical; however, because we are discussing intentional conflict, recognizing and understanding the target is paramount. Realizing that the ultimate agents and targets are human, does not exclude using other intermediate targets as a way to influence humans. Using intermediate targets requires adding understanding of the relationship between these targets and humans to the problem. Some of these are individual hackers with varying motivations and some operate as groups. Clarke and Knake labeled the worst of the groups as advanced persistent threat (APT) actors because they are not only highly capable, but also steadfast in their efforts (Clarke & Knake 2019). (Note that Rothrock uses APT to refer to malware that is implanted and remains resident in the system for long periods of time (Rothrock 2018).) There are also middlemen who buy and sell information—data brokers and persuasion merchants.

Figure 4.1 shows an Individual Actor Ontology, including a target person, a persuader and several kinds of hackers. Figure 4.2 shows a portion of the Significant Group Actor Ontology with several groups that perform malicious or potentially malicious acts and a target organization.

D. S. Hartley III, K. O. Jobson, *Cognitive Superiority*,
https://doi.org/10.1007/978-3-030-60184-3_4

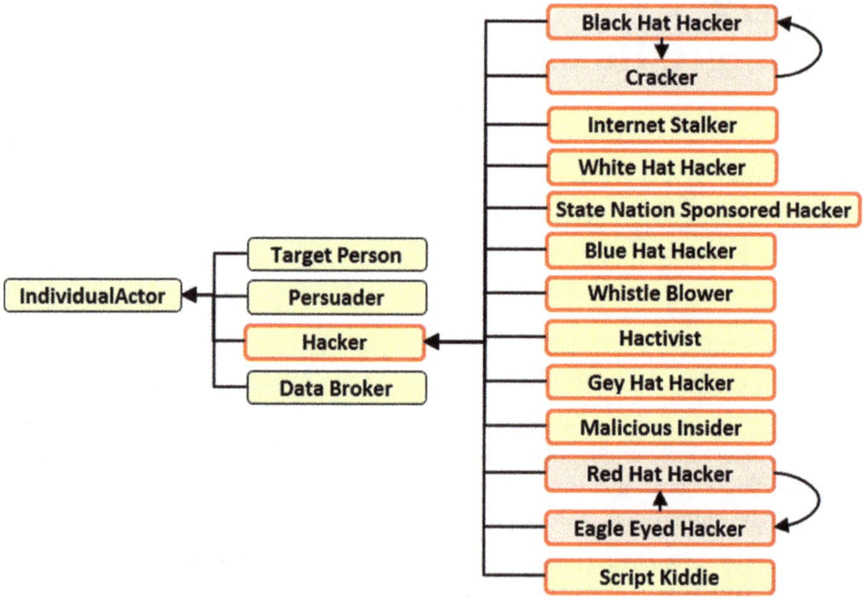

Fig. 4.1 Individual actor classes

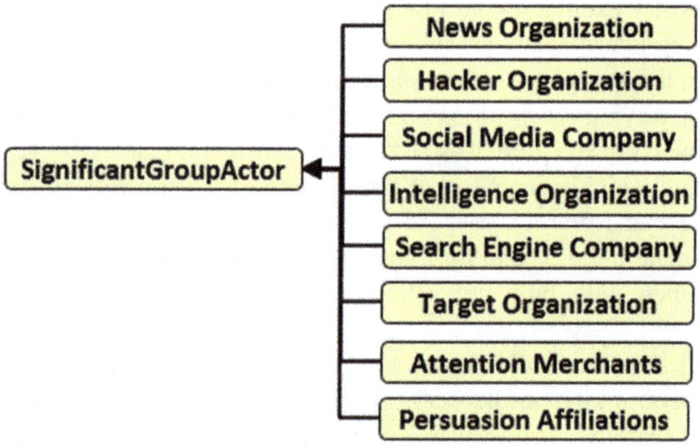

Fig. 4.2 Significant group actor classes

Modeling Humans

Humans are emergent (more than the sum of the parts) bio-psycho-socio-techno-info beings. Three of the many domains of study that describe people are sociology, social psychology and psychology. Each of us is unique in some ways, like some other people in some ways, and like all other people in many ways. Parts of the following discussions are modified from an earlier article by the authors (Hartley & Jobson 2014).

Understanding Human Behavior

Human nature has been regarded as consisting of three parts: the human as an emergent biological being, overlaid with the human as a psychological being, and overlaid with the human as a social being, all within the context of the external world. Clearly there were changes in human nature as humans evolved; but basic human nature is thought to have been nearly constant during recorded history. However, there is reason to believe that the (pre-historic) invention of agriculture (9500–8500 BC,), writing (3500–3000 BC,), and money (~3000 BC) changed human societies (Harari 2015), introducing the possibilities of cities and civilization and inducing changes in human nature through the necessity of dealing with denser populations and more complex networks (Wikipedia 2018d).

Very recently there are indications that human nature may be undergoing further changes. We now know that the cognitive capabilities involved in reading are shaped by the medium (books versus digital media) (Wolf 2018). This implies a large plasticity within humanity. Human nature may be less stable and more fluid than previously believed. Humans are complex adaptive systems within complex adaptive systems (societies) and contain complex adaptive systems (organs, cells, organelles, etc.)—a system of systems (SoS).

Advances in medicine and neuroscience are creating the fields of cognitive optimization/cognitive enhancement and ***nootropics***, pharmacological agents for cognitive enhancement or modification (Sahakian & Morein-Zamir 2007; Mohammed & Sahakian 2011). Mind- and mood-altering chemical agents have been known at least as far back as the Pythian oracles of ancient Greece (Wikipedia 2018a, 2018b, 2018c, 2018d, 2018e, 2018f, 2018g). However, these limited agents had uncertain effects and were not used generally. Further, the creation of computers, smart phones and other information services appears to be having a profound effect on at least some humans. These digitally immersed people have different initial reactions to stimuli and different modes of ***cognition*** (the mental action or process of acquiring knowledge and understanding through thought, experience, and the senses) and decision-making from those of their non-digitally enhanced peers (Fogg & Eckles 2014; Seife 2014).

This means that models of humans as bio-psycho-social beings are inadequate. As suggested in Fig. 4.3 [adapted from Hartley and Jobson (2014)], we should be modeled as emergent bio-psycho-social-techno-info beings, more than the sum of these parts. Emergence is a qualitative change, not a simple quantitative, step-by-step or continuous change.

The time scale of forces that influence our behavior stretches from the evolutionary pace to the fraction of a second before we act (Sapolsky 2017). Though we as a

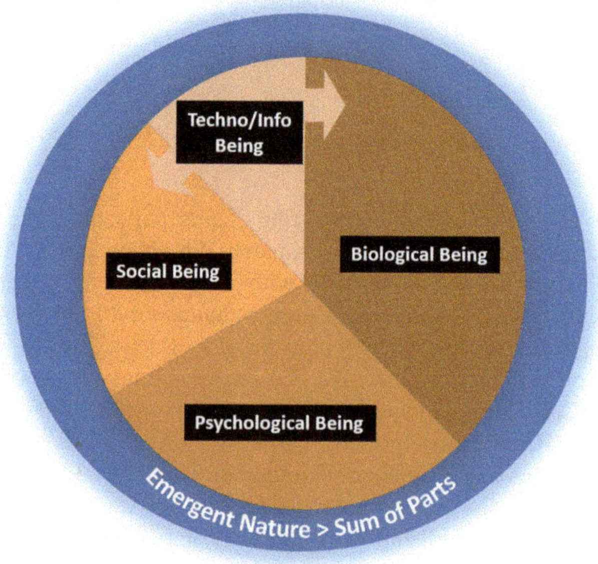

Fig. 4.3 Humans as emergent bio-psycho-social-techno-info beings

species have developed the Internet, split the atom and written the Jupiter symphony, our predictably, systematically irrational aspects are many and obvious (Ariely 2009). Today's matrix of accelerating change includes expansion of our understanding of human potential, default rules and vulnerabilities. Understanding, advancing, and influencing this expanded knowledge must be part of the core curriculum of our lifelong, polythetic education.

Rationality, Mathematics and the Human Mind

Humans can exhibit rational behaviors and can think rationally—exhibited by the human creation of mathematics. Mathematics is obsessed with order. This is evidenced in both the definitions of numbers and in the basics of mathematical inquiry.

Numbers: The natural numbers (1, 2, 3, …) are closed under addition (that is, the sum of two natural numbers is a natural number). However, the addition operator implies an inverse: subtraction. Since 2 minus 4 is not a natural number, the "unnatural" (zero and negative) numbers had to be added, producing the integers, which are closed under addition and subtraction. Again, adding a number to itself several times induces a new concept: multiplication. The integers are closed under multiplication, but not its inverse, division. The result is the rational numbers, which are just those numbers that can be represented as one integer divided by another (when the divisor is the number 1, the integers appear). A special rule had to be introduced forbidding division by zero. Multiplying a number by itself induces the concept of squaring a number. The rational numbers are closed under squaring (and cubing, etc.), but not under the inverse operations (square root, etc.). The problem of square roots of positive rational numbers was handled by adding irrational numbers; however, taking square roots of negative rational numbers required imaginary numbers. (Note the implied denials in the sequence, unnatural, irrational, and imaginary.)

Inquiry: Mathematical inquiry is founded on the concept of proof. That is, a statement will be accepted as true, if and only if it can be showed to follow logically from previously known true statements. Working this logic chain backwards leads to the requirement for a small set of axioms that are assumed or defined to be true (the word choice depends on your philosophical view of mathematics). To a certain extent the choice of axioms is not fixed; however, the set of axioms must not be self-contradictory and none should be provable from the others. As a result, all of the proved statements of a mathematical system (its theorems) must be internally consistent. [Unfortunately for mathematics' obsession with order, Gödel showed that if the mathematical system is complex enough to contain the natural numbers, it cannot be complete. That is, there will be true statements that cannot be proven within the system. Moreover, it cannot be shown *within the system* that the system is consistent (Wikipedia 2018a, 2018b, 2018c, 2018d, 2018e, 2018f, 2018g).]

Irrationality and the Human Mind

On the other hand, despite the fact that mathematics is a human creation, the human mind appears not to be obsessed with order. Truth is malleable; consistency is not required and generally not even checked in a cursory manner; and the human mind even has trouble learning the concepts of mathematical order. Mathematicians are human. This is why you can find mathematicians who are rigorously logical in their professional endeavors and who believe in mutually contradictory things in their personal lives.

In economic theory, rationality is presumed to be a significant part of human nature. Many economic theories presume that, although individual choices may be irrational, on the whole, rational choices prevail. Dan Ariely, in *Predictably Irrational*, showed evidence (through a large number of experiments) that many types of decisions are not rational. However, they are irrational in predictable ways. For example, people distinguish between social and economic settings and apply different behavioral rules in each setting. Some experiments show that introducing money into a social setting can cause a shift in the applicable rules. Other examples include the seemingly magical effect a zero price has and some irrational effects of price: "Why a 50-cent aspirin can do what a penny aspirin can't (Ariely 2009)."

Because Ariely's thesis is that these irrational aspects of human nature are *predictable*, he is not invalidating the heart of economics; rather, he is requiring that its basis needs expansion to include a larger portion of human nature. However, as he pointed out in the book, these irrational parts of human nature expose our decision-making to many forms of deception and manipulation.

Human's Manifold Biases

Of course, every aspect of man can influence our behavior, biases, and vulnerabilities and limit our rationality, including mood, alertness, intellect, knowledge base, and short-term drives, etc. In turn, these affect each other. Psychology has identified a number of biases (Table 4.1) that pervade human thinking and all are context-dependent.

Table 4.1 Salient human biases

Our brain has a rapid prioritized initial automatic ***attentional focus on novelty***.
Humans have a need to grasp and complete patterns (a "mad dash to order"), a bias toward ***pattern completion***, often even without sufficient information. For example, stories provide a powerful way of uniting an idea with an emotion and presenting a complete pattern (Harvard Business Review Staff 2017). Stories, speeches, ceremonies, and symbols are fundamental (Duarte 2012; Duarte & Sanchez 2016).
We have an ***anchoring bias*** for our initial opinion and generally maintain that initial assessment. The anchoring bias of initial opinion is the basis for Warren Buffett's admonition about PR response in a crisis: "get it right, get it fast, get it out and get it over (Muller 2014)."
Following the above bias, we adhere to what is called "***arbitrary coherence***."
Much of human thinking (and communication) is for ***affiliation***, ***affirmation*** and ***confirmation*** of negative opinions of out-groups, as opposed to truth seeking.
A bias toward ***belonging***, ***conforming***, and often ***obeying*** is related to this (Moffett 2018).
Another related bias is our bias toward ***homophily***, the tendency to form social bonds with those who are similar in defining characteristics, beliefs, ethnicity, socioeconomic status, age, etc., (Singer & Brooking 2018).
We have a bias called ***loss aversion***. We often will go to inordinate length or expense to avoid loss, even when the loss is minor in amount.
Our ***preconceptions*** and ***expectations*** shape our experiences so that we experience what we expect to a surprising degree (***confirmation bias***). This predictably irrational part of our nature leaves us open to manipulation by public relations, advertising, propaganda, and attention merchants, which influence our experiences by molding our expectations (Ariely 2009). We "often dismiss objective data when the information is not what we want to see (Brafman & Brafman 2008)."
Our evaluation of a message can be overly influenced by our assessment of the messenger, a ***messenger bias*** (Martin & Marks 2019).
A fundamental humans bias is our ***default to truth bias*** or initial assumption of truthfulness (Gladwell 2019). This default bias can aid in adaptive affiliation but leaves us vulnerable as described in *The Misinformation Age* (O'Connor & Weatherall 2019) and *Weaponized Lies* (Levitin 2016). However, Mercier, in *Not Born Yesterday*, tells us it is more complicated. We judge whether or not the message has interests aligned with our interests and our preconceptions and expected and established ideas have an inertia. "Virtually all attempts at mass persuasion fail miserably." "Humans veer to the side of resistance to new ideas." Our species has a limited "open vigilance guarding against (some) harmful ideas" while being open enough to change our minds when presented with the right evidence. When confronting the established, we must deal with "great chains of trust and argumentation. Long established, carefully maintained trust" in the messengers with "clearly demonstrated expertise and sound arguments" are required (Mercier 2020). See also Berger's book, *The Catalyst: How to Change Anyone's Mind* (Berger 2020).

(continued)

Table 4.1 (continued)

Thaler and Sunstein point out that humans also have ***perceptual biases*** in which perceptions are biased by environmental cues (Thaler & Sunstein 2008). Many optical illusions fall into this category. This was also reviewed by Centola (Centola 2018b). We have to deal with the "inverse optics problem"—"the impossibility of knowing the world directly by virtue of light patterns projected onto the retina." What we in fact see is not a facsimile of the physical world, "but a subjective world fully determined by associations made between images and successful behaviors over the course of species and individual history," a wholly empirical perception (Purves & Lotto 2011).
The ***negativity bias*** describes "the universal tendency for negative events and emotions to affect us more strongly than positive ones." It can spread "bogus scares" or "promote tribalism." Though it is active throughout our life it is even more powerful earlier in our lives. "[T]here are many purveyors of fear and vitriol." The four critical features of this negativity bias are: potency (negativity has more effect than positivity), a steeper negativity gradient (it grows more rapidly), dominance (it dominates in mixtures of positives and negatives), and differentiation (it is more varied, with a wider response repertoire) (Rozin & Royzman 2001; Tierney & Baumeister 2019).

Mental Capacity

Intelligence can be parsed as analytic, creative, and practical (Robson 2019). When a person's "high intelligence" is measured solely as analytical intelligence, as on a traditional IQ test (such as the SAT or ACT), the person may be "less likely to learn from their mistakes or take advice from others. And when they do err, they are better able to build elaborate arguments to justify their own reasoning … or be more dogmatic in their view." (see the subsection on talent recruitment in the section on Organizational Principles in Chap. 7). "Fortunately, there are pedagogical approaches to improving practical and creative intelligence (Robson 2019)." Intelligence must be understood from at least three aspects: analytic, creative and practical.

Cognitive capital consists of intellectual capital, emotional capital and social capital (Sahakian 2018). Humans have varied, but always limited memory, attentional bandwidth and computational ability and yet we often evince an "illusion of knowledge" and think we know more than we do (Sloman & Fernbach 2017). Intuition is notoriously inaccurate outside our limited area of specialized experience. Humans can only pay attention to one thing at a time. Shifting focus from one thing to another thing results in about a half a second of dead time (Cialdini 2016).

Choice

We "rarely choose things in absolute terms." "Rather, we focus on the relative advantage of one thing over another, and estimate value accordingly (Ariely 2009)." We generally use frugal heuristics ("rules of thumb") as opposed to exhaustive search. And we generally use an easy comparison such as one adjacent or immediately available rather than a *de novo* assessment in making our decisions when fully assaying the situation would probably result in a better outcome. The discussion of Thaler and Sunstein's human choice architecture in the Persuasion Fundamentals section later in this chapter augments the examination of choice.

Groups

Man has evolved to form groups and cooperate (Tomasello 2009; Tufekci 2018). The bias is to belong, conform, and often obey. "The markers of social membership are stringent and fragile (Moffett 2018)." Although individuals maintain various levels of standards, the tendency is toward a primal sense of team identity for conformance and often obedience. This bias toward obedience is made clear in the work of Yale professor Stanley Milgram in Obedience to Authority (Milgram 1974). In his landmark research experiment, students followed his authority, repeatedly inflicting what they believed was agonal pain on volunteer experimental subjects, even as those subjects begged to stop the experiment.

Man is predictably, systematically irrational in his thinking, judgement, sense-making, and behavior. Much of our thinking is for affiliation (group membership), validation, affirmation and confirmation of our negative opinions of out groups (Ariely 2009). It takes only "minimal arbitrary groupings to elicit "us-them-ism (Sapolsky 2017)." (*Cf.* "You're not one of us, are you?" "Not from around here, are you?") Moderators of group obedience include proximity, prestige, legitimacy, stability, stress, knowledge of the individual or individuals and criticality of the social process (Sapolsky 2017). Moderators span the bio-psycho-socio-techno-info aspects of man (Sapolsky 2017).

Singer and Brooking described the rise of strange groups on the Internet. "Today, the World Wide Web has given the flat-earth belief a dramatic comeback. Proponents now have an active online community and an aggressive marketing scheme. They spread stories that claim government conspiracy, and produce slick videos that discredit bedrock scientific principles. Simply pushing back at the belief only aids it, giving proponents more attention and more followers. 'YouTube cannot contain this thing,' declared one flat-earther. 'The internet cannot contain it. The dam is broken; we are everywhere (Singer & Brooking 2018).'" While the flat-earthers may be dismissed as irrelevant, a similar group advocates the idea that vaccinations cause autism. "Their passion has also made them a potent online force." The result is that "vaccines have never faced so much public doubt (Singer & Brooking 2018)." (For counter-measures, see the section on Confronting the Established later in this chapter.)

Singer and Brooking described the impact of ***homophily*** (the tendency to form social bonds with those who are similar in defining characteristics, beliefs, ethnicity, socioeconomic status, age, etc.). "Homophily is an inescapable fact of online life. If you've ever shared a piece of content after seeing it on a friend's newsfeed, you've become part of the process. Most people don't ponder deeply when they click 'share.' They're just passing on things that they find notable or that might sway others. Yet it shapes them all the same. As users respond positively to certain types of content, the algorithms that drive social media's persuasion profile-armed newsfeeds ensure that they see more of it. As they see more, they share more, affecting all others in their extended network. Like ripples in a pond, each of these small decisions expands outward, altering the flow of information across the entire system." "But there's a catch: these ripples also reverberate back toward you. When you decide to share a particular piece of content, you are not only influencing the future information environment, you are also being influenced by any information that has passed your way already (Singer & Brooking 2018)."

Violence in Human Evolution

Human aggression comes in two anthropological forms, reactive aggression (impulsive, hot, defensive) and proactive aggression (premeditated, cold, offensive). Having a low level of reactive aggression is no predictor of one's capacity to perpetrate premeditated proactive aggression. "A low propensity for reactive aggression enhances the capacity for tolerant cooperation" within the in-group (family, tribe, nation, etc.). History provides many examples of "peace at home and war abroad." "Understanding this separate nature of proactive and reactive aggression" is critical in profiling, predictions and persuasion (Wrangham 2019).

"Personal Nature"

If "human nature" describes those things that are common to all of us, "personal nature" describes those things that make us different. The relevant differences arise as an emergent individual from the confluence of innumerable bio-psycho-socio-techno-info influences. These differences are genetic, epigenetic and environmental. They manifest in the psychology and behavior of the individual. Figure 4.4 [adapted from (Hartley & Jobson 2014)] shows the categories of influences on a person's behavior. Genetics, epigenetics (the expression of genetics that is modified by the environment), and psychopharmaceuticals can produce biological influences (indicated with green fill). The physical environment and pharmaceuticals in the environment (brown fill) are also influences. The social environment and personal history (blue fill) are social influences. These latter three influences are also influenced by various random events (gray fill). Technology (red fill), both as a creator of pharmaceuticals and as a filter for other influences, affects the personal behavior and acts as a feed-back mechanism from the personal to the social environment.

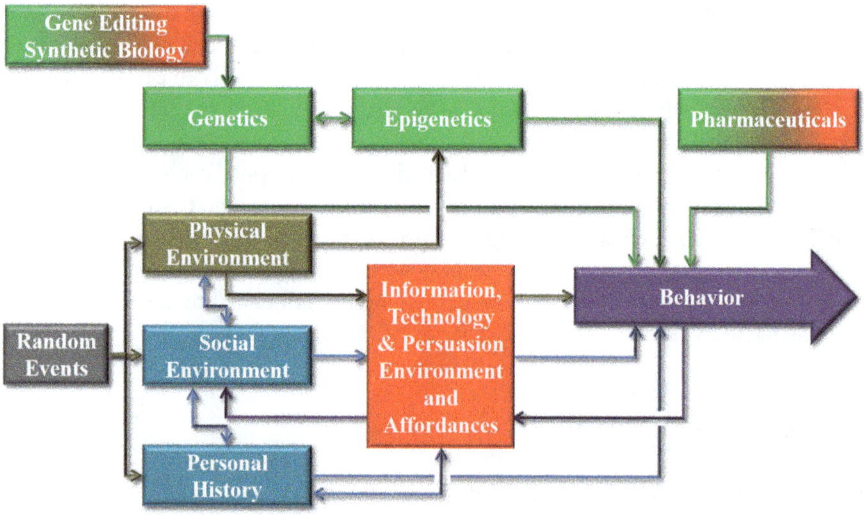

Fig. 4.4 Influences on a person's behavior

Advanced gene editing and synthetic biology are nascent. The modified CRISPR gene-drive technology cuts and splices large segments of the genome, not just short contiguous segments (Service 2019). Further advances, such as the 'prime' gene-editing system (Boussard, Belluck, & Wirz 2019; Cohen 2019), will hasten the spread of genetic changes. Somatic changes will undoubtedly affect behavior.

A person's cognitive state and inherent traits lead to biases that are now better understood. For example, even the incomplete or attenuated manifestation of depression brings a negative bias. The person's ***chronotype*** (morning or evening-person) may advise when in the day the person is more likely to say "yes" (Diaz-Morales 2007). Genetics explains approximately half of the variance in human aggression (Moffitt 2005; Larson 2014) and there is research indicating a specific MAOA gene allele influences anger control (Denson, Dobson-Stone, Ronay, von Hippel, & Schira 2014). The physical environment can even influence the heritable expression (up- or down-regulating or silencing) of genes. These genetic-environmental interactions are called ***epigenetics***.

A person's history, social and physical environment influence his psychology. For example, these can combine in the potential for hubris in political leaders, often increasing with the duration of power (Owen & Davidson 2009). Recent progress in understanding the complexity of human communication in general and within the digital matrix is helpful in prediction and influence. Alex Pentland's work at MIT on the dialectic of social signals, discussed in the books *Honest Signals* (Pentland 2008) and *Social Physics* (Pentland 2014), addresses this. "Nonlinguistic social signals (e.g., tone of voice) are often as important as linguistic content in predicting behavioral outcomes (Pentland 2004)." Benjamin Powers, writing in The Wall Street Journal, discussed computer software that is being trained to identify social signals—"read human emotions." The field, called "affective AI," is still new;

however, there are companies that are using it for commercial purposes (Powers 2018). MIT has an Affective Computing group that is performing research in the area (MIT Affective Computing Group 2020).

Psychological traits are also subject to drug influence. Even casual tetrahydrocannabinol (THC) use influences types of impulsivity (McDonald, Schleifer, Richards, & DeWitt 2003). There are also medications designed for such influence, such as agents with serenic (anti-aggression) effects and others that influence impulsivity.

The last influence in the diagram is "Information, Technology & Persuasion Environment and Affordances." The digitally immersed are subject to influence, search for and evaluate data, and make decisions differently from non-digitally immersed people. Increasingly, they even connect with others differently. The human-computer interfaces and extended reality (xR) of our world are expanding and their human interaction dynamics are not yet well researched (Stanford University VHIL 2019).

Human Communications

We have discussed communications apropos the technium and the noosphere in Chaps. 2 and 3. Here we focus on the human aspects.

Every aspect of man the emergent bio-psycho-socio-techno-info being participates in communication. We are simultaneously children of the word, children of the book and children of the screen. We use many forms of communication: social signals, spoken and written words, mathematical symbols, binary digital communication, musical notation, choreographical marking and a world of semiotics. We fashion stories, speeches, ceremonies, symbols, and memes. If we use elegant listening, we may occasionally learn more in what is *not* said than in what *is* said (Baker 2011). The closest we have to a universal language is seen in the dialectic of social signals, facial expressions, voice, and arm and body movement [paraphrase from (Pentland 2014)]. Our thinking and speech are often for affiliation, affirmation, or confirmation about shared negative feelings toward "outgroups," not truth seeking (Ariely 2009). However, we also communicate to pass information from one to another and to support our goals.

The complexity of communication is reflected in the large portion of the human brain allocated to communication, especially language (Boroditsky 2019; Hines & Stern 2019). Human brain fuses communication with sensing and computation.

Simple Communication

Claude Shannon, the father of information theory, described static or noise as a major problem in communication (Shannon 1948a, 1948b). Although he was describing the nature of electrical transmission of information, his theory is applicable to all communications, including written and verbal communications. Figure 2.5 (Chap. 2) elucidates the feedback from the receiver to the sender to illustrate two-way communication (Shannon's Loop).

The channels of communication are many and the human capacity to discern signal from noise is limited amidst the Niagara Falls of incoming digital information. In 2017, the average computer-connected professional received over 300 digital messages a day, taking 2½ s or 10 words to decide whether to open the messages, parsing the source into friend or foe, seller or helper (Gargan 2017). Here we again face the human "mad dash for order." Our brains bias toward pattern completion. In *The Drunkard's Walk*, Leonard Mlodinow said, "The human mind is built to identify for each event a definite cause and can therefore have a hard time accepting the influence of unrelated or random factors." He also observed that, "Random processes are fundamental in nature and are ubiquitous in our everyday lives," and often underestimated in frequency (Mlodinow 2008). The implication is that Levitin's second method of acquiring information (Fig. 3.8 in Chap. 3), implicitly absorbing it, is likely to result in flawed information. We uncritically infer from a series of good stock picks by a friend that the next pick will also be good and are burned when it isn't good. Levitin's first method of acquiring information, discovering it for ourselves, does support (but not guarantee) critical thinking about the impact of random events, which can result in a lower incidence of acquiring flawed information.

We can generally transfer explicit information. We have some difficulty transferring implicit information. Expert or contextualized knowledge is known as tacit knowledge. It is the most difficult type of knowledge to transfer and generally requires extended personal, one-on-one contact as in a mentor-mentee relationship. The mentee is in context, participating, observing the mentor and ingesting, how, why, when, not just the what. To wit, would you hire a chemist who had memorized the entire textbook but had never worked in a chemistry lab? Interface points and nodes of processing are opportunities for degradation of the information, emphasized by Nicholas Negroponte in "Where People and Bits Meet," that provides examples of problems with interfaces (Negroponte 1995).

Communication Quality

With our limited perception, we rarely respond to the full complexity of incoming signals in the environment. Beyond signal-to-noise ratio, our individual preconceptions, our biases, even our preferences, fears, and immediate needs may cloud interpretation or cause us to ignore information we don't want to hear, prioritize what we prefer, and be overly biased by who is the messenger (Martin & Marks 2019).

"Questioning is a powerful tool for unlocking value in companies: it spurs learning and the exchange of ideas; it fuels innovation and better performance; and it builds trust among team members. And it can mitigate business risk by uncovering unforeseen pitfalls and hazards." "[R]esearch suggests that people have conversations to accomplish some combination of two major goals: information exchange (learning) and impression management (liking) (Brooks & John 2018)." Listening is an important and often neglected topic in communication. The late Howard Baker, former U.S. Senator, ambassador to Japan, official counsellor to one U.S. President and unofficial counsellor to multiple Presidents, considered "elegant listening" and listening for "what they don't say" as requisite communication and leadership skills (Baker 2011).

Communication between disparate communities of knowledge, such as, cyber with traditional military, cyber with foreign policy and statecraft, cyber with politicians, cyber with Silicon Valley, poses challenges and can be a source of "mistranslation" or misunderstanding (Leenen, Aschman, Grobler, & van Heerden 2018). Translation, inherently problematic, should always be considered as a source of falsity, error, intentional bias, or inexactness in meaning. Translation is difficult; professional translators "have the longest apprenticeship of any profession (Baker 2018)." "How is it at all possible to convey and decipher meaning, the most problematic of philosophic notions, across time, across space, across the more or less yawning gap between vocabularies, grammars, networks of diachronic and synchronic systems of sense with separate languages, communities and civilizations (Steiner 1997)?"

The amazing thing is not that we miscommunicate, but that we can, from time to time communicate. We each have different vocabularies, different privacies of reference, different idiolects [derived from George Steiner (Steiner 1997)]. "The single biggest problem in communication is the illusion that it has taken place," [George Bernard Shaw (Shaw 2018)].

Network Communication

Niall Ferguson, in his book *The Square and the Tower*, introduced human networks as a counterweight to hierarchical organizations (Ferguson 2018). Technically, the hierarchical structure of an organization is a network. Ferguson, however, distinguished this structure from the unofficial connections that people make within any organization and its affiliates. He described the difference that organizational principles make to power structures and innovation, introducing the scientific concepts related to network theory to show the distinctions. Broadly speaking, hierarchies are good for control and emphasize vertical communication. Some network structures emphasize lateral communication. The structure and dynamics of network communications are addressed in the Network Science section in Chap. 5.

Negotiation

Negotiation is a form of communication with the aim of resolving differences. As a process, it involves, but is not limited to, decision-making as a subsidiary and may invoke persuasion as a tool. It may or may not lead to a resolution of differences. Fisher, Ury and Patton of the Harvard Negotiation Project prescribed a methodology for negotiation called principled negotiation and described its four points, shown in Table 4.2 (Fisher, Ury, & Patton 2011).

Table 4.2 Fisher, Ury & Patton's "principled negotiation"

Separate the people from the problem.
Focus on interests, not positions.
Invent multiple options looking for mutual gains before deciding what to do.
Insist that the result be based on some objective standard.

Table 4.3 Fisher, Ury & Patton's drivers of emotions

Autonomy is the "desire to make your own choices and control your own fate."
Affirmation is the "desire to be recognized and valued."
Affiliation is the "desire to belong as an accepted member of some peer group." (Recall Moffett's assertion, "The markers of social membership are stringent and fragile (Moffett 2018).")
Role is the "desire to have a meaningful purpose."
Status is the "desire to feel fairly seen and acknowledged."

Sloman and Fernbach gave an example that supports the need for the first two points (Sloman & Fernbach 2017).

> "'If only they understood.' If only they understood how much we care, how open we are, and how our ideas could help, they would see things our way. But here's the rub: While it's true that your opponents don't understand the problem in all its subtlety and complexity, neither do you."

Fisher, Ury and Patton said that emotions, a factor in negotiation, may be driven by a core set of five interests, shown in Table 4.3 (Fisher et al. 2011).

Persuasion

In this section, we discuss general principles and selected types of persuasion, expanding on the concepts introduced in Chap. 2.

Persuasion is the act of causing someone to change his beliefs or actions (Fig. 4.5).

Persuasion Background

Anecdotes

Persuasion takes many forms in the business world. Advertisements and commercials are direct attempts to persuade an individual to buy a product or service. Persuading an organization may require two steps: gaining the attention of a

Fig. 4.5 Persuasion

responsible individual(s) and getting the sale. With respect to gaining attention, Erin Gargan, in *Digital Persuasion*, said, "Today's buyer fields an average of three hundred digital messages a day… to capture attention you have ten words, two and one half seconds of reading… (Gargan 2017)" Her book gave advice on both steps. The businesses also attempt to persuade people to view the business favorably. These attempts include advertising, general marketing, public relations, and crisis management. Warren Buffett's advice on public relations crisis management is succinct, "When you have a problem, get it right, get it fast, get it out and get it over (Muller 2014)."

Why Does It Work?

"Persuasion works by appealing to a basic set of deeply rooted human drives and needs, and does so in predictable ways (Harvard Business Review Staff 2017)." And we have built the technium (technology as a whole system) to reflect our selves, so it is a vehicle for and subject to persuasion.

Persuasion takes place within the domain of human cognition, which presents an increasing number of surfaces of influence. These surfaces include conflict ecosystems, cognified objects, information filters and frames, and default rules. The opportunities, or vulnerabilities, abound across multiordinal dimensions of time, from evolutionary and social biases to the physiology of the seconds before behavior. Whether the target is the Internet governance system, a massive audience, a key influencer, or an avatar, the intent can be specific or to develop a cognitive model, which in turn may constrain or advance a number of subsequent actions (Canan & Warren 2018).

How Does It Work?

The surveilled society (the Panopticon) gathers information and provides manifold metrics, physiological and behavioral biometrics and sociometrics. This is ubiquitous, continuous and adaptive. In our Age of Experimentation, web sites and platforms continually use randomized, controlled experiments by adjusting information access and structure to learn about us and influence us (Luca & Bazerman 2020). The two forces above are armed with AI/ML and big data analytics. New fields of knowledge contribute to modeling, profiling, manipulating, and predicting our future behavior. Human dynamics (Pentland 2014), persuasion science, etc., and new collective structures (attention merchants, persuasion services and bot armies) are extant and active. Immersive technologies, such as xR, are beginning to be important. The Stanford Virtual Human Interaction Lab provides information on the social consequences of emergent xR (Stanford University VHIL 2019).

Persuasion is a particular type of communication. Thinking and communication are often for affiliation and affirmation, as opposed to truth-seeking. New information updates beliefs, it doesn't determine them de novo. This underpins the importance of understanding manifold "priors," our preconceptions and biases. Persuasion is communication with the goal of obtaining something from a person or group. We are all familiar with this at the personal level, starting with a child attempting to persuade a parent to do something and vice versa. It is part of human nature. This continues in school, as always via explicit, implicit, and tacit knowledge transfer. In school, one encounters the pedagogy of choice.

In the pursuit of influence, taking advantage of more than one human predictably irrational aspect at a time produces even more powerful persuasive force (Ariely 2009). An example would be combining our loss aversion with the anchoring bias of initial opinion (Brafman & Brafman 2008). Loss aversion is generally centrally important to those operating at a subsistence level (Kilcullen 2013).

There is still "art" in persuasion; however, there is an increasing element of science, too. The psychologist, Robert Cialdini, in *Pre-suasion,* emphasized the importance of influencing the target prior to making the request, i.e., altering their preconceptions and channeling their attention just before the request (Cialdini 2016). In *Influence Science and Practice*, he discussed six methods of persuasion: ***reciprocity***, ***commitment and consistency***, ***social proof***, ***liking***, ***authority*** and ***scarcity*** (Cialdini 2009). B. J. Fogg's behavior model, the Fogg Behavior Model, says that "three elements must converge at the same moment for a behavior to occur: **motivation**, **ability**, and a **prompt** (or **trigger**) (Fogg 2018)" [emphasis in the source]. Thaler and Sunstein, in *Nudge*, defined the human choice architecture in terms of system design (Thaler & Sunstein 2008). However, these elements are also useful persuasion mechanisms. ***Defaults*** (pre-selected options) are the paths of least resistance. ***Expect error***: humans are fallible; a system that does not take this into account is poorly designed. ***Give feedback***: human performance will improve if feedback of correct and incorrect actions is provided. ***Understand mappings***: mappings are connections between choice and results. ***Structure complex choices***: this architecture element refers to the system required to support complex choices. ***Incentives*** are rewards to move a choice in a desired direction. In his book, *DRiVE*, Daniel Pink discussed the things that motivate us (Pink 2009). According to Pink, the previous standards of motivation were ***carrots*** and ***sticks***. Pink said that sometimes carrots don't work because they turn an interesting task into drudgery or play into work. Sticks sometimes don't work when they convert a motivation into an economic transaction in which other economic factors may outweigh the punishment. Pink emphasized ***autonomy***, ***mastery*** and ***purpose*** (or meaning) as intrinsic motivators of human drive (Pink 2009).

When we generalize the concept of attack surfaces to all human activities, we find every aspect of man is a surface point of potential persuasion: biological, psychological, sociological, technological, and information aspects. The underlying reason for this multiplicity of vulnerable points is complexity and emergent properties. Using our modes of cognition, abstraction, hierarchy, heuristic search, the construction of cognitive artifacts, and collective learning, we consider evidence, point of view, feature of arrangement, ask what if (using inductive, abductive, deductive and seductive reasoning) and ask so what (salience) Each mode has surface points and the combinations add additional vulnerabilities. The ramifications of the complexity are untold in detail, but certain commonalities are observable in general.

How we can now be influenced lies in each of the aspects that are used to model a person (bio-psycho-techno-info beings). The methods and power of persuasion now constitute an Archimedean lever that changes the balance of power. There is a complementarity in persuasion-the-Art and persuasion-the-Science. With more complexity (e.g., the internet of things) come even more attack surfaces. We must consider the persuadee's world view and other preconceptions, and the context, including the messenger as well as the message. The resolute can be made sequacious.

Persuasion Fundamentals

Table 4.4 repeats the earlier table on the fundamentals of persuasion. Note that today the nascent Panopticon, now often with experimentation, provides the information to increase the effectiveness of persuasion. The details are discussed below.

Table 4.4 Persuasion fundamentals (repeated)

Persuasion

The Panopticon:

In our surveilled world, sensing (as surveillance), when fused with computation and communication, enables the garnering and direction of attention, can influence default rules, provide biometrics and sociometrics, and fashion persuasion science strategies, all in an iteratively adaptive propitious manner. The massive data sets of the panopticon provide the raw material for the future of AI/ML, armed with experimentation.

Central Forms	Aristotle	Cicero	Cialdini	Sharot	Fogg	Thaler & Sundstein	Pink	Berger	Martin & Marks	Centola/ Jackson	Digital Attention Merchants
Personal Contact	*Ethos*	Knowledge of Audience	Liking	Priors	Motivation	Incentives	Carrots	Reduce Reactance	Messenger Bias	Network Structure	Garnering attention
Stories	*Logos*	Understand-ing the Case	Reciprocity	Emotion	Ability	Understand-ing mapping	Sticks	Ease Endowment	Hard Messenger	Network Dynamics	Addictive technology
Speeches	*Pathos*	Arranging the Argument	Authority	Incentives	Prompts /Triggers	Structure complex choices	Autonomy	Shrink Distance	Soft Messenger	Diffusion: Information Behavior	Persuasion profiles
Ceremonies	*Kairos*	Emotions	Social Proof	Agency	Captology	Defaults	Mastery	Alleviate Uncertainty		Human & Digital	Always On
Symbols		Eloquent Delivery	Consistency	Curiosity	MIP	Give feedback	Meaning	Corroborat-ing Evidence		Fulcrum of connectivity	Micro-targeting
Social Signals		Practice	Scarcity	State		Expect error				Centrality	Swarms
			Unity	Others						Virality	Global scale
			Pre-suasion								

Technology's New Ecology, Mix and Match: Adaptive, Combinatorial, AI/ML Augmented, Synchronic or Diachronic, nascent xR

Assessment of Credibility, Character and Ability underlies Trust (trust technologies are nascent)

Diachronic (occurring over time or for future effect, as opposed to synchronic or contemporaneous effect)

- ***Shi***: A central ancient Chinese stratagem of warfare, a deception involving influencing the present as part of a larger or grand strategy to influence the future at a propitious moment, often for a long-term, zero-sum game.
- **Apple of Discord**: Sowing a small disagreement to create growth to a major conflict, e.g., election interference for trust, polarization & outcomes.
- **Sleeper software**: Implanted malware to be activated at a later time.
- **Parable of the seed in the Bible**: The seed is sown in various environments with different effects at a later time.

Central Forms

The traditional central forms of persuasion are stories, speeches, ceremonies, symbols (Duarte 2012; Duarte & Sanchez 2016), and social signals. Social signals are the non-verbal clues to thinking and feeling that parallel our speech (Pentland 2008, 2014). Machiavelli's book, *The Prince*, prescribed methods of political persuasion using these central forms (Machiavelli 1966). Video and xR expand the reach of the central forms.

The continuum of influence spans persuasion, manifold forms of manipulation, falsity—including perfidy, coercion and control. Within this continuum, lies, blackmail and sex can be powerful elements. Each can be used to gain desired ends, despite the wishes of the target.

Aristotle and His Classic Four Pillars of Rhetoric

In the West, we first had Aristotle (384–322 B.C.). In his book, *Rhetoric*, Aristotle defined his subject matter, "as the faculty of observing in any given case the available means of persuasion (Aristotle 2004)." ***Rhetoric*** is persuasion through verbal means. He began his discourse by listing the three characteristics of persuasion. "The first kind depends on the personal character [credibility] of the speaker [***ethos***]; the second on putting the audience into a certain [emotional] frame of mind [***pathos***]; the third on the logic, or apparent proof, provided by the words of the speech itself [***logos***]." However, the choice of mode or the choice of combinations depends on the situation and timing, choosing the opportune (propitious) moment [***kairos***].

Cicero

Cicero (106–43 B.C.), in *How to Win an Argument*, emphasized knowing the audience, the natural ability of the speaker, and the art and skill of delivery with eloquence. This has been taught as elocution. He also stressed understanding the case and how it is best arranged and logically presented (Aristotle's *logos*). He insisted on consistency between the emotional tone of delivery and the content. Finally, Cicero advocated repeated practicing of the speech as necessary preparation (Cicero 2016).

Cialdini

The psychologist, Robert Cialdini, in *Influence Science and Practice*, discussed six methods of persuasion: reciprocation, commitment and consistency, social proof, liking, authority and scarcity (Cialdini 2009) (Table 4.5).

Cialdini turned his focus from persuasion to what he called pre-suasion. The idea is that setting conditions that will be favorable to persuasion increases the chance of

Table 4.5 Cialdini's six methods of persuasion

Reciprocation is very commonly seen in requests for donations that include a "gift," such as a pen, a set of address labels, or a calendar. It works when we feel obligated because we have accepted the gift.
Commitment and consistency involve using our desire for self-consistency to persuade us. The plan is to gain an initial commitment and then rely on this desire to cause us to become convinced the commitment must be followed through.
Social proof uses our desire to agree with what others think. Canned laughter used in a television show leads us to think that others like the show, inducing us to do likewise.
Liking uses our desire to accommodate someone we like. A con artist will often try to be likable before presenting the persuasion argument.
Authority uses our desire to defer to someone who is in a position of authority.
Scarcity rests on the economic principle of an inverse relationship between availability and value. Thus, presenting an opportunity as restricted to just a few or available for a limited time implies scarcity and thus high value.

Table 4.6 Cialdini's elements of pre-suasion

Unity refers to affiliation or unity of identity or *We* relationships. These relationships can be formed through family or place (genealogy or geography) or through acting together synchronously or collaboratively, such as in a team (Cialdini 2016).
The ***moment*** is a point or period in time in which the potential persuade is most receptive to being persuaded. This is precisely Aristotle's *kairos*.
Attention—focusing attention increases the perceived importance of the item being focused on. This is also sometimes called the "setting the agenda" method.
Attention **Attractors**—sexual and violent references can attract attention. However, the follow-on message should consider the opposite responses. A message couched as "be one of the few" works well with a sexual pre-suasion message, but not with a violent one. On the other hand, a "join the crowd" message works better with the violent pre-suasion message than with the sexual one. The third attractor is novelty—a rapid change in the environmental circumstances is a powerful attractor or distractor.
Attention **Magnetizers**—self-relevant information (recipient's name, age, health status, etc.) attracts attention and holds it. Similarly, unfinished tasks, presentations, whatever, can hold attention. Mysteries also hold attention.
Association—choosing the right words or images prior to the persuasion attempt increases the likelihood of success. The words or images draw attention to the associations in the mind of the recipient that are likely to help with the persuasion. Metaphors are good for this.
Geography (or environment)—the physical surroundings can influence everything from word choice (of the persuader) to the mood of the engagement.

accomplishing the persuasion. In *Pre-Suasion*, Cialdini added a seventh method of persuasion: unity (Table 4.6).

Sharot

In her book, *The Influential Mind*, Dr. Sharot discussed seven factors that affect influence. She labeled these priors, emotion, incentives, agency, curiosity, state, and others (Sharot 2017) (Table 4.7).

Table 4.7 Sharot's seven factors affecting influence

Priors—the beliefs one holds prior to obtaining new information or being subjected to persuasion are the priors. Sharot explains that confirmation bias makes it easy to accept information or persuasion that agrees with ones priors and leads to strong resistance to change that contradicts the priors.
Emotion—the emotions that are evoked (or not) by a persuasion argument can be very strong persuasive forces because emotions are part of humanities' earliest cognitive structure. This factor can be compared to Aristotle's *pathos*.
Incentives—the use of incentives often works better than the use of warnings (the carrot versus the stick).
Agency—the agency factor relates to the shift in control from the persuader to the persuadee. The perception of external control inhibits influence, while the feeling of self-control or autonomy can facilitate influence.
Curiosity—the curiosity factor can induce people to do things they wouldn't ordinarily do and so it can be a powerful persuasion tool.
State—the environment in which a decision is made is important. Sharot says, "under stress and intimidation, the way in which our brains process information changes dramatically (Sharot 2017)."
Others—the first part of this factor concerns our basic program for learning. Naturally, we learn from our own experience, but we also learn from observing others (with a caveat for messenger bias). This means that we are programmed to be influenced by others. This combines with our desire for affiliation. As Sharot puts it, we consciously look at Yelp ratings in picking a restaurant and unconsciously make wine preference decisions based on the 2004 movie *Sideways*, choosing pinot noir over merlot. The second part of the Others factor concerns unanimity and the "wisdom of crowds." This also relates to crowdsourcing. Sharot points out a crowd is only "wise" if it is composed of people with independent opinions. That is, each individual guess is not influenced by the guesses of others. In this case, the mean of the guesses is likely to be close to the true answer. In more complex cases, it helps if some in the crowd have knowledge of the subject.

Table 4.8 Fogg's behavior model

The core ***motivators*** are	Pleasure/pain, Hope/fear, and Social acceptance/rejection.
Ability is divided into ***simplicity factors***	Time, Money, Physical effort, Brain cycles, Social deviance, and Non-routine.
Prompts or ***Triggers*** are divided into	Facilitator, Spark, and Signal

Fogg

B. J. Fogg's behavior model, the Fogg Behavior Model, says that "three elements must converge at the same moment for a behavior to occur: **Motivation**, **Ability**, and a **Prompt** [emphasis in the original] (Fogg 2018) (Table 4.8)."

Table 4.9 Thaler and Sunstein choice architecture

Defaults are decisions that are preprogrammed or happen normally in the absence of an active intervention. They are ubiquitous and powerful.
Expect error: humans are fallible; a system that does not take this into account is poorly designed.
Give feedback: human performance will improve if feedback of correct and incorrect actions is provided.
Understand mappings: mappings are connections between choice and results. Some mappings are simple, with a clear utility relationship among the results. Others are more complex and require a system to support the choice.
Structure complex choices: this architecture element refers to the system required to support complex choices.
Incentives are nudges to move a choice in a desired direction. These include prices, price changes, and non-monetary elements, such as "free shipping."

Table 4.10 Pink's motivators

Carrots are rewards that are offered for good performance. Pink says that sometimes they don't work because they turn an interesting task into drudgery or play into work.
Sticks are punishments that are offered for poor performance. These also sometimes don't work when they convert a motivation into an economic transaction in which other economic factors may outweigh the punishment.
Autonomy as a motivator works by assuming that people will be self-motivated and ensuring that the environment supports self-motivation.
Mastery is the "desire to get better and better at something that matters."
Purpose is the part of motivation that defines meaning or what "matters."

Fogg also has greatly contributed to the practice of persuasion through computers (see the section on Persuasion in Chap. 2).

Thaler and Sunstein

Thaler and Sunstein, in *Nudge*, defined the human choice architecture in terms of system design (Thaler & Sunstein 2008). However, these elements are also useful persuasion mechanisms (Table 4.9).

Pink

In his book, *DRiVE*, Daniel Pink discussed the things that motivate us (Pink 2009). According to Pink, the previous standards of motivation were only carrots and sticks. Pink defined a new trio of motivation: autonomy, mastery, and purpose (Table 4.10).

Table 4.11 Berger's catalyst factors

Reduce ***reactance*** is defined as reducing the innate anti-persuasion reaction. Start by understanding the person and circumstance of the established system of thought. Trust and concern must be created. Don't demand, ask for change (what to do differently). Then get them to decide for themselves. The target must keep their sense of agency (control) or autonomy. Providing a menu of multiple options supports this effort. Highlight the gap between someone's thought and actions and what they would recommend to others and what they are doing.
Ease ***endowment***. The endowment effect refers to an attachment to the *status quo*. Bringing the cost of inaction to the fore reduces endowment.
Shrink the ***distance*** between existing views and the proposed change. Breaking the change into chunks can lead to eventual acceptance of the entire proposal.
Alleviate ***uncertainty***. Change often involves risk. Lowering the barrier to trying the new proposal can reduce the uncertainty. For example, providing free software with reduced capabilities allows the person to decide whether buying a version with greater capabilities is worth the cost of change. Proposing a trial or making the decision reversible can help.
Find ***corroborating evidence***. This often involves showing examples of other people who have made the proposed change. Berger gives an example of persistant personal contact with mutual concern bringing change in an extremist.

Berger

Jonah Berger described a set of catalyst factors (Berger 2020). The idea is to remove barriers to persuasion (Table 4.11).

Martin and Marks

In their book, *Messengers*, Martin and Marks taught that "we tend to judge an idea not on its merits, but how we judge the person putting it forward" and discussed the traits that determine our assessments (Martin & Marks 2019).

All signals are context dependent. Here we learn that part of the context entails our perception of the messenger (***messenger bias***) and that it is essential in persuasion. The type of messenger, hard or soft, and four specific traits of each of these two types of messenger are important. For the "***hard messenger***," socio-economic position, competence, dominance, and attractiveness are salient. For the "***soft messenger***," warmth, vulnerability, trustworthiness, and charisma are important. Frugal decision heuristics, clustered about the messenger, are known, are predictive, and are vulnerable to manipulation.

Centola

Damon Centola addressed how diffusion works in both human and digital networks: "Here the dynamics of both informational and behavioral diffusion are explained within a framework that allows each to be understood on its own terms (Centola

2018b)." Simple ideas and facts can spread (diffuse) virally from a single contact and use long and weak ties (for example, contacts with acquaintances in distant parts of the country). The spread of behavioral change and diffusion of complex information follow different dynamics, using tight entangled lattice networks and strong ties, "structurally clustered, they are relationally proximate, homophilous, often affect laden and high frequency." Importantly, networks that are "ideal conduits for the spread of simple contagions" are "less well suited for spreading complex (behavioral contagions." Centola further addressed experiments in social design, motivating "high risk social action" in various circumstances and successful methods for diffusion in the face of opposition.

Diffusion is important when the persuasion effort is directed toward a group, rather than an individual, or when the results of the persuasion of an individual depend on the persuasion of others. A simplified recounting of his explanation is given in Chap. 5 in the Network Science section.

Jackson

Matthew Jackson approached network science by orienting, teaching about context (externalities), and explaining network formation ("why certain patterns form and how those patterns determine our opinions, opportunities, behavior, and accomplishments"). Importantly, he described forms of connectedness or ***centrality*** of position: degree centrality or popularity identifies direct influence; eigenvector centrality speaks to the power of our friends; diffusion centrality tracks the reach that someone has in spreading information; and betweenness centrality measures the number of others who must communicate through a node to reach a large number of others. He helped in understanding our power, social position and behavior.

Digital Attention/Information Merchants

A digital attention merchant is a digital platform that makes money by selling your attention. The platform records the attention you pay to advertisements it supplies on its web site. Giant social media platforms, such as Amazon, Facebook, Google, are examples using some or all of the following methods. Horwitz and Seetharaman reported in The Wall Street Journal that Facebook studied the effects of its algorithms on divisiveness. The algorithms aggravated polarization; however, changing them was projected to reduce attention paid to Facebook (Horwitz & Seetharaman 2020). Such changes might also reduce Facebook's income (Table 4.12).

Figure 4.6 lists several of the most popular digital attention and information merchants. The sources with monthly active user (MAU) and monthly unique visitor (MUV) annotations are taken from Alfred Lua's 2019 article, "21 Top Social Media Sites to Consider for Your Brand," on the Buffer Marketing Library site (Lua 2019). The other entries come from various other searches. The monthly usage (where available) is staggering—note the numbers are in units of a billion! The scale is

Table 4.12 Digital attention merchants' methods

Attention merchants use the brain's attentional bias to ***novelty*** with "startling images and evocative words" celebrity, warfare, sex, and the markers of social membership (Wu 2016).
Garnering attention: Cialdini's research shows that focusing attention increases the perceived importance of the item being focused on.
Addictive technology: According to Alter, many of these media are engineered to be addictive for massive engagement (Alter 2018).
Persuasion profiles: Kaptein has performed research that shows that both simple preference profiles and persuasion profiles work in personal encounters and work on the Internet to increase persuasion. His research also shows that personal persuasion profiles (a record of which persuasion techniques work best on the person) are relatively stable across different types of products and environments and that using the wrong method may be counterproductive (Kaptein 2015) (see Vulnerability section in this chapter).
Micro-targeting: Individualized advertisements are selectively placed on the web search results based on previously collected information on the searcher's activities (see (Fogg, Home, n.d.)).
Affective computing (related to affective AI (Powers 2018)) is the nascent digital approach to human emotional intelligence, allowing a program to immediately adapt to the user's activational level and emotional state, with recognition, interpretation, processing, and simulation. Many elements of affective computing are being developed by the MIT Affective Computing group (MIT Affective Computing Group 2020).
Global scale: These digital attention merchants are globally available on the Internet. "Every course is charted (Wu 2016)."
Always on: And they are always on, always available, and with your profile, know the propitious moment and the optimal combination of "mixed incentives (Wu 2016)."

- Facebook – social networking - 2.2 billion MAU
- YouTube – video sharing – 1.9 billion MAU
- WhatsApp – instant messaging - 1.5 billion MAU
- Messenger – instant messaging – 1.3 billion MAU
- WeChat – messaging, all-in-one - 1.1 billion MAU
- Instagram – photo sharing - 1.0 billion MAU
- QQ – instant messaging - .9 billion MAU
- Tumblr – blogging platform - .6 billion MUV
- QZone – social networking - .6 billion MAU
- TikTok – music videos, popular with kids - .5 billion MAU
- Sina Weibo – microblogging - .4 billion MAU
- Twitter – text message posting - .3 billion MAU
- Reddit – social media - .3 billion MAU
- Baidu Tieba – social forum network - .3 billion MAU
- LinkedIn – professional social networking - .3 billion MAU
- Viber – multi-lingual instant messaging - .3 billion MAU
- Snapchat – image messaging - .3 billion MAU
- Pinterest – photo sharing - .3 billion MAU
- Skype – communication - .3 billion
- Line – messaging - .2 billion MAU
- Telegram – instant messaging (encrypted) - .2 billion
- YY – video chat - .1 billion
- VKontakte – social networking - .1 billion
- Taringa – social networking
- Foursquare – local search and discovery
- Renren - social networking
- Tagged – social media
- Badoo – dating social networking
- Myspace – music social networking
- StumbleUpon – recommends content
- The-Dots – collaborative platform
- Snapfish – photo sharing
- Zoom – video conferencing
- Search Engines:
  - Google,
  - Bing,
  - Yahoo,
  - Baidu,
  - Yandex.ru,
  - DuckDuckGo,
  - Ask.com,
  - AOL.com
- Online Shopping:
  - Amazon,
  - Ebay,
  - Etsy,
  - Overstock,
  - Zappos,
  - Wish,
  - Alibaba
- Streaming services:
  - Netflix,
  - HBO GO,
  - Disney Plus,
  - Hulu,
  - Amazon Prime Video
- Wikis

black – US; red – China; brown – Russia; green – Latin America; blue - UK

Fig. 4.6 Digital attention/information merchants

global in reach and global in source, as indicated by the color coding, including the United States, China, Russia, Latin America, and the United Kingdom. This list omits "adult" sites and many smaller digital information merchants. Similar lists for earlier years have smaller user numbers, as the popularity of these sites is growing. The rankings change as sites are growing at different rates and new entries appear.

All of the entities in Fig. 4.6 are attention merchants, but some are information merchants, providing a service by supplying information. Many professional societies have websites with portals to permit access to information (such as digital copies of journals) to members only. These are information merchants that are not attention merchants. However, the rapidly morphing knowledge infrastructure, with its variant information access is presenting vast new ways to influence. It does this by alerting or allowing versus disallowing access, or changing information flows, or potentially creating monopolistic "bundled information and analytics" in "information arbitrage markets (Aspesi & Brand 2020)."

Persuasion is now adaptive, cognified, combinatorial, and multi-ordinal, addressing every aspect of our emergent bio-psycho-socio-techno-info being.

Diachronic: *Shi* and the Apple of Discord

There is a long written history of persuasion, both oriental and occidental. Sun-Tzu's *The Art of War* is dated sometime after 400 B.C. (Sun-Tzu 1963), roughly contemporaneous with Aristotle. Oriental persuasion is often more complex, more nuanced, more combinatorial, more holistic, and more patient than Western persuasion. Oriental persuasion embraces deception and favors the zero-sum game and the strategies of Sun-Tsu. "*Shi*" is a principle of Eastern persuasive strategy. *Shi* is a deceptive strategy involving influencing the present as part of a larger or grand strategy to influence the future at a propitious moment, often for a long-term, zero-sum game. It is described in *The Hundred-Year Marathon* (Pillsbury 2015). This stratagem also is evident without being named in *The New Rules of Warfare* (McFate 2019) and *The Science of Military Strategy (2013)* (Chinese Academy of Military Science 2018).

Shi has a partial analog in the western myth of the Apple of Discord. The Greek myth involves the goddess Eris (Discordia in Roman mythology) tossing a golden apple inscribed "for the fairest" into a wedding feast, causing a dispute among Hera, Athena, and Aphrodite as to who was the fairest, which led to the Trojan War. This myth illustrates that a small disagreement can later grow into a major conflict. Another partial analogy lies in the Biblical parable of the sower or the seeds. The seeds are sown on a path, on rocky ground, among thorns, and on good soil. The effects are discovered later when the seeds sprout. Sleeper software, such as sleeper bots and logic bombs embrace this same delayed or diachronic effect.

Others

The Internet has enlarged the reach of information warfare and its cousins, narrative warfare and psychological warfare or psychological operations (PSYOPS) (Headquarters, Department of the Army 2005). In the days of the Trojan Horse, lies, deceptions and story-telling were limited in space and time by the available communications media. The necessary psychological forces employed were the same because humans have not changed their basic nature, but the impacts on operations were limited to those who could see or hear the messages. (In certain cases, such as the tales of the *Odyssey* (Homer 1946 and *Aeneid*; Virgil 1969), the messages have transcended the local time.) Today, lies, deceptions and story-telling can be delivered around the world, not only to large audiences, but also to tailored audiences, ripe to receive them. Further, these messages can extend for large periods of time because, it seems, nothing is ever forgotten in the Internet. Even more significantly, our understanding of persuasion has been vastly improved through massive efforts to make persuasion more effective. The importance of story-telling has been rediscovered, now named narratology or narrative warfare. The story need not be "true," but it must resonate with the audience. It may be effective because it bypasses critical thinking and shapes the identity of the receptive audience, and thus its beliefs and actions. "This is not information warfare; it is warfare over the meaning of the information (Maan 2018)."

Computer assisted persuasion (***captology***), social media with its potential for ***MIP*** (mass interpersonal persuasion), mobile persuasion, and expanded digital and social information sources (Fogg 2003; Fogg & Eckles 2014) now influence people and are methods for externally manipulating people through information technology. Mimicry of human behavior (acting similarly to the behaviors of the other person) and mood contagion lead to more successful negotiations (Maddux, Mullen, & Galinsky 2008; Ariely 2009). The available information matrix and the individual's facility to use it lead to self-modification, such as affecting the individual's openness to iterative inductive discovery versus fixity of mind, even fixity of world view.

Here enters *Kairos*, the god of the propitious moment. In order to influence, you might change the urgency of a decision or give timely new information. With urgency, you often use frugal heuristics or default rules as opposed to exhaustive research to make a decision.

The scientific study of persuasion has engaged scholars for generations. The 2002 book, *The Persuasion Handbook: Developments in Theory and Practice*, edited by Dillard and Pfau illustrates the range of the domain. It contains 34 chapters by more than 60 authors and comprises almost 900 pages (Dillard & Pfau 2002). In this section, we have reviewed the work of several scientists. There are similarities and differences among the factors that they address. We have chosen not to attempt a meta-analysis to determine who has it "right." Rather, we make the point that now there is a science of persuasion and that educated persuaders can gain probabilistic success in persuading their targets.

Confronting the Established

The full array of the art/science of persuasion at the individual and system dynamics levels is relevant in confronting established opinion, but also there are special factors to be considered and employed regarding the message(s), the context, the messenger(s), and those that are to be addressed. We must always remember that those we address have a matrix of the established "truth" and a bias toward their presuppositions and the familiar. Our message will not so much determine their opinion, but may amend or augment it.

One must not simply directly refute the installed narrative, as that may reinforce the fixity. We must tell better stories. Fashioning the message as a metanarrative encompassing the established, reframing, redefining, or even furthering an aspect of the installed narrative, if feasible, is recommended. Acknowledging the complexity of the issue may be helpful. Word choice, turns of phrase and metaphors should be chosen to match with the view and fixity or flexibility of the established narrative. It is essential to establish trust in the messenger, commonality, even homophily if possible. A setting conducive to trust should be chosen. If the messenger is seen as an authority, a faint self-denouncement may be in order to put the other person at ease.

Mercier, in *Not Born Yesterday*, described our resistance to changing our opinions, our persuasion radar or "reactance" and open vigilance (Mercier 2020). Berger, on the other hand, gave strategies for changing minds in his book, *The Catalyst: How to Change Anyone's Mind* (Berger 2020). Many of these contending forces and vulnerabilities are only recently illuminated.

Vulnerability Points and Surfaces of Humans

Every aspect of man (biological, psychological, sociological, technological, and informational) offers potentials for persuasion. Using our modes of cognition (abstraction, hierarchy, heuristic search, the construction of cognitive artifacts, and collective learning), we consider evidence, point of view, feature of arrangement, ask what if and so what? Each cognition mode has vulnerabilities.

John Keegan, the historian of war, understood fear, need and loss of face as causes of war (Keegan 1994). The three provide streams of influence. There is power in perfidy, as there is in legitimate trust. And Aristotle knew that *pathos* often trumps *logos*. These are not new.

New knowledge of aspects of man's predictably, systematically, irrational aspects offers opportunities for and vulnerabilities to persuasion, learning and engagement. Thinking and speech are often for affiliation, affirmation, and/or for confirmation of negative feelings toward the Out-group, instead of truth-seeking. "Your cognitive capital is not only your intellectual capital, but also your emotional and social capital and each can be manipulated (Sahakian 2018)." David Michaels said in his book

The Triumph of Doubt that there is a well-worn playbook of denial and misdirection that has been proven effective by bad actors (Michaels 2020b).

Further, new understanding of the interactions of biology and cognition present new methods for addressing vulnerability points. Serenics, medications that lessen aggression, and medications that can influence impulsivity exist. We are on the cusp of using nootropic interventions that improve selected aspects of cognition.

Addictive Technology

Adam Alter quoted Stanton Peele's definition of addiction as "an extreme, dysfunctional attachment to an experience that is acutely harmful to a person, but that is an essential part of the person's ecology and that the person cannot relinquish (Alter 2018)." This definition covers addictions to substances, such as alcohol, heroin or opioids. It also can involve addictions to behaviors such as gambling, shopping and sex. Alter said that "behavioral addiction consists of six ingredients: compelling goals that are just beyond reach; irresistible and unpredictable positive feedback; a sense of incremental progress and improvement; tasks that become slowly more difficult over time; unresolved tensions that demand resolution; and strong social connections."

Computer games appear to have used these ingredients as design specifications. Just as there are people who have gambled and not become addicted, there are people who have played computer games and not become addicted. However, there are many computer-game addicts. Alter described research that showed that everyone can become addicted to something under the right (or wrong) circumstances. According to Alter, the physical tools of the computer world, such as smart phones, contain at least one of the ingredients that can lead to addiction—consider the people who cannot be separated from their phone—and the apps on the physical tools, such as Instagram and Facebook are similarly addictive. Moreover, these addictive ingredients have been consciously added to technology to increase use (Alter 2018)—or "optimize" user engagement. "Gamification" is entering education and mass entertainment, providing further surfaces of influence (McGonigal 2011).

The Range of Vulnerability Surfaces

The surfaces of vulnerability become more numerous with the cognifying of ever more objects (the IoT) and as we move from the individual target to the group, be it a dyad or a social platform with 100 million or more users, and as the technium grows. Vulnerabilities are plentiful including mass biases and default behaviors, such as fan affiliation, affirmation, and desire for a sense of belonging, conformity and often obedience. Understanding the psychology and anatomy of social or

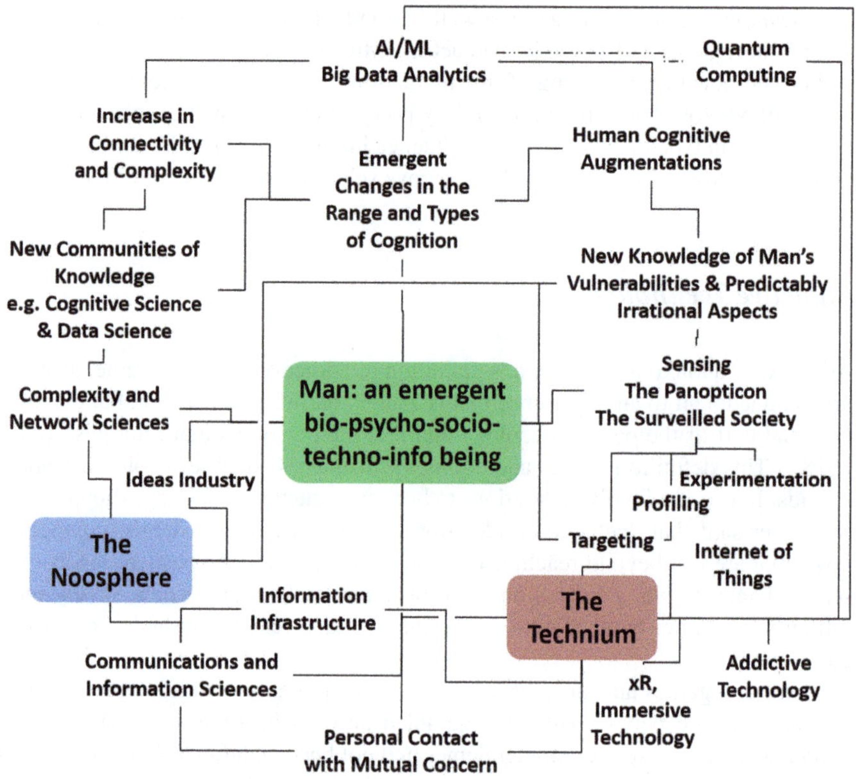

Fig. 4.7 Persuasion entanglements

collective persuasion is critical. The relevant interactive dynamics span the distance from individual persuasion profiles to group or swarm persuasion.

Human vulnerabilities lie at the heart of and magnify most technical vulnerabilities. First, the systems of the technium have been created by humans and have flaws because humans have flaws. Second, most systems are modeled on pre-existing systems, often recasting them with new technology without examination of the implications of doing so: assumptions of the existing system may not match those required for the new system; security or resilience features embodied in the old technology may not carry over to the new technology (or even may not be understood as valuable); and the new technology may introduce new vulnerabilities of which the old technologies were incapable. Third, in today's networked environment, the human interface is often the most effective attack point. "Most successful attacks on computer networks use Trojan horses that are introduced into the network," by human users (Rothrock 2018).

Figure 4.7 illustrate persuasion science's morphing entanglements amidst accelerating change and a motif of connectivity.

Profiles

A profile is a model of a person, which by definition is an abstraction of reality, containing only what is needed and no more. The contents of the profile depend on its expected use.

Simple Profiles

The bare profile will contain a set of attributes and their values with respect to the particular person. For example, the Minnesota Multiphasic Personality Inventory (MMPI), first published in 1943, defines a set of attributes and a test for developing the values (Hartley & Jobson 2014). The resulting "inventory" is a profile.

Commercial profiles contain more prosaic information. For example, one of the authors buys ~100 science fiction novels per year. A simple recommender profile, such as used on Amazon, will show him science fiction books when he logs on. However, this author also orders books for his wife. Suppose they were "bodice-rippers;" that would make profiling his tastes harder. Then, as research for this book, he has bought numerous books on persuasion, social media, the Internet, and so forth (see the Bibliography), so suddenly his profile has changed. Clearly an adaptive profile that changes over time will generate better results.

Persuasion Profiles

A more ambitious profile might include a connection between the bare profile and expected behaviors in pre-defined scenarios. For example, a profile that predicts which sales tactics are most likely to work in a given situation would be quite useful to a salesman. Persuasion profiles exist. Just which sites (individual, corporate or governmental) are creating and using them is not open information; however, if a website makes money from your activity, money that comes from a third party, then you can assume that website is using persuasion metrics to influence your decisions. Which of Cialdini's persuasion methods, singly or in combinations, should be emphasized to work best on each of us? Our persuasion profiles contain that as part of a multi-dimensional, conditional probability profile.

Personal persuasion profiles use all of the "persuasion surfaces" of our emergent bio-psycho-socio-techno-info- self. Biometrics are both physiologic and behavioral, monitoring and influencing our cognition, temperament and character (Cloninger, Przybeck, Svrakic, & Wetzel 1994), sentiment (mood and drive) (Mercier 2020), behavior and trust. Our sociometrics include data from network analytics, membership and the markers of social membership, which are fragile and stringent. Our digital aspects allow monitoring, experimentation, and influence from our attention profile, click stream and with a user facing camera, our dialectic of social signals. All of these profiles are contextualized in our basic drives, needs, fears, biases, and irrationalities. Further, beyond profiling our current status, they are predictive. Each of the three parts of our triune brain (ancient regulatory, limbic or emotional, and neocortical or abstract levels) can be monitored and influenced.

Kaptein has performed research that shows that both simple and persuasion profiles work in personal encounters **and** on the Internet to increase persuasion. His research also showed that personal persuasion profiles are relatively stable across different types of products and environments and that using the wrong method may be counterproductive (Kaptein 2015).

We are each providing the data for our own psychological dossiers. "Social media can also provide a surprisingly clear window into our psychological and neurological states. Luke Stark, a researcher in the sociology department at Dartmouth College, explains that accumulated online postings provide 'something much more akin to medical data or psychiatric data.' Even the most trivial details can be unexpectedly revealing. Consistent use of black-and-white Instagram filters and single-face photos, for instance, has proven a fairly good identifier of clinical depression (Singer & Brooking 2018)."

"Through the clever use of this mountain of information, one could infer much more through 'psychometrics,' which crosses the insights of psychology with the tools of big data. Teams of psychometric analysts had already shown how patterns of Facebook 'likes' could be used to predict characteristics of someone's life, from their sexual orientation to whether their parents had divorced. The researchers had concluded that it took only ten 'likes' to know more about someone than a work colleague knew and just seventy to know more than their real-world friends (Singer & Brooking 2018)."

Micro-targeting for profiling, persuasion or predictive analytics can be augmented with knowledge from our other natural language, man's universal language, the dialectic of social signals pioneered at the MIT Human Dynamics Laboratory (Pentland 2014).

Useful metrics of deception detection are limited, but probabilistically accurate metrics are available. Contextualized analysis of facial micro-expressions, whether by machine or read by "experts," is extant. Mark G. Frank of the SUNY University at Buffalo is a pioneer in this field (Wikipedia 2020).

The Panopticon's Contribution to Persuasion

Added to traditional modeling of a person using the history and psychologic assessment (Hartley & Jobson 2014), today's persuasion technology combines near ubiquitous AI/ML augmented biometrics, sociometrics, geolocation, and contact maps with continuous sensing and analysis with adaptive feedback loops to target the individual or group recipient.

The panopticon gathers metrics—biometrics (physiologic and behavioral), neurometrics, psychometrics, sociometrics (how we interact with our lattice of close associates and our social network structure)—and uses techno-informatics such as our click stream and other patterns of Internet usage. These metrics are analyzed more and more with AI/ML (augmented human hybrid methods). Multiple communities of knowledge are utilized. Every aspect of man's emergent bio-psycho-socio-techno-info being should be considered. The results are persuasion, profiles and predictive analytics. This profiling approach empowers the subsequent sequence of garnering attention using addictive technology to more precisely target the persuasion effort. Knowing the ecology of location using GPS furthers the aggregate persuasion effort.

Having fore-knowledge of a behavioral, demographic, sociometrics, and biometric profile (Hosnagar 2019) and the preconceptions of the person to be influenced provide advantages as a base upon which iterative, adaptive surveilled analytics is attached. A profile often contains a cornucopia of opportunities and vulnerabilities.

Single photon detection (Hadfield 2009; Migdall, Polyakov, Fan, & Bienfang 2013) with ultra-rapid processing and bioinformatics about man's plumes and tracks for identification, profiling, persuasion, and predictive analytics: genomic, epigenomic, proteomic, microbiomic will soon be extant.

Over a longer time scale (persuasion before persuasion), Cialdini's book *Pre-Suasion* described the stage before the effort to persuade, before the opportune moment (*kairos*) has arrived (Cialdini 2016). The Chinese concept of *shi* must be understood. *Shi* is a principal deceptive stratagem of influencing the present for its effect in the future at a propitious time, often as part of a long-term zero-sum game (Pillsbury 2015).

Robert Cloniger's work on temperament and character (e.g. harm/conflict avoidance, novelty seeking/aversion, reward dependence, persistence, self-directedness, cooperativeness, and self-transcendence) indicated useful profile dimensions (Wikipedia 2019a, 2019b, 2019c, 2019d). Thaler's Nobel work on choice architecture and structuring complex choices was seen with the reports of "manipulation that changed people's beliefs about malleability of groups in influencing peace negotiations across political and regional divides (Halperin, Russell, Trzensniewski, Gross, & Dweck 2011)." Physiologic biometrics, behavioral biometrics, and sociometrics are also extant. Sensing dimensional metrics may come from outside the body, on the body, or within the body, depending on context. An augmented-human feeding of AI/Machine Learning (AI/ML) with these metrics can augment profiles.

Zeynep Tufekci, said, "…The capacity to spread ideas is only limited by one's ability to garner and distribute attention… The flow of the world's attention is structured to a vast and overwhelming degree by just a few digital platforms. They use massive surveillance of our behaviors on and off line…optimized for engagement… We are susceptible to glimmers of novelty, messages of affirmation and belonging and message of outrage toward our perceived enemies… The most effective forms of censorship today involve meddling with trust and attention not muzzling speech itself… (Tufekci 2018)"

Carole Cadwallader reported in *The Guardian* that Cambridge Analytica harvested more than 50 million Facebook users' profiles between June and August 2014. These profiles were used to "create sophisticated psychological profiles" for use in political ads that were "designed to work on their particular psychological makeup." These ads were purportedly used in the U.S. 2016 presidential campaigns

Table 4.13 Uses of experimentation

1. Testing theory and mechanism,
2. Understanding magnitude and tradeoffs,
3. Evaluating specific policies and products, and
4. Explicative fact finding in cases where they don't have a theory.

and in the UK "Brexit" campaign (The Cambridge Analytica Files: 'I made Steve Bannon's psychological warfare tool': meet the data war whistleblower 2019).

Recent advances in combinatorial persuasion, armed with AI, augmented with personal and group metrics can make many individuals and the masses more prone to follow. The resolute can be made sequacious.

The Experimental Revolution

This section could have been part of sections on learning, education, change in cognition, sensing, or persuasion. We placed it here because of the exploitation of human vulnerabilities when there is no full transparency. Also, although there is a long and storied history of randomized controlled trials (RCT), their recent digital network ubiquity, scale, effectiveness and high power at low profile is revolutionary.

Big technology companies now routinely use experimentation, generally without full transparency (Fry 2020). Providing two versions of a website and analyzing the effectiveness (e.g., for generating sales), segmented by user characteristics, is one example. Table 4.13 lists the ways they use experimentation (Luca & Bazerman 2020)..

Evidence trumps intuition but the combination is desired. Leaders must have knowledge of statistics, including big data analytics, experimental design, pitfalls and limits, and interpretive discernment. Typically, a series of experiments is necessary for sagacity that must extend from interpretation through the frameworks of the desired action (Luca & Bazerman 2020).

The Ideas Industry and Thought Leadership Activities

In the "market place of ideas" "we rarely take the time to examine the people and institutions that give rise to them [the ideas]." Instead, we see the ideas industry "disproportionally empowering issue evangelists over broadly trained experts (Drezner 2017; Lee 2017)." We must understand that the new complex adaptive systems encompassing the evolving information infrastructure, the rise of the dazzling effectiveness of persuasion as a science/art, the ideas industry, with its thought leadership activities (Drezner 2017), network dynamics, AI, and experimentation, constitute the "combining well" for effective persuasion at any scale.

Trends in Understanding Humanity

Our understanding of man has increased and is accelerating. We now know that each person is enveloped in a chemical genomic, epigenomic, proteomic, and microbiomic plume and leaves a trail when moving. Automated methods of tracking individuals are being developed. (Did you think bloodhounds track people by magic?) This understanding brings new opportunities and vulnerabilities.

Would-be creators of utopias are accused of believing in the perfectibility of man—that is, that human nature can change within a time-frame of years to decades. Others, including some historians, philosophers, Christian theologians, and biologists maintain that human nature has been relatively constant throughout the span of human history. We posit that the biological component of human nature has not dramatically changed over this time span, but that some sociological and psychological components have changed as man has altered his own environment (*viz.* the creation of cities and the rapid development of connecting, augmenting information technologies).

We certainly try to change others' behaviors. Traditionally, the manifold forces of persuasion were found in stories, speeches, ceremonies, and symbols. We have added chemical modifiers such as serenics to probabilistically reduce aggression and may add nootropics and genetic manipulation to enhance or modify cognitive functions. Now Humu (Humu, Inc. 2018) has merged the learning science, persuasion science, and motivational science of Thaler's and Sunstein's *Nudge* (Thaler & Sunstein 2008) with network science to produce an automated system to change behaviors. We can motivate, persuade, augment, degrade, inform at scale, induce the viral spread of information, and increase affiliation or induce violence. To wit, the resolute can often be made sequacious—ready to be led.

Advances, often requiring transdisciplinary, even new, communities of knowledge, can now more often change man. Currently our understanding of man does not rest in some monolithic science, but is scattered over many areas and transdisciplinary communities of knowledge. The relevant fields cover such domains as our new understanding of man's predictably, systematically irrational aspects (Ariely 2009). As we create small, agile, transdisciplinary teams, we can expect to further increase our understanding of man, his potential and vulnerabilities.

We know that this understanding armed with big data analytics from the Panopticon (surveillance state), can micro-target and sway a group. We know that using psychopharmacology, impulsivity and aggression in man can be changed. Understanding and inducing intergroup hostility and aggression is a current topic of study (Sapolsky 2017)! Academic discussions of such potentialities exist. However, the authors envision those who might want to reduce the will to fight or induce group violence in others.

Even cognition is changing; new forms are emerging. In 1994, Arturo Escobar reported on changes he saw then, "Significant changes in the nature of social life are being brought about by computer, information, and biological technologies, to the extent that—some argue—a new cultural order, 'cyberculture,' is coming into being (Escobar 1994)." Considering that the iPhone wasn't introduced until 2007, it is safe to say that the changes that Escobar observed have only grown larger.

Figure 3.9 (Chap. 3) introduced changes to cognition. The top level represents the augmentation of humans with new forms of collective learning, AI/ML and "cognified objects"—the introduction of some version of cognition into objects. Some systems are simply pre-programmed decision systems. At the simplest, these programs receive situation inputs and calculate results. More complex programs make adaptive decisions based on the inputs and pre-programmed tests to develop their results. The programs can be immensely complex in detail; however, they make deterministic decisions, which are trackable and repeatable. AI systems vary in their computational nature; however, they are generally less trackable, but are repeatable. Human-machine hybrid systems include a human-in-the-loop element, so that they are not necessarily trackable or repeatable. Quantum AI systems are conjectural at this time. The introduction of a quantum computer into the system is supposed to allow the consideration of "all" possible solutions simultaneously, rather than serially, as with standard digital computers. Quantum computing will boost AI and AI changes paradigms. This simultaneous consideration would produce results more quickly with more computational power, permitting the solution to problems that are currently essentially insoluble.

However, Malone (Malone 2018) suggested thinking of machine-in-the-loop (rather than man-in-the-loop) as the appropriate model for human-machine hybrids. He said, "Virtually all human achievements have been made by groups of people, not lone individuals. As we incorporate smart technologies further into traditionally human processes, an even more powerful form of collective learning is emerging."

Figure 4.8 illustrates a cognified version of the OODA loop. In this case, AI/ML support is provided for the human decision maker. The observation is supported by AI pattern recognition, which can be improved through experimentation and analytics. The orientation is supported by data filtering and matching (requiring knowledge access with analytics) to generate possible courses of action (COAs). The decision is supported by COA evaluation, requiring superior connectivity. Finally, the results are used to update the pattern recognition through AI learning (connecting arrows not displayed).

Figure 4.9 illustrates an automated OODA loop in which the AI support is tightly linked to the OODA steps, so that the system performs the steps without human intervention.

For less time-sensitive decisions and general cognition, we still have stories, speeches, ceremonies, and symbols and we still have personal contact with people with mutual concern. Individual cognition is improved through education and training, reskilling, upskilling and multiple forms of cognitive optimization.

Human ***augmentation*** began in prehistory when people (or perhaps pre-humans) developed weapons from sticks, rocks and fire, augmenting their physical abilities

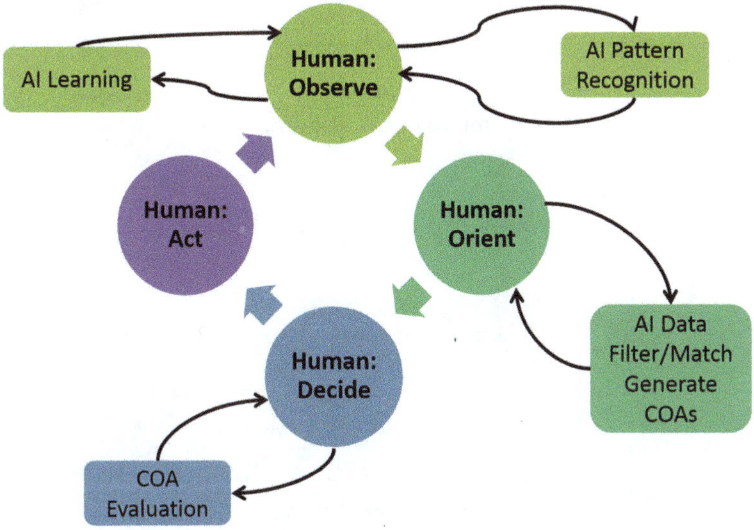

Fig. 4.8 The cognified OODA loop

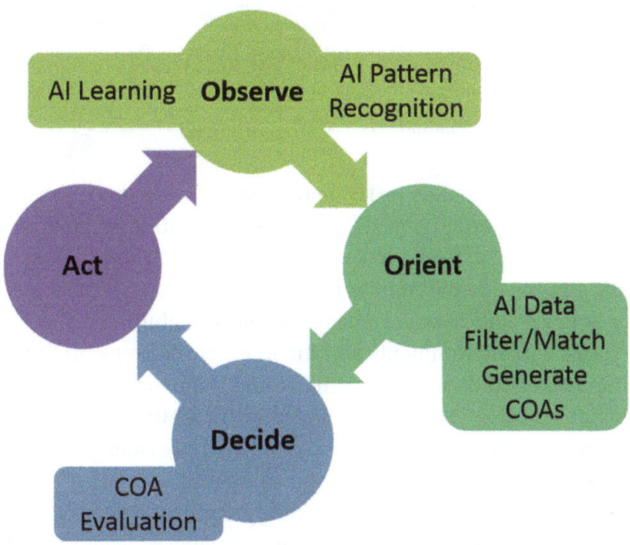

Fig. 4.9 The automated OODA loop

(lately including exoskeletons (Pons 2019)). The creation of language augmented human cognition by supporting group cognition. Story-telling and then written storage supported time-binding, further enhancing native human cognition. We are now adding machine-supported augmentations such as xR, searchable databases

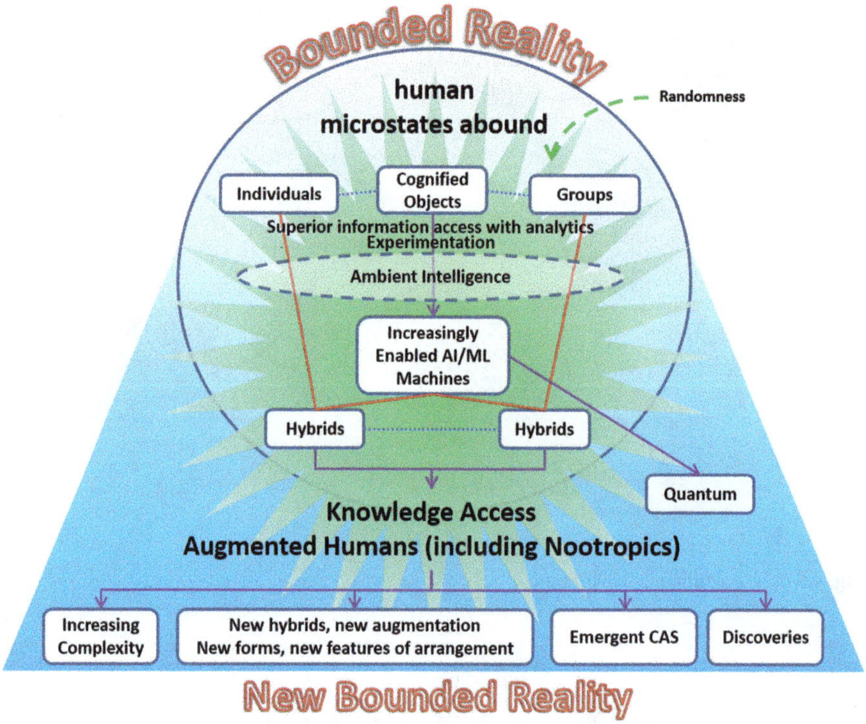

Fig. 4.10 Bounded reality and randomness

and AI devices, such as Apple's Siri™ and Amazon's Alexa. Ambient intelligence refers to a system of cognified objects and processes within an environment.

Figure 4.10 shows a different view of cognition, which emphasizes our bounded reality and the impact of randomness on the noosphere (within the ellipse in the figure). Data science and now AI change cognitive abilities. The cognifying of objects, processes and environments and the internet of things bring further opportunities. Using these affordances individually and with augmented collective learning bring further abilities. Abductive reasoning (modeling the simplest and most likely explanation) by the prepared mind can yield previously unrecognized patterns of reality, expanding the ellipse of bounded reality.

Advances in psychology, social psychology, neuroscience, cognitive science, and information science are salient. Complexity science fosters the understanding of transdisciplinary knowledge and creativity. Major advances in measurement and monitoring bring new optics for thought. Virtual and augmented reality are already selectively useful. The use of selected ***nootropics*** (drugs that enhance or modify mental functioning), advanced genetic engineering and synthetic biology are extant. Psychometric, biometric and sociometric analytics and ambient learning design are available to advance cognition. Optimal access to the fractal frontier of science will bring further enhancement.

Chapter 5
The Technium—Plus, Redux

In this chapter, we look more deeply at the sciences and technologies that are significant parts of the technium. These include complex adaptive systems, AI and the human brain, network science, quantum computing, and other technologies that may be transformative in the future.

Our inchoate cognified world

We see the direct and consequential impact of accelerating **change** in the technium (technology as a whole system), the exponentially expanding noosphere (the total information available to humanity), and in our increasing knowledge of people, who are the ultimate target of this conflict. Accelerating change is likely to contain both good and bad elements and elements that are too rapid to quickly assimilate and socialize.

Figure 5.1 suffers from one problem: the arrow of change and the axes give the impression of smooth change. The changes in humans, the noosphere and the technium are expected to be anything but smooth. There will be increases in each, but also increases in the number and types of categories in each. These axes each therefore represent a multiplicity of dimensions, meaning that the arrow of change will actually be a jagged path through multiple dimensions. Accompanying the changes will be changes in scale, connectivity, complexity, and the impact of randomness. As the changes grow, multiple paradigm shifts can be expected.

Some of this change is the predictable change of observable trends such as described in the "Trends" sections in Chaps. 2, 3 and 4. Theoretically, predictable changes can be addressed and mitigated (if appropriate). It should be noted, however, that there is no guarantee that predictable changes actually will be addressed and mitigated.

Some change is not clearly predictable. The nature of a Complex Adaptive System (CAS) is that it generates emergent behaviors—unexpected behaviors given what is initially known about the CAS itself.

D. S. Hartley III, K. O. Jobson, *Cognitive Superiority*,
https://doi.org/10.1007/978-3-030-60184-3_5

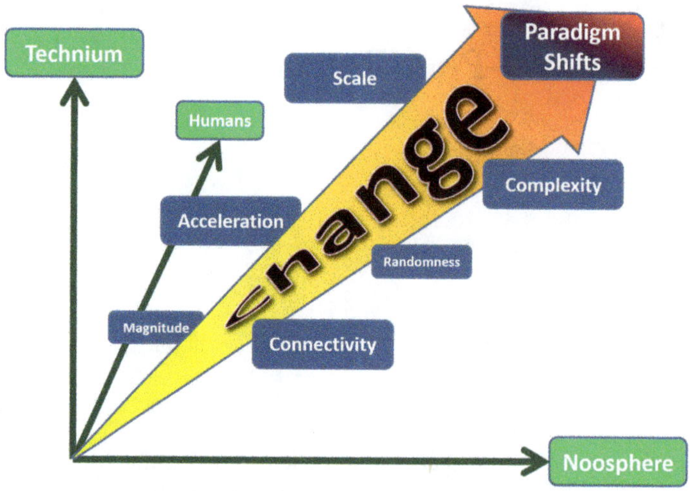

Fig. 5.1 Accelerating change affects everything

Complex Adaptive Systems

With ***Complex Adaptive Systems*** (CAS), behavior of the whole is different from that of its parts and different from the sum of those parts. Further, a CAS cannot really be understood by itself, but must be considered within its environment and will probably act differently in different environments (Moffat, 2003). Not only are the systems complex, but their adaptive responses are complex.

Serena Chan of MIT said that "The definition of complex adaptive systems seems to change with the different attempts at application (Chan, 2001)." Table 5.1 gives her characteristics of CASs.

Table 5.2 lists characterizing statements for CASs from other sources.

We live in a complex and emergent universe. In his book on complexity theory, Moffat provided a lucid description of some of these characteristics and the mathematics behind them (Moffat, 2003).

There are four areas that are fundamental to the study of CAS (Table 5.3). However, the study must be interdisciplinary.

"Life exists at the edge of chaos," Stuart Kauffman (Kauffman, 1995). Kauffman reasoned that, "for an organism to be both alive and stable, [their regime had to be] not too rigid or 'frozen' and not too chaotic or 'gaseous.'" (Mitchell, 2009)

Emergence and Novelty

The nature of a Complex Adaptive Systems (CAS) is that it generates emergent behaviors—unexpected behaviors given what is known about the CAS itself. Chemistry is an example. Atoms have electrons with specified energy levels—a nice

Table 5.1 Chan's characterization of complex adaptive systems

• Distributed Control
– No single centralized control mechanism
– The interrelationships among elements produce coherence
– The overall behavior is not simply the sum of the parts
• Connectivity (complexity)
– The elements are inter-related, interact, and are interconnected within the system
– And have similar connections between the system and its environment
• Co-evolution (adaptivity)
– Elements can change based on interactions with each other and the environment
– Patterns of behavior can change over time
• Critically sensitive to initial conditions
– Outcomes are not linearly correlated with inputs
– Long-term prediction and control are believed to be impossible to predict
• Emergent order
– Individual interactions lead to global properties or patterns
– This is anentropic
• Far from equilibrium
– When pushed from equilibrium, the CAS may survive and thrive
– Combine order and chaos in an appropriate measure
• State of paradox
– Stability and instability
– Competition and cooperation
– Order and disorder

physical property, worthy of study. However, this physical property governs how atoms bind together. A new set of "rules" emerge that creates the field of chemistry. It is hard to see how the behaviors of organic chemistry could be predicted from knowing about electron energy levels, yet these behaviors nevertheless emerge.

Emergent properties are evident when they are full blown. For example, chemistry emerges from physics and biology emerges from chemistry. In particular, living beings emerge from organic (carbon-based) chemistry (Fig. 5.2). With each step in the figure there is more connectivity, more complexity and more information. There are those who argue that we may need another step, labeled "AI Superbeings." For now, we will just leave "Augmented Humans" to include augmentation by AI.

Table 5.2 CAS characteristics from other sources

• CASs have hierarchical organization with subsystems constructed of subsystems:
– CASs have irreducibility;
– CASs have anentropic subsystems;
– CASs have vigorous connectivity (dynamic networks of interactions—multiple feedback and feed-forward loops) with non-linear interactions (small changes can have large effects); and
– CASs often show elements of symmetry.
• The higher in the hierarchy the responses, the less prescriptive and more predictive they are (decentralized, distributed control).
• CASs exhibit non-equilibrium order and can demonstrate un-computability.
• CASs are involved in manifold competition and cooperation. They
– Show continuous adaptive learning improvement;
– Undergo progressive adaptive revisions and evolve; and
– Generally, have robust failure tolerance.
• CASs demonstrate self-organization and selection:
– E.g., flocks of birds, schools of fish, human organizations, cities, all with no central control;
– Self-organized, collective phenomena that are not present in the individual parts (***emergence***), e.g., human consciousness;
– Can exhibit cooperation and competition (co-evolution) with other CASs;
– Can result in self-replication;
– Frequently use microstates; and
• With CASs more is different.

Table 5.3 Fundamental areas in the study of CASs

Information,
Computation,
Dynamics and chaos, and
Evolution.

Tyler Volk supplied a list of emergences that roughly parallels this figure and supplies more information (Table 5.4). Each item emerges from the previous one and comprises increased connectivity and complexity (Volk, 2017).

However, not all change that is "not clearly predictable" has to be as a result of emergence from a CAS. The explosion of personal computers was not clearly predictable from the existence of mainframe computers. In fact, one of the authors (a professional user of computers) thought the Apple II was a fun toy, but did not see any major uses for it or its ilk. (Society is a CAS and thus changes in activities in society can be emergent phenomena; however, the normal view of a society as a CAS would discuss such things as the development of hierarchical societies or democratic societies as the direct emergent phenomena related to the CAS.) While the

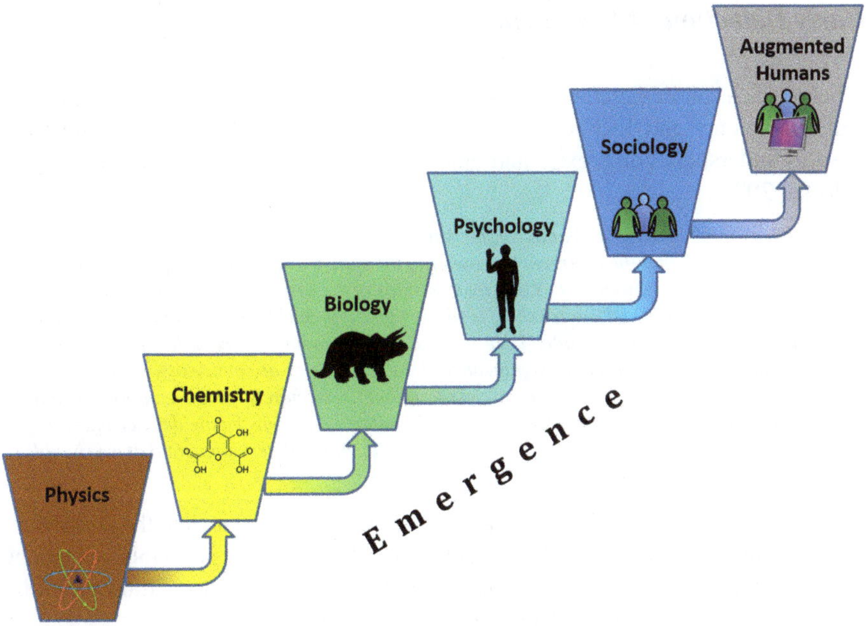

Fig. 5.2 Emergence

Table 5.4 Volk's list of emergences

1.	Individual quanta,
2.	Protons and neutrons,
3.	Atoms,
4.	Molecules,
5.	Prokaryotic cells,
6.	Eukaryotic cells,
7.	Multicellular organisms,
8.	Animal social groups,
9.	Language,
10.	Cities and culture, and
11.	Geopolitical states.

creation of personal computers may not represent emergence, the development of uses for them may.

Novelty, the quality of being new or original can exist within or outside of complex adaptive systems. Early detection or favored access to a novelty, with sufficient sagacity, can bring competitive advantage in commerce, science, education, homeland security, or defense when the advances are germane to the domain's field of action. The accelerating frontier of science and technology is likely where Archimedes would place the fulcrum to change the world.

Early Detection of Emergence and Novelty

Emergence is unpredictable. James Moffat quoted the Chief Analyst of the UK Defence Science and Technology Laboratory (Dstl), Roger Forder, concerning the need to understand complexity and emergence in the domain of defense analysis (Moffat, 2003).

> *One effect of the human element in conflict situations is to bring a degree of complexity into the situation such that the emergent behaviour of the system as a whole is extremely difficult to predict from the characteristics and relationships of the system elements. Detailed simulation, using agent-based approaches, is always possible but the highly situation-specific results that it provides may offer little general understanding for carrying forward into robust conclusions of practical significance. Usable theories of complexity, which would allow understanding of emergent behaviour rather than merely its observation, would therefore have a great deal to offer to some of the central problems facing defence analysis. Indeed they might well be the single most desirable theoretical development that we should seek over the next few years.*

"Emergence can be both beneficial and harmful to the system and the constituent agents." Emergence though unpredictable, its early detection is possible and can be critically important. Nascent awareness of emergence must be decentralized, utilizing augmented, distributed detection (O'Toole, 2015).

The process by which emergent properties emerge is not understood; however, their existence is evident. Suppose one were observing the earth as living creatures were just emerging. How would we detect this? Especially, how would we detect this emergence if we had no idea that this was the event we wished to detect or had no good definition of what a living creature might be? In Eamonn O'Toole's thesis, he exploited the feedback from emergence that "constrains the agents at the micro-level of the system. This thesis demonstrates that this feedback results in a different statistical relationship between the agent and its environment when emergence is present compared to when there is no emergence in the system." (O'Toole, 2015).

How can we organize to systematically detect a novelty when it is first conceived or first introduced? We must have sufficient discernment and sagacity to see its potential. The brain's first neurophysiologic topic of attention is toward novelty. The brain utilizes multiple types of sensors and its wetware features massive connectivity with flickering microstates (Jobson, Hartley, & Martin, 2011). A grand wish for such an early detection of emergence will require multiple polythetic optics. From the individual point of view, it requires a mind prepared to meet the unexpected with discernment. From the technical vantage point, the work of O'Toole with multiple distributed detectors is a helpful start. The most problematic prospect may entail the vortices combining human and machines (man and his matrix). Here we offer Eratosthenes (see the sections on creating a team in Chaps. 7 and 8) and on a larger scale, the imperative of cognitive superiority.

The definition of complex adaptive systems includes a requirement that emergent properties are generated. This implies that there are complicated systems that are not **complex** systems. What is it that converts a complicated system into a complex system? If a complicated system becomes a complex system, how would one detect the emergent properties? Can the nature of the emergent properties be predicted beforehand?

It is conjectured the AI systems might become self-aware under some conditions (Tegmark, 2017). This would be an emergent property. How would one detect this event? It would certainly help if we had a good definition of "self-awareness."

AI and the Human Brain

The ascension of artificial intelligence/machine learning (AI/ML) is the "story behind all stories (Kelly, 2016)"

Kai-Fu Lee spoke of two broad approaches to artificial intelligence: rule-based and neural networks (Lee, 2018). The rule-based approach set out to list if-then-else-type rules to describe the behavior that the AI system should exhibit. At one point, these rules were created by asking experts in a domain what the situations of interest were and what would they do in those situations. Hence this approach is often called the expert systems approach. This approach has had intermittent successes, but no real commercial applications.

John Launchbury of DARPA called this the "first wave" of AI (J-Wave 1). He described this as "handcrafted knowledge" and characterized it as being poor at perceiving the outside world, learning and abstracting, but is able to reason over narrowly defined problem spaces. Recently, it succeeded at the Cyber Grand Challenge by identifying code characteristics related to flaws (Launchbury, 2017).

Neural Nets

The neural net approach was defined by creating artificial neural nets that were supposed to mimic the neural networks in the human brain. This approach has had some successes, but has undergone periods of disfavor. However, recently, it has had great commercial successes due to sufficient computing power to handle large networks and very large data sets, especially with the development of deep learning (Lee, 2018). Seabrook reported that the "compute" (the complete ability to do computing) is growing faster than the "rate suggested by Moore's Law, which holds that the processing power of computers doubles every two years. Innovations in chip design, network architecture, and cloud-based resources are making the total available compute ten times larger each year (Seabrook, 2019)."

Figure 5.3 illustrates the construction of one type of artificial neural net. The intent is to replicate the ability of humans to recognize something, given an input set. The input set entries are fed to a series of nodes in the first layer, here labeled 01 through 09. Each of these nodes passes its data to each of the nodes in the second layer (sometimes called the hidden layer), here labeled 11 through 19. Each node in the second layer applies a weight to the input it receives, potentially different for

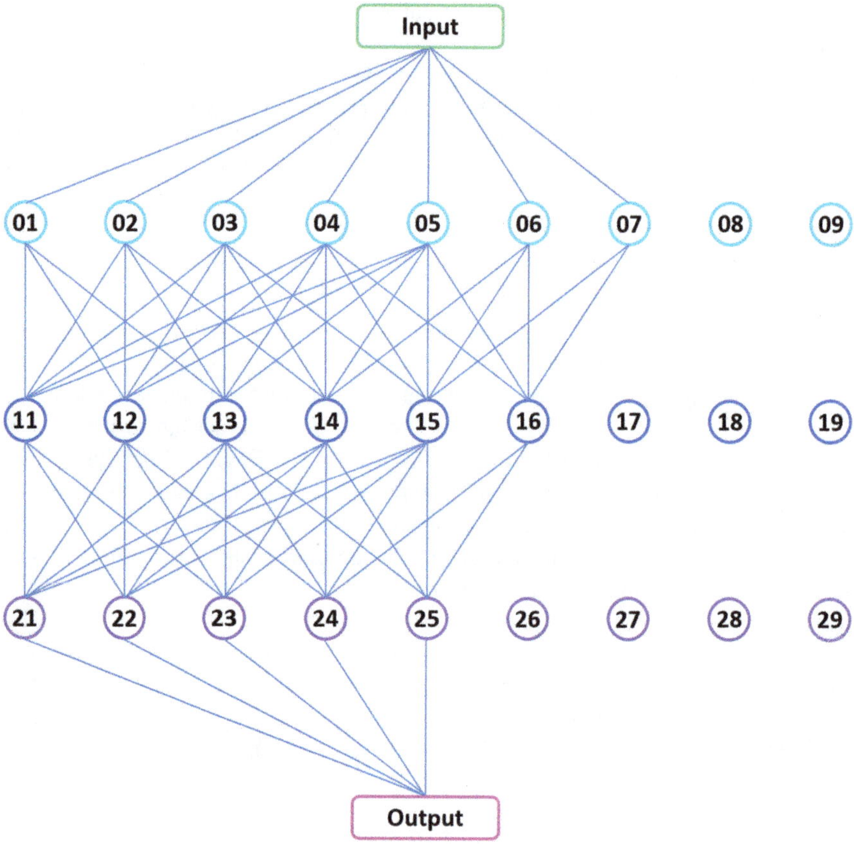

Fig. 5.3 Neural net layers

each source and combines the inputs using some function, such as the weighted average. Each node of the second layer passes its results to the third layer, here labeled 21 through 29. Each node in the third layer applies a weight to the input it receives, potentially different for each source and combines the inputs using some function, such as the weighted average. The results from the third layer comprise the output of the artificial neural net, weighted by source. (Note that the connections in the figure are only partially illustrated. Note also, that the outputs from a node in one layer need not connect to all the nodes in the next layer or might have a zero weighting.)

Suppose the goal is to determine whether a given picture is a picture of a tiger and the output is a yes or no answer. The input data consist of some set of information about the picture. With arbitrary weights, the system is unlikely to be able to discriminate among a set of pictures. However, such a system can be "trained." Each time a picture is "shown" to the system, the output is "graded" and the weights are allowed to change. It has been shown that, with sufficient training and a methodology for changing the weights applied, such a system can correctly identify the pictures that contain a tiger as the subject. Further, such systems can be built and trained that correctly identify each of several animals, not just a single type of animal. Not only can such a system correctly identify the animals in the pictures from the training set of pictures, but also it can correctly identify these same animals from pictures not in the training set, with some probability of success. This is simple machine learning.

Simple machine learning works; however, it didn't work well enough. The deep learning Lee talks about works much better. A digression into how the human brain works will be informative.

The Brain

The human brain uses sensing, abstraction, hierarchy, heuristic search, individual and collective learning, and the construction of cognitive artifacts for adaptation. AI is not there yet. Hawkins and Blakeslee wrote *On Intelligence*, with a chapter on how the cortex works (Hawkins & Blakeslee, 2004). Several points are directly pertinent to our discussion here. First, the brain uses similar internal structures (generally in different parts of the brain) to classify sensory input of all types. For example, the pixel-like inputs from the eyes are classified into images and the letters of words and the frequency-based inputs from the ears are classified into phonemes and words using the same hardware (well, wetware) and algorithms. It also uses the same structures to learn how to do the classification. The primitive hierarchical structure is the neural net with real neurons. However, as Hawkins and Blakeslee explained, the actual neural processing is more sophisticated, hierarchical in fact. The layers are critical in subdividing the work. Early layers do things like detecting edges. Later layers identify letters. Final layers work on putting things together. There are many complexities, such as using feedback from upper layers to lower layers to supply predictions for what may be coming next. However, the point is that the structure of the brain works. Deep learning has added more hierarchical processing. Moreover, the evidence of the brain's use of the same structure for multiple things implies that deep learning will have many applications. In fact, Lee described many commercially important applications.

AI Systems' Bounded Reality

Despite the successes of some AI systems, we haven't discovered the emergent capacity for broad contextualized adaptation. Both simple machine learning and AI deep learning (neural net) suffer from bounded reality. The first set of bounds is defined by the domain of interest: the system is only defined for that domain. The second set of bounds is defined in the rule-based approach by the creativity of the

Table 5.5 "Real-world" AI training data

x	y	Used for training
1	1	Yes
2	2.5	Yes
3	3	Yes
4	3.5	Yes
5	5	Yes
6	5.7	No
7	6.6	No
8	7.5	No
9	8.4	No

authors in defining situations and the completeness of the rule sets. For the neural net approach, the second set of bounds is defined by the training data used.

The concept of training an AI system is similar to that of this example: a training set is used to set the system parameters so that it generates the appropriate responses. "Curve fitting" or fitting a curve to a data set provides the example. Consider the data in Table 5.5.

For each x value, there is one proper y value. Suppose only the first five pairs are known when the system is created. Thus, only the first five pairs are used to train the system. These data were fit with a linear equation: $y = 0.9x + .03$, $R^2 = 0.9529$. This is a very good fit for data that probably has measurement error in it. However, in "training" an AI system, there will be a search for a better fit. The equation in Fig. 5.4 is found that has $R^2 = 1$, a perfect fit!

When new input data are submitted to the system ($x = 6$, 7, 8, and 9), the green curve results. It fits the training data perfectly and yields a curve growing dramatically as the x value increases. However, the remainder of the data from Table 5.5 is now discovered, showing that the "perfect" curve is seriously flawed. (In fact, the original "imperfect" curve fits the new data very well.) AI systems that are created through a training regimen can suffer from bounded reality, just as humans can.

This example is contrived to make its point; however, it illustrates a truth for the general case: if the training data do not cover the entire domain of intended use of the AI system, the system can fail spectacularly for situations outside of the domain. A similar case can be created for interpolated situations, although the failures will (in most cases) not be as dramatic.

John Launchbury called this "statistical learning" and labeled it the second wave of AI (J-Wave 2). For a given problem domain it is good at perceiving and learning, but not so good at abstracting or reasoning. As mentioned by Hutson below, it can be spoofed and if it undergoes continuous learning as it is used it can become unusable. Launchbury described a system that was designed to be a chat bot that began to take on the hateful characteristics of the users with whom it was chatting (Launchbury, 2017).

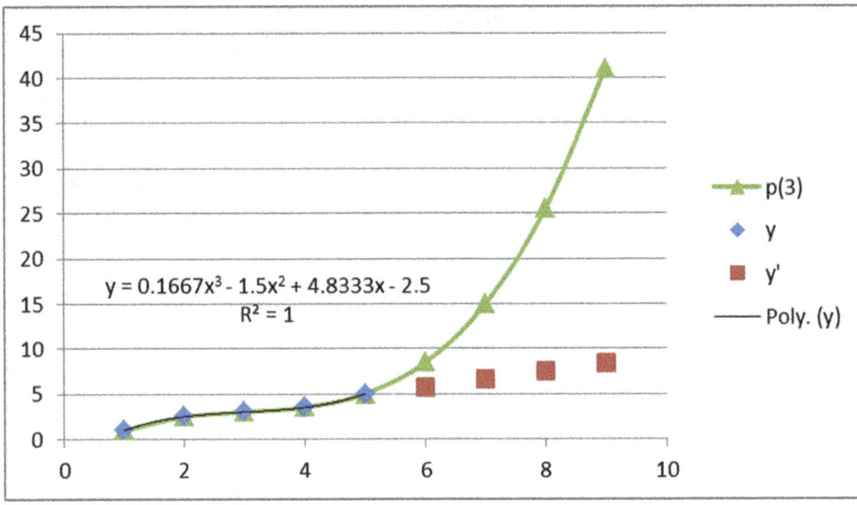

Fig. 5.4 Results with extrapolation

Other AI Limits

Matthew Hutson described some problems with AI learning (Hutson, 2018b). There are known problems with AI learning algorithms, such as reproducibility of results "because of inconsistent experimental and publication practices," and interpretability, "the difficulty of explaining how a particular AI has come to its conclusions." However, Hutson described work by Ali Rahimi and his collaborators in which they argued that many AIs are created without "deep understanding of the basic tools needed to build and train new algorithms." Researchers often do not know which parts of the algorithm yield which benefits and thus do not know which parts are superfluous or counterproductive. The potential unintended consequences of using AI which is not understood range from nil to catastrophic, depending on the application.

In another article, Hutson described alterations to physical objects that fool AI figure recognition (Hutson, 2018a). One example is pictured in which a stop sign appears to have the words "love" and "hate" added; however, "a common type of image recognition AI" thought "it was a 45-mile-per-hour speed limit sign."

Hernandez and Greenwald reported in The Wall Street Journal about problems with IBM's famous Watson AI system. They said, "Big Blue promised its AI platform would be a big step forward in treating cancer. But after pouring billions into the project, the diagnosis is gloomy (Hernandez & Greenwald, 2018)." This article is about AI and cancer; however, it generalizes to AI and any other complex problem.

This discussion seems to be one about flaws in AI; however, it is really about flaws in the humans who create the AI and about the vast unmeasured complexity of human nature. Absent flaws in the underlying computer system, AI and other computer programs do exactly what they are told to do, no more and no less. It is a human responsibility to decide what to tell them to do.

On the other hand, Rodrick Wallace argued that ambitious plans for AI dominated systems will face problems having levels of subtlety and ubiquity unimagined by the purveyors of the plans. His title, *Carl von Clausewitz, the Fog-of-War, and the AI Revolution: The Real World Is Not A Game Of Go*, expressed his thesis (Wallace, 2018). The problem of defeating human masters at chess was difficult. Winning at Go was regarded as much more difficult, yet an AI system was built that did just that. However, Wallace argued that the real world is so much more complex than Go that this achievement, while real, is not dispositive. As he saw it, the Fog-of-War problem described by Clausewitz has not been solved by humans and will afflict AI systems as well. In fact, he said, "We argue here that, in the real world, Artificial Intelligence will face similar challenges with similar or greater ineptitude." Wallace discussed this in mathematical terms in the body of the book, showing why he drew such an extraordinary conclusion. He might describe the AI bounded reality problem as the difficulty for AI to see reality at all.

What Can AI Do?

John Launchbury of DARPA categorized AI capabilities in terms of "waves." Two of these were mentioned above. Kai-Fu Lee also described AI in terms of waves, based on functionality. Kai-Fu Lee described his view of the coming AI revolution in his book *AI Super-Powers* (Lee, 2018). (Lee's view is more optimistic than that of Wallace, above.) For clarity, we will henceforward label Launchbury's waves, J-waves, and Lee's waves, K-waves, using their first initials to distinguish the referent.

Table 5.6 describes Launchbury's J-waves (Launchbury, 2017).

Table 5.7 describes Lee's K-waves (Lee, 2018).

J-Wave 1: Rule-Based

Launchbury's first wave consists of rule-based, expert systems. He described this as "handcrafted knowledge" and characterized it as being poor at perceiving the outside world, learning and abstracting, but is able to reason over narrowly defined problem spaces.

J-Wave 2: Statistical Learning

John Launchbury called his second wave "statistical learning." The second wave consists of neural nets with training. For a given problem domain it is good at perceiving and learning, but not so good at abstracting or reasoning.

Table 5.6 Launchbury's AI waves

J-wave 1	**Rule-based** (expert system) Perceiving outside world: poor Learning: poor Abstracting: poor Reasoning: over narrowly defined problem spaces
J-wave 2	**Statistical learning** Perceiving: good in a given problem domain Learning: good in a given problem domain Abstracting: poor Reasoning: poor
J-wave 3	**Contextual adaptation**: construct explanatory models, explain results, train from few examples Perceiving: good Learning: good Abstracting: not good, but better than previous waves Reasoning: good

Table 5.7 Lee's AI waves

K-wave 1	**Internet AI** Is here Recommendation engines using profiles
K-wave 2	**Business AI** Developed for selected domains Deep learning of data already collected by businesses Uses weak features (possible problems)
K-wave 3	**Perception AI** Examples are here Connected with sensors to the real world Amazon's Echo
K-wave 4	**Autonomous AI** Has started Gives systems autonomy Autonomous stock picking vehicles at Amazon

J-Wave 3: Contextual Adaptation

Launchbury described a developing third wave of AI that he called contextual adaptation. This type of AI is meant to "construct explanatory models for classes of real-world phenomena," adding to its classification ability the ability to explain why it gets the results it displays. The desire is to train it from very few examples, rather than the thousands or hundreds of thousands required for second wave AI. It should be good a perceiving, learning, and reasoning and better at abstracting than either of the previous waves of AI.

K-Wave 1: Internet AI

Internet AI is already here. It includes recommendation engines that use simple profiles to recommend products and simple AI products to curate news stories that fit a user's preferences, such as the Chinese Toutiao. Toutiao created an AI system to "sniff out 'fake news.'" It also created an AI system to create fake news and pitted the two against each other, allowing each to learn and get better (co-evolution). These are referred to as generative adversarial networks (GAN) because the two adversarial networks generate outputs used in the competition.

K-Wave 2: Business AI

Business AI is concerned with using the data already collected by a business to figure out how the business can be operated more efficiently. Conventional optimization methods concentrate on strong features; whereas AI optimization using deep learning can analyze massive amounts of data and discover weak features that will produce superior results. Having the data in structured formats helps this process greatly. [One concern that Lee omitted is the problem of significance or lack thereof of weak features. If the quantity of data is not sufficient, the AI produced results will be good predictors of the training data, but poor predictors of data going forward—the problem illustrated in Fig. 5.4.]

Business AI includes more than just industrial operations. Financial services, such as credit-worthiness for lending money, provide an example. The Chinese Smart Finance is using the massive amounts of financial transaction data available on Chinese systems to make small loans to individuals. Algorithms are being built for providing medical diagnoses and advice to judges on evidence and sentencing (in China).

Seabrook added some AI skills that belong in this wave. These range from spell check and translation software, to predictive texts, to code completion, to Smart Compose, which is an optional feature of Google's Gmail that will fill in a predicted sentence to complete what the user has already written. GPT (generative pretrained transformers), by OpenAI, has more ambitious goals. It is being designed to "write prose as well as, or better than, most people can (Seabrook, 2019)." Seabrook tested the current version, GPT-2, and found that it can, indeed, write prose. However, in its current state, it creates grammatical prose with "gaps in the kind of common-sense knowledge that tells you overcoats aren't shaped like the body of a ship." The output of GPT-2 had a consistent tone, but no causal structure in the flow of the contents; however, it would do fine for producing fake Tweets or fake reviews on Yelp (Seabrook, 2019).

K-Wave 3: Perception AI

Perception AI connects AI to the real world by allowing an AI system to perceive the real world. "Amazon Echo is digitizing the audio environment of people's homes. Alibaba's City Brain is digitizing urban traffic flows through cameras and object-recognition AI. Apple's iPhone X and Face++ cameras perform that same digitization for faces, using the perception data to safeguard your phone or digital wallet." This is where the cognified refrigerator will not only know what is in it, but can order something when it gets low. A cognified shopping cart can identify you when you arrive at the grocery store, connect to the refrigerator's information on what has been ordered already, connect to your buying profile, and recommend things you should buy—including specials on things that you might be tempted to buy.

Commercial applications are just the start. Education can be transformed into private tutoring in a classroom environment. AI can monitor every step of the education process and ensure that each student learns at his or her own pace, even providing advice to procure extra tutoring where necessary. A Wall Street Journal article described the Chinese efforts to employ headbands with electrodes to monitor student focus (Wang, Hong, & Tai, 2019).

Previous K-waves depend heavily on software applications, with little hardware dependence. Perception AI will depend heavily on hardware to provide the interfaces to the real-world—the sensors and output interfaces that are customized for the refrigerators, police eyeglasses or shopping carts. At some point, the Panopticon will have arrived, with every home, office and public space filled with cognified, Internet-connected sensors and output interfaces.

K-Wave 4: Autonomous AI

Autonomous AI is the last wave; however, that doesn't mean it hasn't already started. Amazon has autonomous vehicles that bring items to humans to scan and box. California-based Traptic has created a robot that can find strawberries in the field, check the color for ripeness, and pluck the ripe ones. Self-driving cars are being tested and are the subject of numerous news articles. Lee mentioned two approaches to their development: the "Google" and "Tesla" approaches. He characterized the Google approach as cautious—test extensively, build the perfect product, and jump straight to full autonomy. The Tesla approach is to build incrementally, test through use by customers, and add on features as they become available.

Profiles

In earlier descriptions of profiles, machine learning is described as determining which things a person is more likely to be willing to buy (simple profile) and which types of persuasion are more likely to be effective for a person (persuasion profile). Those discussions were couched in a way that implies rule-based AI implementations. For example, "if this is person X and persuasion technique Y is used, then a high level of persuasion is expected" and "if this is person X and persuasion technique Z is used, then a low level of persuasion is expected." Such a profile is based on examination of *strong features*, that is, labeled data with high correlations to the desired outcome. Persuasion profiles built this way are easily understood.

However, in Lee's discussions of deep learning, he made clear that deep learning also uses weak features, attributes that appear unrelated to the outcome but with some predictive power. Algorithms that contain both weak and strong features may be indecipherable to humans. Such an algorithm might skip past any decision on which of Cialdini's (for example) persuasion techniques should be used and produce uniquely tailored techniques of persuasion.

Take Over the World?

Can AI take over the world? We don't worry about that in this book; however, there are serious AI researchers who are thinking about this. This topic is considered in *The Singularity is Near* by Ray Kurzweil (Kurzweil, 2005) and James Barrat's *Our Final Invention: Artificial Intelligence and the End of the Human Era* (Barrat, 2013). Max Tegmark's book *Life 3.0* presented an interesting discussion of thinking on this topic as of 2017 (Tegmark, 2017).

Network Science

Networks are vital parts of the human condition and communication within society. The human nervous system is a system of networks (partially described in the section on the brain, above). Networks are also critical elements in computer usage.

Human Social Networks

Niall Ferguson discussed human social networks, contrasting them to human hierarchies in the history of human power structures (Ferguson, 2018). As an historian, he said that most accounts of history concentrate on the hierarchies (typically housed in high towers), omitting the social networks (typically in the town square below the towers), which he said are the true drivers of change. He made the case that networks are just as important as hierarchies in understanding human history, and by implication, the human future.

Networks are a central part of all human endeavors. Networks consist of signals, boundaries, nodes, and links. Not surprisingly, with human networks all aspects are dazzlingly complex. The science of networks "cuts across fields … from sociology, economics, mathematics, physics, computer science, anthropology" as well as war, psychology and data science (Holland, 2012). "How networks form and why they exhibit certain key patterns, and how those patterns determine our power, opinion, opportunities, behaviors, and accomplishments" is part of the cannon of cognitive superiority (Jackson, 2019).

Matthew O. Jackson in his book, The Human Network, described the impact of networks on human society and its members (Jackson, 2019). In particular, there are certain positions in a network that provide greater influence for the person occupying the position than for people in other positions. The person occupying such a position may have achieved the position through talent or random factors. Through successful individual behavioral adaptation, the individual's position may be enhanced, creating the position of influence. This, in turn, allows the person to build an even stronger network.

Network science has been useful in identifying positions of influence. Jackson defined four centrality (connectedness) measures, shown in Table 5.8 (Jackson, 2019). Positions with a high score in any of these measures have greater influence than positions with lower scores; however, each measure correlates with a different type of influence.

Network science requires a polythetic, multiordinal approach. An example is the concept of "externalities." All signals are context dependent. One person's behavior affects the well-being of others. Externalities are fundamental to network understanding. The hierarchical and modular feature of networks, the human bias toward getting into groups for affiliation and affirmation, and the ease of induction of us-them-ism has produced stringent and fragile markers of social (network) membership. These markers are among many surfaces of vulnerability to persuasion (Moffett, 2018).

Christakis and Fowler's book, *Connected*, discussed network science, particularly as applied to social networks (Christakis & Fowler, 2009). They emphasized the many types of connections and the fact that these connections carry influence and spread information, with an obvious relationship to the spread of contagious

Table 5.8 Jackson's network centrality measures

Degree centrality measures the number of connections of a node. "Being able to get a message out to millions of followers on a social medium gives a person the potential to influence what many people think or know."
Eigenvector centrality measures the quality of the connections in terms of their connections. "Having many friends can be useful, but it can be equally or even more important to have a few well-positioned friends."
Diffusion centrality measures the ability to reach many others through a small number of intermediaries. "How well positioned is a person to spread information and to be one of the first to hear it?"
Betweenness centrality measures the number of others who must communicate through a node to reach a large number of others. "Is someone a powerful broker, essential intermediary, or in a unique position to coordinate others?"

diseases. It is important to note the fundamental difference in the spread dynamics of information versus behavior, which is discussed below.

Networks of Individuals

Damon Centola explained the distinction between the diffusion of simple things like information (***simple diffusion***) and the diffusion of complex things like behavior (***complex diffusion***) and their significance in his book, *How Behavior Spreads* (Centola, 2018b). In this sense, a simple thing is something that is immediately contagious. That doesn't mean 100% contagious, only that one contact may be sufficient. Generally, diseases such as measles or the common cold only require exposure from one person for another person to contract it, although any particular contact may not transmit the disease. Complex things, like behavioral change, require contact from multiple sources. In general, the adoption of a new technology may require exposure to more than one other person who has adopted it. (Technology adoption is also influenced by ease of use and usefulness in addition to network dynamics.)

If you think of society as a set of nodes (people), connected by their associations, you will perceive that these connections are not all the same. Some are strong bonds between closely associated people and some are weak bonds of acquaintance. In a non-mobile society, almost all of the strong bonds will connect people who are geographically close. Even in a mobile society, a large fraction of the strong bonds will connect geographically close people. However, weak bonds can span continents (think of your Facebook connections). The presence of these weak bonds is what creates the "six degrees of separation" effect, in which almost anyone is connected to every other person (say Kevin Bacon) by a very few links.

As Centola explained it, simple things, like information, can diffuse through both strong connections and weak connections; however, it is the weak connections that allow for explosive contagion (going *viral*). A local diffusion is passed on through the weak connections to different areas (Fig. 5.5), allowing simultaneous growth throughout the society. In the figure, node 22 starts the contagion (the solo "1" identifier); its neighbors (the area marked "2") and the weakly connected node 18 (the solo "2" identifier) contracts it next; and then their neighbors contract it (the areas marked "3"). The figure shows that in four stages almost all of the nodes have embraced the idea (or contracted the disease).

On the other hand, complex things, like behavior, require reinforcement from multiple sources, which weak connections don't generally provide. The distant person doesn't generally have other connections that receive the message at the same (or nearly the same) time and so does not receive reinforcement, resulting in no conversion. Complex things spread (mostly) through the strong connections, often in geographically contiguous areas, because the people connected by strong connections are connected to others who have strong connections to multiple sources (Fig. 5.6). In this example, two sources are required for a node to embrace the behavior (or contract the disease). Nodes 22 and 23 are the initial sources (marked

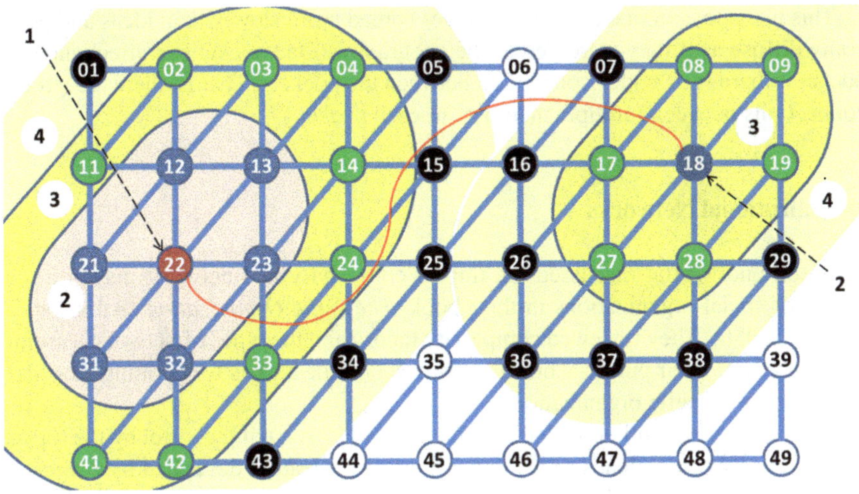

Fig. 5.5 Simple diffusion

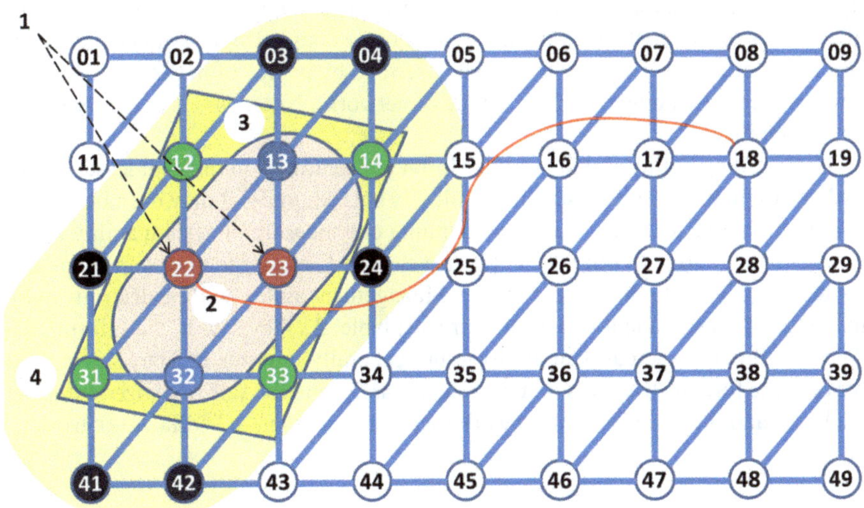

Fig. 5.6 Complex diffusion

with the "1" identifier). Because the network connections do not connect all nearest neighbors in this network, node 13 is infected in stage 2, but other close nodes, like node 14 are not infected. However, in stage 3, node 14 has two infected neighbors (node 13 and node 23) and is infected. Similarly, node 24 is not infected until stage 4. After four stages, less than half the network is infected. Note that node 18 has not been infected, despite its connection to node 22—node 18 has only one infected connection through stage 4.

This is the reason that behavior changes spread more slowly than ideas and generally diffuse as if they were tied to the geography. (One pocket can affect another pocket if there is a "wide" connection between the pockets. That is, there are strong connections between multiple members in each pocket.)

Organizational Networks

Atkinson and Moffat discussed the impact complexity and networks have on the agility of social organizations in their book, *The Agile Organization* (Atkinson & Moffat, 2005b). They reviewed complexity theory and the types of networks (useful to any reader). Their purpose, however, was to provide a basis for defining the characteristics of an agile organization.

They defined a tightly coupled management style as having control by the top as a high priority, which leads to the hierarchical organization described by Ferguson above. On the other hand, a loosely coupled management style is one that tolerates and encourages self-organizing informal networks, similar to the social networks of Ferguson. Atkinson and Moffat compared the effectiveness of the two management styles in times of stability and in times of turbulence: the tightly coupled style provides better results in the first and the more loosely coupled style works better in the second. In either case, the styles can be described by choice of network type (a traditional hierarchy being a particular type of network). Note, ours is certainly not an age of stability!

In describing agility, Atkinson and Moffat concentrated on times of lesser stability because in times of high stability, agility is not required—it may even be a negative, frictional factor. They started by defining one measure of system agility as the number of states or condition available in a system. Clearly, the management agility should correspond to the system agility. Management agility will be determined by the range of management actions that are available. As they saw it, the Information Age recommends increases in agility—and generally requires it. They saw a need for both the formal structures of a flexible hierarchy and the self-organized informal networks and the need for both to work together (Atkinson & Moffat, 2005b).

Computer Networks

The Internet is a network of networks. It uses a set of protocols to support messages between computers, including addressing protocols and domain servers to route the messages.

Internet Protocol version 4 (IPv4) defines slightly more than four billion addresses (2^{32}). When you enter a URL for a website, you normally type something like "www.drdeanhartley.com," a set of characters. However, the machinery of the Internet converts this into a numerical address, such as "nnn.nnn.nnn.nnn," where the numbers between the periods range from 0 to 256, giving the four billion +

addresses. A new version of the protocol, IPv6, will have 2^{128} addresses, approximately 3.4×10^{38} or about 340,000,000,000,000,000,000,000,000,000,000,000,000 addresses. This huge number of addresses will allow almost everything to be connected—an internet of things.

Some computers and devices are connected directly to a network (hard-wired). These may be connected by coaxial cables, fiber optics or copper wires. The connection method determines (in part) the speed of the connection. Actually, speed is something of a misnomer. The signals all travel near the speed of light; however, the bandwidth differs. That is, the capacity for parallel signals can vary dramatically. Thus, the total amount of information that is transferred per second varies.

Devices may also be connected by cellular telephone technology. The new fifth generation (5G) networks provides higher speed connections than previous generations. It will also allow for direct connections between all of those (almost) innumerable things in the internet of things). The implications and emergent properties are still being pondered as 6G is being envisioned (Davis, 2020).

Quantum Technologies

Quantum physics requires deep mathematics for its description. It includes counterintuitive results because our intuition is based on our experiences in the "classical" world, which is distinctly different from the quantum world. Table 5.9, comparing the two worlds, is derived from Crease and Goldhaber's book, The Quantum Moment (Crease & Goldhaber, 2015).

- The first entry in the table declares that different laws of physics apply at different scales. The macroworld has no concept that corresponds to the identicality of all electrons. They can be in different states, but otherwise they are all the same! "For an electron bound in an atom these states are specified by a set of numbers, called 'quantum numbers.' Four quantum numbers specify a state, and that's it—nothing else." The four quantum numbers are energy, angular momentum, magnetic moment, and spin. Each quantum number can take on only discrete sets of integers or half-integers. There are two categories of identical particles. Fermions obey the Pauli Exclusion Principle, which says that no two identical fermions (such as electrons) can occupy the same quantum state. Fermions can't

Table 5.9 Comparing the classical world to the quantum world

	Classical	Quantum
Scale	Macroworld laws	Microworld laws
Inhomogeneity	One type of presence	Wave and particle
Discontinuity	Continuous	Discrete
Uncertainty	Deterministic	Heisenberg
Unpredictability	Causality	Randomness
Observer effect	None	Dependent

be "mashed together." (Pauli was given the Nobel Prize for this result.) Bosons (e.g., photons) can be "mashed together." In fact, a sufficient number mashed together become a Bose-Einstein condensate—a classical wave. Liquid helium, with its strange properties, provides a visible example in which helium atoms act like bosons.

- The second entry refers to the concept that in the classical world, each thing has a "definite identity and is located at a specific place at a specific time"—ghosts and phantoms to not appear do not "pop up and disappear unpredictably." In the quantum world, pairs of particles and anti-particles do pop up and disappear unpredictably and things can act like waves or particles and thus must be regarded as having dual natures.
- The classical world is imagined to be constructed of or described by three physical dimensions and a single time dimension, each continuous. In a continuous dimension, between any two points there is always another point—there are no gaps. The quantum world is defined by gaps: electrons jump (or fall) from one energy level to another, with nothing in between. [At this point there is no evidence that time or space is quantized, fundamentally discontinuous; however, many variables that can be expressed as being continuous in the classical world are discrete in the quantum world.]
- In the classical world, uncertainty is "epistemological uncertainty—uncertainty in what we know about the objects of study." In the quantum world, "ontological uncertainty or uncertainty in nature itself" is added. Thus, things are deterministic in the classical world, even though we cannot precisely measure them. But in the quantum world there exist things that **cannot** be determined, such as simultaneous exact knowledge of position and momentum—Heisenberg uncertainty.
- One of the clearest breaks between the classical world and the quantum world lies in the realm of causality. The classical world is based on causality—if something happens, something caused it. In the quantum world, some things just happen—a radioactive atom decays or not; a light wave reflects or refracts. The best you can do is determine a probability of occurrence.
- The most disturbing difference lies in the significance of the observer. In the classical world, an observer can interfere with an effect—the measuring instrument might be too obtrusive. However, successively finer instruments would reduce the interference and measuring the successive changes might allow for accounting for the interference. In the quantum world, the effect may not occur until it is observed! Schroedinger's cat provides the familiar example. The cat is neither dead nor alive, but is has the two states superposed until the box is opened and the state observed.

An ordinary (classical) computer is based on bits with two possible states, "on" and "off" or "1" and "0," instantiated in hardware. A quantum computer is based on qubits, in which both states are superposed (a possibility described in quantum theory). The qubits of a quantum computer are also instantiated in hardware (to date using superconducting technologies, see below). Computations in both types of computers are performed by algorithms in computer programs. However, the algorithms for quantum computers depend on probabilistic logic based in quantum theory. Theory says that quantum computers can outperform ordinary computers for certain tasks (***quantum supremacy***). Recent tests of a quantum processer were compared with the (currently) fastest supercomputer in the world, showing that this theory is correct (Cho, 2019; Jones, 2019). For our purposes, the technical details are not relevant. However, the known and possible impacts of this coming technology on information are relevant.

Experimental, small scale quantum computers have been built and work has been done on algorithms that will use the nature of quantum computing to solve problems (Waliden & Kashefi, 2019). At this time, it is known that IBM, Google AI and Honeywell are working to build quantum computers. Working computers are expected to be available in late 2020 (Lang, 2020).

Currently, we are in the Noisy Intermediate-Scale Quantum (NISQ) era (Preskill, 2018). The "intermediate-scale" modifier refers to the number of qubits—large enough to demonstrated proof-of-principle, but not large enough to perform the envisaged, valuable tasks. "Noisy" refers to the impact of having too few qubits—there are not enough qubits to perform adequate error correction. Insufficient error correction is referred to as noise. In any case, quantum computers will use classical computers as front-ends and back-ends to prepare the problems for the quantum computer and to interpret the results.

One of the areas that quantum computing will disrupt is encryption/decryption. Secure communication and storage of data currently depends on the difficulty involved in finding the factors of very large numbers (on the order of 300 digits). Conventional computers, even large super computers are incapable of doing this in reasonable amounts of time. Full scale quantum computers will be able to do this easily.

Experts are working on different encryption schemes that will be unbreakable by quantum computers (or conventional computers). However, there have been and continue to be thefts of massive amounts of stored data from computer systems. Where these data are encrypted, the thefts seem to be senseless—until one accounts for future quantum computer capabilities. In the future, these data can and will be easily decrypted. This is called retrospective decryption. In that future, some of the data will have been rendered useless by the passage of time. However, some will retain tremendous value, such as social security numbers tied to identities, financial transactions, and identities of spies (Mims, 2019b).

Beyond the threat to data security, the ability of quantum computers to break current encryption methods threatens economic security. The authors of a 2018 article in Nature said, "By 2025, up to 10% of global gross domestic product is likely to be stored on blockchains. A blockchain is a digital tool that uses cryptography techniques to protect information from unauthorized changes. It lies at the root of the Bitcoin cryptocurrency. Blockchain-related products are used everywhere from finance and manufacturing to health care, in a market worth more than US$150 billion." The authors continued, "within a decade, quantum computers will be able to break a blockchain's cryptographic codes." They included recommendation for making blockchains more secure, such as tightening the encryption techniques and ultimately using quantum communications to ensure security (Fedorov, Kiktenko, & Lvovsky, 2018).

Beyond the limits of our "rational" bounded reality, beyond our inability to predict emergence in our manifold complex adaptive systems, faintly aware of randomness, passing through our limits, defaults, preconceptions, and the systematic predictably irrational aspects of our cognition, we have evolved and mathematically described a Newtonian world-view. The Newtonian world-view is as deterministic and dependable as a game of billiards. Unfortunately, we have also evolved and mathematically described an unpredictable and discontinuous quantum world-view that underlies the Newtonian world. Its effects exist, but the "effects are not directly noticeable (Crease & Goldhaber, 2015)." Rapidly unfolding quantum understanding is likely to become a more central part of cognitive superiority.

xR—Immersive Technologies

Extended Reality (xR) stands for a collection of software and hardware technologies that provides a combination of digital and biological realities. It can contain augmented reality (AR) by including wearable "intelligence," virtual reality (VR), now with the potential for avatars, and 360° video. AR is spreading to most corners of society, including commerce, education, entertainment, and warfare. The augmented warrior is extant. The Stanford University Virtual Human Interaction Lab is a pioneer in VR (Stanford University VHIL, 2019). There is minimal knowledge of the effects and potentials of xR. What will be the persuasive potential of a companion avatar?

Genetic Engineering and Synthetic Biology

Advanced genetic engineering and synthetic biology are extant. Genetic engineering includes adding sections of genetic code to confer desirable properties (e.g., disease resistant plants) and replacing errors in genes that cause diseases (gene therapy). The idea is to replace sections of DNA or RNA with corrected sections. Synthetic biology includes this and goes farther. The idea is to create new biological systems or redesign those found in nature. The use of these technologies for purposeful attacks requires a vastly increased commitment to biosecurity.

The modified CRISPR plus gene-drive technology cuts and splices large segments of the genome, not just short contiguous segments, and spreads them more rapidly than the traditional genetic transmission dynamics (Service, 2019). The 'prime' gene-editing system could surpass first generation CRISPR. David Liu, a chemist at the Broad Institute in Cambridge, Massachusetts, said "Prime editors offer more targeting flexibility and greater editing precision (Champer, Bushman, & Akbari, 2016; Cohen, 2019)."

The uses for biological technology include: improved treatments for disease and medical impairments; possible human augmentations, such as nootropics and physical enhancements (consider the various kinds of athletic "doping"); and biological war. Whether the biological agents are feral diseases, come from unintended releases, or are purposefully released, they can produce massive health and economic effects, as evidenced by the COVID-19 pandemic of 2020. A low barrier to entry into the bio-war domain, the potentially problematic attribution, and the ability to scale an attack make this an area of essential and increased focus, needing best-in-class expertise and ability. Genomic science, advanced genetic engineering, synthetic biology, and augmented computational biology contribute to the problem. They, together with big data analytics, network science, persuasion science, logistical and communication expertise, must be coordinated for security and defense (Desai, 2020). Further, no knowledgeable adversary will miss the opportunity to superimpose an "infodemic" [coined by the World Health Organization (WHO) (World Health Organization (WHO), 2020)] on an epidemic. With purposeful biosecurity threats we must consider multiple releases (vectors) in form, location and timing in parallel with infodemics and hybrid, multi-domain attacks. Synthetic DNA and RNA can make many diseases, including new forms, into software problems or opportunities.

Other Possibly Transformative Technologies

AI and quantum technologies are six-hundred-pound gorillas. Kahn says AI "will be the most important technology developed in human history (Kahn, 2020)." Quantum technologies are based in an area of physics that is literally incomprehensible to most people today. The impacts may include things currently thought of as impossible. Three other technologies have the prospect of revolutionizing society: superconductivity, nuclear thermal propulsion, and 3D printing.

Superconductivity

Some materials conduct electricity so poorly that they are used as insulators to prevent electrical flows in undesired directions. Some materials, such as silver, copper, and aluminum are very good conductors and are used for wires. Other materials, when cooled to near absolute zero (0 Kelvin), have no resistance at all and are termed ***superconductors***. The first superconductors required cooling by liquid helium (around 4 Kelvin). Later high-temperature superconductors were produced that only needed the cooling provided by liquid nitrogen (around 77 Kelvin) (Wikipedia, 2019a).

Superconducting magnets are like electro-magnets, but much stronger and have a persistent magnetic field. The strength of these superconducting magnets is sufficient to levitate very large masses, resulting in the term ***Maglev***. Numerous applications have been proposed in the book, *Maglev America*, such as transportation, energy storage, and space launch (Danby, Powell, & Jordan, 2013).

Superconducting Enabled Transportation

James R. Powell and Gordon T. Danby created and patented a number of inventions in the field of superconducting magnetic levitation. Powell and Danby presented their original concepts in 1966 and received a patent in 1968. This concept has been **implemented** in Japan in an ultra-high-speed train (up to 360 miles per hour) (Powell & Danby, 2013).

Superconducting Enabled Energy Storage

The same Maglev technology used in transportation can be used to store power. The mass that is raised to a higher level and then returned to a lower level can be water, as in pumped hydro systems, or it can be any other substance. A given mass of water requires a large storage area compared to a denser substance like concrete. A Maglev system can move large amounts of mass to great heights and recover the energy with 90% efficiency (a 10% loss), with cheaper infrastructure costs and greater efficiency than pumped hydro systems (70% efficiency) (Powell, Danby, & Coullahan, 2013; Rather, 2013; Rather & Hartley, 2017).

Superconducting Enabled Space Launch

The superconducting technology of Maglev can also be used to launch payloads, including manned vehicles, into space—and do it at a fraction of the cost of chemical rocket launches. Chapter 13 of the *Maglev America* book introduced the technology and cost estimates (Powell, Maise, & Jordan, 2013).

The book, *StarTram: The New Race to Space*, by James Powell, George Maise, and Charles Pellegrino, expanded the description and discussion (Powell, Maise, & Pellegrino, 2013). This book goes beyond the launch system to discuss technologies for exploring and colonizing the solar system.

Nuclear Thermal Propulsion

In the 1980s, a team of nuclear engineers, led by James Powell, at Brookhaven National Laboratory began work on a particle bed reactor. This design consisted of 400-micron diameter nuclear fuel particles packed in an annular bed. Hydrogen flowing through the center was heated by the nuclear fuel and expelled as the propelling gas. Later this project transitioned to the classified Space Nuclear Thermal Propulsion program. In 1992, the Cold War ended and the program was discontinued (Powell, Maise, & Pellegrino, 2013).

Recently, work on nuclear thermal propulsion has been revived by NASA (NASA, 2018). Vehicles using this type of propulsion would be extremely useful both in providing cislunar travel (avoiding any possible venting of radioactive material on the Earth's surface) and to reduce the time required for travel to Mars by a very large factor (Rather & Hartley, 2018b).

3D Printing

Additive manufacturing (known as 3D printing) consists of building an artifact by adding material to form specified shapes. Traditional techniques involve subtractive manufacturing in which the shape is milled from a block, removing unwanted material. Carving a sculpture from marble is an example of subtractive "manufacturing," whereas molding a sculpture from clay is an example of additive "manufacturing." 3D printing gets all of the attention, although most commercial applications will require both additive and subtractive manufacturing.

The Oak Ridge National Laboratory (ORNL) has one of the most advanced 3D printing facility in the world. This facility has printers for manufacturing the familiar plastic (polymer) articles. However, metal artifacts can also be formed using metal powders and wires. An extremely important advantage of 3D printing lies in the ability to characterize the desired nature of the artifact (composition, heat history, etc., by 3D boxel [cf., pixel in 2D images]) and to ensure the actual artifact meets that characterization. The facility has produced an entire car (including engine) (Peter, 2019). It is possible that asteroidal and lunar regolith materials can be used as the material to be used in 3D printing (Rather & Hartley, 2018b).

Technology Readiness

The National Aeronautics and Space Administration (NASA) needed a "method for estimating the maturity of technologies during the acquisition phase of a program (Wikipedia, 2019b)." NASA developed the concept of technology readiness levels (TRLs) during the 1970s to meet this need. Since that time, the concept has been adapted and adopted by the U.S. Department of Defense, the European Space Agency, and finally established as an ISO standard in 2013.

The TRL scale ranges from 1 to 9, with 9 representing the most mature technology. Although the definitions may vary with the organization, the NASA definitions provide a solid basis for understanding the definitions of the levels (Table 5.10).

Conceptually, a technology concept moves through the levels from basic principles to commercial (or government) implementation. However, not all technology

Table 5.10 NASA's technology readiness levels

1. Basic principles observed and reported;
2. Technology concept and/or application formulated;
3. Analytical and experimental critical function and/or characteristic proof-of concept;
4. Component and/or breadboard validation in laboratory environment;
5. Component and/or breadboard validation in relevant environment;
6. System/subsystem model or prototype demonstration in a relevant environment (ground or space);
7. System prototype demonstration in a space environment;
8. Actual system completed and "flight qualified" through test and demonstration (ground or space); and
9. Actual system "flight proven" through successful mission operations.

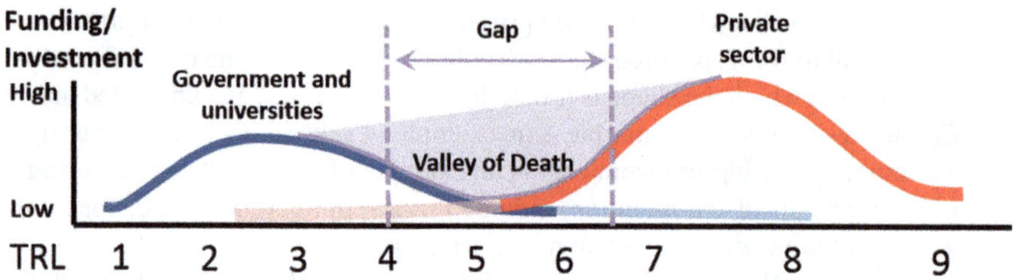

Fig. 5.7 The valley (gap) of death

concepts actually reach commercial implementation. Some prove to be impractical or too costly. A Government Accountability Office (GAO) forum on nanomanufacturing identified another reason for some failures—a systemic funding gap, called the Valley of Death (U.S. Government Accountability Office, 2014).

Figure 5.7, adapted from the forum report, shows the funding gap in the Valley of Death in terms TRLs. Essentially the problem is that early stages of research and development of concepts can often find funding from the government or universities and late stage implementation funding of some technologies is provided by the private sector.

However, there is no general system in place to provide funding for technologies to carry them from the laboratory environment to systems development in the relevant environment. The figure shows why this gap is called the Valley of Death. Many promising technology concepts die from lack of funding. Some may have been doomed in any case; however, some may have died that would have proved to be immensely valuable.

Chapter 6
The Adversarial Environment

Who are our adversaries? What do they want? Why should we be concerned now?

We are facing today a multi-pronged, multi-faceted attack on our civilization. This is not a coordinated attack by a single enemy. There are multiple national opponents, who, acting individually, are using a variety of modes of attack over broad scales of time on multiple facets of our national life. There are also many non-nation-state opponents, both external to our country and within it, who are doing the same. There are individuals and small groups of individuals, acting on economic motives, doing the same. Additionally, our social media have created an environment that fosters individual attacks. There are the traditional corporate activities that seek to further their own ends through influence operations. Together, these actors present a vast matrix of competing interests and influence and create an environment of constant conflict.

"The modern internet is not just a network, but an ecosystem of nearly 4 billion souls, each with their own thoughts and aspirations, each capable of imprinting a tiny piece of themselves on the vast digital commons. They are targets not of a single information war but of thousands and potentially millions of them (Singer & Brooking, 2018)."

This conflict involves the individual, the social organizations, the corporate organizations, and the government, using and exacerbating the changing environment. While the technium and the noosphere are the means, media, and immediate and long-term targets, the cognitive domain is the actual domain of conflict.

Much of human history is red n tooth and claw, kill and eat. Frederick the Great said, "Every man has a wild beast within him." "The question is what releases the beast (Wrangham, 2019)." We humans "have a rare and perplexing combination of moral tendencies. We can be the nastiest of species and also the nicest." "Peace at home and war abroad" is not rare. "We now recognize that aggression comes in not one but two major forms, each with its own biological underpinnings and its own evolutionary story." "Reactive (hot, defensive, or impulsive) aggression is a response to a threat." Proactive aggression (cold, premeditated, offensive) is the aggression of

D. S. Hartley III, K. O. Jobson, *Cognitive Superiority*,
https://doi.org/10.1007/978-3-030-60184-3_6

war (coalitionary proactive aggression) or the deliberate aggression of the sociopath, or, at times, the offended and unrestrained. The proactive individual protagonist typically acts when he can "assess a high likelihood of cost free success." It is essential that those charged with our security and defense clearly understand that we are low on the scale of one type of aggression (reactive aggression) and high on the other type (proactive aggression) and that "the separate nature of proactive and reactive" aggression helps to explain warfare. Methods of influence, prediction and furtherance of human violence are extant and can be used for dissociative ends (Wrangham, 2019).

Adversaries

Adversaries come in many configurations and sizes. All contribute to the environment of conflict in the noosphere and technium.

Individuals

Individuals range from the perpetrators of individual defamatory attacks on others to swindlers or the hackers who use their skills to attack the computers of others. The resources of individuals range from having an account on social media to access or control of thousands of computers, with funding ranging from pocket change to millions of dollars.

Malicious individuals or groups may act on their own or may be associated, either informally or formally as proxies, with groups, corporations, or governments. These individuals may penetrate all of the layers of security or may start from a privileged position within a corporation, such as a recent case in which an employee of Amazon's cloud division is reported to have stolen more than 100 million customers' data from the Capital One data stored in the Amazon cloud (Mattioli, McMillan, & Herrera, 2019). Another privileged position is created by the creators of applications (apps) that perform useful functions either on smartphones or in web browsers. Some browser apps, called browser extensions, have been found to conduct surveillance. They sell information on "where you surf and what you view into a murky data economy … to be harvested for marketers, data brokers or hackers (Fowler, 2019a)."

Groups

Some groups are civic organizations with a benevolent public agenda. There are also both organized groups and loose affiliations of hackers. There are groups who use the Internet almost exclusively and groups who use it to aid their real-world activism. Clarke and Knake labeled the worst of these groups "advanced persistent threats (APT)" because they are not only highly capable, but also steadfast in their efforts (Clarke & Knake, 2019). Group resources can be expected to be generally larger than individual resources.

Companies

Virtually all companies advertise. Some companies engage in industrial espionage. Some companies are captive instruments of their governments and some hold governments captive. Corporate resources can be enormous, with many having millions or billions of dollars in available funds, with commensurate technical resources.

Recently, social media companies have provided a special concern. As described earlier, social media provide vehicles for influence attacks and have been accused of fostering their own agendas in influence operations (McNamee, 2019). However, in an opinion article, Andy Kessler of the Wall Street Journal argued that these risks are exaggerated. He argued that the social media themselves are training people to be more alert to these attacks and more discerning in their acceptance of fake news. He said that, "For all its flaws, social networks and artificial intelligence keep delivering value and utility to users, training people for a world that moves in nanoseconds. Better to teach the next generation how to keep up (Kessler, 2020)." This debate continues.

Non-State Actors

Non-state actors are groups that have ambitions in the international arena, some acting independently and some acting as proxies. Some are supposed to be benign, such as United Nations organizations, and some are distinctly malignant, such as Al Qaeda. The resources of most non-state actors are comparable to those of general groups, although some have very large funding bases.

"'Terrorism is theater,' declared RAND Corporation analyst Brian Jenkins in a 1974 report that become one of terrorism's foundational studies. Command enough attention and it didn't matter how weak or strong you were: you could bend populations to your will and cow the most powerful adversaries into submission (Singer & Brooking, 2018)." "ISIS's legacy will live on long after the group has lost all its physical territory, because it was one of the first conflict actors to fuse warfare with the foundations of attention in the social media age. It mastered the key elements of *narrative*, *emotion*, *authenticity*, *community*, and *inundation* [emphasis in the source] (Singer & Brooking, 2018)." (***Authenticity*** means engendering the belief that the persona of the social media person is really that of the real-life person animating the social media person.)

Nation-States

Nation-states have full access to national funding. Their technical and financial resources can be huge. Their goals can range from gaining economic advantages to global dominance. Their methods can range from theft of intellectual property to industrial espionage to war. For some countries, divining intent from methods can be difficult. A translated Chinese document titled *Unrestricted Warfare* made this clear. Their methods for war include, lawfare (using and bending laws to advantage), "hacking into websites, targeting financial institutions, using the media, and conducting terrorism and urban warfare (Qiao & Wang, 1999)."

The U.S. Department of Defense cyber strategy said, "We are engaged in a long-term strategic competition with China and Russia. These States have expanded that competition to include persistent campaigns in and through cyberspace that pose long-term strategic risk to the Nation as well as to our allies and partners. China is eroding U.S. military overmatch and the Nation's economic vitality by persistently exfiltrating sensitive information from U.S. public and private sector institutions. Russia has used cyber-enabled information operations to influence our population and challenge our democratic processes. Other actors, such as North Korea and Iran, have similarly employed malicious cyber activities to harm U.S. citizens and threaten U.S. interests. Globally, the scope and pace of malicious cyber activity continue to rise. The United States' growing dependence on the cyberspace domain for nearly every essential civilian and military function makes this an urgent and unacceptable risk to the Nation (Department of Defense, 2018)."

Digital Adversaries

Singer and Brooking added an additional type of adversary. "The way the Internet affects its human users makes it hard enough for them to distinguish truth from falsehood. Yet these 4 billion flesh-and-blood netizens have now been joined by a vast number of digital beings, designed to distort and amplify, to confuse and distract. The attention economy may have been built by humans, but it is now ruled by algorithms—some with agendas all their own (Singer & Brooking, 2018)."

Goals and Intents

The goals and intents of the adversaries are various and differ within types of adversaries as well as between them. However, some categories of goals and intents are common among adversaries.

Personal Enmity

Some people take advantage of social media to conduct personal attacks. They are acting on personal enmity.

Other adversaries seek to create enmity. Singer and Brooking, explaining emotion and purpose of trolls, repeated the words of a well-known troll, 'Ironghazi,' who explained, "'The key to being a good troll is being just stupid enough to be believable, keeping in mind that the ultimate goal is making people mad online (Singer & Brooking, 2018).'"

Influence

The desire to gain attention and influence is common among many types of adversaries. Their actions may seek current influence or be positioned for the future.

Individual and Group Influence

Malicious individuals and groups may seek to influence their targets to gain current access. Or they may use influence as an indirect means to further their ultimate goals.

Corporate Influence

Generally, companies use advertising and similar activities to obtain influence, leading to economic gains. Some companies, such as Google and Facebook, have privileged positions with respect to external data, gathering enormous amounts of personal data from their users. They also are in the information business, selling access to users and their data. Some have been accused of using their positions to exercise political influence on their users (Copeland, 2019b). In 2019, Rep. Tulsi Gabbard, a candidate for the Democrat nominee for President in 2020, accused Google of censoring her by suspending her advertisements (Carlson, 2019).

Singer and Brooking described a company, Breitbart, acting to increase influence, "Bannon embraced social media as a tool to dominate the changing media marketplace, as well as to remake the right-wing. The modern internet wasn't just a communications medium, he lectured his staff, it was a 'powerful weapon of war,' or what he called '#War' (Singer & Brooking, 2018)."

National Influence

Sean McFate cited the Russian Troll Factory, illustrating that the power of cyberwarfare lies in delivering disinformation. "Trolls are anonymous *agents provocateur* that stalk the internet, throwing seditious hand grenades into chatrooms and on news sites (McFate, 2019)."

Michael Pillsbury described the Chinese use of *shi* in its hundred-year war to replace America as the global superpower. China has been positioning itself and using influence over others to create a situation that will yield Chinese influence over future events (Pillsbury, 2015).

The U.S. also seeks influence. For example, as Lt Col Patrick McClintock said in a National Defense University capstone report, "The US conducts and supports [Humanitarian Assistance/Disaster Relief] HA/DR operations in the Indo-Pacific to: (1) provide humanitarian relief that alleviates suffering, (2) create a positive image of the US and its military among leaders and inhabitants of the region, (3) build relationships and advance military interoperability with other countries and militaries that support US regional presence, (4) lay the foundation for other forms of security cooperation, and (5) demonstrate the US military's commitment to allies and partners, to include exposing them to new capabilities (e.g., strategic airlift) (McClintock, 2020)."

Surveillance (the Panopticon)

Clearly, almost ubiquitous surveillance exists now. All of our social media are analyzed for use by the companies who own the social media; devices like Alexa require AI analysis to produce the desired answers and actions; our newest televisions have voice activated controls, which require similar surveillance and analysis; we can expect our security cameras to be merged into systems, perhaps with external surveillance and analysis; and companies are selling refrigerator surveillance systems!

An article on the front page of the Wall Street Journal in November of 2019 was titled. "Google Amasses Personal Medical Records." The article described how one of the largest health-care systems has teamed with Google to "collect and crunch the detailed personal-health information of millions of people across 21 states." "The data involved in the initiative encompasses lab results, doctor diagnoses and hospitalization records, among other categories, and amounts to a complete health history, including patient names and dates of birth." "Neither patients nor doctors have been notified (Copeland, 2019a)." The purpose is to improve health care. However, other benefits are certainly expected by the two parties to accrue to themselves.

Big Brother can be a nation-state or a corporation. However, integrating these various data sources will yield more profitable results than any one stand-alone data feed. The enormous quantity of data spanning all aspects of personal life will provide excellent input for big data analytics and AI/ML processing, prediction and influence. China is internally deploying that integration now (Lee, 2018).

Today your smartphone tracks your location and reports it to various recipients (depending on the apps you have installed and the connections they make to third parties). If you turn off the tracking feature, your phone still records your locations (with times). When you turn the tracking feature back on, your phone uploads the history of your locations to the recipients so that they have all the information they would have had if you had not ever turned tracking off. If you have any medical apps that record history, these apps may be sending the information to multiple places. If you use a browser on your phone, this information is recorded and sent. Probably there are things you do on your phone today that are not recorded and disseminated. You can assume that one day everything you do on your phone may be disseminated to someone.

If your computer is connected to the Internet, many of your activities are recorded and disseminated. You can assume that one day, unless your computer is never connected to the Internet, everything you do or say (assuming your computer has a microphone and camera) with or around your computer may be recorded and disseminated.

If you have a smart TV, smart appliances, new car, or Internet connected security system, you can assume eventually everything may be recorded and disseminated. Eventually, everything in your house will be "smart." Already it is difficult to buy a "dumb" TV.

If you purchase groceries or gas with a store-affiliated card, all of your purchases are recorded. That's how they know to send you those nice coupons that correspond to the things you buy frequently. Credit card companies not only know where you use them and how much you spend, but they also know what these purchases mean—your bill shows the expenses categorized by things such as food, entertainment, and travel.

In the future, you can expect that someone will know everything that you do and draw conclusions about your activities. (Currently, it is possible to live "off the grid;" however, there are places now that don't accept cash. It will get harder.) Right now, the things about you that someone knows are divided among multiple corporations and the government (unless you live in China, where it is all being collected by the government (Lee, 2018)). No one knows when or if the current division of knowledge about you will be consolidated. That will be the arrival of the Panopticon.

In the United States, there is some push-back against state surveillance. In an article in the Wall Street Journal, Restuccia and Volz described discussions concerning an overhaul of the program that surveils U.S. citizens suspected of posing national-security risks. The Foreign Intelligence Surveillance Act (FISA) was first adopted after Watergate and modified by the post-9/11 Patriot Act. It codifies this type of surveillance. The abuses that took place before and after the Trump inauguration are motivating these concerns (Restuccia & Volz, 2020).

Economic Gain

There are individuals and groups who use conventional telephone calls, email, and social media to extort money from others using various swindles. Malicious individuals act for economic gain by using such tools as ransomware for direct economic gain and obtaining control of insufficiently protected computers to support economic motives indirectly.

Information brokers exist, as do companies selling political persuasion services. These entities use data collected through surveillance as the commodity they sell.

Corporations have both external and internal rationales for engaging in information activities. External reasons include acquisition and prevention of the acquisition of economic, scientific, and personal data. The acquisition of external data includes data acquisition from other corporations, governments, selective scientific advances, and customers or potential customers. Internal reasons include acquisition of personal data on employees for business improvement, control of employees, and prevention of internal data theft or other malicious activities. These may all be classified as driven by a desire for economic gain.

Philosophical and Ideological Motives

Malicious individuals act for ideological reasons (such as antipathy toward corporations or governments).

Maliciousness

There are individuals who act maliciously to display their prowess or create havoc as an enjoyable activity.

Control of Society

Nation-states have both external and internal rationales for engaging in information activities, both offensive and defensive. External reasons include acquisition and prevention of the acquisition of military, economic, scientific, and personal data. External reasons can include influence, coercion or control of other countries. Internal reasons include the acquisition of personal data for defensive reasons, such as identification of spies, terrorists and common criminals, and for the control of internal populations and groups.

One reason for intentional conflicts can be stated as "control of society." The commercial version is controlling actions for profit. The national version is controlling society for power or "for its own good." In this communications age, control of society begins with control of the narrative. (Histories describe wars for the control of territory sometimes as if one day a king decided to conquer his neighbor and then set out to do so. However, we suspect that the king generally had to prepare the ground to get his followers to engage in the war. Thus, the king had to try to create and control the narrative.)

Singer and Brooking discussed the Chinese view of internal control. "Mao [Zedong] envisioned a political cycle in which the will of the masses would be refracted through the lens of Marxism and then shaped into policy, only to be returned to the people for further refinement." "To achieve this goal, even stronger programs of control lurk on the horizon. In the restive Muslim-majority region of Xinjiang, residents have been forced to install the Jingwang (web-cleansing) app on their smartphones. The app not only allows their messages to be tracked or blocked, but it also comes with a remote-control feature, allowing authorities direct access to residents' phones and home networks. To ensure that people were installing these 'electronic handcuffs,' the police have set up roving checkpoints in the streets to inspect people's phones for the app (Singer & Brooking, 2018)."

"The most ambitious realization of the mass line, though, is China's 'social credit' system. Unveiled in 2015, the vision document for the system explains how it will create and 'upward, charitable, sincere and mutually helpful social atmosphere'—one characterized by unwavering loyalty to the state. To accomplish this goal, all Chinese citizens will receive a numerical score reflecting their 'trustworthiness … in all facets of life, from business deals to social behavior (Singer & Brooking, 2018).'" Buckley warned that social credit could come to the United States (Buckley, 2019).

Concerning Russia, Singer and Brooking discussed its methodologies for internal control. "Since Putin consolidated power in 1999, dozens of independent journalists have been killed under circumstances as suspicious as those that have befallen his political opponents (Singer & Brooking, 2018)." "The outcome has been an illusion of free speech within a newfangled Potemkin village. 'The Kremlin's idea is to own all forms of political discourse, to not let any independent movements develop outside its walls,' writes Peter Pomerantsev, author of *Nothing is True and Everything is Possible*. 'Moscow can feel like an oligarchy in the morning and a democracy in the afternoon, a monarchy for dinner and a totalitarian state by bedtime (Singer & Brooking, 2018).'"

Singer and Brooking continued with Russia's external efforts. "But importantly, the [Potemkin] village's border no longer stops at Russia's frontier." "The aim of Russia's new strategy, and its military essence, was best articulated by Valery Gerasimov, the country's top-ranking general at the time." Gerasimov delivered a speech saying, "the role of nonmilitary means of achieving political and strategic goals has grown. In many cases, they have exceeded the power of force of weapons in their effectiveness (Singer & Brooking, 2018)."

Hvistendahl, writing in *Science*, discussed the Chinese government's efforts at societal control (Hvistendahl, 2018). China is using modern digital surveillance techniques to instrument the infrastructure, together with systems analysis and other sophisticated analysis techniques, to effect control of its society. Microsoft is worried about the use of facial-recognition software and is urging governments to regulate its use, especially to prohibit "ongoing surveillance of specific people without a court order (Greene & MacMillan, 2018)." This same article called out China, "where the government uses it [facial-recognition] extensively for surveillance."

In 2014, Alex Pentland wrote the book *Social Physics* about an attempt to develop a science of how humans behave in society. Part of the book details extremely large data collection experiments using cell-phone type technology to monitor millions of person hours of activities. The point of the book is that such data can be used to design corporate and city environments (Pentland, 2014). During the COVID-19 pandemic, use of cell-phone tracking has been proposed for use in "contact tracing" to help reduce the spread of infection. However, it has been also argued that this could be used to monitor and control the spread of ideas (Servick, 2020).

War

Intentional conflict up to and including war can be direct or indirect, momentary or a marathon, monothetic or polythetic, overt or covert, and fixed or adaptive. It can involve any of the actor pairs shown in Table 6.1.

David Sanger described the current U.S. thinking, "In almost every classified Pentagon scenario for how a future confrontation with Russia and China, even Iran and North Korea, might play out, the adversary's first strike against the United States would include a cyber barrage aimed at civilians. It would fry power grids, stop trains, silence cell phones, and overwhelm the Internet. In the worst-case scenarios, food and water would begin to run out; hospitals would turn people away. Separated from their electronics, and thus their connections, Americans would panic, or turn against one another (Sanger, 2018b)."

Christian Brose in his book *The Kill Chain* described a conversation in which a former Pentagon official said about war games, "When we fight China or Russia,

Table 6.1 Conflict actor pairs

Nation versus nation (direct or via proxies),
Faction or corporation versus nation,
Faction or corporation versus faction or corporation,
Individual versus nation,
Individual versus faction or corporation, or
Some combination of the above.

blue [our side] gets its ass handed to it. We lose a lot of people. We lose a lot of equipment. We usually fail to achieve our objective of preventing aggression by the adversary (Brose, 2020b)."

These scenarios do not look as incredible now as they once did. As this book is being written, the COVID-19 pandemic is beginning to wane in the U.S. ; however, the economic effects of the shutdown, initiated to fight the pandemic, are just beginning to be felt. The repercussions have not yet been assessed, but already can be measured in the trillions of dollars. Because this was a voluntary shutdown, infrastructure is untouched. A cyberattack is capable of destroying generators and large power transformers (LPT) (Clarke & Knake, 2019). According to a Department of Energy report on large power transformers, the average lead time for a single LPT is between five and 16 months and only 15% of them are made in the U.S. The cost for each LPT ranges from $2 to $7.5 million, plus transportation and installation, for another 25–30% (an LPT can weigh 410 tons) (U.S. Department of Energy Infrastructure Security and Energy Restoration Office of Electricity and Energy Reliability, 2012). The situation for generators is similar. A major cyberattack would not destroy just one or two LPTs and generators—it would destroy hundreds and thousands of them. The United States would be without electric power for at least a year.

An article in the *MIT Technology Review* described a contract to be awarded for cloud computing for the U.S. Department of Defense, worth up to $10 billion. Potential winners of the contract included Amazon, Microsoft, Oracle, and IBM (Weinberger, 2019). (As of March 13, 2020, the contract had been awarded to Microsoft; however, the Department of Defense had asked a judge to let it reconsider the award (Feiner, 2020).] Traditional defense contractors, such as Lockheed Martin, Boeing and Raytheon are known for producing weapons, which Sean McFate (below) believes will be or already are of little importance in the new wars; however, information will be critical. The bidders for this and similar contracts may become the new powers in defense contracting.

New Rules (or No Rules)

Sean McFate believes the old method of warfare, conventional war, is obsolete. In his book, *The New Rules of War*, he described how war as actually practiced differs from conventional war. For example, he said, "there is no such thing as war or peace—both coexist, always." By this he meant that actors are working to push the limits to obtain their objectives, using methods that fall short of acts that provoke adversaries into declaring war. He claimed, "technology will not save us," and "the best weapons do not fire bullets." Purchasing more sophisticated and expensive weapons will not win wars, but persuasion will (where brute force is not desirable). Shadow wars will be frequent, in which forces wage war but use narrative warfare to obscure the identity of the principal actor and even that a war is taking place (McFate, 2019).

Current wars are using mercenaries (contractors) and this trend will grow. The concept of nation states as the sole actors capable and allowed (by international law) to wage war (the Westphalian Order) has become obsolete. Many of the approximately 194 nations recognized today are nations in name only. Many are narco-states, run by fabulously wealthy drug organizations, or states run by warlords as their personal adjuncts, or essentially lawless areas, denoted by names and boundaries for reference purposes and historical reasons, but not acting as nation-states serving a populace. Corporations and individual billionaires can afford to hire armies and wage wars as they see fit (McFate, 2019).

Kilcullen provided an important image of something he calls *competitive control*:

> "Insurgents make fish traps, as do militias, gangs, warlords, mass social movements, religions (Jesus, for instance, called his apostles to be 'fishers of men') and, of course, governments. Like real fish traps, these metaphorical traps are woven of many strands—persuasive, administrative, and coercive. Though each of the strands may be brittle, their combined effect creates a control structure that's easy and attractive for people to enter, but then locks them into a system of persuasion and coercion: a set of incentives and disincentives from which they find it extremely difficult to break out (Kilcullen, 2013)."

David Sanger opened his book, *The Perfect Weapon*, saying, "A Year into Donald J. Trump's presidency, his defense secretary, Jim Mattis, sent the new commander-in-chief a startling recommendation: with nations around the world threatening to use cyberweapons to bring down America's power grids, cell-phone networks, and water supplies, Trump should declare he was ready to take extraordinary steps to protect the country. If any nation hit America's critical infrastructure with a devastating strike, even a non-nuclear one, it should be forewarned that the United States might reach for a nuclear weapon in response." "Trump accepted Mattis's nuclear recommendation without a moment of debate (Sanger, 2018b)."

"Detecting" War

On a national level, how does a nation determine when malware attacks [or other information attacks] rise to the level of war, even if not officially declared as such by the opposition? In an article in the New York Times, David Sanger said, "State-sponsored Russian hackers appear far more interested this year in demonstrating that they can disrupt the American electric utility grid than the midterm elections, according to United States intelligence officials and technology company executives (Sanger, 2018a)." Two articles in The Wall Street Journal described hacking attacks attributed to the Chinese and potential communications grid problems from Chinese equipment (Lubold & Volz, 2018; Taylor & Germano, 2018). The hacking involved theft of classified information and weapons plans. The potential communications problems involved the use of Chinese-made telecommunications equipment in national networks. Visner described two events as cyber weapons testing: the 2014 North Korean attack on Sony Pictures, in which a hacker group released confidential personnel information and copies of unreleased films and employed malware to erase Sony computer files; and the 2014 unattributed attack on a German steel mill, in which malware was introduced into the industrial control systems, causing an explosion and significant damage (Visner, 2018). In his book, *The Perfect Weapon*, Sanger said, "After a decade of hearings in Congress, there is still little agreement on whether and when cyberstrikes constitute an act of war (Sanger, 2018b)."

Visner described sovereignty problems in differing views of cyberspace (Table 6.2) (Visner, 2018).

Visner drew some inferences, "If cyberspace is sovereign territory, can a state acquire more of it? Can cyberspace be governed and controlled? How can it be acquired? By force? We know Russia tried to influence US elections. If Russia was successful in influencing US elections by 'seizing' cyberspace, was that a military victory? What has Russia gained? What have we lost?"

Visner also discussed the thinking of Dr. Joseph Nye, the former Chairman of the National Intelligence Council, who described the world as a three-level chessboard. At the first level, information technology (IT) is applied through military power, where the US remains the dominant leader (although not unchallenged). Here the barriers to entry are high. At the second level, IT is applied in the world of commerce, which is multi-polar. Middle range powers are able to overcome the barriers to entry here. At the third level, IT is available to groups and individuals, with no one dominant. The barriers here are incredibly low and shrinking. According to Visner, Dr. Nye argued that US policy-makers and decision-makers need to understand the use of the last two levels and the power in them. The reason is that in the past it was believed that the nation with the largest military would prevail in conflict, but that in the information age it could be the state—or non-state actor—*with the best story that prevails*.

"Today, online battles are no longer just the stuff of science fiction or wonky think tank reports, but an integral part of global conflict. As a result, governments around the world have begun to adapt to it. Russia is the most obvious example—a government whose state media, troll factories, and botnets all conspire to wage (in the words of its own military doctrine) 'global information warfare.' Echoing the

Table 6.2 Sovereignty and cyberspace

For the US and western democracies, cyberspace is a global commons
We operate in cyberspace
We defend cyberspace—personal information, intellectual property, business, research, infrastructure, our military operations
We even fight in cyberspace (Department of Defense, 2015)
We don't "own" cyberspace
Think of the Law of the Sea—in this instance, we control cyber assets in our physical space
Beyond territorial waters—universal jurisdiction
For China, Russia, and possibly others:
Cyberspace is territory in which the government has sovereign prerogatives
Cybersecurity is about defending the state's legitimacy and the government's sovereign prerogatives

language of ISIS propagandists, Russian military strategists describe how a strong information offensive can have a strategic impact on a par with the release of an atomic bomb." "[T]he Russian government doesn't resort to netwar because it wants to. Rather, it sees no other choice. The best defense, after all, is a good offense (Singer & Brooking, 2018)."

China

The noted historian Keegan said, "Oriental warmaking … is something different from and apart from European warfare it is characterized by … evasion, delay and indirectness … wearing down the enemy." "It includes the ideological and intellectual (Keegan, 1994)."

"Since 2003, the Chinese military has followed an information policy built on the 'three warfares': psychological warfare (manipulation of perception and beliefs), legal warfare (manipulation of treaties and international law) [lawfare], and public opinion warfare (manipulation of both Chinese and foreign populations) (Singer & Brooking, 2018)."

Holly South, in a National Defense University capstone report, discussed China's use of arms sales to gain influence over other countries, not only in South Asia, but also in Africa. For example, she said, "China made its first arms transfer to Djibouti in 2014. A year later, negotiations began for China's first overseas naval base in the country. China made additional transfers in 2015 and 2016 prior to the base formally opening in 2017 (South, 2020)."

Brose, in *The Kill Chain*, described a scenario he and his boss, Senator McCain, conceived. In this scenario, some kind of incident with the Chinese precipitated an escalation to war. The Chinese would employ cyberattacks and antisatellite actions early. They would then proceed to defeat our kinetic forces. The argument is that we depend on very expensive platforms (ships, aircraft, etc.) for our military operations. Because they are so expensive, we have relatively few of them. Brose argued that China has achieved technical parity (or nearly so) and that its numbers of less expensive weapons, together with an aggressive pace of operations would overwhelm and defeat our forces in detail (Brose, 2020b). This scenario was just a thought experiment. However, it is a plausible one.

Of special note is the Chinese government's effort called "military-civil fusion" that aims to harness advances from China's tech sector for military might. The larger goals are evident in its entanglement with iFlytek efforts toward ubiquitous interpretive surveillance fused with predictive, "prevention and control systems," voice and facial identification, audio-visual translation technology coupled with sociometrics and biometrics (Hvistendahl, How a Chinese AI Giant Made Chatting—and Surveillance—Easy, 2020). The reach of the Chinese has become more evident in the uncovering of China's Thousand Talents program, utilizing clandestine financial support for selected American research scientists (Mervis, 2020a).

On a larger scale, China sees the United States as a hegemonic power seeking to "encircle China with a network of offensive alliances." "Chinese leaders believe the United States has been trying to dominate China for more than 150 years, and China's plan is to do everything possible to dominate us instead (Pillsbury, 2015)." China's perception is not wholly incorrect. The U.S. and its allies are working to prevent China's domination. Captain Aaron Nye of the Royal Australian Navy, in a National Defense University capstone paper, suggested that "Australia should promote itself as a member of a "Middle Power Concert" to balance against rising US-China tensions, and to promote community and regional security building (Nye, 2020)."

Their grand marathon strategy is "relatively stable (Chinese Academy of Military Science, 2018)." It utilizes the wisdom and deception of Sun-Tsu and methods of the ancient warring states where "the only rule is that there are no rules." It is unrestricted warfare by all possible means (Qiao & Wang, 1999). It is also described in McFate's book, *The New Rules of Warfare* (McFate, 2019). The battlefields beyond-the-battlefield use "10,000 methods combined that transcend boundaries." "The winner is the one who combined well (Qiao & Wang, 1999)."

The concept of *shi* is paramount. *Shi* is a principal deceptive stratagem of influencing the present for its effect in the future, often as part of a long-term zero-sum game. Spanning the psychological diplomatic cultural economic and religious domains, the matrix of conflict is combinatorial, adaptive, complex, polythetic, multi-ordinal, and nuanced. It is often trans-domain, using lawfare (the bending of law to achieve desired ends), the media, the military, ecologic warfare, and cyber techniques. The conflict utilizes proxies of many stripes, including mercenaries and temporary alliances. It steals intellectual and strategic secrets, uses narratology, persuasion science, and fake news; it is offensive and defensive, public and private. Evoking local war and conflict at scale, it creates confusion, operates semi-warfare and quasi-warfare, can be preemptive or reactive and approaches from supply and/or demand.

The "gray zone" is a relatively new term for competition below the threshold of armed conflict. (It has obvious overlaps with unconventional conflict.) China uses many techniques, as mentioned above, that lie in the gray zone. Kaleb Redden, in a National Defense University capstone paper, examined these in relation to the U.S. National Defense Strategy (NDS). He said we should "ask which elements of gray zone behavior would undermine DoD's ability to ensure conventional deterrence and a favorable regional balance of power, either by setting conditions for regional conflict or by allowing China to take measures to make U.S. success less likely if conflict occurs." He suggested that there are four criteria for actions of particular concern: "Activities that erode the perception of U.S. credibility among regional allies and partners"; "Non-kinetic activities that impede effective U.S. power projection"; "Activities that erode the will of the U.S. populace to intervene in a crisis"; and "Activities that erode America's long-term technological advantages (Redden, 2020)."

China now not only publishes many more scientific papers than the United States "but its annual growth in publications is ten times that of the United States." "China last year likely topped the United States in overall research spending for the first time in history (Mervis, 2020b)." China is also producing more graduates in science, technology, engineering, and mathematics (STEM) than the United States and as of 2016 was building "the equivalent of one university per week." According to the World Economic Forum, the numbers of STEM graduates for 2016 were 4.7 million for China, 2.6 million for India and 568 thousand for the United States (McCarthy, 2017).

Regarding cognitive competition, China has repeatedly announced its goal of being the dominant AI power by 2030 (Larson, 2018). Toward that end it is spending massively, developing an unrivaled size of big data sets, developing AI for education, sensing, psychometrics and sociometrics and control from kindergarten to university. AI-augmented education has become a national priority (Wang, 2019). China was the first to demonstrate the feasibility of international Quantum communication via satellite connecting China and Australia (Popkin, 2017). China obviously seeks cognitive superiority.

On the other hand, there are those who point out that China has its own problems. LtCol Nathan Packard, in a National Defense University capstone paper, concluded that "The dominant narrative within the U.S. defense establishment misunderstands the trajectory of Chinese power. In reality, critical economic, demographic, and social drivers are trending negatively for the Chinese. In the coming years, China's economy will not meet the expectations of its population. The [Chinese Communist Party] CCP's Great Firewall, state censorship, social credit system, and other repressive measures, are an indication of regime weakness, not strength. The current U.S. approach reduces a complex relationship to a matter of black and white. While China is certainly a strategic competitor, threat inflation impedes good strategy making by narrowing the available options and perspectives (Packard, 2020)." If this conclusion is correct, China might be weaker in the future; however, seeing this, it might be more aggressive in the short-term to counteract its internal problems.

Russia

"In early 2014, a policy paper began circulating in the Kremlin, outlining what steps Russia should take if President Victor Yanukoviych, the pro-Russian autocrat who controlled Ukraine, was toppled from power. Russia had to be ready, the memorandum's author urged, to create a new set of political conditions on the ground—to manipulate the 'centrifugal aspirations' of ethnic Russians, pushing them to declare independence from Ukraine. In essence, if their guy was ever forced from power, Russia had to be ready to start a war (Singer & Brooking, 2018)." And that is what happened.

The Gerasimov doctrine was openly published in 2013 (Gerasimov, 2013). "The Gerasimov doctrine combines old and new: Stalinist propaganda, magnified by the power of Twitter and Facebook, and backed up by brute force." It was implemented in the Ukraine, "the country that has become a test-bed for techniques Russia later used against the United States and its allies (Sanger, 2018b)."

The Gerasimov doctrine is grand strategy; however, Russia is also active at the tactical end of the spectrum. Patrick Tucker wrote in Defense One about a new tool for an internet attack. Leaked Russian documents claimed that Russia has developed a botnet toolset that enables hacking of the cognified objects of the internet of things (IoT). Once hacked, these objects are coordinated as a botnet to conduct a distributed denial of service (DDoS) capable of shutting down the internet of a small country for several hours. The claims of these leaked documents have not been independently verified (Tucker, 2020). However, the existence of the Mirai botnet, used by Russia against Estonia in 2007 and cited by Rothrock as being used in a 2016 exploit that largely used internet of things devices (Rothrock, 2018) lends credence to the claims.

The United States

The authors were told that those who cannot comment "on the record" recommend that one should read David Sanger's book, *The Perfect Weapon* (Hall, 2020). Sanger said that many of the U.S. war plans open with "paralyzing cyberattacks on our adversaries." In lesser contingencies, such as replying to Russian cyberattacks, the U.S. could "unplug Russia from the world's financial system; reveal Putin's links to the oligarchs; make some of his own money—and there was plenty hidden around the world—disappear." However, the problem would be in dealing with Russia's responses - escalation.

Sanger said, "The irony is that the United States remains the world's stealthiest, most skillful cyberpower, as the Iranians discovered when their centrifuges spun out of control and the North Koreans suspected as their missiles fell out of the sky. But the gap is closing (Sanger, 2018b)."

General Paul Nakasone, Commander of the United States Cyber Command (USCYBERCOMMAND), testified before the Senate Committee on Armed Services on February 14, 2019. His statement discussed the environment and mission of his command. Part of his testimony concerned changes in strategic guidance and authorities, "USCYBERCOMMAND has recently improved the scope, speed, and effectiveness of its operations with the help of legal and policy changes. I want to thank Congress for its support of DoD's cyberspace operations as reflected in provisions of the FY19 National Defense Authorization Act (NDAA) that enhanced our agility to execute missions consistent with law. We also received updated policy guidance that, in conjunction with the NDAA provisions, significantly streamlined the interagency process for approval of cyber operations and thus facilitated recent activities (Nakasone, 2019)."

Patrick Tucker, Technology Editor for *Defense One*, in the Foreword of the November 2019 issue of *Cyber in the Era of Great Power Competition*, said, "The United States has long enjoyed supremacy in every warfare domain: on land, sea, air, and space. But the new domain of cyber is the one where the U.S. lead could erode the fastest. The barriers of entry are cheap and the rules for the use of new tools and weapons are few and difficult to enforce. Moreover, information technology now touches everything in modern life. So the digital battles of the future will play out in the robotic weapons and vehicles of the future as well as across the phones and internet-connected devices of individuals and businesses around the world. With very little cost, it's possible to have a huge and disturbing impact on a given nation's physical and economic security (Tucker, 2019a)."

Winning

"The thread that runs through all these strange internet skirmishes is that they take place simultaneously, in the same space. Sometimes, the conflict is between feuding celebrities; other times, nations embroiled in a life-and-death struggle. Sometimes, these battles dominate social media chatter completely; other times, they pass with nary a mention." "There aren't two or ten of these conflicts, but many thousands, all unfolding at once and leaving no one and nothing untouched. By merely giving them our attention, we become a part of them. Like cyberwar, these LikeWars are also about hacking. But they're not targeting computer networks—they're targeting human minds." "There's one more aspect that makes them different from conflicts of the past. Anyone can fight in them, but all the combatants are equally powerless in one key, new way. For while these warriors of LikeWar each fight their own personal and global wars across the internet, they aren't the ones writing its rules (Singer & Brooking, 2018)."

David Sanger listed some prescriptions, shown in Table 6.3 (Sanger, 2018b).

Packard's view on China's power trajectory (in the section on China above), is more sanguine than the views of other experts; however, he did not find the current U.S. approach to China to be effective. Table 6.4 repeats Packard's conclusions with regard to China. His paper includes more detailed recommendations, all with regard to China; however, all appear to be more broadly applicable.

The importance of *cognitive superiority*, including information and persuasion, in war is ascending. War itself is changing. At its heart, war is not about breaking things and people; it is about imposing the will of one group on another. The changes in the noosphere and technium are changing the relative utility of the means of war.

Table 6.3 Sanger's prescriptions for cyber security

We must acknowledge that "our cyber capabilities are no longer unique."
We need a "playbook for responding to attacks, and we need to demonstrate a willingness to use it."
We must "develop our abilities to attribute attacks and make calling out any adversary the standard response to cyber aggression."
We need "to rethink the wisdom of reflexive secrecy around our cyber capabilities."
We need to help the world to "move ahead with setting … norms of behavior even if governments are not yet ready."

Table 6.4 Packard's blueprint for global leadership

Our actions thus far have been strategically incoherent, episodic, overly militarized, and, for the most part, ineffective.
Fresh military approaches, particularly in the areas of cyber and operational concepts, are needed to restore the U.S. deterrence posture.
The United States must focus more attention on using economic, diplomatic, and informational means to shape the world system in accordance with its interests (Packard, 2020).

Why Do We Care—Now More than Ever Before?

Our national history warns us about the need for preparation. We have a limited history to draw from because of the brevity of experience with the digital world, its accelerating rate of change and new scale of time, and the preference for secrecy concerning adverse experiences with the digital world. In the past, we have repeatedly been unprepared when facing wars that threatened our survival and only after significant delays did we adapt to defend and defeat the enemy. The digital "attack" will be at the speed of the electron, enormously faster than the Blitzkrieg of World War II. Our fate may be determined in nanoseconds after a clandestine polythetic prologue. Warfare, how it is waged, by whom it is waged, and its time frame have changed. We are all "newbies" and with the accelerating frontier of knowledge we will continue to be newbies. Further, the barrier to entry and scaling is lower, especially in cyberwar, biological warfare and in cognitive conflict writ large. Increasingly cognitively enabled machines and the drop in the barrier between expert knowledge and end user has changed the paradigm.

Further, in a cognitive conflict, our "near peers" (those we consider worthy of concern) consist of more than just other countries. We know of non-state actors with near-peer capabilities in cyber war and there may be others of which we are ignorant. "*We're all part of the battle*." No matter who the initial protagonists are, once the conflict is open on the Internet, any attention paid to it—by anyone—becomes part of the conflict (Singer & Brooking, 2018). The changes and rate of change in conflict have never been so mixed, so complex, so great. Kinetic superiority is no longer a certain guarantor of security. Now with multiple weapons and layers hidden by method and their "local habitation and name," we must have cognitive superiority (Table 6.5).

Some Considerations

Some examples of persuasion efforts are relatively benign:

- That used-car salesman who wants to sell you that car.
- That politicians who wants you to vote for them.
- You want to get her to date you.

Table 6.5 Why the urgency

Warfare
How and by whom it is fought; the time frames have changed; and the change is accelerating
We have near peers
The matrix is more intertwined and ever more complex
Information is ascendant in power
In the past we have not been prepared
Axis of accelerated changes
The sum of human knowledge is increasing exponentially
The knowledge infrastructure is morphing
The frontier of science and technology is accelerating
More rapid increase in the transformative power of AI in the critical security domain
More rapid obsolescence of knowledge and skills
There are low barriers to entry, easy to scale size of effects, and potential problematic attribution in cognitive conflict, writ large, in cyberattacks and in bio-attacks
China's 2030 AI Manhattan Project-level goal and advantages (graduating ten times the number of computer science engineers versus the U.S., plus there are advantages in the size of big data sets to feed AI/ML) and a zero-sum world view
Aspects that are faster than Blitzkrieg
Persuasion
Even more effective with new forms and forces
Ubiquitous, continuous, targeted, orchestrated across scale
Humankind—new knowledge
Of our vulnerabilities
Of our potentials

Persuasion is more and more effective and powerful than ever and the surfaces for its implementation and cycle speed of new opportunities and vulnerabilities are increasing. We live within a matrix of connectivity, with a central axis of accelerating change in the noosphere (sum of knowledge known to man), in the technium (modern system of technology), and in the expanding understanding of man. We even see change in man himself through advanced augmentations. Each of these changes allow new potential opportunities for persuasion and coercion, even control.

Man is a complex adaptive system of and within other complex adaptive systems. The currency of these systems is information, but information has been weaponized. We have information conflict with its attendant ascendency of the importance of persuasion. Personal data has emerged as a new asset class (Hardjono, Shrier, & Pentland, 2016). According to a Harvard Business Review article, "Persuasion depends mostly on the audience (Chamorro-Premuzic, 2015)." The Panopticon, a vast array of information-gathering methods and metrics, armed with experimentation, fused with Artificial Intelligence (AI) and Machine Learning (AI/ML), human-curated conditional probabilities, and other augmented human analytics, allows would-be persuaders to know the audience. With research, surveillance and analysis, messages can be personalized (micro-targeted using new persuasion profiles) for the optimal density of learning moments (Aristotle's propitious moment—*kairos*) . Surveillance and rhetoric are informed by new advances in multiple disciplines such as AI, behavioral and social psychology, social signals, captology, dynamics, and cognitive and information sciences.

Persuasion forces are ubiquitous. Possibilities exist at levels of communication from word choice to metanarrative, all simultaneously and across time, space and scale. Persuasion operates at all levels of power: political, diplomatic, commercial, military, financial, educational, and personal. The low barrier of entry into persuasion battles means there are many players. With these changes come increased connectivity and complexity, resulting in lessened predictability. This necessitates more rapid iterations of persuasion forces and counterforces. Persuasion *science* has joined the *art* of persuasion, thereby increasing effectiveness.

Potentially Malignant

Some persuasion efforts are potentially malignant. When the civility and argumentative complexity of public discourse declines, then trust in democratic institutions decreases. "The more polarized (and uncivil) political environments get, the less citizens listen to the content the message and the more they follow partisan cues or simply drop out of participating." The new "science of deliberation" provides some mitigating counterforce (Dryzek, et al., 2019).

Facebook, Twitter, LinkedIn, Google, YouTube, Instagram, Snapchat and WhatsApp are among the dozens of platforms that influence directly, using persuasion science, by their default rules, and by what they crowd out. Defaults influence without visible persuasion or coercion. Social media is engineered to be addictive for massive engagement (Alter, 2018). In the book *Irresistible*, Alter sketched addictive technology's use of compelling goals that are just beyond reach, irresistible and unpredictable positive feedback, a sense of incremental progress and improvement, tasks that become slowly more difficult, unresolved tensions that demand resolution and strong social ties (Alter, 2018). "Through the technology embedded in almost every major tech platform and every web-based device, algorithms and the artificial intelligence that underlies them make a staggering number of everyday choices for us…[even] how we consume our news…and search (Hosnagar, 2019)."

We have worried that our devices provide surfaces for surveillance and opportunities for experimentation and persuasion. Voice activated devices must listen and process words to activate. The software control for activation is designed elsewhere. Smart TVs can be created with hidden cameras so that not just conversations, but also video images could be captured to read social signals and other data. We didn't realize that someone has just such a device, asking us to install a spying device in our own homes—and pay for the privilege of being spied upon. Figure 6.1 shows this device.

People with concerns about Facebook's past privacy actions must have had an impact. (See Roger McNamee's book, *Zucked* (McNamee, 2019).) The Facebook

Fig. 6.1 The Facebook Portal

Table 6.6 Facebook's Portal privacy

You can completely disable the camera and microphone with a single tap, or block the camera lens with the camera cover provided.
Facebook doesn't listen to, view or keep the contents of your Portal video calls. Your Portal conversations stay between you and the people you're calling.
For added security, Smart Camera uses AI technology that runs locally on Portal, not on Facebook servers. Portal's camera does not use facial recognition and does not identify who you are.
Like other voice-enabled devices, Portal only sends voice commands to Facebook servers after you say, "Hey Portal." You can delete Portal's voice history in your Facebook Activity Log.

page on Portal privacy (Facebook, 2019), retrieved in March of 2019, included the privacy declarations shown in Table 6.6.

This is fine until Facebook decides to change what it is actually doing, with or without telling the customers (perhaps embedding the change in little-viewed legalistic terms of use). Further, like all internet connected objects, if you don't set good passwords in all the right places, Portal can be hacked.

Malignant

Additionally, we are seeing increasing examples of distinctively malignant persuasion efforts (internationally and nationally).

"Social media platforms have been implicated as a key vector for the transmission of fake news (Grinberg, Joseph, Friedland, Swire-Thompson, & Lazer, 2019)." Audio fakeries exist (see Montreal-based company *Lyrebird*) and visual fakeries are nascent (see Chinese company iFlytek) (Fontaine & Frederick, 2019). Vision is man's dominant sense and we now live with "deepfakes," videos altered to make it appear that a person says or does something he or she never said or did. AI-generated fake news makes truth elusive. "A machine designed to create realistic fakes is a perfect weapon for purveyors of fake news (Giles, 2018)."

Psychological Operations (PSYOPS) now operates in our world of ever accelerating changes in the noosphere and the technium (Kelly, 2016). Understanding and inducing intergroup hostility and aggression is a current topic of study (Sapolsky, 2017)! AI and machine learning (ML) are changing man's cognitive and behavioral decision dynamics. This morphology of increased complexity and adaptive connectivity spans new communities of knowledge requiring more trans-disciplinary expertise and collective lifelong learning. This broader knowledge of those accelerating changes must be coupled with the tacit knowledge of the local complex adaptive systems, e.g. with understanding of the ecologic spheres of influence and conflict and battles for "competitive control (Kilcullen, 2013)."

Information and Cyber Superiority

Even as AI emerges, the intelligence is not in the machine. Intelligence resides in individuals and teams with tools. "Fundamentally there are two levels of information—the lower level is comprised of what we will define as either instructive or descriptive information and the higher level contains meaning or semantics. Computers work at the lower level. We work from above (Sapolsky, 2017)." Currently, humans using intelligence augmentation (IA) train AI systems prior to AI augmenting human intelligence—increased IA.

Given the accelerating changes in the noosphere, the technium, and therefore humans, adaptive changes in management, structure and talent will be necessary for information superiority. Some questions to be considered—are we operating to address the facts in Table 6.7?

In the domain of cybersecurity, extremely high classification levels prevail. This presents problems, as a comparison with the information security domain indicates (Table 6.8).

Certain characteristics of cyberweapons are significant (Table 6.9).

The country has to worry about more effective spying and manipulation by foreign actors. However, we also have to worry about more effective surveillance and manipulation by technology corporations, data brokers, attention merchants, and perfidious persuasive political entities.

Table 6.7 Facts about information superiority

Knowledge is power.
We must have superior information access at both an individual and a systems level.
Education excellence must be a national priority
We must be superior at using persuasion.
Malware implants may now make us vulnerable (the prepared battlefield).
With increasing complexity, there will be more competing ideals and new decisions regarding balancing these ideals, e.g., control versus operational freedom.
There is need for more agile, flexible and adaptable organizations.
More creativity, more passionate curiosity, more questioning of defaults, and more originality is necessary.
More multidisciplinary talent must be recruited, developed, empowered, and rewarded.
Continuous education for all is required.
More selective connectivity is necessary.
Management must structure narratives and the taxonomy of information for external relations, as well as for internal use.

Table 6.8 Classification—too much and too little

With too little security you end up dying;
With too much security you fail because you can't learn or create or act quickly enough; and
There must be sagacity in handling these competing ideals.

Table 6.9 Cyberweapon characteristics

They often become ineffective after first use (if we have sharing);
Their path through the Internet is unknown;
The time of effect can be uncertain;
Attribution of author/user can be problematic;
The scale (and sometimes the nature) of the effect is uncertain;
The collateral damage can vary from none to extensive and uncontrollable, and can include blowback; and
Understanding and interpreting escalation dynamics of offensive cyber operations are complex and critical (Lin & Zegart, 2018).

Threat Analysis

Samuelson discussed how wargaming and analysis can complement each other in investigating cybersecurity issues (Samuelson, 2018). (This discussion is also directly applicable to the larger cognition domain.) ***Wargaming*** is a process of considering attacks and defenses by pitting two humans or groups against each other.

Table 6.10 Sample threat analysis questions

What weapons are aimed at which targets?
Who is doing what?
How are they doing it?
How competent are they?
What are their motives and plans?
What (forces, capabilities, policies, etc.) is contained in the emergent near future?

The process is definitely not exhaustive in considering all possibilities; however, the competition often stimulates people to create novel solutions and imagine new problems. ***Analysis*** is also a process of considering attacks and defenses; however, it is structured to either be exhaustive or to sample the entire space of possibilities with a rational plan. Analysis uses predetermined algorithms to compute results. Together, they can discover more than either can separately. Samuelson concluded, "Wargaming may offer considerable potential to identify key issues and policy options in information security. Wargaming is better suited to illuminating decision-making than to assessing technical capabilities and possibilities. Engineering analysis, ideally including penetration testing, is more appropriate as the basis for risk assessments and adjudication (Samuelson, 2018)."

Threat analysis is needed to define the nature and potency of current and possible threats. (Note that while we have emphasized the information threats, such as cyber-attacks, in this book, the threat analysis must also include kinetic threats.) We must have "foresight, for insight, for action (Johansen, 2007)." Questions to be asked are shown in Table 6.10.

Table 6.11 illustrates the concept with broad target categories in the first column and broad threat categories in the first row. The contents of the cells indicate whether the column entry is threatened by the row entry (T = target), contains the actor doing the threatening (A = Actor), or provides support for the threat (S = Support). Human actors include individuals, corporations, non-nation-state actors, and nations. This table is a sketch of a real analysis. For example, it omits information on combinations and second or third order effects.

Defense analysis consists of ongoing, iterative enumeration of the targets and defenses, estimations of the defense quality, and other useful information. Questions to be asked are shown in Table 6.12.

We will assume that the target is the entire U.S. society and its components. That is, the target includes individuals, various groups, and corporations. We must consider collateral damage to social media by bots, reducing trust, engendering legal actions, causing costly monitoring and removal, etc.

Once each iteration of the threat and defense analyses is complete, an analysis of the shortfalls is required to determine what should be done to mitigate the problems. Table 6.13 lists possible areas of concern.

Table 6.11 Threat analysis

	Corruption	Malware	Surveillance	Persuasion	Control
Humans	T, A	A	T, A	T, A	T, A
Noosphere	T, S	T	T	S	T, S
Technium	A	T, A	T, A	A	T, A

Table 6.12 Sample defense analysis questions

What is to be defended?
What point defenses are available?
What area defenses are available?
What does each defend against?
How competent is each?
Who is responsible for each?
How competent are they?
What is the coordination plan?
What future forces will be available and when?

Table 6.13 Shortfall concerns

Technium Arena	Missing defenses Inadequate defenses Defenses against future weapons Counterattack situation First attack situation
Noosphere Arena	Known vulnerabilitiesSearch for unknown vulnerabilities Do we have superior information access, individually and as a system? Are we learning faster than the adversaries?
Human Arena	Individual vulnerabilities Human augmentation Corporate (private and public) vulnerabilities Corporate (private and public) info security organizations National information warfare organizations Coordination plans
Integration	Are things combined well?

The threats to our national security are manifold and growing. The Army Cyber Institute and Arizona State University sponsored a workshop, called Threatcasting Workshop West 2017, in May of 2017. In this workshop the participants forecast threats (threatcasting) "to create 22 futures regarding complex issues: the advancement of AI, the diminishing ability to conduct covert intelligence gathering, the growing complexity of code, the future division of work roles between humans and machines, and more (Vanatta, 2017)." The group thought about life in 10 years, taking a whole-of-society approach to envision what might happen and which organizations might take various actions in response to the changed situation. Their conclusions included the statement that "the future environment will be complex,

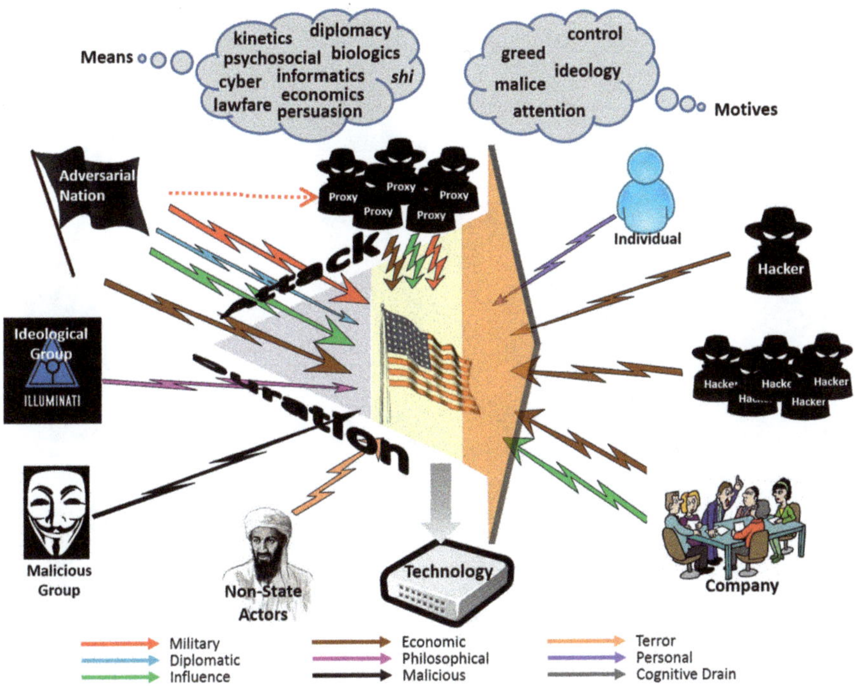

Fig. 6.2 The adversarial environment

and the threats and attack vectors will be diverse. Therefore, our solutions must also be diverse and interconnected."

Figure 6.2 recapitulates our overview of the adversarial environment. It shows multiple types of adversaries and attacks (counting the cognitive drain of our technological "servants" as an attack). For simplicity, the multiple targets are subsumed with a national symbol because all can have national effects. The means are varied, as are the motives. The attacks can be singular or mixed, overt or covert. The attack durations vary from nearly instantaneous to decades. The attacks may not be simultaneous when measured in a time-frame of hours; however, over periods of months to years, they can be characterized as simultaneous.

Chapter 7
Engagement

The conflict has already begun

"The United States is fully engaged in combat operations in the cyber realm, according to a panel of military officials at the AFCEA-USNI West conference in San Diego (Seffers 2019)." This panel in 2019 included flag officers of the Navy, Marine Corps, ecCoast Guard, and the Joint Staff.

The complexity of conflict spans a time range from milliseconds to "the 100 Year Marathon;" is occidental and oriental, personal and global; is waged by "ten thousand means" and memes, with no rules. The ecology of conflict now involves new emergent forms of cognition. The conflict is a complex adaptive system of complex adaptive systems, with accelerating changes.

> *This is not information warfare; it is warfare over the meaning of information.*—Ajit Maan (Maan 2018)

> *Every pixel on every screen of every internet app has been tuned for maximum persuasion.*—Roger McNamee (McNamee 2019)

Attention and trust have become commodities. Information, an asset category, has ascended in power.

"The internet has become the most consequential battlefield of the 21st century, the pre-eminent medium of global communication (Singer & Brooking 2018)." "Artificial intelligence is today's story—the story behind all other stories (Kelly 2016)." Technology is becoming persuasion's accelerant. Information has become weaponized. The Internet has reshaped war. "Diplomacy has become less private and policy-oriented, and more public and performative (Singer & Brooking 2018)." Half the world is on social media and the other half is rapidly following. This digital world "…is a place where wars are fought, elections won, and terror is promoted." An example of the scale and power of Internet recruitment is the "yellow jacket" protests in France following a political misstep. In one week, three hundred

D. S. Hartley III, K. O. Jobson, *Cognitive Superiority*,
https://doi.org/10.1007/978-3-030-60184-3_7

thousand people were mobilized over the Internet to set up barricades on the thoroughfares throughout France (Wall Street Journal 2019).

The Web is "deeply susceptible to fraud, rife with fake views, fake clicks, and fake eyeballs (Tufekci 2019)," fake identities (see the website https://thispersondoesnotexist.com (Wang 2019) and (Simonite 2019)), and now totally lifelike fake video and xR birthed through immersive computer generated imagery (CGI) (Rubin 2019).

As with any complex adaptive system, our defense and security systems must have a large number of subsystems supporting resilience and adaptation. These subsystems although coordinated upon need, must possess the autonomy to provide for adaptation, as opposed to relying on a few massive legacy platforms of such expanse that repeated change in the face of accelerating technology and cognitive paradigm changes is prevented. This model of many small autonomous expendables versus a large, tightly-coupled system is analogous to the severe acute respiratory syndrome coronavirus 2 (SAR-CoV-2), with its 15 genes attacking, in mass, a human with 30,000 genes, who is unprepared for the new adversary (Berwick 2020).

Kinetic warfare superiority is no longer a certain guarantor of freedom. (Note that while we have emphasized the information threats, such as cyberattacks, in this book, the threat analysis must also include kinetic threats.) Now we encounter multiple weapons and layers hidden by method and by "local habitation and name."

In this chapter, we look at parallel tracks. The first consists of the strategy of achieving cognitive superiority. The second consists of continuing actions to address the ongoing conflict. Figure 7.1 divides activities into quadrants by their consideration of use and quest for fundamental understanding. The upper right quadrant is labeled "Pasteur's Quadrant" because Pasteur's work involved a high level of searching for fundamental understanding, driven by a high consideration of utility. The strategy section of this chapter falls in this quadrant because it is directed at increasing our knowledge to solve real problems. The parallel section on addressing the ongoing conflict falls into the lower right quadrant, "Applied Research," as it is directed at using what we already know to address real problems.

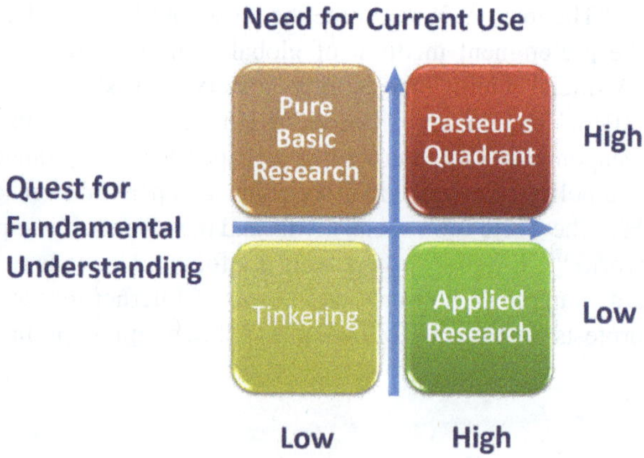

Fig. 7.1 Pasteur's quadrant

Strategy

Our thesis is that cognitive superiority is the key to the future.

Christian Brose, in *The Kill Chain*, argued that we need to focus on the kill chain, not platforms. He said that we need to redesign "the American military from a military built around small numbers of large, expensive, exquisite, heavily manned, and hard-to-replace platforms to a military built around large numbers of smaller, lower-cost, expendable, and highly autonomous machines. Put simply, is should be a military defined less by the strength and quantities of its platforms than by the efficacy, speed, flexibility, adaptability, and overall dynamism of its kill chains (Brose 2020b)." Sean McFate, in *The New Rules of War*, also argued against reliance on large, expensive platforms. He said. "we should invest in people rather than machines, since cunning triumphs over brute force, and since technology is no longer decisive on the battlefield. We also need a new breed of strategist—I call them war artists—to contend with the new forms of conflict (McFate 2019)." The solutions for winning in kinetic warfare, hybrid warfare and all new forms of conflict will require effective thought.

Accordingly, we need a strategy that will produce and maintain cognitive superiority. AI superiority is required and "A team" recruitment, including for military AI, is a central component of cognitive superiority. The following sub-sections will describe the general principles. The application of the principles will be described in Chap. 8.

Education

Education must be a national priority with public-private partnerships supporting lifelong learning using interoperable learning and networked, modern, pedagogy-driven technology. Liberal arts is needed as part of a foundation to teach critical thinking, analytical problem solving, and understanding of humanity to enlarge our horizons so that we are aware of a greater part of reality than is apparent in our daily lives. The second part of the foundational educational path is STEM. STEM support should include statistical literacy and advanced placement computer science courses in all U.S. high schools and later support for reskilling and upskilling for fundamental skills, craft, and theory. The curricula of our schools are important; however, the quality of the teachers is arguably more important. Assuring that teaching is a highly honored profession is a requirement for having good teachers.

An example of the U.S. military's concerns in the area of education is exhibited in a March 2020 article about the Navy's overhaul of its education system. The Navy education system includes the Naval War College, the Marine Corps University, the Naval Postgraduate School, and the Naval Academy. The Navy now wants to "create a naval community college to provide associate's degrees to tens of thousands of young sailors and Marines, at no cost." The Navy is doing this "because the nation no longer has a large economic and technological edge over potential adversaries." John Kroger, the Navy's first chief learning officer said, "'In a world where potential adversaries are peers economically and technologically, how do you win?' Kroger said, 'We think we can out-fight potential opponents because we can out-think them. In order to do that, we must have, by far, the best military education program in the world (Mcdermott 2020).'" This is embracing cognitive superiority.

Lifelong Learning

In their book, *The Future of Professions* (Susskind & Susskind 2017), the authors emphasized the importance of lifelong learning, upskilling, reskilling, and cross training as necessities in today's employment matrix. Most people will not spend their entire careers in one job, company or even industry. This is seen as a response to increasingly enabled machines and the drop in the barrier between expert knowledge and the end user. Further, knowledge is increasing exponentially.

Daniel Michaels quoted Alain Dehaze for the Wall Street Journal, "due to the acceleration of technology, people are losing around 40% of their skills every three years." Mr. Dehaze advocated for individuals having personal training/educational accounts, funded by the government, companies, or the individual, to provide for upskilling or reskilling as needed (Michaels 2020a).

Motivated learning is the center of adaptation. We should always be a student and always be a teacher, for in teaching we see our limits, expand our understanding and improve our emotional and social capital. Learning involves knowing, doing and teaching. Our goal should be to know "best in class" and exceed it.

Education, like catalysis, is a surface phenomenon. To wit, there should be lots of surface to advance learning: the surface between the student & teacher (providing the igniting power of personal contact with mutual concern and the site of tacit knowledge transfer) and the surface between what the student knows and what is just beyond. The next step is Steiner's approval of the material presented that was "aimed just above my head." The desiderata are fostering not only analytical intelligence, but also creative intelligence and practical intelligence, understanding that "cognitive capital is not just intellectual capital, but also emotional capital and social capital (Sahakian 2018)."

The culture of creativity and originality is central in today's age of accelerating change. "…on average, creative geniuses weren't qualitatively better in their field than their peers. They simply produced a greater volume of work, which gave them more variation and a higher chance of originality (Grant 2017)." But there is more to the influence diagram of creating "the originals": different experiences including cultural experiences, cooperative sharing across different domains of knowledge, developing multiple interests and avocations, such as the arts, writing, music, allowing questioning of defaults, asking "what if?" and "so what?" all contributing to "what now?" All are important to engendering originality. The experiential content should encompass values, communication, logic, quantitative skills, creative skills, and practical intelligence, utterly interwoven with learning how to learn.

For adults, including in security and defense, learning how to learn may be envisioned as having a model of how best to structure a personalized adaptive system of information feeds for explicit, implicit and tacit knowledge. What books, journals, MOOCS, MOOSECS, and other rich affordances, such as Ted Talks, adult education classes, reskilling and upskilling offerings, which mentors, which peers and groups will foster personalized adaptive learning and how to nurture and utilize this necessary enriching cornucopia are important questions. This should be augmented at a systems level with what we describe as an Eratosthenes Affiliation.

Teaching

Our educational systems should attract, affirm, support, and reward teachers who are talented, motivated and motivating—teachers that model the engaged joy of sharing lifelong learning. Teachers should understand Yeats's "Education is not the filling of a pail, but the lighting of a fire." Teaching talent must be given sufficient autonomy to find meaning in teaching and to develop a level of mastery (Pink 2009).

Levitin said, "One of the main purposes of training [more properly, educating] someone for a PhD, a law or medical degree, an MBA, or military leadership is to teach them to identify and think systematically about what they don't know, to turn unknown unknowns into known unknowns (Levitin 2016)." The deterioration of our education with respect to critical thinking has allowed lies to be easily weaponized (Levitin 2016). The ammunition consists of words, numbers, metaphors, pictures, statistics, and narratives.

The center of teaching must be personal contact with mutual concern. The ability to teach the material presented at each intermediate and higher level of advancement (grade) to those immediately below should be a requirement for promotion. Teaching not only demonstrates the teachers' knowledge, but also advances that knowledge with new questions and improves emotional and social capital, while modeling for the more junior students.

Learning

We have institutionalized education, but should not forget that we are also self-educating beings. For example, as part of our human learning process we internalize our notions of cause and effect by observation, not only through school courses. Beyond that, we learn by using logic. In ***deductive logic***, we begin with a general premise and conclude that it holds for a particular instance. In ***inductive logic***, we make observations and create rules, hypotheses and theories that incorporate and explain the observations. In ***abductive logic***, we gather evidence and create a model or conclusion that is the most probable explanation for the evidence. In "***seductive logic***," we are led astray by our own preconceptions, biases and fallacious arguments that lead us to a false conclusion (Schweitzer 2019).

Questioning is another method of learning. "Questioning is a powerful tool for unlocking value in companies: it spurs learning and the exchange of ideas; it fuels innovation and better performance; and it builds trust among team members. And it can mitigate business risk by uncovering unforeseen pitfalls and hazards." "[R] esearch suggests that people frequently have conversations to accomplish some combination of two major goals: information exchange (learning) and impression management (liking) (Brooks & John 2018)." We must always be able to ask ourselves, "could I/we be wrong?"

In learning how to learn (meta-learning), we must develop a prepared mind with the capacity to meet the unexpected; avoid a mad dash for order fueled by too urgent seductive reasoning; tolerate the unexpected disruption to our previous understanding; and with passion and sagacity, penetrate that disruption, that island of chaos; for it is in this discernment that we reach much of discovery and invention (Kotelnikov 2019).

Learning and Teaching Methodologies

Our pedagogy should drive the technology of learning, as opposed to picking the latest learning technologies. When learning technology is used, it should be personalized, adaptive, adjusting to the student's learning speed and style. Examples of creative, Internet delivered learning technology include CS50 at Harvard and MIT that is free through the Internet via the multi-university alliance, edX. CS50 has been taken by over 1,000,000 students worldwide. A second example is the Kahn Academy. Relevant sciences and technologies include learning science, modern pedagogy, and augmented (human hybrid), adaptive, collective, and immersive technologies.

Learning technology can be counterproductive. Adaptive education is not equivalent to personalized education. There is hard evidence that human mentoring and one-on-one personal contact with mutual concern is powerfully predictive in learning. One computer to one pupil is not the same (Wexler 2020). China's massive investments in AI driven, surveilled digital "intelligent education" "has impressive granularity and scale. It is adaptive but not fully personalized. It tends to focus on 'knowledge points' and 'knowledge maps' with apparent areas of impressive results. The concern is that it may not be imbuing creativity and motivation in the students for minds prepared to meet the unexpected (Hao 2020)."

Learning should be a "demanding festival." Demanding is a characteristic that shows up in the description of CS50 as it did in polymathic, polyglot Oxford University professor George Steiner's book, *Errata* (Steiner 1997). As Cicero said, "Practice. practice, practice (Cicero 2016)." Practice that is both deep and effective, informed by learning science (Grant 2017), error focused, and, when possible, focused on the maximum density of learning moments (times of need in challenge). Teaching should be held accountable with demonstrable results, e.g. Duke's Team LEAD (Learn, Engage, Apply, Develop) as described by Krishnan (Krishnan 2015), while avoiding "teaching for the test."

Institutional Education

Because the technium is changing, people are reconsidering educational structures and methods. For example, Beetham and Sharpe contended that pedagogy for the digital age must be supported from the top, valuing a learning environment, the learning sciences, lifelong learning, recruiting motivated talent with intellectual, emotional and social capital (Beetham & Sharpe 2013) . The system should utilize learning designs with sufficient social and physical support, optimizing new digital learning technologies. The power of the mentor-mentee relationship, especially for tacit knowledge transfer, continues to be central in traditional and newer forms. There is power in personal contact and mutual concern.

Post-doctoral students and faculty need education in new trans-domain fields and access to monitoring and use of ultra-expensive technology and methods only available in the private sector. A current example is the Rapid Online Analysis of Reactions (ROAR) training in automated chemical analysis described in *Chemical and Engineering News* (Peplow 2019).

Sean McFate decried the military practice of introducing strategic education too late. "Leaders must learn to think strategically as cadets, not as colonels. It's often too late by then. This is because tactics and strategy require two different kinds of thinking, and they are diametrically opposed. One is complicated while the other is complex (McFate 2019)." Complicated things can be decomposed and reassembled. Complex things are more than the sum of their parts.

A joint initiative between Harvard and MIT created edX to make faculties and courses available free over the Internet. The creation of new interactive, somewhat adaptive internet affordances such as Kahn Academy, Coursera and edX constitute "the single biggest revolution in education since the printing press (Rosen 2012)." See *Rethinking Pedagogy for the Digital Age* (Beetham & Sharpe 2013), *Rethinking Learning for a Digital Age*, (Sharpe, Beetham, & De Freitas 2010), and *The Cambridge Handbook of the Learning Sciences*, 2nd Edition, R. Keith Sawyer (Sawyer 2014).

Information (Knowledge) Access

Information is the currency of the twenty-first century. It is the new power. As Aspesi and Brand said in a *Science* article, "The struggle for control over information and knowledge looms large (Aspesi & Brand 2020)." Within the vast system of systems of the noosphere, there are links, barriers, brokers, filters, and tolls. Some sources are obvious and others more difficult to find, some with analytics and some without. The complexity and hierarchy of information access is enormous. According to Aspesi and Brand, knowledge infrastructure is rapidly consolidating, new portals are being created. New consortia of academic institutions, publishers, and scientific societies are forming to reify "information arbitrage" with "bundling of access and analytics (Aspesi & Brand 2020)."

This book emphasizes two exemplars of favored information access, Eratosthenes for systemic gathering information from the frontiers of science and technology and personalized adult adaptive learning systems (PAALS) for individual learning (in the section on Cognitive Enhancement in Chap. 8). Management excellence requires advantages in formative access for supply chains, regulatory and political ecologies, talent pools, etc. This topic will be amplified in Chap. 8.

Communications Recap

Table 7.1 captures the aspects of communications from the technium, the noosphere and humanity.

Organizational Principles

Our past U.S. history has been one of reaction. We urgently need a grand proactive response to the overall conflict. This will require a dedicated organization that can shape the situation to our advantage, not just respond to attacks. It will need to be able to address the current situation and detect changes requiring new activities. Some such organizations exist or are nascent. However, many of these suffer from problems (Burke 2018).

The Agile Organization

An organization that is dedicated to cognitive superiority requires agile structure, management, talent, and operations. "Agility" is a popular buzzword in the business community, with many definitions, prescriptions, and case studies of successes and failures.

Agility: Three defining dimensions of agility are "internal," "lateral" and "over." "Internal" agility refers to optimal entrusted operational freedom and originality. "Lateral" agility addresses the increasing need for talent (consultant microstates), discovery and emergence detection. "Over" agility refers to connecting to hierarchical authority and policy. The capacity to deal with accelerating change requires all three. An article in *Harvard Business Review* is relevant, "Agile at Scale: How to Create a truly flexible organization," (Rigby, Sutherland, & Noble 2018).

Table 7.1 Aspects of communications

The motif of the universe is connectivity, up and down the scale from quantum to sociology (Schweitzer 2019).
"The biggest single problem in communication is the illusion that it has taken place [George Bernard Shaw (Shaw 2018)]."
"The amazing thing is not that we often miscommunicate, but that, from time to time, we can communicate. We each have a different idiolect, different vocabulary and privacies of reference (Steiner 1997)."
Much of our communication is for affiliation, affirmation and confirmation of negative assessments of out-groups, as opposed to truth seeking (Ariely 2009). This is particularly important because the markers of social membership are fragile and stringent (Moffett 2018).
Listening is a neglected topic in communication. The late Howard Baker, Jr., former U.S. Senator, ambassador to Japan, official council to one U.S. president and unofficial council for multiple presidents, considered "elegant listening" and listening for "what they don't say" requisite communication skills (Baker 2011).
The complexity of communication is reflected in the large portion of the human brain allocated to communications, especially language (Boroditsky 2019).
Human communication is fused with sensing and computation. In our world of binary digits(bits), n represents information and 2^n represents the amount of information communicated (Shannon 1948a, 1948b). All signals are context dependent. Signal-to-noise ratio is a part of context. With the Niagara Falls of incoming information, it is hard to distinguish the salient or even the relevant from the noise (indigestion from apocalypse). Shannon's admonition that technical accuracy and semantic precision do not equate to effectiveness is significant.
Incoming information may update our current beliefs and preconceptions. It does not determine our beliefs (Bayesian Logic). Beyond signal-to-noise ratio, our individual preconceptions, our biases, even our preferences and fears may cloud our interpretation or cause us to ignore information we don't want to hear and to prioritize what we prefer. (See Irrationality and the Human Mind, in Chap. 4.) With our limited perception, we rarely respond to the full complexity of the message. Messenger assessment is essential (Martin & Marks 2019). Our assessment of the messenger can bias our interpretation of the message
Every aspect of man, the emergent bio-psycho-socio-techno-info being, participates in communication, including our predictable, systematic irrational aspects. Every hierarchical level of language can inform—from word choice, turn of phrase, metaphor, narrative, and metanarrative. The closest we have to universal language is seen in the dialectic of social signals, facial expressions, qualities of voice, arm and body movements (Pentland 2008, 2014). The manifold structure of our communications includes a dialectic of social signals, spoken language, written language, mathematical symbols, musical symbols, choreographic notation, the bits and bytes of our digital world, and the broader field of semiotics.
We are story-tellers. We communicate with stories, speech, ceremonies, and symbols. But stories are primal and video stories are rising in importance. Video has become central in communications and xR brings immersion and mixing of new communication technologies.
The categories of explicit, implicit and tacit knowledge are listed in increasing difficulty for communication. Expert or contextualized knowledge is known as tacit knowledge. It is the most difficult type of knowledge to transfer and generally requires personal one-on-one contact as in a mentor-mentee relationship. The mentee is in context, participating, observing the mentor and ingesting, how, why, when, not just the what.

(continued)

Table 7.1 (continued)

Translation, inherently problematic, should always be considered as a source of error or inexactness in meaning. "How is it at all possible to convey and decipher meaning, the most problematic of philosophic notions across time, across space, across the more or less yawning gap between vocabularies, grammars, networks of diachronic and synchronic systems of sense which separate languages, communities and civilizations? (Steiner 1997)" Bias in translation can come from the biases of human translators, including societal biases, as well as training set bias in AI-mediated translation or with AI-human curated systems. An example of authority designated word choice is found in "politically sensitive translation," as when the Chinese government insists on translation technology referring to the "China Sea" and the Koreans expect the same body of water to be translated as the "Eastern Sea."
Truth detection is also problematic. We have a tendency to "default to truth" (assume truthfulness), within limits and with many exceptions, even in our misinformation age of fake news, deepfakes, attention merchants, and perfidious bot armies and can have an illusion of transparency, believing that our interpersonal interactions and reading of social signals provide a valid understanding of character and honesty (Gladwell 2019). Truth detection is currently widely studied and now aided by training and technology. However, it continues to be imperfect and is still often accompanied by the illusion of knowledge.
Mercier, in *Not Born Yesterday*, tells us we judge whether or not a message has interests aligned with our interests and our preconceptions and expected and established ideas have an inertia. "Virtually all attempts at mass persuasion fail miserably." "Humans veer to the side of resistance to new ideas." Our species has a limited "open vigilance guarding against (some) harmful ideas" while being open enough to change our minds when presented with the right evidence. When confronting the established, we must deal with "great chains of trust and argumentation. Long established, carefully maintained trust" in the messengers with "clearly demonstrated expertise and sound arguments" are required (Mercier 2020). See also Berger's book, *The Catalyst: How to Change Anyone's Mind* (Berger 2020).
Our communication is evermore computerized. AI-writing is extant from spell-check and translation software, prediction texts, code completion, to Smart Compose GPT (generative pretrained transformers) which can "write prose as well as or better than most people can (Seabrook 2019)." The internet has brought manifold changes in languages. Internet communication 'is making our language change faster, in more interesting ways, than ever before (McCulloch 2019)." The internet as the backbone of the digital matrix, brings network diffusion dynamics to the fore. With new abbreviations, multiple genres from text, email, blogs, podcasts to emojis and keysmashes convey markers of social membership. The "always on" mobile, ubiquitous nature of this phenomenon exponentally increases communication volume, copying, accessing, sharing, filtering remixing, and questioning. In text-based communication like email and instant messaging, we are unable to convey as much meaning as we can express through vocal tones and cadence, facial expression and physical gestures—tools we normally take for granted (Johnson 2020). Brain-computer interfaces are in the laboratory. Current corporate and DOD nascent efforts to effect a direct brain/computer interface (BCI), the place where silicon and carbon meet, will revolutionize communication (Tullis 2019). A current corporate example of this is Elon Musk's Neuralink (Neuralink Corp 2018).
Group (network) communication, with scale, structure and dynamics, introduces additional complexity, beyond the already complex subject of person-to-person or dyadic communication. The dynamics of network communication are addressed under the heading of Network Science in Chap. 5, above.
"Too little communication, and there is no learning and no synergy. Too much communication, and all the minds end up in the same place, focusing on the same types of solutions (Bernstein, Shore, & Lazer 2019)."

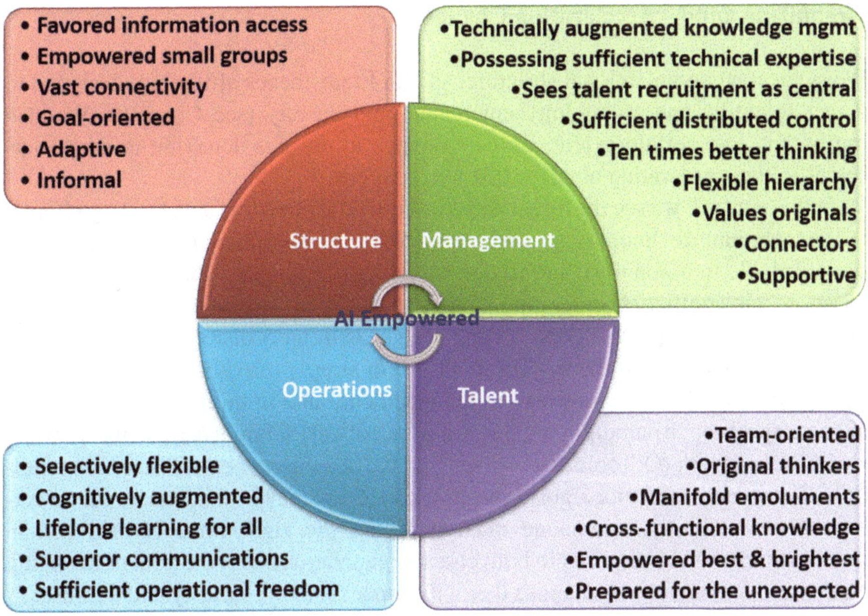

Fig. 7.2 Agile organization

Figure 7.2 represents a distillation of many sources, some concentrating on improving scale, others looking to improve quality. The structure of the organization must be informal (adaptive, yet connected) and goal-oriented. The management must be supportive, connecting the operations with hierarchical authority and policy with a minimum of control. Managers should be connectors who select and foster the creative, the originals, who may more often question defaults and expect more autonomy versus strict hierarchical control. Management must also ensure that people with the right talents are hired, retained and developed. The people (talent) must be bright and original thinkers, yet also team players. Although leaders may say they want inquisitive minds and "originals," in fact, they most often stifle curiosity, fearing risk, inefficiency, or loss of face (Gino 2018). The operations should be constructed so that the people are entrusted with the optimal operational freedom and freedom to be original. A fixated or slow bureaucracy will kill the capacity to deal with accelerating change.

Rigby, Sutherland and Noble wrote about the problems and techniques of moving from a few agile teams to a large, corporate-wide set of agile teams (Rigby et al. 2018). The talent should not just have expertise but also "enthusiasm for work on a collaborative team." Further, "Too little communication, and there is no learning and no synergy. Too much communication, and all the minds end up in the same place, focusing on the same types of solutions (Bernstein et al. 2019)."

Organizing amidst Accelerating Change

We suggest an organizational structure, and an Eratosthenes affiliation, designed to detect scientific and technology emergence and novelty (see Chap. 8). We also imply that, to a certain extent, we can manage to use this detection to adapt ourselves to the accelerating changes that will beset us.

In this context, we see the direct and consequential impact of accelerating **change** in the technium (technology as a whole system), the noosphere (the total information available to humanity), and in our knowledge of people, who are the ultimate target of this conflict. Accelerating change is likely to contain both good and bad elements. Even long-term "good" change can be extremely disruptive when it is too rapid or too massive for the system to absorb or simply too different from the current status quo. "Smart creatives" in management, able to think in first principles and manage through paradigmatic shifts, will be critical (Schmidt & Rosenberg 2017).

O'Toole's work (O'Toole 2015) discussed the detection of emergence using multiple, distributed computer algorithms; however, these may be inadequate for detecting novelties. Further, someone must be using the algorithms. Hybrid human organizations will be required in both cases, organizations with the goal of detecting emergence and novelties: changes that will impact society, security and defense.

The Army is setting up a Futures Command, which one might imagine as having a goal of combining with the sixth domain, including an Eratosthenes affordance. The National Cybersecurity FFRDC at MITRE might also have this goal. There has been considerable discussion about the value of agile organizations and what is meant by the term (Atkinson & Moffat 2005a) (Rigby et al. 2018). What are the required characteristics that an organization dedicated to the early detection of paradigmatic changes? Table 7.2 lists some of these characteristics.

Table 7.2 Organizational properties amidst accelerating change

The organization should possess superior knowledge management technology, have an organic structure, and an agile management team with superior intellectual, emotional, and social capital that is adept at dealing with diverse communities of knowledge.
It might have a steering committee of graybeards to oversee and comment on the work.
The organization should act as a hybrid intelligence of diverse human experts augmented with AI/ML and other cognitive artifacts.
The team should consist of motivated, empowered "smart creatives (Schmidt & Rosenberg 2017)" that are recruited and encouraged to recruit more talent.
The team should have knowledge of what systems are currently being utilized: there is no excuse for not knowing current "best in class" as a starting point with a goal of exceeding it.
The organization's network should have access to content experts and the traditional and newer sciences, such as AI/ML, quantum technologies, persuasion and motivation science, information science, network science, learning science, data science, molecular biology, and neuropsychosocial expertise.
The network structure will have to utilize a variety of affiliations from brief and limited connections to ongoing alliances.

Management: Redefining Leadership

"How you structure information is a source of power. It is one of the most important but least understood skills in business …humans split the world into arbitrary mental categories in order to tame the wild profusion of existing things" "when we flip these around we apprehend in one great leap … the exotic charm of another system of thought." A few astute bosses know how to remold taxonomies and bend the current perception. This classification brings power of perception and persuasion for multiple uses (Ryder 2018).

In an article in *MIT Sloan Management Review*, Groysberg and Gregg discussed the need for lifelong learning for leaders (Groysberg & Gregg 2020). Leaders "… need to constantly reinvent" themselves "every three to five years." "[L]eadership skills are depreciating at twice the rate of only a decade earlier." "They must continually expand their base of knowledge." "But knowing that you have to stay relevant is not the same as knowing how." In a separate article, Deborah Ancona advised leaders to spend time with start-ups, "where new creative ideas come from," polish communications and persuasion skills, recruit top talent, create meaning, form "X-teams to foster speed, innovation and execution," and be a connector for internal collaboration links to knowledge resources and innovation partners in the outside world (Ancona 2020)."

"The context of leadership has changed." The matrix of constant change requires the operation must be able to operate with "more interdependence". Less hierarchically static, less rigid organizational charts, leaders must give themselves extensively to the work "mixing confidence and humility, intensity and vision (Rigby et al. 2018)?" Table 7.3 lists some leadership characteristics.

Figure 7.3 illustrates the Menninger morale curve, which describes the typical progress of morale in the face of challenges. Management must be prepared for this and manage through it and have a realistic view of the environment for retention (Carter 2019).

Table 7.3 Leadership characteristics for an agile organization

The best managers are connectors (not just teaching managers, not "always on" managers, and not just cheerleader managers).
They optimize the balance of freedom and responsibility, "freedom within framework," resolve the tension between empowered employees and organizational discipline. They create mechanisms for questioning defaults and allowing dissent.
They understand that small multidisciplinary teams, "microstates," generally out-perform large hierarchy of control in solving new problems.
They ask more questions and know how to question and ask more follow-up questions. They know that questions are the "wellspring of innovation" and the tone and type of framing of questions are important. It is often a virtue to invite feedback.
They believe in talent uber alles—talent with passionate curiosity (Conaty & Charan 2010).
Management must understand how to help the smartest of people stay on an optimal course of learning and collaboration (Argyris 2019).

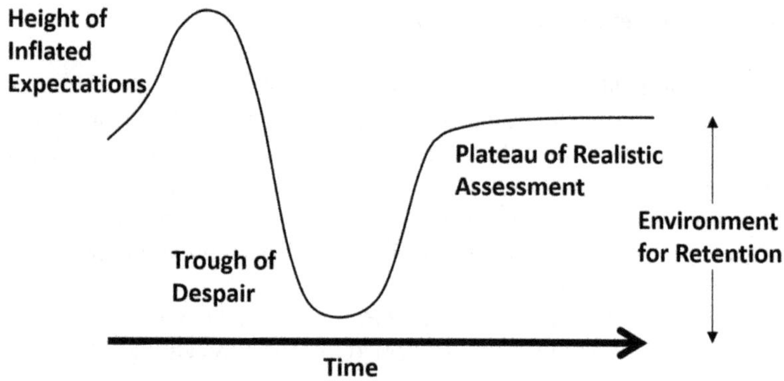

Fig. 7.3 Menninger morale curve

Talent Recruitment

Recruitment and maintaining A-team personnel is essential for success. Essential recruiting skills include talent identification and connecting to that talent. Recruitment will need to have affiliative abilities and a flexible structure. Experts in new domains are needed. Talent will reside both internal to the organization and external to it. The relationships will vary from joining the organization to consulting to giving secondary connections. The relationships may progress in a sequence of steps.

Capelli talked about the fact that talent has to be recruited: "the majority of people who took a new job last year weren't searching for one: someone came and got them (Capelli 2019)." Talent awareness and a recruitment, of consultants and internal employees, is both essential and more complex in today's connected, politically correct, competitive world with the financial opportunities of the silicon clusters and with the novelty of danger with near-peers' cyber abilities and goals. However, we should not wait until we have the perfect talent, but start with the best that is available, grow that talent (Coyle 2009), and evolve toward talent superiority. Table 7.4 lists some characteristics for creating an environment for successful talent recruitment.

Talented individuals can be disruptive. They have had evidence of their superior talents and may assume their opinions are always superior to those of others. There is value in this disruption, but also dangers to the organizational culture. Seeking "cultural fit" is a valid recruiting goal; however, beware that in seeking "cultural fit," that fit doesn't just mean "people like us."

Human cognitive capital is central to cognitive superiority. Considered at the level of "intelligence," cognitive capital can be measured as "g" general intelligence, as reported by IQ tests. This metric has some predictive value for academic and career success. Dr. Barbara Sahakian of Cambridge University cautioned that we must view cognitive capital as intellectual capital, emotional capital, and social capital (Sahakian 2018). More recently, Dr. Robert Sternberg of Cornell University has shown an increased predictable value for success in commerce and the military

Table 7.4 Environment for successful talent recruitment/management

The environment needs proper recruiters, managers, persuasion, messages, frames, images, and metanarratives to avoid having large groups of digital A-Team talent eschew contributing to advancement of needed AI for security and defense.
An environment must be one where learning for all is valued, continuous and supported and favored information access is available.
It must offer a new learning science with pedagogy for the digital age, including developing actual growth in two of the three types of intelligence, practical and creative intelligence.
It must contain a stable of proactive recruiters informed with and having the talent of persuasion, enabled and armed with the environment for the individual recruit. These recruiting teams should be internal and external
The environment must have a culture of creativity and originality, where default positions can be questioned, where people can learn to be original. Creativity and originality should not just come from outside but also fostered by the organization. "… although leaders might say they want inquisitive minds, in fact most stifle curiosity, fearing it will increase risk and inefficiency." Five ways to bolster curiosity are: (1) Hire for curiosity; (2) Model inquisitiveness; (3) Emphasize learning goals; (4) Let employees experiment, explore and broaden their interest; and (5) Have "why?" "what if?" and "How might we?" days (Gino 2018).

Table 7.5 Talent characteristics

The best and brightest (internal and consultant), including multidimensional "smart creatives," with technical skills and team skills (Schmidt & Rosenberg 2017).
Motivation, intrinsic and rewarded "as much as talent counts, motivation counts twice"
Grit: "perseverance and passion for long-term goals," a concept highlighted by the work of Angela Duckworth of the University of Pennsylvania (Robson 2019).
The understanding that much of our intelligence is not in individual brains but in the collective mind utilizing technical tools of thought (Sloman & Fernbach 2017).
Talent that can work in teams that invite feedback
Originals that question defaults, ask what if? And so what?

using tests that divide intelligence into analytical intelligence, creative intelligence and practical intelligence (Robson 2019). Table 7.5 lists some characteristics that will be required for talent superiority.

Recruitment should be empowered with persuasion for the digital age (there are manifested salient advances) and personal contact with mutual concern. The illumination of the salience of need and rightness of cause requires persuasion on all scales (public opinion, public relations, organizational and individual recruitments). This requires priority, an ensemble of talent and favored information access.

Excellent emoluments are also required to recruit the best and brightest talent (Table 7.6).

It is likely that more talents, especially for temporary and episodic consulting will be external to the organization, to wit, flexible agile recruitment offering a variety of types of relationships, will become even more important.

Smart groups require more than smart people. These groups must avoid mitigated speech, may employ flexible hierarchy and contain talent attuned to collective learning. Further, "smart" people don't stay smart in a vacuum. Individual cognitive

Table 7.6 Emoluments for recruiting and retaining talent

Emoluments for recruiting and retaining talent
Ranked, titled, recognized and rewarded
Sufficient financial rewards
The opportunity to work with top internal and external talent
Favored access to the frontier of science and technology (see the section on Eratosthenes Affiliation in Chap. 8)
Work that offers meaning, making a difference
Challenge with sufficient operational freedom
Lifelong learning and ambient intelligence with managers with the requisite engineering prowess for recruitment and optimization
Recruiters that are informed, empowered, making recruitment propitious and easy, and on occasion serving as mentors
Individualized combinations of emoluments often work best

optimization requires best-in-class lifelong education, favored information access, superior ongoing learning speed, invitations for feedback, and multi-level cognitive augmentation.

Addressing the Ongoing Enlarging Conflict

The first track of this chapter consisted of laying out a general strategy of achieving cognitive superiority. This section focuses on actions for addressing the enlarging arc of ongoing conflict.

The expanding complexity of the conflict requires sagacity and planning. Singer and Brooking said, "social media has created a new environment for conflict. It has transformed the speed, spread, and accessibility of information, changing the very nature of secrecy. Yet, while the truth is more widely available than ever before, it can be buried in a sea of 'likes' and lies (Singer & Brooking 2018)."

Past, Current and Proposed Organizations

We have divided these organizations into commercial, government, and hybrid organizations. It is worth noting that the government and hybrid organizations focus on cyber operations, some apparently omitting consideration of influence operations, while the commercial organizations slide into censorship when they address influence operations.

Existing Commercial Organizations

"Early in its corporate existence, AOL recognized two truths that every web company would eventually confront. The first was that the Internet was a teeming hive of scum and villainy. The second was that there was no way AOL could afford to hire enough employees to police it. Instead, AOL executives stumbled upon a novel solution. Instead of trying to police their sprawling digital commonwealth, why not enlist their most passionate users to do it for them (Singer & Brooking 2018)?" Legal action forced them to quit. Other companies have hired paid content moderators. There are two problems, first "it comes at the cost of resources that might otherwise be plowed into profit generators (Singer & Brooking 2018)." And the "second problem is scale (Singer & Brooking 2018)." There is just too much content. "Every minute, Facebook users post 500,000 new comments, 293,000 new statuses, and 450,000 new photos (Singer & Brooking 2018)." Other platforms have similar figures.

"At the end of 2016, Facebook, Microsoft, Twitter, and Google circled back to where online censorship had begun. Emulating the success of Content ID and PhotoDNA, which had curbed copyright violations and child porn respectively, the companies now applied the same automated technique to terrorist propaganda, jointly launching a database for 'violent terrorist imagery.' Just a few years before, they had insisted that such a system was impossible, that the definition of 'terrorism' was too subjective to ever be defined by a program (Singer & Brooking 2018)." Silicon Valley (and similar) companies "*must proactively consider the political, social, and moral ramifications of the services* (Singer & Brooking 2018)." Or should they?

Christopher Mims discussed the problems with social media organizations' addressing unacceptable posting on social media. The central problem is stated in the question, "Where is the line between maintaining quality of information and flat-out censorship?" Mims described some of the positions taken by social media with respect to removing malicious content and "shadow banning" unpopular political positions and individuals. He also said that there exists an official organization, the Global Internet Forum on Countering Terrorism, which is tasked with some of this responsibility. Another possibility is non-profit consortia that share information about cyber threats. Despite these possibilities, politics is an obstacle. Who decides what is unacceptable (Mims 2018)?

According to Shan Li, writing in The Wall Street Journal, the digital information platforms in China are using and selling censorship under the name of "content moderation." The software goes beyond screening out pornography, hate speech and violence, to screening political content. The analyses include both text and images. The article quoted Matt Perault, a former director of public policy at Facebook Inc. and now director of Duke University's Center on Science & Technology as saying, "The global norm is trending toward censorship over expression." "Many countries looking to import the tools and policy to govern their internet will pick China's off-the-shelf technology (Li 2020)."

Government Organizations

The US Government is concerned about cyber war and the Department of Defense (DoD) is a key player in this conflict. Within DoD, the Services (Army, Navy, Air Force, Marine Corps, and now Space Force) furnish the capabilities by recruiting, training and equipping the forces and then providing them to the Combatant Commands for use. A large portion of the non-kinetic capabilities are currently maintained within National Guard units. With the potential for "fast war," this may be a vulnerability.

This same philosophy is employed in the cyber and information domains. For example, ARCYBER, AFCYBER, MARFORCYBER, CG Cyber, and FLTCYBER are the Army, Air Force, Marine Corps, Coast Guard, and Navy cyber commands. Each of these commands has two roles: provide protection for its own Service's particular systems (for example, ship systems within the Navy); and provide capabilities to the Combatant Commands (Hall 2020). More information about the Army (Gallagher 2018), Navy (Department of the Navy 2018) (Seffers 2020), and Air Force (Air Forces Cyber 2018; Underwood 2019c) is available. Steven Stover provided some relevant information about the National Guard's contributions to cyber activities in Task Force Echo (Stover 2019).

There is concern about the implementation of these organizations in the area of personnel: can they be staffed with personnel with the right talents and training (Corrigan 2019)? In his testimony to Congress, General Paul Nakasone, Commander of the United States Cyber Command (USCYBERCOMMAND), addressed this topic, saying, "To help sustain an advanced cyber force, all of the Services are applying hiring and retention incentives (especially for high-demand, low density skill sets) as well as utilizing the flexibility in managing talent that Congress recently granted us by authorizing the new Cyber Excepted Service. The retention of top talent—particularly in some critical, high-skill jobs—is a significant concern because it will be crucial to our continued success. We track attrition closely, as the competition with the private sector and other government agencies for talent will be an enduring challenge. An important element of building certain low-density skill sets, moreover, is outreach to and utilization of our Reserve Component (Nakasone 2019)."

Each of the Service organizations is organized differently; however, a deeper look at ARCYBER (as of April 2019) provides a useful example. This organization had about 16,500 soldiers, civilian employees and contractors for global operations 24 h a day, seven days a week (U.S. Army Cyber Command 2019). The command includes offensive operations at Fort Meade under the 780th Military Intelligence Brigade (Cyber) (U.S. Army Cyber Command 2020), defensive operations at Fort Gordon by the Cyber Protection Brigade, and other operations at Fort Belvoir and Fort Huachuca.

In addition to the Service commands, there are organizations within DoD, such as USCYBERCOMMAND (Wikipedia 2018g), dedicated to the problem. There are also external organizations that provide support, such as the National Cybersecurity Federally Funded Research and Development Center (FFRDC) at MITRE and the Military Operations Research Society (MORS).

In October of 2018, MORS held a Cyber Wargaming Workshop (Timian 2018). The organization of the workshop illustrates some of the approaches to the conflict.

- Working Group 1 provided an introduction to wargaming and its theory. It covered how to research and design wargames, how to design an analytic framework, and how to present the results. The focus was on education.
- Working Group 2 discussed more advanced techniques, such as red teaming. The focus was also on education.
- Working Group 3 focused on cyberspace and information operations and wargaming techniques. Again, the focus was on education.
- Working Group 4 focused on cyberspace operations analytics. It discussed current measures, metrics and data structures and the development of new metrics, operational and system level taxonomies, effects categorization, and support tools. The focus was on education and development of new concepts.
- Working Group 5 focused on cyberspace operations modeling and simulation. Like Working Group 4, there was a dual focus on education and developing new concepts.

Samuel Visner presented a vision of cybersecurity at a MORS conference in December 2018 (Visner 2018). The mission of the National Cybersecurity FFRDC at MITRE is to "Accelerate adoption of secure technologies: collaborate with innovators to provide real-world, standards-based cybersecurity capabilities that address business needs." What they do is

> "Develop, publish, and reach out to stakeholder and adopters cybersecurity architectures—comprised of commercial cybersecurity technologies—that can be applied to the 'verticals' comprising the United States private sector and critical infrastructures …

- Drive innovation
- Support standards

> … in support of US economic competitiveness and security."

The engagement and business model of the National Cybersecurity FFRDC consists of four steps, shown in Table 7.7.

The constraints they place on the results are shown in Table 7.8.

The Transportation Security Administration (TSA) has recognized the needs to address cybersecurity for its systems and users. Accordingly, it is developing procedures and implementing them (Transportation Security Administration 2018). It is likely that this will be a typical bureaucratic stove-piped effort.

Table 7.7 Visner's cybersecurity engagement and business model

1. Define a scope of work with industry to solve a pressing cybersecurity challenge;
2. Assemble teams of industry organizations, government agencies, and academic institutions to address all aspects of the cybersecurity challenge;
3. Build a practical, usable, repeatable implementation to address the cybersecurity challenge; and
4. Advocate adoption of the example implantation using the practice guide.

Table 7.8 Visner's cybersecurity results constraints

Standards-based: Apply relevant local, national and international standards to each security implementation and account for each sector's individual needs; demonstrate reference designs for new standards.
Modular: Develop reference designs with individual components that can be easily substituted with alternates that offer equivalent input-output specifications.
Repeatable: Enable anyone to recreate the NCCoE [National Cybersecurity Center of Excellence] builds and achieve the same results by providing a complete practice guide including a reference design, bill of materials, configuration files, relevant code, diagrams, tutorials and instructions.
Commercially available: Work with the technology community to identify commercially available products that can be brought together in reference designs to address the challenges identified by industry.
Usable: Design usable blueprints that end users can easily and cost-effectively adopt and integrate into their businesses without disrupting day-to-day operations.
Open and transparent: Use open and transparent processes to complete work, and seek and incorporate public comments on NCCoE documentation, artifacts and results.

Fort Polk, Louisiana, has a laboratory for training for information warfare, the Social Media Environment and Internet Replication (SMEIR). It is an internet of fake digital activity on top of fake real activity that acts as a simulation of potential conflict that combines the digital world with the real world. This organization actively embraces the weaponization of social media, its effects and its potentialities (Singer & Brooking 2018).

Singer and Brooking reported responses by other countries. Finland, Estonia, Latvia, Lithuania, and Sweden have moved to "the creation of 'whole-of-nation' efforts intended to inoculate their societies against information threats (Singer & Brooking 2018)." "Their inoculation efforts include citizen education programs, public tracking and notices of foreign disinformation campaigns, election protections and force transparency of political campaign activities, and legal action to limit the effect of poisonous super-spreaders (Singer & Brooking 2018)."

Government/Civil Hybrid Organization

After the 1988 malware attacks, the U.S. federal government created the Computer Emergency Response Team (CERT) at Carnegie Mellon University, operating under the direction of DARPA. "CERT was established to promote the security of the United States' rapidly growing national digital network. That was admirable. Unfortunately, CERT also established a model of a reactive rather than a preemptive approach to computer and network security (Rothrock 2018)."

According to Singer and Brooking, Russia's approach to the conflict has been unified and massive. "A conglomerate of nearly seventy-five education and research institutions was devoted to the study and weaponization of information, coordinated by the Federal Security Service, the successor to the KGB. It was a radical new way to think about conflict …, premised on defanging adversaries abroad before they are able to threaten Russia at home. Ben Nimmo, who has studied this issue for NATO and the Atlantic Council, has described the resultant strategy as the '4 Ds: dismiss the critic, distort the facts, distract from the main issue, and dismay the audience (Singer & Brooking 2018).'"

Cohen and Singer called for the formation of a Civilian Cybersecurity Corps (CCC) (Cohen & Singer 2018). They proposed an analog to the Civil Air Patrol and the Coast Guard Auxiliary that were formed in World War II. The CCC would function as an auxiliary to the Department of Homeland Security, with national scale and coordination and local subunits in each state. Cohen and Singer envisioned three roles: education and outreach; testing, assessments, and exercises; and on-call expertise and emergency response.

General Nakasone, in his testimony to Congress, addressed the U.S. approach, "Securing the nation in cyberspace requires whole-of-nation efforts and effective collaboration with allies. It is a priority for USCYBERCOMMAND to expand its ability to collaborate effectively with other government agencies, the private sector, academia, and allies. We must do this because they directly and indirectly complement and enhance our warfighting capabilities; indeed, enabling our partners is a key element of persistent engagement. We are working with a range of partners who support, enable, and assist our operations (Nakasone 2019)."

Action Portfolio

The shift to cognitive conflict and the understanding of the need for cognitive superiority is not easy. Cyber defensive and offensive actions are the easiest to prescribe because they are the most nearly concrete actions in this conflict. However, cyber actions are not the only possible actions and may not be the most important. Kimberly Underwood described a shift in emphasis from cyber to information in the Army's multidomain operations (Underwood 2019b). In fact, Underwood also reported that the Army Cyber Command (ARCYBER) will probably change its name to something like the Army Information Warfare Operations Command (Underwood 2019a). Lt. Gen. Stephen Fogarty recommended doing the same for the U.S. Cyber Command (Seffers 2018).

Addressing Technology Demands

AI superiority is essential. Technology is becoming equal to biology and culture in demanding our time and attention. Our technological "servants" demand that we serve them: reset the clocks when the power goes out; update our phone and computer apps; deal with both unwanted and useful e-mail in great quantities; and learn how to operate ever-changing technology. Further, persuasion in the technium has a massively complex, rapidly expanding ecology. We face search default control, social media tyranny, suggestion engines, and, in China, legally-required, aggregating, surveilled apps. Now we meet the 600 pound gorilla of hybrid AI/ML, utilizing big data analytics from our surveilled world, armed with experimentation, to orchestrate multiordinal persuasion, coercion and collective control.

Addressing Influence Attacks

Persuasion attempts can come through any of our means of communication and address multiple facets of man. We need foresight to orchestrate the metanarratives of influence within the cyber domain and beyond. This requires minds prepared to meet the unexpected and knowledge of the game and its players. The surveilled world and superior analytics provide the incoming feed. "Combining well" from grand strategy to individual action is required. In the continuum of persuasion, coercion and control, the Persuasion Fundamentals (see Chap. 4), as well as the section in the Appendix on persuasion sources should be mastered. The work of Cialdini offers an example of this content.

The psychologist, Robert Cialdini, in *Influence Science and Practice*, discussed six methods of persuasion: reciprocation, commitment and consistency, social proof, liking, authority and scarcity (Cialdini 2009). He discussed why each one works and what the defenses are. The bracketed comments remind of the definition of the persuasion method (Table 7.9).

Lazer, et al, identified two defenses against fake news: empowering individuals to detect fake news and preventing exposure to fake news. They described various fact-checking efforts as elegant, but having only mixed scientifically established efficacy. In some cases, fact-checking appears to be counterproductive by reinforcing the memory of the false information. They described educating individuals on improving their evaluation of the quality of information sources as a second approach. However, this could reduce the perceived credibility of all news sources. Because fake news largely originates on the Internet (the authors do not mention "tabloid journalism"),

Table 7.9 Cialdini's defenses against persuasion

Reciprocation [very commonly seen in requests for donations that include a "gift"] *The primary defense involves rejecting our feeling of obligation.*
Commitment and consistency [using our desire for consistency to persuade us] *The defense is to realize that there is such a thing as a foolish commitment.*
Social proof [our desire to agree with what others think] *Cialdini advises using disruption, such as sending letters to the perpetrators of deliberate rigging of social evidence. In cases of bad social evidence "going viral," he advises researching the claim.*
Liking [our desire to accommodate someone we like] *The defense is to become aware of unwarranted liking and concentrate on the proposed deal.*
Authority [our desire to defer someone who is in a position of authority] *The defense is to be aware of the power of this desire and be prepared to resist, if necessary.*
Scarcity [the economic principle of an inverse relationship between availability and value] Cialdini says that this works on us viscerally, bypassing our cognition. *He suggests using this arousal as a cue that something is wrong as a defense.*

there may be some methods for reducing its dissemination. Automated social media accounts that impersonate humans—bots—provide one method of multiplying the number of messages spreading the fake news content. These automated methods provide clues to their identity, which could be used to reduce their effectiveness. However, attempts to do this will lead to evolving strategies in automation (Lazer et al. 2018). An audience armed with critical thinking is the best defense.

Abigail Summerville wrote in The Wall Street Journal about approaches to battle manipulated photos and videos (deepfakes) (Summerville 2019). She reported that Jeffrey McGregor of Truepic said, "While synthetically generated videos are still easily detectable by most humans, that window is closing rapidly. I'd predict we see visually undetectable deepfakes in less than 12 months." Truepic is working to create hardware for mobile phones to "automatically mark photos and videos when they are taken with data such as time and location, so that they can be verified later. Truepic also offers a free app consumers can use to take verified pictures on their smartphones." Summerville also reported that the Defense Department "is researching forensic technology that can be used to detect whether a photo or video was manipulated after it was made."

"Newer, more advanced forms of deep learning involve the use of 'generative adversarial networks [GAN] .' In this type of system, two neural networks are paired off against each other in a potentially endless sparring match. The first network strains to create something that seems real—and image, a video, a human conversation—while the second network struggles to determine if it's fake. At the end of each match, the networks receive their results and adjust to get just a little bit better. Although this process teaches networks to produce increasingly accurate forgeries, it also leaves open the potential for networks to get better and better at detecting fakes (Singer & Brooking 2018)."

Christopher Mims reported in The Wall Street Journal about attempts to detect the accounts of malicious actors on social media. Some of these attempts use content or language filters to identify terrorists and their disinformation campaigns; however, these have been proved subject to being confused. A graduate student, Hamidreza Alvari, at Arizona State University has produced an algorithm that "looks for accounts that spread content further and faster than expected." However, "Humans still need to make the final determination to avoid false positives." Mims also reported, "Many tools exist that could help identify bad actors on the Internet. There's just no consensus on how to use them (Mims 2018)."

Addressing Narrative Warfare

"We need an influence containment strategy." "[Narrative warfare] is not information warfare; this is warfare over the *meaning* of the information (Maan 2018)." According to Maan, counter-narratives—messages that essentially start out, "X is false," are not just ineffective, but actually reinforce message X. The optimal approach if the narrative requires response is to destabilize the narrative. To destabilize a narrative Maan asked the questions in Table 7.10.

Table 7.10 Maan's advice for destabilizing a narrative

1. What assumptions do portrayals of the situation rest upon? Can those assumptions be challenged? Can the enemy's story be encompassed in a new metanarrative?
2. How does it encourage the audience to mis-identify themselves? What techniques? What are the identity triggers?
3. How does it impart meaning to events? How does it express causality? The example of implication we just discussed is the causality implied by sequential ordering. I [Maan] have referred to these sorts of implications as moral contraband. They are snuck in and often go unperceived and unchallenged (Maan 2018).

Table 7.11 Maan's narrative hierarchy

1. A *Metanarrative* influences how the international community regards a situation—one that encourages a perspective that is consistent with coalition interests.
2. A *Strategic* (Master) narrative describes what we are doing, why we are doing it, how it will help the situation, and how the target audience—national/international community should respond and how they will benefit from such a response.
3. *Operational* narratives connect and synchronize the micro and macro narratives in action.
4. *Tactical* (personal/micro) level narratives address the concerns of local populations, domestic audiences, and soldiers on the ground.

"Challenge the implications of the descriptions. What information has been deleted? If you add in the deleted information, can you disrupt the causal implication of the narrative? (Maan 2018)"

However, the preferred approach is one of building a proper initial narrative and let the enemy try to counter it. She said, "Our narrative needs to reach from bottom up—micro to macro." (The narrative hierarchy in Table 7.11 is listed from top to bottom.)

She gave one example of a counter-narrative:

> "*The brutality of ISIS and their violence against civilians demonstrate the moral depravity of their leaders who recruit and exploit vulnerable people to use as pawns. We recognize that we played a part in Iraq that allowed ISIS to develop. It is therefor* [sic] *the moral responsibility of the United States and an international coalition to intervene and stop the spread of ISIS militarily and to offer humanitarian and development assistance to those affected. There is a better alternative to the miserable future ISIS envisions for the territories it seeks to dominate. The people of this region, regardless of religion or ethnicity, deserve stability and security*. (Maan 2018)"

Passive Cyber Defense

Our innovation and connectivity have outpaced security. We would like to lock down our cyber systems, filtering out implants and malware, hardening vulnerabilities in electrical grids and infrastructure and communication from ocean to space. We would also like to establish a preventive cost of cyber intrusions. However, we must balance our inmost and enduring desire for peace with the knowledge of the advantage of first strike in cyber conflict and the unavoidable risk inherent in escalation of the conflict.

Government organizations, corporations and individuals can protect themselves from some attacks through the Internet. Generally, there have been two levels of protection; software (firewalls) and hardware (routers) as the first layer of defense and software (anti-virus software) as the second layer, providing some resilience. More recent thinking has increased the number of levels. For example, institutions with their own networks (or networks of networks) now must consider network protection. Additionally, there is the problem of zero-trust networks (the assumption that all networks, including internal networks, cannot be trusted). However, most penetrations in well-protected systems occur because people open the doors (e.g., respond to phishing emails). This corresponds to raising the visor in Fig. 7.4.

Table 7.12 describes a number of cyber defense activities.

Active Cyber Defense

An editorial in the Wall Street Journal by Brian Finch described a method used by French cybersecurity personnel to foil Russian hackers. The French created dummy accounts with faked documents. The Russian hackers accessed the accounts and stole the documents and released them, hoping to embarrass the French. However, the French then exposed these as spurious documents, invalidating the Russian attempt. Not only did this foil the immediate attack, but it also reduced the effectiveness of future exploits by obligating hackers to validate stolen materials before using them, imposing time costs on their attempts. These time costs reduce the productivity of hackers and increase their dwell time in the system, increasing the likelihood of detection (Finch 2019). The editorial called this method "cyber blurring." It is also part of what is known as a "honey pot trap." A honey pot trap can be as simple as a dummy account or as complex as specifically created server systems, which are separated from the actual systems.

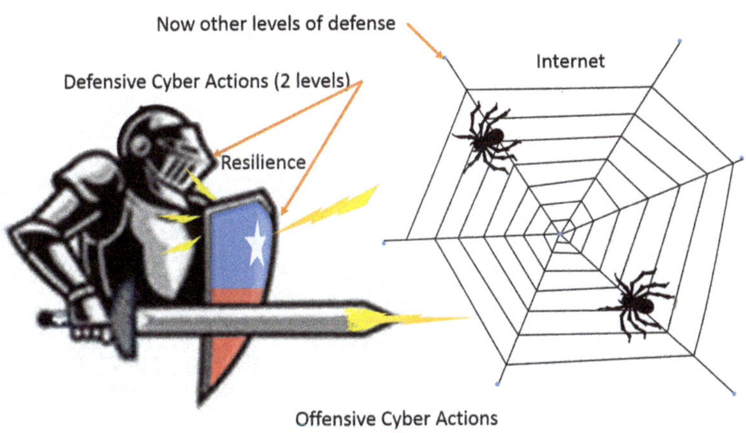

Fig. 7.4 Cyber defense and offense

Table 7.12 Cyber defense activities

Cyber defense activities
Anchoring and adaptive defense/cyber resilience: The waning advantages of cyber-offense over cyber-defense is being brought about by the development of concepts and strategies that mirror adaption in biologic CASs. We hear of various forms of immunity (intrinsic, event induced, and herd immunity), collective learning, sharing knowledge and counter-measures, and swarms of cognified agents using distributed execution.
Build zero-trust architecture: segment the network according to type of access and categories of information carried; enhance identity and access management; implement least privilege at the firewall; add application context to the firewall (content rules); and log and analyze security events (Trinos 2019).
Constantly changing the attack surfaces and modifying the structure
Using red team testing
Threat hunting inside the organization
"Continuous behavior-based authentication"
Teaching the team cyber-hygiene
Rapid detection, containment and analysis
Looking for and fixing software and employee vulnerabilities
Reciprocal information sharing, including
attack profiles—sharing knowledge of past and ongoing attacks with partners in defense (Falco et al. 2019)
vulnerability reporting—defining procedures for accepting the information on vulnerabilities from an organization with a problem
Finding, fixing and finishing adversaries within the network
Understanding the larger "cyber-defense matrix (Rothrock 2018)."

Note: In all of the above it will be essential to selectively share the tacit knowledge not just the explicit and implicit knowledge

Drew Hinshaw and Valentina Pop described how difficult it is to identify and convict cyber criminals. Two hackers took control of Washington DC's street cameras eight days before Donald Trump's inauguration in 2017. The US Secret Service was in charge and took the matter seriously. Yet, it still took the efforts of the Secret Service, the Federal Bureau of Investigation, and Dutch, British and Europol investigators to identify, arrest and convict the culprits. It also took more than a year and a half to do it (Hinshaw & Pop 2019).

Cyber Offense

"Offensive security is a proactive and adversarial approach to protecting computer systems, networks and individuals from attacks (Rouse 2012)." The three components are annoyance, attribution and attack. "The annoyance component consists of frustrating the attacker's attempt through tools that establish false ports, services and directories. Once the attacker is lured into the false system, he ends up looping endlessly through it." The attribution component is comprised of software that identifies the system that attempts the access. The attack component consists of extensions of the annoyance and attribution components. Malicious assaults on the attacker are currently illegal in the U.S.

However, the U.S. government may have special rules permitting various offensive actions under some circumstances (Volz 2018). Ellen Nakashima reported that the U.S. Cyber Command might expose the personal information of senior Russian officials and oligarchs if Russia tries to interfere in U.S. elections (Nakashima 2019).

According to Sean McFate, "there are even mercenaries in cyberspace, called 'hack back' companies. These computer companies attack hackers, or 'hack back,' those who assail their client's networks. Hack back companies cannot undo the damage of a network breach, but that's not the point. They serve as a deterrent. … Also known as active defense, this practice is currently illegal in many countries, including the United States, but some are questioning this wisdom, since the National Security Agency offers scant protection for nongovernment entities (McFate 2019)."

Government organizations also have offensive capabilities that may be used to attack the systems that are attempting a penetration, including selected cyber-counterattacks and hybrid physical/cyber counterattacks. Offensive cyber operations and understanding "escalation dynamics" are becoming "increasingly prominent in US policy and international security more broadly (Lin & Zegart 2018)." See Herman Kahn's classic *On Escalation: Metaphors and Scenarios* for a thorough treatment of escalation (Kahn 2012). Cyber resilience is also being recognized more broadly as a requirement (Rothrock 2018).

The U.S. Army has created an organization to engage in the cyber war that is ongoing. Matt Gallagher's article on the Cyber Battalion at Fort Gordon described a part of this organization (Gallagher 2018). Soldiers are selected by aptitude and engage in offensive and defensive operations. The Fort Polk laboratory for training for information warfare, the Social Media Environment and Internet Replication (SMEIR) is a training center for the conflicts seething on the internet. It acts as a simulation of potential conflict that combines the digital world with the real world. From this training may come the warriors who will engage in the real thing (Singer & Brooking 2018).

In an opinion piece in The Wall Street Journal, Dave Weinstein stated that the rules governing the use of cyberweapons have been relaxed (Weinstein 2018). He then described some of the considerations regarding their use. On the one hand the threat of their use has a deterrent effect on opponents. On the other hand, their use could endanger ongoing intelligence collection operations and may lessen the credibility of diplomats calling for a free and open Internet. Weinstein outlined three practical problems with cyber-weapons (after attribution of the opponent). First, they may not be as precise as planned: a 2017 Russian cyberattack metastasized and spread far beyond its original target. Second, cyberweapons can be captured, reverse-engineered, and used against the originator. Third, their use may expose the originator's defensive vulnerabilities.

Weinstein advised that the use of cyberweapons not be restricted to cyber war and that the use of conventional weapons should not be restricted to conventional war. Whatever the nature of an attack, The U.S. should respond with cyber or conventional weapons as it deems appropriate. Weinstein also advised that two scenarios, one offensive and one defensive, are appropriate for cyberweapons.

"Cyber-weapons are an effective first-strike capability when conventional conflict is imminent or has already commenced." On the defensive side, "The U.S. should not hesitate to disable infrastructure that is facilitating the digital invasion of our sovereignty." He closed with a defense of the threat to use cyberweapons (Weinstein 2018).

Cyber Deterrence

"To deter, we must detect (Visner 2018)." The questions that must be answered are shown in Table 7.13.

COL Andrew Hall, Director of the Army Cyber Institute at West Point, said that some of our offensive efforts are purposefully described in the open literature specifically to support deterrence (Hall 2020).

Resilience

Resilience is "the capacity of a system, enterprise, or a person to maintain its core purpose and integrity in the face of dramatically changed circumstances (Rothrock 2018)." Cyber resilience is benefiting from lessons imported from our understanding of physiologic, psychologic and social (community) resilience (Southwick & Charney 2018; Zolli & Healy 2012). These three disciplines reveal the adaptive advantages of supportive connectivity, collective learning, expecting and embracing change, flexibility, and at times disconnected redundancy.

The point of cyber resilience rests on the realization that successful cyberattacks are inevitable and measures must be taken to avoid a resultant catastrophe. These measures include mundane personal, technical, and procedural actions. A mundane example is maintaining paper records. A personal measure is training to avoid phishing email attacks. A technical example is off-site electronic backups. A procedural example is the use of the Parkerian hexad to evaluate risk reduction opportunities. This procedure uses "six elements of information security: confidentiality, possession or control, integrity, authenticity, availability, and utility (Falco et al. 2019)."

Cyberattacks are illegal—crimes; however, Rothrock said, "Business leaders, however, may be better served by thinking of the attackers as especially ruthless and unethical competitors. Mounting and maintaining an aggressive defense against

Table 7.13 Visner's cyber detection and deterrence

What are the effects of cyberweapons on our national security and critical civilian infrastructures?
What are the characteristics of cyberweapons tests?
Are there side effects of weapons testing that can be detected (monitored)?
What are the actual intentions of cyberattacks and what are their actual effects on our mission effectiveness and strategic interests?
Do we understand our adversaries well enough to relate their national interests, goals, and strategies to the types and timing of cyberattacks?

them requires more than cyber-*security* measures. It requires *business* measures—decisions and policies that involve the entire enterprise. Digital resilience is a whole-business strategy (emphasis in the original)." Although the Internet was designed for decentralization, not security, this "decentralization turned out to be one of the sources of the Internet's security through resilience (Rothrock 2018)."

Greenberg discussed resilience at a macro-level that goes beyond the impact on a single small company or system to the system of systems that comprise a large, systemically important company or an entire nation. An interconnected system is subject to failure cascades as have occurred in the U.S. power grid, plunging entire quadrants of the U.S. into darkness. He quoted Dan Geer, "Quenching cascade failure, like quenching a forest fire, requires an otherwise uninvolved area to be cleared of the mechanisms of transit, which is to say it requires the opposite of interdependence." We have to build and maintain independent back-up systems (Greenberg 2019). Our hope is that on a national scale, current efforts toward alternative grids will be transformative for security and resilience (Rather & Hartley 2017; Roberts 2019).

As cognition is changing, cognitive superiority must be multiordinal and polythetic. We must have smart people, smart groups, AI superiority, smart machines and smart hybrid entities (humans augmented with AI) and ambient intelligence. They must continually learn, utilizing the pedagogy and technology of learning science and have favored access to the frontier of knowledge. The smart people must have analytic, creative and practical intelligence and intellectual, emotional and social capital (together cognitive capital).

Sun-Tsu has been adapted to the twenty first century (Sun-Tzu 1963), e.g., AI with big data analytics, augmented micro-targeting and denying the enemy information. The work of Richard Thaler, 2017 Noble Laureate in the Science of choice and choice and architecture, further expanded the persuasion system (Thaler & Sunstein 2008). Narratology resilience requires addressing the established narratives. The battleground for cognitive superiority is composed of complex adaptive systems and systems of systems (SoS), with intelligent nodes, links, signals, and boundaries.

Multi-Domain Operations

Multi-Domain Operations is the U.S. Army concept for countering and defeating a near-peer adversary that is capable of contesting with the U.S. in all domains—land, sea, air, space, and cyber. Part of the operational concept is a Theater Information Command. This concept will be tested in major military exercises (Koester 2019).

The U.S. has invested considerable resources in space over the last 60+ years. More than the investment, however, the value of space assets in terms of utility is large and growing. Satellites provide standard voice and television communications, location data through GPS systems, and internet connectivity. Hardware in space is vulnerable to kinetic attack. For example, in January of 2007, China tested an anti-satellite system (Zissis 2007). More recently, in April of 2020, Russia also tested an anti-satellite missile system (Gohd 2020). Military systems, including satellites also have hacking vulnerabilities. In 2019, Air Force tests showed that hackers could break into an F-15 fighter. In 2020, the Air Force is testing satellite vulnerabilities to hacking (Whittaker 2020). Military operations must become multi-domain and combining well is a necessity.

Perfection

We are going to be talking about or including by implication the concept of perfection. Some thinking on this concept is in order.

When we see a painting of a tree, it is not usually a sapling. You may have never planted a sapling, but you have probably seen them for sale at a garden center. The one you want is "perfect." It has a straight trunk, straight, unbroken limbs and smooth bark. Now visualize an old oak tree, one that might be the subject of a painting: it has rough bark, perhaps a swirl in the bark where a limb used to be, and distinctive crooked, even gnarled limbs or perhaps a broken limb. The tree worth painting for its beauty is not perfect. This aesthetic is not a European artifact. One of the authors has a Japanese scroll with a flowering tree as its subject. The tree has pretty pink flowers. It also has grey-green lichen patches on the branches and one branch stub visible in the painting. Again, the tree worth painting for its beauty is not perfect. One last example should be sufficient. Many years ago, Hollywood discovered that an actress with a perfectly symmetrical face and flawless skin required a "beauty mark" to be beautiful.

In aesthetics, either perfection is not the same as beauty or we are using the wrong definition for perfection. A similar thing holds for human systems: a perfect system (using a standard definition) is often too brittle to handle reality. We might wish to create an AI system that automatically scours all electronic sources and is fed all non-electronic sources manually. The system reports all threats and displays options for countering each one. **Caveat**: as with all stories of djinns, etc., there is a catch; what you say you want may not be what you really want; computers are exactly as literal minded as the djinns of fiction. The goal is not to create a "perfect" system, but to create a robust system that may not achieve optimum performance under ideal conditions, but achieves excellent performance under all conditions. Again, we should consider that we may have the wrong definition of perfection.

Change the Environment: The Box and Out of It

The "box" is the multi-agent, multi-pronged set of conflicts, immersed in an environment of accelerating change that we have described. We must address this situation—successfully. However, "out of the box" thinking can yield game-changing results by "flipping" the problem (Johansen 2007).

Stratagems

One flipping strategy involves changing the rules of a conflict. Suppose there are two ranked teams: A—F, as shown in Fig. 7.5. Our team is inferior by paired rank. The 'X' marks a pairing where we lose. If we play our best against their second best, leaving our worst to play their best, we may do better. If we play our best against their third best, we may win. In sports this may be cheating. In war, this is strategy. A Chinese general is reported to have used a similar strategy in racing three horses on one side versus three horse on the other (Qiao & Wang 1999). We need strategies for this conflict.

Reconstructing the contests and goal as cognitive superiority is the initial necessary and central paradigm-changing recommendation. It is simply the recognition of what is extant on the largest scale. Further, this will emphasize the need for major derivative "out of the box" creative disruptions. The field is ripe: toward generalized AI, true, useful quantum computation, communication and sensing, new forms of cognition, advances in detection, from single photon to cryo-electron microscopy, advanced directed energy, DNA-based data storage (Bomgardner 2020), and a cislunar economy (see description below). One or more of these may be sufficient to reshape the battlefield to our advantage.

Space as a New Frontier

Another flipping strategy involves changing the basic environment of the conflict. Creating a new frontier in space has the potential to be a game-changer. Historians cite the open frontier as a major factor in US cultural development as an adventurous, indi-

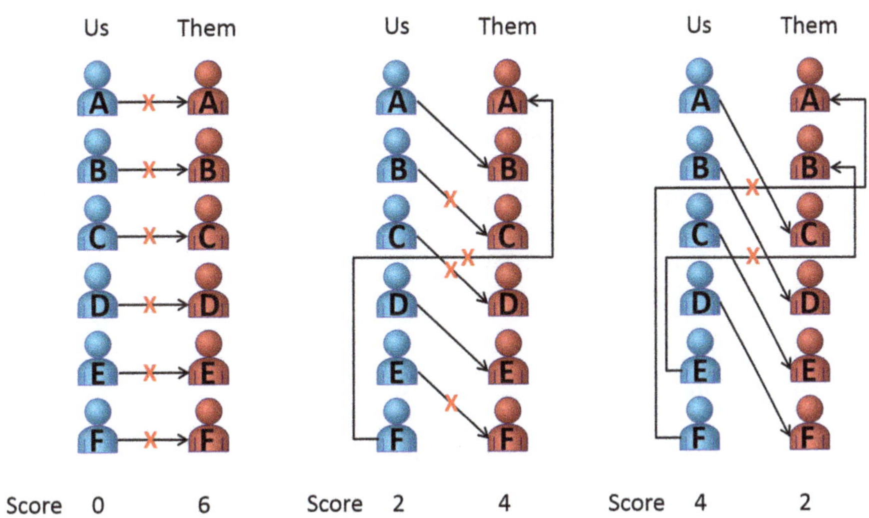

Fig. 7.5 Thinking out of the box

vidualistic, creative society. "*Opening space for full-scale development will provide the same advantages for our future* (Rather & Hartley 2018a)." John D. G. Rather pulled together a symposium on rapidly developing space using the synergies of nascent technologies. The eminent speakers described and discussed such topics as applications of superconductivity, nuclear thermal propulsion, capture and use of small, near-Earth asteroids, directed energy propulsion and power beaming, closed human ecosystems, large-scale 3D printing, solutions to low gravity effects on humans, quantum universe properties, and the visions that science fiction has provided and continues to provide for scientific and technical development. The conclusion of the symposium was that we can initiate a cis-lunar economy and reach Mars by 2030, using the technologies that we are developing today (Rather & Hartley 2018b).

The CIA analyst, Julia Curlee, suggested that the U.S. can "(1) *shape* the competitive environment to favor the US by driving down the cost of launch and space operations; (2) *enable* US allies and collective security through joint space operations, infrastructure development and diplomacy; (3) *induce* China toward adherence to wester norms in space operations by offering greater cooperation, while preparing to (4) *coerce* China by enhancing counterspace capabilities (Curlee 2020)."

Operating in the Conflict—As It Evolves

We are operating in the conflict now and it is evolving. The various "teams" we have are not perfect, but they are the ones we have. In the next chapter we will discuss how we can create better teams. But now, as the conflict evolves, the teams we have must evolve to match the challenges.

Innovate

Security for boundary and signal control will be necessary and the team will utilize hybrid human/AI/ML systems and be a facilitator for AI/ML dominance. The team can address human predictably systematically irrational aspects (Ariely 2009) as evinced by the work of Herbert Simon, Daniel Kahneman, and Richard Thaler, all Nobel laureates. The work of Michael Bernstein, PhD at Stanford on team optimization is relevant as is the work of Alex Pentland, MIT Human Dynamics Lab, in the field of social intelligence optimization.

Affiliation for Recruitment

We must control the metanarratives relevant to recruitment for us and our adversaries. We need our A-Teams to support our goals. From this perspective, we would consider the Google employees and Stanford students who objected to working on Department of Defense projects as "radicalized (Baron 2018)." Sufficient distributed authority and operational freedom with a flexible hierarchy are essential to rapidly react in order to reduce radicalization: "timing is critical: by the time potential recruits are sold on the ideology, it's too late to influence." The micro-targeting method developed by Google Jigsaw may prevent the sympathetic from becoming radicalized. To wit, there is an advantage in getting your story in first. There has been some success with radicalization avoidance using personal engagement by individuals attuned to their social conditions (Altran, Axelrod, Davis, & Fischhoff 2017). Rapid, ultra-concise personalization is required. This is similar to the off-line world where "A persuader should make a concentrated effort to meet one-on-one with all key people he or she plans to persuade (Conger 1998)." To be able to influence behavioral swarms one must address the structure and language (at times coded language) of connectivity and the swarm's capacity to migrate to a different venue (Ganesh 2018). Interrupting connectivity is often a powerful way to prevent group action. In conflict ecosystems, orchestrating persuasion, coercion, and effective administration often provides control (Kilcullen 2013).

Persuade

Certainly, the individual can and should act to identify and rebuff personal persuasion attacks; however, that is not enough. As a society, we must use persuasion to fight malevolent persuaders. To win, we must have organizational persuasion superiority.

Persuasion superiority must encompass the Oriental and the Occidental. From the Orient we learn from Sun-Tsu and learn about *shi*. In the West, understanding persuasion starts Aristotle's *Rhetoric* (Aristotle 2004) and includes the art/science of the narrative (narratology) (Maan 2018), and the persuasion principles of Cialdini (Cialdini 2009; Cialdini 2016), Fogg (Fogg 2003), and Thaler (Thaler & Sunstein 2008). Trans-domain AI/ML-augmented persuasion science has been added to rhetoric and narratology.

The surfaces of conflict are expanding as the metrics of time and scale accelerate and vulnerabilities and opportunities increase. Information superiority is imperative to enable persuasion superiority and persuasion superiority is imperative to enable information superiority.

The pedagogy of choice, the massive power of the largest search engines, the preconceptions of the sender and receiver, and innumerable default rules and frugal heuristics—all can amend, augment, and/or degrade persuasive forces.

Even if we were to be successful in stopping current Panopticon increases (through directly gathering information about customers), there is so much information already extant on Internet pages, indirect methods combined with the data that have already been collected will be sufficient to produce increasingly sophisticated persuasion profiles (Narayanan & Shmatikov 2008; Berinato 2015; Bettilyon 2019). We must also address such issues as data ownership (Hardjono, Shrier, & Pentland 2016). Understanding persuasive forces and critical thinking skills are even more important.

Chapter 8
Conclusion

> ***There is a tide in the affairs of men,***
> ***Which, taken at the flood, leads on to fortune;***
> ***Omitted, all the voyage of their life***
> ***Is bound in shallows and in miseries.***
> ***On such a full sea are we now afloat;***
> ***And we must take the current when it serves,***
> ***Or lose our ventures—***(Shakespeare, 1919)."

At this point the authors would like to wrap up with a neat package of recommended actions, based on data and analyses, that addresses each component of the problem, their interactions, and the emergent features that together make up the situation. That is the wrong approach. The conflicts we face are too diverse and changing too rapidly for simple algorithmic solutions. We contend that cognitive superiority is the means to the solutions. We must be algorithmically armed but not algorithmic ridden.

In this chapter we offer a synopsis of current conflicts, warfare in a information age, and propose requirements for achieving ongoing **cognitive superiority**.

The War

We are engaged in warfare the unlike any before. Instability increases, change accelerates in the technium and the noosphere, strategic spaces expand, and many battles don't have a physical battlefield. The cycle time is both faster and slower. The time scale has expanded and now ranges from milliseconds to the 100-year marathon (Pillsbury, 2015). This warfare is occidental and oriental and exploits our increasing understanding of human vulnerabilities and potentials. Some combatants are familiar,

D. S. Hartley III, K. O. Jobson, *Cognitive Superiority*,
https://doi.org/10.1007/978-3-030-60184-3_8

some new and they are many. Bits and atoms—digital and kinetic conflict—are utterly intertwined. AI/ML and the panopticon, augmented by experiments performed on unsuspecting internet users, provide adaptive predictive analytics for use by captology, narratology and *shi*. We encounter surrogation, bot armies, proxies, information arbitrage markets, and merchants of information and attention using persuasion science for micro-targeting and massive interpersonal persuasion (MIP), strategic deception and confusion strategies. We have near peers who seek our total domination and fight with "10,000 means" where the only rule is that there are no rules (Chinese Academy of Military Science, 2018; Qiao & Wang, 1999). The old paradigms are replaced by the new (Table 8.1). Just as in Darwinian survival of the fittest, "If environmental conditions change, the struggle begins anew (Max, 2003)."

We are at war, a multi-agent, multi-pronged attack (Fig. 8.1). This is partially a metaphorical war, as when advertisers work with addictive technology to persuade us to buy their product or change our political views. However, this is also a literal war, a life-and-death struggle for existence, with kinetic, economic, information, and diplomatic operations. This war affects more people, more severely, more quickly, and more certainly than climate change. We have seen many discussions about coping with the attacks, but few about winning the war. This may not be a short war, but we can win it.

We have a limited history to draw from because of the brevity of experience with the digital world, its accelerating rate of change, and the preference for secrecy concerning adverse experiences with the digital world. We have repeatedly been unprepared when facing wars that threatened our survival and only after significant

Table 8.1 Toward new paradigms

The central axis of our time is accelerating change
The sum of human knowledge is increasing exponentially
The motif is connectivity
Increasingly cognitively enabled machines and the drop in the learning barriers between expert knowledge and end-user is changing us and the matrix of our age (Susskind & Susskind, 2017).
New knowledge of man, including our vulnerabilities and potentials and advances in persuasion science, are increasing the effectiveness of persuasion
We have a surveilled world with experimentation amidst a vast infrastructure of knowledge access.
Tracking is ubiquitous; knowledge brokers abound.
Sensing is fused with computation and communication.
Information is ascendant in power, favored information access, and analytics and superior learning speed are critical.
Three clusters of emergence are preeminent.
Cognition: AI (AI supremacy will determine who decides the rules of the future), big data analytics, "software is eating the world," etc.
Biology has advanced genetic engineering and synthetic biology.
"Reality" is increasingly represented by immersive technologies: xR, VR, AR, 360° video, and mixed reality, often scripted with persuasion science and metanarratives.

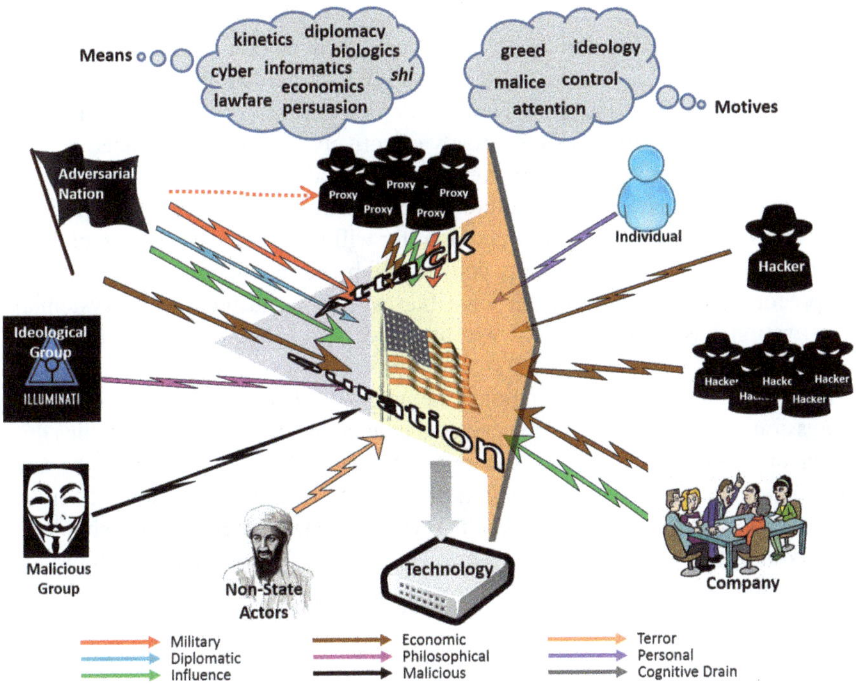

Fig. 8.1 Multi-agent, multi-pronged attack

delays did we adapt to defend against and defeat the enemy. A massive digital "attack" would be at the speed of the electron. Our fate could be determined in nanoseconds after a clandestine polythetic prologue. Kinetic superiority is no longer a certain guarantor. "For the first time since World War II, an adversary managed to knock a U.S. Navy aircraft carrier out of service. Only this time the enemy was a virus, not a nation-state (Koblentz, 2020)." Now with multiple weapons and layers hidden by method and problematic attribution, augmented with features unique to the digital world, we must have cognitive superiority.

Accelerating Change

The changes are in the technium (our technology), the noosphere (the sum of our knowledge), and in man and our knowledge of man. The motif of that change is connectivity with increase in the complexity of the complex adaptive systems that constitute our world.

Advances in AI, the biological sciences, cognitive science, computer science, data science, the learning sciences, information science, network science, neuroscience, psychology, and social psychology are salient. Complexity science fosters the understanding of transdisciplinary knowledge and creativity. Major advances in monitoring, measurement (e.g., single photon detection (Migdall, Polyakov, Fan, & Bienfang 2013)) and experimentation (e.g., high-throughput experimentation with automation and robotization (Peplow, 2019)) bring new optics for thought. Extended reality (xR) is already selectively useful and advanced genetic engineering, nootropics (drugs that enhance or modify mental functioning), and synthetic biology are extant. A future of accelerating change (Fig. 8.2) causes a remixing of these topics: quantum computing will boost AI and AI is prepared to boost all fields. As always these are constrained by our bounded reality–limited by our preconceptions, cognitive capacity, biases, fixity, and predictable systematically irrational aspects—however, we should work to enlarge our views of reality, and expand the bounds.

Figure 8.2 suffers from limitations: the arrow of change and the axes give the impression of smooth change. However, the content in Chaps. 2, 3, and 4 belies this. The changes in humans, the noosphere and the technium are expected to be anything but smooth. There will be increasing change in each, with increases in the number and types of categories in each. These axes each therefore represent a multiplicity of dimensions. The arrow of change will actually be a jagged path through multiple dimensions.

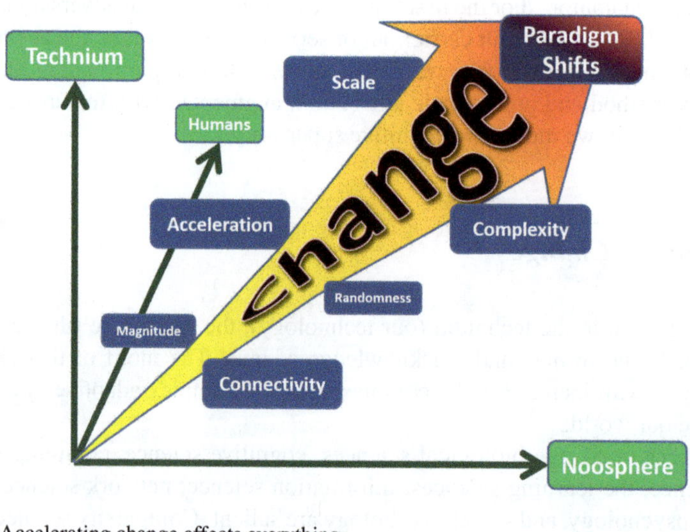

Fig. 8.2 Accelerating change affects everything

Its from Bits (The Age of Cognification)

Although information is orthogonal to matter and energy, information relates to and can represent matter and energy ($F = MA$, $E = MC^2$, etc.). John A. Wheeler, the physicist who popularized the term "black hole," suggested that each thing in the universe, starting with the basic particles derives its existence from information—bits (Wheeler, 1989).

Information in the eye of the beholder and the hands of the user, can be the ingredients for the acquisition of knowledge for

- the sake of learning or advancement of man,
- property in the ideas industry (Drezner, 2017),
- profit for the arbitrage of ideas market (Aspesi & Brand, 2020),
- weapons for cyber warfare
- in the event of kinetic war, to assure our kill chain is combined well (CAS integrated) with superior speed (Brose, 2020b), or
- for cognitive superiority, and thus all of the above.

Evolution is the competition and cooperation of information. There is no love, peace, war, or meaning without information. Knowledge is the coin of the realm in our information age and it is increasing exponentially. Data can bring information, which can bring knowledge, which can bring wisdom; but wisdom comes in very small packages. As the radius of our knowledge increases, the circumference of our ignorance increases six-fold.

LTG Michael Flynn said, "Publicly available information is now probably the greatest means of intelligence we could bring to bear (Singer & Brooking, 2018)." This new aspect of the taxonomy of intelligence is obviously relevant to all learning ecosystems including education and propaganda. Controlling the morphing misinformation processes can be accomplished only with knowledge of authors, articles, rumors, images, the publishers and platforms. There is too much information and diversity for a single person or a standard team.

We are complex adaptive systems living in complex adaptive systems that are becoming more information-dense, more complex. Cognitive superiority, the cognitive domination of one side over others illustrated in Fig. 8.3, is now essential in war and necessary to flourish in peace.

Humanity and Its Matrix

Man is an emergent bio-psycho-socio-techno-info being. We are in an age when the very nature of cognition is morphing with AI/ML, the cognification of objects, processes, environments, and the cognitive augmentation of man.

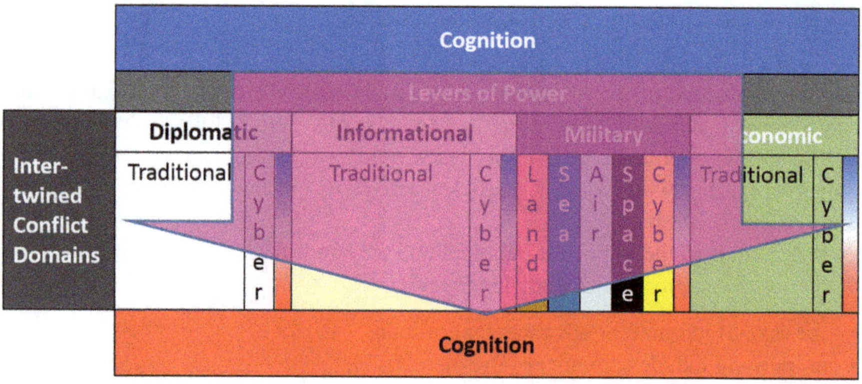

Fig. 8.3 Conflicts are within the cognitive domain

We have predictably systematically irrational aspects with manifold vulnerabilities and potentials. The new science of persuasion, armed with new knowledge of man's irrationalities and vulnerabilities, using big data analytics from new surveilled mobile biometrics and sociometrics, allows targeted direction of attention and induction of doubt with probabilistic persuasive control. Warfare and peace are not exempt.

The conflicts that permeate our environment utilize the panopticon, open or hidden. Deception can be simple or as complex as part of *shi*. The participants, means, and memes, are utterly intertwined. Narrative warfare is joined by computational propaganda, election tampering, and stealing intellectual secrets. Fake news can use AI-augmented sociometrics and biometrics to direct attention and micro-target or expand for mass interpersonal persuasion (MIP), employing computer assisted persuasion (captology). Persuasion art/science should be understood as combining the oriental and occidental traditions, brought into the twenty-first century. Sun-Tsu, Aristotle, Cicero, Cialdini, Centola, Fogg, Maan, Sapolsky, Sunstein and Thaler, and Martin and Marks are central in this community of knowledge of persuasion.

Drawing from Fig. 8.1, we see that among the myriad persuasive competitors, there are national attacks whose fundamental long-term grand strategy is a zero-sum game for domination. There are also attacks with economic gain as the motive. There are attacks designed to influence opinions and behaviors. There are attacks based on philosophical and purely malicious motives. There are personal attacks and demands on our cognitive capacities by our cognified "servants." The targets include the operations of physical systems and human cognition.

The Imperative—Cognitive Superiority

Prerequisite: Executive level vision, with announced political/power buy-in; a Manhattan Project level of funding and empowerment; and a senior leader with recognized expertise in science and technology management and experience in dealing with government (for example, Vannevar Bush, during World War II (Dyson, 2012)).

There is a complementarity about cognitive superiority: it is both an emergent sixth domain and part of the other five domains, for as the Chinese said, we are in a new world of cognification (Chinese Academy of Military Science, 2018) and "the winner is the one who combined well (Qiao & Wang, 1999)." We must combine well to support the imperative of Cognitive Superiority.

Requirements

Table 8.2 lists the requirements for cognitive superiority. Each is described in the text following the table.

1. An executive and bipartisan supported **vision and grand strategy** to address the enlarging arc of cognitive conflict is required. The arc of the conflict includes competition for superior information access, cyber war, economic warfare, "lawfare," narrative warfare, and conventional military warfare. The pressures arrayed against us are generated simultaneously by multiple actors with different agendas. The means include diplomacy, meme and media conflict, network dynamics, persuasion science, and warfare for supremacy in the emergent new forms of cognition. All of these must be coordinated and interoperable across hierarchical levels of abstraction, vision, policy, strategy, operations and tactics in a world of

Table 8.2 Requirements for achieving cognitive superiority

1. An executive, bipartisan supported vision and grand strategy for a Manhattan Project level of national commitment to Cognitive Superiority, including AI and quantum superiority
2. Talent, the best and brightest
3. Education, lifelong for all, with superior learning speed
4. Favored information access both for the individual and on a systems level to the frontier of science and technology
5. Persuasion science superiority
6. Superior cyber-sensing security resilience and capacity for our global networks;
7. Cognitive augmentation for individuals and groups
8. All of the above "combined well."

unending paradigm shifting disruptive change (Kelly, 2016; McFate, 2019; Maan, 2018). Central to the vision is a Manhattan Project level of national commitment to **Cognitive Superiority** is required, including:

(a) **AI/ML superiority,** with third J-wave AI/ML (DARPA, 2019) (within five years the country with the superior military AI may determine the rules of the future), **quantum superiority**, and cognified objects and systems (IoT) on earth and in space;
(b) **Recognition of and formal Establishment** of the *de facto*, extant, **Cognitive (Sixth) Domain of Warfare**;
(c) **Talent**: The best and brightest talent: recruited, recognized, and remunerated;
(d) **Persuasion science**: Persuasion and influence superiority, both for external use and internal use in recruitment and management;
(e) **Major cognitive augmentation systems**: With superior analytic information access, a dedicated Eratosthenes affiliation, PAALS, and removing barriers to information access;
(f) **Process**: Operations using flexible multidisciplinary approaches, resilient cyber security, embedded lifelong education both for the team and throughout the nation, and favored access to the frontiers of science and technology; and
(g) **Adaptive integration**: Policy, diplomacy, strategy, and tactics, with the motif of connectivity for the vision.

2. **Talent**: The best and brightest, "smart creatives (Schmidt & Rosenberg, 2017)," must be recruited (see the subsection on talent recruitment in Chap. 7 and the section on talent below), recognized with emoluments, ranked, and offered selected relationship flexibility across multiple significant domains of knowledge. It will be critical to craft the metanarrative and persuasion arguments to recruit Silicon Valley's A-team for America's military AI superiority.
3. **Education** as a national priority should be understood as extending from womb to tomb. Teaching should be a more honored profession. Education involves filling the bucket of knowledge, lighting the fire of the "demanding festival" of lifelong learning and preparing the mind to meet the unexpected. This cognitive adaptation for today's matrix of accelerating change and exponential increase in the sum of human knowledge (with new forms of cognition) is for intellectual enrichment and increasingly sequential employment, but now necessary for national defense. (For more on education, see the education section in Chap. 7.

   (a) **Liberal arts** and **STEM** education are required, as is **training in the trades**. The evidence for the benefit of choice in education is overwhelming. The goal of a "liberal arts education" is to teach critical thinking, analytical problem solving, and understanding of humanity. This goal is impeded by politics, political correctness, greed and fixity, which must be called out and overcome. STEM support must include statistical literacy and advanced placement computer science courses in all U.S. high schools and later work-life adult education support for reskilling and upskilling for fundamental skills, craft, and theory. The current 40% of post high school students attending college, as currently constructed, should be re-thought. A large percentage of these students should be offered training for likely employment skills and then at the time when creative destruction causes that job to disappear, be offered reskilling or upskilling. Minds must be prepared to meet the unexpected (see the subsection on serendipity and sagacity in Chap. 3).

(b) **Life-long learning** is required. This includes transdisciplinary reskilling and upskilling as we face the automating workplace. Our technical and scientific expertise are becoming obsolete ever more quickly. The pedagogy should be optimally matched to the student's individual learning style, the topic and matrix. Urgently needed adult education must be expanded. It should encompass all workers, from the factory floor through "white collar" jobs to academia, with easy logistical and financial availability. Post-doctoral students and faculty need education in new trans-domain fields and access to monitoring and use of ultra-expensive technology and methods only available in the private sector. This requires bipartisan political will with public-private partnerships supporting lifelong learning, using interoperable, learning networked, modern personalized pedagogy-driven learning technology, a foundational educational path that is a hierarchically selective system.

(c) **Learning speed superiority** is critical, as we experience accelerating change, both in the civilian and military world (this may be our only long-term adaptive advantage) (Anderson, 2019).

(d) **Meta-learning skills** are needed for defense, security and beyond to hone personalized adult adaptive learning systems to optimize the incoming information and support tacit knowledge transfer. These skills include learning, knowing how to learn, understanding the sources of invention and discovery (Polya, 1945), and content expertise.

4. **Favored information access including access to the frontier of science and technology**—both for the individual and on a systems level are obligatory. (The items are amplified in the section on cognitive enhancement below.)

   (a) The system needs an **Eratosthenes Affiliation** for cognitive augmentation that will harvest, winnow down and make convenient salient knowledge from the expanding frontier of science and technology for system-wide use by defense and security. Besides providing cognitive enhancement, this will serve as an enticement for talent recruitment.

   (b) Personnel should be taught to develop personalized adult adaptive learning systems (**PAALS**) to optimize their lifelong learning including use of their collective learning opportunities and optimized use of the available cognitive artifacts (computer search expertise, MOOCS, MOOSECS, etc.). They should understand the power of collecting and nurturing mentorships, hone the skills of problem solving taught by Polya, and understand the complexity of tacit knowledge transfer.

(c) It will be necessary to **remove barriers** to the improvement of research reporting and deal with information access portals and tolls.

5. **Persuasion science superiority** is required a priori to bring this vision of the urgent necessity for cognitive superiority to those in power, then to establish meta-narratives in international relations, for recruitment of previously reluctant AI/ML expertise, and for the cognitive superiority agenda, including the military.
6. **Superior cyber-sensing security resilience and capacity**: David Sanger's prescriptions for cyber security are relevant (see Table 6.3 in Chap. 6). We certainly need defenses of various types; however, we also require resilience to bounce back from successful attacks. This will require superior knowledge management, including security, robustness, resilience and provenance of data, selected modularity, capacity for dynamic reorganization, facility for cooperation, and access control (Rothrock, 2018; Zolli & Healy, 2012).
7. **Cognition augmentation for individuals and groups**: Cognified, individual and networked digital augmentation across domains is advised. Intelligence amplification or augmentation (IA), ambient, processes, group and individual are part of this. It will be necessary to minimize neurotoxicants (substances capable of causing adverse effects in the nervous system and sense organs) in our exposome (the environment, that is, non-genetic drivers of health and disease) (Vermeulen, Schymanski, Barabasi, & Miller, 2020). Attention must be paid to the manifold factors that optimize cognition, including nutrition, sleep hygiene, exercise, and psychosocial health. Where possible, we should optimize our integrated stress response (ISR) (Costa-Mattioli & Walter, 2020).
8. All of the above "**combined well** (Qiao & Wang, 1999)."

Cognitive superiority will require our A-Team talent and should be envisioned as continuous, lifelong learning, optimizing information access and learning speed, possessing superior AI (necessary for continued freedom) and intelligence augmentation (IA). Requirements #3, #4, and #7 above can all be advanced with individuals having their own personal training/education accounts, funded by the government, their company, or by themselves, to provide for upskilling or reskilling as needed. "Due to the acceleration of technology, people are losing around 40% of their skills every three years (Michaels 2020a)." Why would we not do this?

Numbered among the impediments will lurk limited knowledge or vision, aversion to feedback, fixity and bureaucracy, and self-interest of many stripes, political, hubristic or greed.

Organizational Implementation: What's Different Now?

Winning this war will not be simple. The diversity of means, targets, protagonists, and motives guarantees this. We need an ensemble of solutions that can address all aspects of the "war."

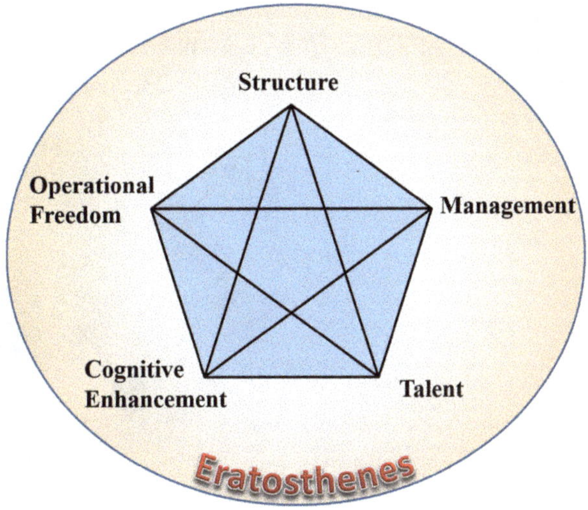

Fig. 8.4 Organizational requirements for cognitive superiority

The art and science of management has changed in the twenty-first century. Empowered by information and technology, individuals and small teams can have enormous impact, far greater than ever before (Schmidt & Rosenberg, 2017). Figure 8.4 begins the description of the ensemble. The ensemble is adapted from the requirements for an agile organization of Fig. 7.2 in Chap. 7. It can be envisioned as having six parts: structure, management, sufficient operational freedom, talent, cognitive augmentation, and an Eratosthenes affiliation. We have added individual cognitive enhancement to the agile organization requirements to take advantage of the human cognitive enhancements that are becoming part of the cognitive landscape. An Eratosthenes affiliation expands the cognitive enhancement from the individual to the organization.

Structure

Organizational structure has at its center trust and candor. It is dedicated to multidisciplinary lifelong learning for all, features connectivity within the team and without. Some connections should be continuous but with the capability for microstates (temporary confluences that inform). With accelerating change, agility is essential. Valuing "adapting to change more than sticking to the plan," flexible hierarchy with agile teams are probabilistically more productive and work differently from strict "chain of command bureaucracies (Rigby, Sutherland, & Noble, 2018)." A transformational mindset and the capacity for rapid response and quick iterations are essential. AI/ML can now be used to enhance the operations of both the talent and the management (Tarafdar, Beath, & Ross, 2019).

The organization can also be viewed as a team or set of teams. Because the breadth of knowledge required is larger than a single person or small team can be expected to possess, the team must have a network of collaborators (Fig. 8.5). Some of these collaborators will be closely linked to the team (C), as shown by the bold

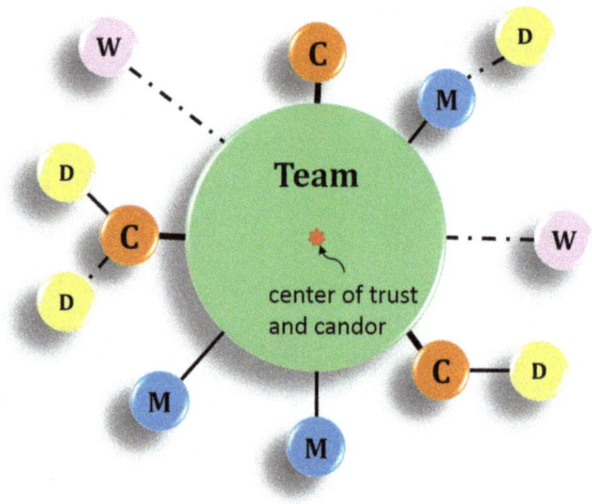

Fig. 8.5 Teams and affiliate support

connections. Some will bc only moderately (M) or weakly linked (W), as shown by the light and dashed connectors. Some collaborators will be more distant (D), only linked through the closer collaborators. The team members and collaborators should be augmented with AI/ML and other cognitive artifacts and supported with superior connectivity within the team, to knowledge resources, and to innovation partners (Ancona, 2020). Crowdsourcing will be one useful team adjunct. Brabham defines crowdsourcing as "an online, distributed problem-solving and production model that leverages the collective intelligence of online communities to serve specific organizational goals (Brabham, 2013)."

Work has been done concerning AI assisted teams (see DARPA ASIST (DARPA, 2019)). The team environment can benefit from all forms of intelligence (ambient, traditional, and xR augmented intelligence). Enhancement by collective learning should flow from the team long-term and short-term with microstates, as well as from the network of "consultants," optimally involving a variety of types of associations from on-call to special projects and lifelong availability of education and upskilling. Ongoing personalized information feeds, both traditional and digital, are needed. A supportive, connected, personalized environment along with the previously mentioned persuasion science change can give great advantage for top talent recruitment.

Each team will need abilities seen in the neurobiology of cognitive science to quickly form microstates with real time recruitment, semi-permeable filtering and rapid analysis, prediction and adaption. In the digital world, "x-teams" "foster speed, innovation, and execution. These teams don't just collaborate internally; they also link to knowledge resources and innovation partners in the outside world (Ancona, 2020)." No static models, no single model, no silo models will be sufficient.

Figure 8.6 combines Figs. 8.4 and 8.5. The Eratosthenes methodology will detect and send information from the frontiers of science and technology to the team and to the network. Its structure will involve AI/ML-augmented computer and

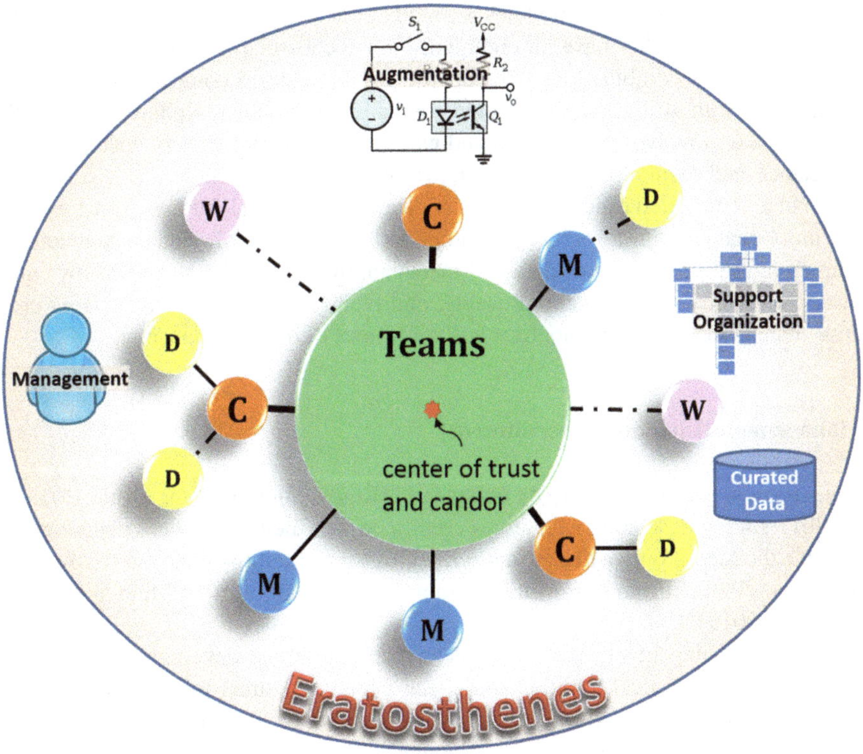

Fig. 8.6 Teams and their myriad support connections

information scientists, experts from academia, military, industry, and security. It will have the capacity for curation and will look for morphing ontologies and salient single advances.

Now, with the surging power attendant to information and accelerating changes in the noosphere, the technium and cognition, including the network science, translation technology, AI/ML, big data analytics and data science, it is possible and it is also urgently essential to have superior information access. Awareness of the scientific and military advantage of having favored access to the frontier of knowledge has a long, storied history, repeatedly brought to the fore at times of conflict or challenge. It has been mitigated and stymied by entanglement with politics, turf battles, unripe fields of knowledge and inadequate technologies (Burke, 2018).

As in the human brain and human hybrid systems in general, the structure's outer boundaries should reflect the adaptive advantage seen in Mother Nature's modular, flexible, hierarchical, cognitively selective semi-permeable membranes. The competing ideals of secrecy and security versus the need for free exchange of information and ideas across traditional and new boundaries to foster creativity and discovery must be addressed. In the past, excessive secrecy, "has retarded development or at least policy integration of digital combat power (Lin & Zegart, 2018)."

Fortunately, many of the modules are ready or nearly ready for collective assembly. It will of necessity have an emergent bio-psycho-socio-techno-info structure. Mother Nature's combinations of cooperation and selected competitive strategies are advised with affiliation bias in envisioning and with quick alpha versions with early end-user involvement, constructed with relevant subdomains of specific fields of science and technology. In parallel, we must develop modules with sufficient distributed, connected executive expertise. The psycho-social, human aspect will be the most challenging. Expert aggregators and "cheerleaders" will be mandatory. Human hybrid processing of data and metadata, the capacity to winnow down and make potentially salient material usable, and facilitation of microstates using creative management and sociometrics will all be part of this affordance.

Management (Including Recruitment)

Leaders must "promote agility by being agile (Rigby, Sutherland, & Noble, 2018)." "A 2017 survey of leading executives confirmed that their skills were depreciating at twice the rate of only a decade earlier." "CEOs must rethink their job (Groysberg & Gregg, 2020)." From senior management on down all must be lifelong learners (Ignatius, 2019).

General Management must view talent recruitment and development as key. It must have the technical abilities and social capital to attract talent. Management must subscribe to the vision of accelerating change in the noosphere, the technium, man, and the knowledge of man. Managers should be connectors, not micromanagers, and employ flexible hierarchy to encourage the questioning of default rules within a challenging, clement environment.

"Your Approach to Hiring is all Wrong," refers to the fact that "the majority of people who took a new job last year weren't searching for one: someone came and got them (Capelli, 2019)." Talent recruitment-development-retention is a central management responsibility. To attract talent there should be trust and candor, meritocracy, recognition, reward, and career development offerings, opportunity to find meaning in their work, mastery in their field, and sufficient operational freedom (Pink, 2009).

Recruitment must be supported using persuasion art/science and by metanarratives to foster participation in these efforts as opposed to the belief in the counternarrative of a "virtuous" avoiding of giving aid to DoD and Homeland Security. In the setting of America's having the best AI/ML companies and the most effective attention and persuasion merchants, there is a dangerous problem with silicon valley's relationship with Homeland Security and the Department of Defense. The attitude of distrust and disjoint metanarratives and narratives are barriers to the recruitment of talent and a prime example of failure of dealing with complexity and competing ideals. Solving this impasse must be urgently addressed from personal contacts to metanarratives. (See the sections on persuasion, including confronting the established, in Chap. 4 above.)

Talent

Talent is required for multiple traditional and new communities of knowledge. For computer sciences, we must have "smart creatives" with deep technical knowledge, hands-on experience, firehoses of new ideas, curious, driven, unafraid to fail, self-directed, and communicative that freely collaborate (Schmidt & Rosenberg, 2017). For persuasion superiority, rhetoric and narratology (mastery of storytelling) including video and narrative warfare, captology, computational propaganda, psychology, data science, learning science, cognitive science, data science, and human and digital network science are required. The talent should also be hired for grit, "a concept that Angela Duckworth of the University of Pennsylvania describes as perseverance and passion for long-term goals (Robson, 2019)." Talent and management must not only teach new content and traditional "how to learn" skills, but also actively improve practical and creative intelligence (Robson, 2019).

An Eratosthenes enabled team can address the science and technology knowledge explosion and will attract talent in today's competitive environment for the best and brightest. Favored access to be in the vanguard of the knowledge explosion will entice talented recruits, even in today's hyper-competitive talent recruitment environment. The opportunity to gain mastery in their fields of knowledge and an opportunity to work with other senior experts will aid motivation and retention. Such a team structure will provide a unique resource that will empower learning and creativity. Providing individual and team multifaceted cognitive enhancement and lifelong transdisciplinary learning will be talent multipliers. Having the talent, connectivity, structure, mentors, and technology to learn, and innovate will capture the creativity of small, smart groups. Utilizing a "stake in the outcome" versus "perks of rank" and an environment where results, not rank, are celebrated and rewarded will produce the desired results (Bahcall, 2019).

Operational Freedom

The operations should be constructed so that the individuals and small teams are entrusted with the optimal operational freedom, the freedom to be original. The organization must be agile because a fixated or slow bureaucracy will kill the capacity to deal with accelerating change, the unexpected.

An environment of collaboration, including collective learning, requires elegant listening, empathy, "making people comfortable with feedback" ("aversion to feedback is common"), teaching people to lead and to follow, clarity of communication, and "training people to have win-win interactions (Gino, 2019)." The difficult problem of dealing with competing ideals of maintaining the core scientific benefits of collaboration (nationally and internationally) and guarding against intellectual espionage will require public-private collective wisdom (Leshner, 2019).

Cognitive Enhancement - Metascience

Cognitive enhancement, including superior information access with analytics, is suggested at three levels: an Eratosthenes Affiliation for favored access to salient information at the systems level; personalized adult adaptive learning systems (PAALS) at the individual level; and removing other barriers. The technology and talent are extant to grasp this set of powerful low-hanging fruit.

There is an exponential increase in the sum of human knowledge. As the radius of our knowledge increases, the circumference of our knowledge (the boundary of our ignorance) increases six-fold. To wit, obsolescence is upon us in an accelerating fashion. John Chambers, former CEO of Cisco Systems, said that without constantly learning the leaders of tech companies are obsolete in three to five years (Groysberg & Gregg, 2020). In medicine, it is estimated that it only takes five years for 50% of treatment algorithms to be out of date. Lifelong efficient learning and superior speed of learning are our only sustainable advantages. It is necessary for cognitive superiority, central to the sixth domain and the maintenance of freedom.

Eratosthenes Affiliation: We are in urgent need of an Eratosthenes Affiliation (named for Eratosthenes, a third century B.C. scientist, mathematician, philosopher, and world-wide information gatherer, arguably the first information scientist).

An Eratosthenes Affiliation requires a multidisciplinary affiliation of library/information scientists, educators, computer scientists, multiple content experts in applicable fields of science and technology, provided with the requisite AI and IA. The purpose is detection and gathering the newest knowledge from the ever-accelerating expansion of the frontier of science and technology for use and empowerment of those in and allied with our security and defense. We now have the requisite technology, talent and metascience for this essential element for enduring cognitive superiority.

The Eratosthenes Affiliation should learn what current systems are extant. There is no excuse for not knowing the current best in class. It will require an organic structure with an agile management team with superior intellectual, emotional and social capital adept at dealing with diverse communities of knowledge. It needs empowered talent to recruit and motivate the recruits to participate in further recruitment. The network will of necessity utilize a variety of types of affiliation, from brief and limited to ongoing. End users should be involved early. Success will entail the proper metanarratives, the use of the art/science of persuasion, and scaling in an incremental fashion. Each of SciFinder (SciFinder, 2019), DataONE (DataONE, 2020), and Google Scholar (Google Scholar, 2019), the national labs, DARPA, IARPA, NASA, commercial and independent labs, knowledge brokers, consultants, academia, library and information science may be parts of the affiliation.

At least one near peer is pursuing its version of an Eratosthenes Affiliation - China (Chinese Academy of Military Science, 2018) and possibly Russia (Singer & Brooking, 2018).

PAALS: Personalized Adult Adaptive Learning Systems are individual systems to aid in learning. They address cumulative education and education at the time of need (with the locus of our maximum density of learning moments). Such a system involves aids in how to learn—heuristics meta-learning, includes guides concerning mentors—how to seek, appreciate, and nurture them and how to locate and transfer tacit knowledge. The system also aids in participating in collective learning, such as groups, microstates, and list serves, and in finding and using cognitive artifacts, traditional, digital and hybrids, such as MOOCs, MOOSECs, Ted talks, digital platforms, and search expediters. We are children of the word, the book, the screen, and now also digital intelligence amplification or augmentation (IA). We should choose topics for our focused learning, know how best to assemble our learning structure and reify that system.

Removing Other Barriers: The rapidly evolving knowledge infrastructure means we must deal with "information arbitrage markets" with portals and "augmented discovery services through artificial intelligence (AI)-powered mining and analysis of full-text (Aspesi & Brand, 2020)."

Another claim is that there are other chronic and current addressable delays in harvesting advances from the frontier of science and technology for deployment and use. The period of delay is less, but present, even when there is obvious advantage to those with vast financial resources, as when the advance is deemed essential for national defense (to be addressed by the Eratosthenes Affiliation) or very lucrative for commerce. There is a yawning gap of delay outside these two areas where, though currently not judged salient to either of those two areas, the discovery may, with time, yield emergent, manifold, national advantage, including defense or commerce. This issue is discussed more fully in the section on Validation and Accessibility in Chap. 3. Table 3.10 in that section lists remedies.

Part of the delay in knowledge transfer from the frontier is because of an accepted practice by even the most prestigious academic journals of allowing publication without sufficient transparency of procedures, data collection, and description of metrics to be readily reproduced for validation. Examples of this can be seen in the short, discovery-announcing articles found in the journals *Science* and *Nature*. This can be remedied by a policy of not publishing without transparency and detail commensurable with reproducibility. (The publisher Wiley and the software firm Scite are teaming up to use the software Scite.ai to use AI to help determine which articles are reproducible (Brainard, 2020). This may be a step in the right direction.) This could be strengthened by an independent certifying body attesting that the article provided sufficient information for reproducibility. Successful pressure for journal article method transparency would speed the path from print to use. Pre-registration of hypothesis *(ex ante predictum)* would also improve the advancement of science (DellaVigna, Pope, & Vivalt, 2019).

These meta-scientific, normative and structural changes can bring great cognitive advantages to those who employ their bounty. We now have the technology, metaknowledge and many of the unassembled subsystems to bring an Eratosthenes Affiliation to life.

Rationale for a Manhattan Project to Achieve Cognitive Superiority

The sum of human knowledge is increasing exponentially. The disruptive impact of technology and new knowledge is felt across the matrix of man (Schmidt & Rosenberg, 2017). Knowledge infrastructure and thought leadership are new battlegrounds. We have near peers in the conventional land, sea and air domains. We have near peers in the newer space and cyber domains. Some are near peers in only one or two domains. Russia and China are near pears in all five domains. Nation-state power is challenged by new capacities for reach and scale in our ever more connected and complex world, as evidenced by Al Qaeda, ISIS and COVID-19. Power has shifted to include large international corporations, swarms and even individuals who are billionaires.

Technology follows from and abets knowledge. The power of information is mounting. Technology, knowledge and skills are becoming obsolete more rapidly. AI is on track to be the most transformative technology in human history and military AI superiority may determine who writes the rules of the future (Karp, 2020). However, there are and will be newer technologies (e.g., quantum technologies), further accelerating change. By numbers of graduates, China leads in science, technology, mathematics, and engineering (McCarthy, 2017). Our ability to learn faster may be our only sustainable advantage.

However, the nature of power, of warfare, and how and by whom it is waged has changed, continues to change, and the change is accelerating. Kinetic power alone is no longer sufficient to guarantee dominance or even freedom (Brose, 2020a). Low barriers to entry, ease of scaling effects, and the potential of problematic attribution guarantee more combatants. This is particularly true in cognitive conflict writ large, in biosecurity and in cyberwar.

We are engaged in ongoing conflicts involving atoms (kinetics) and bits (information). The persuasion wars require the talent to recognize fleeting moments of potential massive influence, digital and otherwise. Persuasion science/art can make the resolute sequacious. This conflict is polythetic, multi-pronged, and pursued by multiple agents with multiple motives for multiple ends. If we fail to see its entirety, but try to address the conflict piecemeal, we will ultimately fail.

The future “dogs of war” will include bits and orbits, atoms, memes and meta-narrative meaning, genes and germs. It’s different now.

Cognitive superiority is the basis for information superiority, technical superiority, economic superiority, diplomatic superiority, and military superiority. The future of conflict is lies in the pursuit for cognitive superiority. Achieving and maintaining cognitive superiority will require a massive and coordinated effort—a Manhattan Project level effort.

Foresight for Formation

"The old order changeth, yielding place to the new (Tennyson, 1842)," and the pace of change accelerates. We change in information infrastructure, technology, affiliation, and biology. Even "reality" and cognition have ever new and more complex forms.

We face an existential threat, challenged like never before. We must define cognitive superiority as the grand central mission. The requisite executive challenge is political system buy-in to this reality for focus and funding. We need a Cognitive Superiority Manhattan Project with a scientific advisory mechanism. We have the people, the technology and many of the subsystems. We executed the original Manhattan Project, the Moonshot, and have organized a whole-of-America response to COVID-19. We are "shovel ready." With an empowered IARPA, with DoD, DARPA, the 17 national labs, proper funding, public-private partnerships, in concert with technology push and demand pull it will be transformative not only for defense, security and freedom, but for vast new wealth that has repeatedly come from technology and information paradigm shifts (Margonelli, 2020).

The proper grand strategy must deal with ten thousand methods from milliseconds to marathon, provide totally integrated superior kill chain dynamics, have talent with the sagacity to deal with the unexpected and possess flexible adaptive management. A lifelong commitment to learning must be algorithmically enabled, not algorithmically ridden. All "combined well" for cognitive superiority.

Most of the knowledge needed to realize this vision is extant but spread across multiple domains of knowledge and unassembled. The alliance would include empowered superior senior management, graybeards, and content experts from multiple domains. Truth and need must prevail over political correctness. Need and commitment to results should trump short-term ego, career advancement and turf wars. Management will need to be connectors between, above—to address politics and power, within—to orchestrate, and without—to foster a variety of consultant relationships.

The first step can be top down or bottom up. Top down might entail a conference with powerful agents: NSA, DOD, Homeland Security, commercial knowledge brokers, senior advisers and graybeards, etc. for buy-in of the vision, its creation and support. Alternatively, one agency could be the genesis to connect and combine wide and well. Such a complex adaptive system of necessity will become a public/private partnership with trans domain talent and include aggregators and persuaders and sufficient authority for the enduring conflict.

These proposals will foster advances in basic research, while solving immediate real-world needs for security, defense and beyond (Pasteur's Quadrant in Fig. 7.1). The weaponization of a *forme fruste* of a cognitive domain is extant but distributed and accelerating in potential province and power. It can be assembled and will be by some, to influence and potentially control any level of oppositional power from National Destiny, Grand Strategy, command and control down to the individual combatant and citizen. It will seek and feed upon the opponent's limited executive vision, poor knowledge management, fixity, insufficient agility, and suboptimal cognitive capital across all domains and hierarchies of warfare.

It's Different Now

"The central axis of our time is unending accelerating change (Kelly, 2016)." The motif is connectivity. The sum of human knowledge is increasing exponentially. There is a new ecology of information access, analytics, and management. The new and unfolding knowledge of man's vulnerabilities and potentials is crucial. We must possess favored information access, superior learning speed, the sagacity to wisely address the unexpected and develop and deploy emerging technology and knowledge. Information ascends in power. There are even emergent new forms of cognition. For continued freedom, cognitive superiority is the central imperative.

If not us, who? If not now, when?

Appendix

The Appendix contains two parts. The first is a discussion of salient contents of selected sources, arranged by topic. The second part contains definitions of selected terms.

Discussion of Selected Sources

The discussion of each of the sources concerns the portions that are relevant to this book and should not be taken as a complete precis of each work. The topic headers are meant to be informative, not definitive, as to the type of content of the sources. Further, many sources provide material relevant to several topics, making the choice of topic in which they appear somewhat arbitrary.

Artificial Intelligence

Barrat, J.: *Our Final Invention: Artificial Intelligence and the End of the Human Era*, (Barrat, 2013).

Barrat describes recursive self-improvement as applied to AI and speculates that this could lead to greater than human intelligence.

Brockman, J. (Ed.): *Possible Minds: 25 Ways of Looking at AI* (Brockman, 2019).

This is a polythetic view of AI, a collection of essays by 25 scientists on the subject of AI.

Kurzweil, R.: *The Singularity is Near*, (Kurzweil, 2005).

This is Kurzweil's classic description of the possibility of artificial intelligence surpassing human intelligence.

Lee, Kai-Fu: *AI Superpowers: China, Silicon Valley, and the New World Order*, (Lee, 2018).

D. S. Hartley III, K. O. Jobson, *Cognitive Superiority*,
https://doi.org/10.1007/978-3-030-60184-3

This former president of Google China reviews AI's structure, progress, and implementation from a US and Chinese perspective. China's 2016 "Sputnik Moment" of AI, its AI frenzy, its internet's alternative universe, and China's advantages in the race for AI supremacy are discussed.

Tegmark, M.: *Life 3.0: Being Human in the Age of Artificial Intelligence*, (Tegmark, 2017).

Tegmark discusses a set of futures involving the possible interactions of humans and intelligent machines.

Wallace, R.: *Carl von Clausewitz, the Fog-of-War, and the AI Revolution: The Real World Is Not A Game of Go*, (Wallace, 2018).

Wallace describes the challenges and successes of AI, but contends that it is mathematically demonstrable that when faced with the complexities that humans face in the real-world, AI systems can do no better than humans.

Cognition

Ariely, D.: *Predictably Irrational: The Hidden Forces that Shape Our Decisions* (Ariely, 2009).

Ariely illustrates many ways in which people do not make rational decision. Yet he also shows that these irrational decisions are consistent and therefore predictable. This predictability allows the creation of an economic description, behavioral economics, that differs from but parallels rational economics.

Berlin, Isaiah: *The Hedgehog and the Fox* (Berlin, 2013).

Berlin describes two approaches to life. The hedgehog approach views the world through a single defining idea. The fox approach is one of multiple ideas. Berlin gives examples of historical writers and thinkers who can be categorized as one or the other. Berlin regarded the division as an intellectual game; however, others have taken it more seriously.

Bock, P.: *The Emergence of Artificial Cognition: An Introduction to Collective Learning* (Bock, 1993).

This is a textbook still salient to understanding cognition and game theory. Peter Bock offers many foundational disambiguaters for anyone with serious interest in information conflict.

Brabham, D. C.: *Crowdsourcing*, (Brabham, 2013).

Brabham defines and illustrates crowdsourcing. Crowdsourcing is a deliberate blend of a bottom-up, open, creative process with top-down organizational goals. It is generally online. He identifies four dominant crowdsourcing types, based on the kind of problem being solved, as the knowledge-discovery and management approach, the broadcast-search approach, the peer-vetted creative-production approach, and the distributed-human-intelligence tasking approach.

Brafman, O. and **Brafman**, R.: *SWAY: The Irresistible Pull of Irrational Behavior* (Brafman & Brafman, 2008).

The two Brafmans discuss human biases and tendencies that lead to irrational behavior and give examples.

Harari, Yuval N.: *Sapiens: A Brief History of Humankind* (Harari, 2015).

This book provides an excellent anthropological view of the history of humanity, including the power of communication, coordination, and collective learning.

Hawkins, J. and **Blakeslee**, S.: *On Intelligence*, (Hawkins & Blakeslee, 2004).

This book is about intelligence, human and artificial. It also provides an excellent description of the biological workings of the brain.

Mlodinow, L.: *The Drunkard's Walk: How Randomness Rules Our Lives*, (Mlodinow, 2008).

Mlodinow discusses the nature of chance the impacts of randomness on various parts of our lives.

Plato (B. Jowett, translator): *The Republic*, (Plato, 2016).

A classic work of philosophy including ideas about justice and human limits.

Polya, G.: *How to Solve It: A New Aspect of Mathematical Method*, (Polya, 1945).

Polya talks about how to learn and teach mathematics and methods of learning beyond mathematics.

Robson, D.: *The Intelligence Trap: Why Smart People Do Stupid Things and How to Avoid Them*, (Robson, 2019).

Robson says that intelligence doesn't guarantee an absence of mistakes, it may make a person more susceptible to making certain types of errors. He does give advice for avoiding these errors.

Sapolsky, R.: *Behave: The Biology of Humans at our Best and Worst* (Sapolsky, 2017).

Professor Sapolsky, a neuroscientist and primatologist, gives a broad, interdisciplinary review of human behavior. From a fundamental evolutionary behavior to the seconds before we decide, he helps us understand the causes of violence, crowd behavior, cognitive strategies, the effects of stress on behavior and behavioral appetites, and sating. *N.b.*, he describes the structure of the associative and dissociative power captured in the biases of us/them-ism, including multiple ways to increase or decrease these irrationalities. The core automatic and emotional character and minimal distinctiveness necessary for eliciting such bias is revealed.

He also provides a very readable description of the brain and nervous system in an appendix, "Neuroscience 101."

Silver, Nate: *The Signal and the Noise: Why so many Predictions Fail—but Some Don't* (Silver, 2012).

Nate Silver presents statistical and human factors to improve prediction and guidance for thinking probabilistically.

Sloman, S. and **Fernbach**, P.: *The Knowledge Illusion, Why We Never Think Alone*, (Sloman & Fernbach, 2017).

Sloman and Fernbach describe many facets of our congenital ignorance, our bias toward overestimating the depth of our understanding, and how our communal intelligence rescues us.

Steiner, G.: *Errata: An Examined Life*, (Steiner, 1997).

This is an autobiography, laced with deep philosophical thought, foundational knowledge of communication, and useful models of pedagogy.

Tierney, J. and **Baumeister**, R. F.: *The Power of Bad: How the Negativity Effect Rules Us and How We Can Rule It*, (Tierney & Baumeister, 2019).

The authors contend that the "negative" has a greater impact on us than the "positive." They describe means for harness this to our benefit.

Tomasello, M.: *Why We Cooperate*, (Tomasello, 2009).

Tomasello argues that we are innately cooperative and that our culture is built on this and reinforces it with learned behaviors.

Volk, T.: *Quarks to Culture: How We Came to Be* (Volk, 2017).

Volk discusses the world as a series of complex adaptive systems that spawn more complex adaptive systems, from physics to chemistry to biology to culture.

Wolf, M.: *Reader, Come Home: The Reading Brain in a Digital World*, (Wolf, 2018).

Wolf discusses the changes in cognitive processing brought about by reading material presented on computers, such as social media content, as opposed to reading books.

Communication

Stories are primal! Stories are evocative and resonate with our need to understand and make sense of the world. They can appeal to our deepest needs, desires and values. If the speaker has the audience's trust, (this requires a positive opinion on his character and competence.) he can illuminate, inspire, captivate with the message, forms of phrase, choice words, with substance and style that is clear, uniting an idea with emotion for the specific audience at the propitious time. Tone, volume, social signal production and matching speech style to the audience all are relevant. From Sumeric, Greco-Judeo-Christian traditions to Shakespeare, Chaucer, and Dickens, the story is central to persuasion.

Centola, D., et al.: "Experimental Evidence for Tipping Points in Social Convention," (Centola, 2018a).

Professor Centola teaches how to use network science to initiate social movements, to mobilize political activism versus the simple viral-like spread of ideas. He reveals how to create online networks that increase the adoption of new behavior. Additionally, he announces that there are "exact broadcast frequencies at which subliminal messages may be effective for activating cognitive and behavioral responses." (p. 196) "The size of the critical mass is expected to vary based on theoretically identifiable features of a social setting."

Conger, S.: "The Necessary Art of Persuasion," (Conger, 1998).

Conger discusses, "the great benefit of one-to-one meetings, powerful stories with vivid language matching the motivational frame of the audience, incorporating their perspective," persuasion being seen as learning and negotiating.

Duarte, N. and **Sanchez**, P.: *Illuminate: Ignite, Change, through Speeches, Stories, Ceremonies, and Symbols*, (Duarte & Sanchez, 2016).

The authors emphasize the time progression and stages of persuasion using stories, speeches, ceremonies, and symbols, utilizing the visual, auditory, spatial, and physical from the "dream to the leap, to the fight and to the climb."

Edelson, M., et al.: "Following the crowd: brain substrates of long-term memory conformity," (Edelson, Sharot, Dolan, & Dudai, 2011).

The authors describe how the power of the crowd, utilizing man's primal desire for affiliation (membership) and affirmation, can be harnessed to change an individual's initial view to that of the crowd.

Forsyth, M.: *The Elements of Eloquence: Secrets of the Perfect Turn of Phrase*, (Forsyth, 2014).

Forsyth dissects famous phrases and shows how to create eloquent, powerful phrases.

Geary, J.: *The World in a Phrase: A Brief History of the Aphorism*, (Geary, 2005).

Geary discusses examples of aphorisms and their power.

Gladwell, M.: *Talking to Strangers: What We Should Know about the People We Don't Know*, (Gladwell, 2019).

Gladwell describes interviews with various people and the problems with the tools and strategies we use to make sense of people we don't know—how they invite conflict and misunderstanding.

Harvard Business Review: *HBR's 10 Must Reads On Communication*, (Harvard Business Review, 2013).

For the executive and aspiring manager, this collection of strategies and examples provides practical advice concerning management and teams.

Johnston, P. *Choice Words: How Our Language Affects Children's Learning*, (Johnston, 2004).

Johnston discusses how teachers use word choice to educate children and, by extension, the importance and power of word choice.

Levin, Mark R.: *Unfreedom of the Press* (Levin, 2019).

This book describes bias of the current news media against President Trump with reference to the history of journalism and, by extension, how stringent and fragile the markers of social membership are.

Matsumoto, D, **Frank**, M. G. and **Hwang**, H. S. (Eds.): *Nonverbal Communication: Science and Applications*, (Matsumoto, Frank, & Hwang, 2013).

The chapters of this book describe the science and applications on nonverbal communications.

McCulloch, G.: *Because Internet: Understanding the New Rules of Language*, (McCulloch, 2019).

McCulloch describes how the internet is changing communication, including a new vocabulary for digital natives.

McKee, R.: *Story: Substance, Structure, Style and the Principles of Screenwriting*, 1997, (McKee, 1997).

"The art of story is the dominant cultural force in the world… …the art of Film is the dominant medium in this grand enterprise." McKee offers a guide to this craft including "the principles of Antagonism." pp. 317-337.

Negroponte, N.: *Being Digital*, (Negroponte, 1995).

Negroponte describes the multiple elements of digital communication, such as bandwidth, virtual reality and the internet.

O'Connor, C. and **Weatherall**, J. O.: *The Misinformation Age: How False Beliefs Spread*, (O'Connor & Weatherall, 2019).

O'Connor and Weatherall argue that social factors, e.g., who you know, determine the beliefs in false things.

Pentland, A.: *Honest Signals: How They Shape Our World*, (Pentland, 2008).

Pentland describes unconscious social signals as a separate communications network. Because these signals are biologically evolved, he calls them "honest signals."

Pentland, A.: *Social Physics: How Good Ideas Spread: The Lessons from a New Science*. (Pentland, 2014).

Professor Pentland (Director of the MIT Human Dynamics Lab) gives us an introduction to the new science of the quantification of the dialectic of social signals, our universal language offering information for profiling, prediction, and persuasion.

Poibeau, T.: *Machine Translation*, (Poibeau, 2017).

Poibeau describes the problems of a computer translating human language and the efforts from rule-based approaches to deep learning.

Polanyi, M.: *Personal Knowledge: Towards a Post-Critical Philosophy*, (Polanyi, 1958).

This is a work on the philosophy of science. Polanyi argues that our personal experiences and ways of sharing knowledge have an effect on scientific discovery.

Polanyi, M.: *The Tacit Dimension*, (Polanyi, 2009).

Professor Polanyi explains how tacit knowledge, expert or contextualized knowledge, is in the mind of the expert, some of which the expert cannot put into words but must demonstrate. This most difficult type of knowledge must be experienced as in a mentor-mentee or apprentice relationship by observing and "doing." It is distinct from explicit and implicit knowledge that are easier to transfer.

Shannon, C. E. and **Weaver**, W.: *The Mathematical Model of Communication*, (Shannon & Weaver, 1963).

This book explains Claude Shannon's mathematical theory of communication. Shannon founded information theory with his quantification of information and its connection to entropy. He connects the quantification to the (at the time) new term "bit" (for binary digit), leading to direct application to digital computer communications. In the popular literature, "Shannon's Loop" is provides an elegant model of the dialectic of communication.

Stephens, M.: *Beyond News: The Future of Journalism*, (Stephens, 2014).

Stephens argues for "wisdom journalism," which adds interpretive, explanatory and opinionated views of events.

Wihbey, J. P.: *The Social Fact: News and Knowledge in a Networked World*, (Wihbey, 2019).

Wihbey argues that journalism can better serve by focusing on ways to foster social connections, as opposed to pure reporting.

Complex Adaptive Systems

Holland, J.: *Signals and boundaries: Building Blocks for Complex Adaptive Systems* (Holland, 2012).

Holland describes the signals and semi-permeable boundaries of complex adaptive systems. He argues that these are important in understanding and steering complex adaptive systems.

Kauffman, S.: *At Home in the Universe: The Search for the Laws of Self-Organization and Complexity*, (Kauffman, 1995).

Kauffman describes how complex adaptive systems work, giving many examples.

Moffat, J.: *Complexity Theory and Network Centric Warfare*, (Moffat, 2003).

Moffat discusses complexity theory and how it relates to network centric warfare.

O'Toole, E.: *Decentralised Detection of Emergence in Complex Adaptive Systems*, (O'Toole, 2015).

O'Toole describes how emergence in complex adaptive systems can be detected by statistical analyses.

Education

Beetham, H. and **Sharpe**, R. (Eds.): *Rethinking Pedagogy for a Digital Age: Designing for 21st Century Learning*, (Beetham & Sharpe, 2013).

This book discusses issues in designing and delivering learning activities, given digital influences. It illustrates the concepts with case studies.

Davidson, C. N.: *The New Education: How to Revolutionize the University to Prepare Students for a World in Flux*, (Davidson, 2017).

Davidson argues that higher education, as it is now designed, is unsuited for the current age.

Ignatius, A. (Ed.): *Harvard Business Review Special Issue: How to Learn Faster and Better*, (Ignatius, 2019).

Erika Andersen advises that "the ability to learn faster than your competitor may be the only sustainable competitive advantage." This issue uses a list of authors to address motivation; self-assessment; avoiding defensive thinking; understanding your personalized learning style; seeking support, guidance, and asking for feedback; setting aside time for learning; and, if you are in management, the need to manage for learning.

Krishnan, K. R.: *The Art of Learning: Learn to Learn*, (Krishnan, 2015).

Krishnan discusses the key principles to learning. Having first armed us with the neuro-ecology of leaning, he emphasizes motivation and awareness of our preconceptions influence on interpretation. He reports that for optimal retention, multiple spaced learning sessions are preferable to cramming. The convergence of top-down processes of knowledge and expectation with bottom-up information derived from our senses lead to new percepts. Ignition of motivation is derived from both intrinsic interest (pull) or gratification and extrinsic factors (push). "Praise is most effective in engendering development of a more intrinsic process." His "golden rule" is to praise or critique the action, never the person. Krishnan provides practical advice for student and teacher.

Sawyer, R. K. (Ed.): *The Cambridge Handbook of The Learning Sciences*, (Sawyer, 2014).

The chapters in this book are divided into sections on foundations, methodologies, practices that foster effective learning, learning together, learning disciplinary knowledge, and moving learning sciences research into the classroom.

Sharpe, R., **Beetham**, H. and **De Freitas**, S. (Eds.): *Rethinking Learning for a Digital Age*, (Sharpe, Beetham, & De Freitas, 2010).

This book discusses education from a learning point of view, with learners as active participants.

Valiant, L.: *Probably Approximately Correct: Nature's Algorithms for Learning and Prospering in a Complex World*, (Valiant, 2013).

Valiant approaches learning from the viewpoint of a computer scientist. He argues that the key is "probably approximately correct" algorithms. These are evolutionary strategies for pragmatic coping with problems.

Human Networks

Centola, D.: *How Behavior Spreads: the Science of Complex Contagions*. (Centola, 2018b).

Professor Centola's ground-breaking work is validated for both digital and offline traditional groups. This is a seminal book on the new field of network science that is revolutionizing social persuasion. He deals with how to induce mobilization of social networks. Although new ideas can spread in networks (like a virus) with remarkable ease, there are often surprising barriers to spreading of complex behaviors such as political activism. He reveals how to understand network structure and design and influence networks to increase the spread of new behaviors.

Christakis, N. A. and **Fowler**, J. H.: *Connected*, (Christakis & Fowler, 2009).

Christakis and Fowler describe how social networks affect you from health to wealth.

Ferguson, Niall: *The Square and the Tower* (Ferguson, 2018).

Ferguson devotes this book to discussing human networks, contrasting them to human hierarchies in the history of human power structures. As an historian, he says that most accounts of history concentrate on the hierarchies (typically housed in high towers), omitting the social networks (typically in the town square below the towers), which he says are the true drivers of change. He makes the case that networks are just as important as hierarchies in understanding human history, and by implication, the human future.

Jackson, Matthew O.: *The Human Network: How Your Social Position Determines Your Power, Beliefs, and Behaviors* (Jackson, 2019).

Jackson discusses how social networks affect power and influence and account for failure to assimilate basic facts. He also discusses contagion, both disease and financial crises.

Jackson, Matthew O.: *Social and Economic Networks* (Jackson, 2008).

This is a textbook on networks and their social and economic applications. Jackson.

Management

Conaty, B. and **Charan**, R.: *The Talent Masters: Why Smart Leaders Put People Before Numbers*, (Conaty & Charan, 2010).

Conaty describes how leaders judge and develop talent in others—and why.

Coyle, D.: *The Talent Code: Greatness Isn't Born. It's Grown*, (Coyle, 2009).

Coyle argues that talent can be created and nurtured and gives advice for this vital endeavor.

Grant, A.: *Originals: How Non-Conformists Move the World*, (Grant, 2017).

Grant describes "originals" as non-conformists by championing novel ideas and values that go against the grain, combat conformity and oppose outdated traditions, moving the world.

Schmidt, E. and **Rosenberg**, J.: *How Google Works*, (Schmidt & Rosenberg, 2017).

Schmidt and Rosenberg discuss the management philosophy of Google and how it differed from that of conventional corporations. They discuss finding and fostering "smart creatives." This book is filled with modern management ideas that fuel Silicon Valley and how to realize their power. The authors describe the power of individual "smart creatives" and small teams empowered by information and technology. They describe sufficient operational freedom and "times ten" thinking to foster leaps in progress. They stress the need for a sufficient number of individuals with technical depth, management savvy and creative flair.

Persuasion, General

The following sources are focused on persuasion. As always, consider context, timing, meta-structures, access to information, simplicity, ease of use, and repetition.

Aristotle (W. Rhys Roberts, translator): *Rhetoric* (Aristotle, 2004).

This work is the classic and still central to our understanding of persuasion.

- *ethos*—credibility
- *pathos*—emotional appeal
- *logos*—logic
- *kairos*—the propitious moment (timing)

Arvatu, A. and **Aberdeen**, A.: *Rhetoric: The Art of Persuasion*, 2015, Bloomsberry (Arvatu & Aberdein, 2016).

Arvatu and Aberdeen describe the elements of rhetoric and how to use them.

Berger, J.: *The Catalyst: How to Change Anyone's Mind*, (Berger, 2020).

Berger argues that the best way to change someone's mind is to remove the barriers set up to oppose the change.

Chamorro-Premuzic, T.: "Persuasion depends mostly on the audience," (Chamorro-Premuzic, 2015).

Here you hear the echo of Cicero to know your audience—do your homework before you begin—their features, memberships and matrix.

Cialdini, R.: *Influence: The Psychology of Persuasion*, (Cialdini, 2007).

This is a "must read" for anyone with a serious interest in persuasion. His persuasion principles (these principles are fundamental on- and off- line) are:

- Reciprocation
- Commitment and consistency
- Social proof
- Liking
- Authority
- Scarcity

Cialdini, R.: *Pre-Suasion*, (Cialdini, 2016).

This book addresses what is said and done before making a request, using the relationship, trust, and setting to make the audience sympathetic to the message before they encounter it

Cicero, M. T. (James M. May, translator): *How to win an Argument by Marcus Tullius Cicero: An Ancient Guide to the Art of Persuasion* (2016) (Cicero, 2016).

From Aristotle's Athens to the renaissance, rhetorical education for civic duty remained a primary element of education. To the Romans, rhetorical efficiency was a component of leadership. The Roman orator spoke of natural ability, training and mastery of precepts and content expertise and then practice. Cicero showed facility in the use of syllogistic reasoning—using a major premise, a minor premise, and a conclusion—but his major focus was on arrangement, style (elocution), memory and delivery. Delivery emphasized voice, movement, gesture and facial expression. Cicero's emphasis on movement was the Roman awareness of the power of social signals now studied at the MIT Human Dynamics Laboratory. To Quintilian, an orator *is Vir bonus dicendi peritus,"* a good (moral) man skilled in speaking. Well known Roman proverb (in Rome).

Cicero emphasizes knowing the audience, the natural ability of the speaker, the art and skill of delivery with elegance, polished with practice, understanding the case and how it is best arranged, utilizing the power of emotions and affirmation, clarity and accuracy, and practice, practice.

Dillard, J. P. and **Pfau**, M. (Eds.): *The Persuasion Handbook: Developments in Theory and Practice*, (Dillard & Pfau, 2002).

This book illustrates the range of the persuasion domain. It contains 34 chapters by more than 60 authors and comprises almost 900 pages.

Eslick, A. et al.: "Ironic effects of drawing attention to story errors," (Eslick, Fazio, & Marsh, 2011).

This article says simply pointing out or highlighting errors may have the unintended effect of increasing the retention of the erroneous view. Error assessment is preferred to identifying the errors.

Fazio, L. et al.: "Knowledge Does Not Protect Against Illusory Truth," (Fazio, Brashier, Payne, & Marsh, 2015).

This gives another view of man's limits and predictable vulnerable aspects.

Fazio, L. and **Marsh**, E.: "Correcting False Memories," (Fazio & Marsh, 2010).

Fazio and Marsh discuss the successful correction using feedback and hypercorrection effects (in which the correction is more likely to be successful when the false memory was strongly held, rather than weakly).

Fazio, L. and **Marsh**, E.: "Slowing presentation speed increases illusions of knowledge," (Fazio & Marsh, 2008).

This modern advice on elocution mimics Cicero in emphasizing the style of the presentation, not just the logic and content.

Fisher, R., **Ury**, W., and **Patton**, B.: *Getting to Yes: Negotiating Agreements Without Giving In*. (Fisher, Ury, & Patton, 2011).

The authors describe a method of negotiating that avoids problems normally found in the process. The elements are the following:

- Separate the people from the problem;
- Focus on interest, not positions;
- Work together to create options that will satisfy both parties;
- Negotiate successfully with people who are more powerful, refuse to play by the rules or resort to dirty tricks"

Halperin, E., et al.: "Promoting the Middle East Peace Process by Changing Beliefs about Group Malleability," (Halperin, Russell, Trzensniewski, Gross, & Dweck, 2011).

This addresses the importance of flexibility and homophily by description and example.

Harvard Business Review Staff: "Emotional Intelligence: Influence and Persuasion," (Harvard Business Review Staff, 2017).

This work contains a collection of articles, written by various authors. This is a practical description and advice for understanding the part of intelligence that frequently determines influence and success. "Sell to Mr. Rational for simple sales and to Mr. Intuitive for complex sales." Here we see "the two basic components of trust, competence and character." "The research shows that persuasion works by appealing to a limited set of deeply rooted human drives and needs."

Headquarters, Department of the Army: *PSYOPS Military Psychological Operations Manual, Field Manual 3-05-30* (Headquarters, Department of the Army, 2005).

This document provides an official, traditional overview of the missions, roles, policies, and strategies of military psychological operations.

Martin, Stephen and **Marks**, Joseph: *Messengers: Who We Listen To, Who We Don't, and Why* (Martin & Marks, 2019).

All signals are context dependent. Here we learn that part of the context entails our perception of the messenger and that it is essential in persuasion. The type of messenger, hard or soft, and four specific traits of each of these two types of messenger are important. For the "hard messenger, " socio-economic position, competence, dominance, and attractiveness are salient. For the "soft messenger," warmth, vulnerability, trustworthiness, and charisma are important. Frugal decision heuristics, clustered about the messenger, are known, are predictive, and are vulnerable to manipulation.

Mercier, H.: *Not Born Yesterday: The Science of Who We Trust and What We Believe*, (Mercier, 2020).

Mercier is adept at illuminating barriers to persuasion. He describes human active vigilance, our radar against persuasion and our resistance or "reactance." He clarifies how we judge whether the messenger and message are aligned with our own interest and if it undermines our autonomy or agency. He reveals why most attempts at mass persuasion fail.

Milgram, S.: *Obedience to Authority: An Experimental View*, (Milgram, 1974).

This is the classic study on how the power of "authority" can make us sequacious.

Moffett, M. W.: *The Human Swarm: How Our Societies Arise, Thrive, and Fall*, (Moffett, 2018).

Moffett understands the human predisposition to join groups, value and guard membership and to be influenced or even controlled by that membership. He reveals how "stringent and fragile" the markers of social membership can be. He points out the "we-ness at the root of riots, ethnic cleansing and holocausts;" how the swarm influences us and society.

Pink, D.: *DRiVE, the Surprising Truth About What Motivates Us*, (Pink, 2009).

This book concerns the power of autonomy, mastery, and purpose or meaning to motivate and discusses when incentives may be counter-productive. Pink presents hard, counterintuitive evidence that without understanding the person and setting, the use of incentives and/or punishments may produce adverse, unintended outcomes.

Pink presents the evidence for purpose, autonomy and mastery motivating people beyond traditional rewards and punishments. He reminds us of the human intrinsic motivation toward activity that ignites "our innate need to direct our own lives, to learn and create new things and to do better by ourselves and our world."

Sharot, T.: *The Influential Mind, What the Brain Reveals About our Power to Change Others*, (Sharot, 2017).

Professor Sharot (Director of the Affective Brain Lab at University College, London) focuses on how we form beliefs and ideas; the use of fear to induce inaction; when to question the crowd's opinion or the unanimous opinion; and how technology cause confirmation bias to influence.

Thaler, R. and **Sunstein**, C.: *Nudge: Improving Decisions About Health, Wealth, and Happiness*, (Thaler & Sunstein, 2008).

Professor Thaler (2017 Nobel Laureate) addresses the "science of choice:"

- Choice architecture,
- Defaults,
- Structuring complex choices,
- Anchoring,
- Expecting error,

- Priming,
- Mapping,
- the Spotlight effect,
- feedback, and
- giving Incentives.

Persuasive Technology

Alter, A.: *Irresistible, The Rise of Addictive Technology and the Business of Keeping You Hooked*. (Alter, 2018).

Alter argues that social media platforms are engineered for maximum addiction. He said that "behavioral addiction consists of six ingredients: compelling goals that are just beyond reach; irresistible and unpredictable positive feedback; a sense of incremental progress and improvement; tasks that become slowly more difficult over time; unresolved tensions that demand resolution; and strong social connections." Computer games appear to have used these ingredients as design specifications.

Canan, M., and **Warren**, R.: "Cognitive Schemas and Disinformation Effects on Decision Making in Lay People," (Canan & Warren, 2018).

Canan and Warren enlighten with the of abetment of influence by addressing the cognitive structure, chain of logic, and metaphors used in narrative understanding.

Dryzek, J. et al.: "The crisis of Democracy and the Science of Deliberation." (Dryzek et al., 2019).

This book describes the urgent need for a scaffolding to foster deliberative critical collective reasoning. The thesis is the importance of honored discussion and fostering thoughtful reflective public dialog in these times of dissociative us-them-ism.

Fogg, B. J.: *Persuasive Technology, Using Computers to change What People think and Do*. (Fogg, 2003).

Professor B. J. Fogg introduces the term captology for Computer Assisted Persuasion and the term MIP for Mass Interpersonal Persuasion referring to using the Internet, including the giant social media platforms, to persuade on a large scale.

See also the section on website credibility (Fogg, Home, n.d.).

Fogg, B. J. and **Eckles**, D.: *Mobile Persuasion: Twenty Perspectives on the Future of Behavior Change*. (Fogg & Eckles, 2014).

See Fogg, B. www.mobilepersuasion,com

B.J. Fogg presents his tripartite "Fogg Behavioral Model" (FBM) of persuasion consisting of motivation, ability and trigger. He posits that motivation deals with pleasure v. pain, hope v. fear, or social acceptance v. rejection. He divides triggers into three types: sparks (increased motivation), facilitators (enhancement of ability) and signals (reminders). He emphasizes the perception of simplicity in engendering the desired behavior. He considers simplicity in terms of time, money, and physical and mental effect, and whether or not the behavior will be socially acceptable. He describes web-site credibility and suggests a policy of launching the effort early and "iterating quickly." (Fogg, 2018) The cultural context is always important. Importantly, he emphasizes that we have a "persuasion profile" similar to a credit report.

Fontaine, R., and **Frederick**, K.: "The Autocrat's New Tool Kit" (Fontaine & Frederick, 2019).

Authoritarian programs, including in China and Russia, are using surveillance, big data analytics, facial recognition, etc., for micro-targeting and the "industrialization" of propaganda to control their citizens, for international influence and, in China's case, as commercial products to sell to other autocrats. The prediction is for the future to see "far more effective influence campaigns."

Gargan, E.: *Digital Persuasion* (Gargan, 2017).

Here the focus is on the mobile decision moment, in which *kairos* applies.

Hardjono, T., et al.: *Trust:: Data: A New Framework for Identity and Data Sharing*. (Hardjono, Shrier, & Pentland, 2016).

The authors call for reinventing societal systems to ensure trust. Further, they describe, in a fair amount of detail, proposals to do that.

Harrell, E.: "Neuromarketing: What You Need to Know," (Harrell, 2019).

Harrell describes biometric parameters for predictive profiles.

Hosanagar, K.: *A Human's Guide to Machine Intelligence*, (Hosnagar, 2019).

Professor Hosanagar describes the staggering number of man's everyday choices that are made by AI as defaults, and he addresses biases in AI and man. Further, he addresses new surfaces of persuasion such as chatbots and avatars.

Kaptein, M.: *Persuasion Profiling, How the Internet Knows What Makes You Tick*. (Kaptein, 2015).

"A persuasion profile is a collection of estimates of the effects of distinct persuasion principles for an individual and the certainty around those estimates." (e.g., Cialdini's six principles.) "People are consistent in their persuasion profile." A persuasion profile can be based on a questionnaire or better yet on actual behavior on- or off-line.

"Every time a response to a persuasion principle is observed, the persuasion profile is improved." "Persuasion profiles are happening right now. They are everywhere."

Lederman, O. et al.: "Rhythm: A Unified Measurement Platform for Human Organizations," (Lederman, Mohan, Calacci, & Pentland, 2018).

The authors present a beginning of the use of digitally derived biometrics and sociometrics for the tracking and surveillance to improve [control?] efficiency, self-awareness and communications in an organization.

Luca, M. and **Bazerman**, M. H.: *The Power of Experiments: Decision-Making in a Data Driven World*, (Luca & Bazerman, 2020).

The authors discuss how continuous sensing allows experimental design and implementation for iterative additive influence. Web sites and platforms continually use randomized, controlled experiments by adjusting information access and structure to learn about us and influence us.

McNamee, R.: *Zucked: Waking Up to the Facebook Catastrophe*, (McNamee, 2019).

McNamee details the damage caused by Facebook and other social media.

Michaels, D.: *The Triumph of Doubt: Dark Money and the Science of Deception*, (Michaels, 2020b).

Michaels discusses manipulated science for corporate profit.

Polson, N and **Scott**, J.: *AIQ: How People and Machines Are Smarter Together* (Polson & Scott, 2018).

Polson and Scott explain the structure, power and ubiquity of suggestion engines.

Seife, C.: *Virtual Unreality: The New Era of Digital Deception*, (Seife, 2014).

Seife discusses "the trickery, fakery and cyber skullduggery that the internet enables."

Resilience Sources

Rothrock, Ray A.: *Digital Resilience: Is Your Company Ready for the Next Cyber Threat?* (Rothrock, 2018).

Rothrock describes how enterprises are attacked through the internet and the fact that successful attacks are almost inevitable. He argues that companies must prepare to survive and thrive despite the attacks. He provides resilience strategies.

Southwick, Steven M. and **Charney**, Dennis S.: *Resilience: The Science of Mastering Life's Greatest Challenges* (Southwick & Charney, 2018).

The authors describe general resilience—bouncing back—from traumas and provide methods to improve resilience.

Zolli, Andrew and **Healy**, Ann Marie: *Resilience: Why Things Bounce Back* (Zolli & Healy, 2012).

The authors define resilience and describe how systems react to traumas. They relate scientific discoveries that explain why some systems bounce back and others fail.

The Future

Kelly, Kevin: *The Inevitable: Understanding the 12 Technological Forces that will Shape Our Future*. (Kelly, 2016).

Becoming, cognifying, flowing, screening, accessing, sharing, filtering, remixing, interacting, tracking, questioning and beginning are the 12 forces identified by Kelly.

With accelerating unending change, "We are in an "upgrade arms race" and "we will be newbies forever." "We are cognifying inert things." He opines that "It's hard to imagine anything that would change everything as much as cheap powerful artificial intelligence."

Johansen, Bob: *Get There Early. Sensing the Future to Compete in the Present* (Johansen, 2007).

Robert Johansen of the Institute for the Future (IFTF) in Palo Alto distinguishes dilemmas that cannot be solved from problems that have a solution. He discusses "dilemma sensemaking" where you can win anyway by reframing, changing the time horizon, learning by immersive experience, decentralizing, and rapid profiling.

Migdall, A., et al. (Eds.): *Single-Photon Generation and Detection*, (Migdall, Polyakov, Fan, & Bienfang, 2013).

The articles in this book describe various aspects and appliations of single-photon generation and detection.

Powell, J, **Maise**, G. and **Pellegrino**, C.: *StarTram: The New Race to Space*, (Powell, Maise, & Pellegrino, 2013).

The authors describe the use and economics of superconducting magnets to launch objects and people into space.

Susskind, R. and **Susskind**, D.: *The Future of the Professions: How Technology Will Transform the Work of Human Experts*, (Susskind & Susskind, 2017).

The Susskinds describe the global societal transformative effects of "increasingly enabled machines and the drop in the barriers between expert knowledge and the end user."

War and Conflict, General

Brose, Christian: *The Kill Chain: Defending America in the Future of High-Tech Warfare* (Brose, 2020b).

This book discusses America's loss of military dominance, especially with respect to China. It proposes that America's "future force be built around smaller, lower-cost, more expendable, and more autonomous systems." This force must be integrated with superior communications.

Brose, Christian: "The New Revolution in Military Affairs." (Brose, 2019).

A discussion of the revolutionary effect of artificial intelligence, autonomous systems, ubiquitous sensors, advanced manufacturing and future quantum science on the preparation for warfare.

Chinese Academy of Military Science: *The Science of Military Strategy (2013)* (Chinese Academy of Military Science, 2018).

This book is an internal description by the Chinese military of its overarching strategy. It provides a view of complexity, deception, patience, utilizing *shi* and the wisdom of Sun-Tsu. Its central orientation is toward cognitive superiority in the service of long-term, zero-sum nation-state domination.

Clausewitz, Carl (Michael Howard, Peter Paret, translators): *On War* (Clausewitz, 1993).

This is a view of the Occidental art of war. However, it has adherents that read into it one view of war, emphasizing his discussion of "absolute war," and adherents who emphasize his discussion of the relationships between political and military objectives. The book was unfinished at his death, leaving room for argument. He also introduced several enduring metaphors, such as the "fog of war," "friction," and "centers of gravity."

Gaddis, J.: *On Grand Strategy* (Gaddis, 2018).

Gaddis provides an erudite, top-level view of strategy, describing the requisite habits of mind needed to deal with complexity, competing ideals, the dangers of anchoring our preconceptions, the relationship between means and ends, and the need to avoid the overreach of our inadequately considered capacity versus our aspirations.

Homer (E. V. Rieu, translator): *The Odyssey*, (Homer, 1946).

This is the classic tale of Odysseus, his travails and conflicts.

Kahn, H.: *On Escalation: Metaphors and Scenarios*, (Kahn, 2012).

Kahn discusses the nature of escalation in warfare and policy.

Keegan, J.: *A History of Warfare*, (Keegan, 1994).

Keegan provides a history of warfare throughout the world.

Kilcullen, D.: *Out of the Mountains: The Coming Age of the Urban Guerrilla.* (Kilcullen, 2013).

Kilcullen outlines the importance of the complex adaptive systems of "conflict ecosystems" and the theory of "competitive control" and its networked connectivity amidst massive demographic shifts.

Laozi (Edmund Ryden, translator): Daodejing (Laozi, 2008).

A Chinese view of complexity, connectivity, time, and control. This is "one of the foundational texts of Chinese thought." The leader is advised that the "difficulty in governing people comes from their knowing too much."

Lewis, M.: *Moneyball: The Art of Winning an Unfair Game*, (Lewis, 2003).

Lewis describes analytics and its application to baseball.

Li, S., & **Wen**, P.: China Casts Broad Net to Collect Data. *The Wall Street Journal* (Li & Wen, 2019a).

This article reports the salience of "Xuexi Quiangguo," and aggregating, legally required app to conflate surveillance data on a massive scale for current social control analytics. This will contribute to an unparalleled big data set to train third K-wave AI.

Machiavelli, Niccolo (D. Donno, translator): *The Prince*, (Machiavelli, 1966).

Machiavelli has been called the father of political science. He advised that deceit, the murder of innocents and other immoral behavior was common and effective in maintenance of political power. In his philosophy the end justifies the means. A close reading of the text, tempers the negative view of his advice.

McFate, Sean: *The New Rules of War: Victory in the Age of Durable Disorder* (McFate, 2019).

This book provides a perspective of China's grand long game, oriental disguise strategy of unrestricted war. It is warfare of any means using the media, economic warfare, stealing intellectual secrets, "lawfare"—bending the rules, cyber tactics, and public opinion. It incorporates Sun-Tsu and *shi*. The book also discusses Russia's use of similar tactics.

Pillsbury, Michael: *The Hundred-Year Marathon* (Pillsbury, 2015).

Pillsbury describes nine aspects of China's strategy:

1. Induce complacency
2. Manipulate your opponent's advisers

3. Be patient—for decades or longer
4. Steal your opponent's ideas and technology
5. Military might is not the critical factor for winning the long-term competition
6. Recognize the hegemon will take extreme, even reckless actions to retain its dominant position
7. Never lose sight of *shi*
8. Establish and employ metrics for measuring your status
9. Always be vigilant to avoid being encircled or deceived

Qiao, Liang and **Wang**, Xiangsui: *Unrestricted Warfare* (Qiao & Wang, 1999).

This document lays out war where, "the only rule is that there are no rules," where all forces are combined, where cultural, ethnic, diplomatic, "semi-warfare," quasi warfare, and sub-warfare are used. Here "military threats are already no longer the major factor affecting national security." This means "achieving means by fair means or foul," "all things are interdependent" and "boundaries relative."

Snyder, T.: *The Road to Unfreedom: Russia, Europe, America*, (Snyder, 2018).

Snyder analyzes the nature of Russian actions (after the fall of the Soviet Union) and describes the threat to democracy and law posed by these actions.

Sun-Tsu (Samuel B. Griffith, translator): *The Art of War* (Sun-Tzu, 1963).

Sun-Tsu and Clausewitz are arguably the most influential authors of military strategy. Whereas, Clausewitz set out to create a narrative description of the necessary concepts, Sun-Tsu's book is a collection of aphorisms and elucidations of the concepts contained in the aphorisms. The following are example aphorisms:

- Appear weak when you are strong, strong when you are weak;
- The supreme art of war is to subdue the enemy without fighting;
- Let you plans be dark and impenetrable as night and when you move fall like a thunderbolt;
- All warfare is based on deception;
- In the midst of chaos is opportunity;
- Build your opponent a golden bridge to retreat across.

Virgil: "The Trojan Horse," (Virgil, 1969).

This is a view of the Oriental art of war—in the West. The tale of the Trojan Horse is a classic story of deception in war.

Wrangham, R.: *The Goodness Paradox: The Strange Relationship Between Virtue and Violence in Human Evolution*, (Wrangham, 2019).

"aggression comes in not one, but two major forms, each with its own biological underpinning and its own evolutionary story." Wrangham helps us understand the difference in impulsive aggression and premeditated proactive aggression. This is centrally important in understanding why we often have "peace at home" and "war abroad" and in understanding the "coalitionary proactive aggression that is war."

War, Information

Burke, C. B.: *America's Information Wars: The Untold Story of Information Systems in America's Conflicts and Politics from World War II to the Internet Age*, (Burke, 2018).

Burke describes the search for an information system by the U.S. intelligence community (the CIA and its predecessors) that would allow successful retrieval of appropriate information while not requiring excessive efforts at cataloging and storing the information.

Clarke, Richard A. and **Knake**, Robert K.: *The Fifth Domain: Defending Our Country, Our Companies, and Ourselves in the Age of Cyber Threats* (Clarke & Knake, 2019).

Clarke and Knake define the elements of cyber offense and defense and describe examples of each. The examples include both national and cybercriminal attacks.

Ganesh, B.: "The ungovernability of digital hate culture." (Ganesh, 2018).

This shines a light on the "downside of the Democratic Digital Media," with low barriers to entry and anonymity where extreme bigotry and dissociative speech can "swarm" "anywhere and anytime."

Gerasimov, V.: "The Value of Science in Prediction," (Gerasimov, 2013).

The Gerasimov doctrine combines old and new: Stalinist propaganda, magnified by the power of Twitter and Facebook, and backed up by brute force. He says "the role of nonmilitary means of achieving political and strategic goals has grown. In many cases, they have exceeded the power of force of weapons in their effectiveness."

Greenberg, A.: *Sandworm: A New Era of Cyberwar and the Hunt for the Kremlin's Most Dangerous Hackers*, (Greenberg, 2019).

Greenberg describes the 2014 set of cyberattacks that targeted companies and countries around the world. The attackers were working in the service of Russia's military intelligence agency.

Kello, Lucas: *The Virtual Weapon and International Order* (Kello, 2017).

Kello approaches the subject of cyberspace and the potential of cyberweapons from the perspective of the international relations community, rather than the military community. He argues that this subject is important because it requires an expansion of the traditional view of state versus state actions to include the actions of non-state actors. It also requires a new theory of conflict that includes indirect damage caused by information that affects the operation of computers and thus extensive aspects of our societies.

Levitin, D.: *Weaponized Lies: How to Think Critically in the Post-Truth Era.* (Levitin, 2016).

Levitin describes how mis-applied statistics and graphs can lie. He extends the description of mathematical lies to verbal lies—seductive logic—that leads away from facts in appealing ways. He argues that the scientific method is the solution for determining when lies are being proffered.

Lin, Herbert and **Zegart**, Amy, eds.: *Bytes, Bombs, and Spies: The Strategic Dimensions of Offensive Cyber Operations* (Lin & Zegart, 2018).

The chapters in this book explore cyber weapons and their strategic dimensions.

Maan, A: *Narrative Warfare*, (Maan, 2018).

Maan explains that narrative warfare is "not so much information warfare, but rather warfare about the meaning of information."

Mervis, J.: "Elite Advisers to help NSF Navigate security concerns," (Mervis, 2019).

Mervis discusses the advisability of providing new methods and scientists to our security entities. This is advocating having multidomain and trans-domain consultants to help the NSF deal with evolving security concerns with its complexity and competing ideals.

Sanger, D. E.: *The Perfect Weapon: War, Sabotage, and Fear in the Cyber Age*, (Sanger, 2018b).

Sanger details the 2015 Russian hack of the Democratic National Committee (DNC) and leaks of the stolen emails and Russian hacks into the White House, the State Department, the Joint Chiefs of Staff, and implantation of logic bombs in U.S. electrical and nuclear plants. He extends his discussion to Chinese, Iranian and North Korean cyber operations. He recalls the destruction of Iran's nuclear centrifuges through cyber weapons. (Declassified testimony by Shawn Henry of Crowdstrike corroborates the attribution of the DNC hack to Russian intelligence agencies (The United States House of Representatives, 2017).)

Singer, P., and **Brooking**, E.: *LikeWar: The Weaponization of Social Media* (Singer & Brooking, 2018).

"War, tech, and politics have blurred into a new kind of battle space." "If you are online, your attention is like a piece of contested territory." "The most prominent part of the Chinese Golden Shield Project is its systems of keyword filtering. Should a word or phrase be added to the list of banned terms, it effectively ceases to be." (p. 138) Singer discusses misinformation caused by "…at least 60,000 Russian accounts in a single 'botnet' (a networked army of bots) that infected Twitter like a cancer." "Fake followers and 'likes' are easy to produce." (p. 79) According to their research, "Whether you're a CEO, a Commander-in-Chief, or a military commander, if you don't have a social media component, you are going to fail."

Tufekci, Z.: "It's the (Democracy-Poisoning) Golden Age of Free Speech." (Tufekci, 2018).

Tufekci discusses the increasing use of media platforms for active disinformation campaigns. She says, "The most effective forms of censorship today involve meddling with trust and attention not muzzling speech itself."

Villasenor, J.: *Artificial intelligence, deepfakes and the uncertain future of truth*. (Villasenor, 2019).

This provides important understanding of the power of depicting people in fake videos that they did not actually appear in.

Woolley, S., **Howard**, P.: (Woolley & Howard, 2019a).

"we can define computational propaganda as the assemblage of social media platforms, autonomous agents, algorithms, and big data tasked with the manipulation of public opinion." Computational propaganda is an "emerging field of study of digital misinformation and manipulation." It is characterized by automation, scalability, anonymity, for "rapid distribution of large amounts of content, sometimes personalized." Human hybrids [bot-aided humans] can "manufacture consensus." or give an "illusion of general support." "Bots generate almost half of web traffic."

Glossary of Selected Terms

The definitions given here are not comprehensive or authoritative, but relate to their use in this book. They are meant to be an *aide memoire* to preclude searching the text for a meaning.

Abductive logic A form of logical inference that starts with a set of observations and seeks to find or create the simplest or most likely explanation (model) for the evidence.
Abstraction Is the process of reducing complexity by keeping certain parts (presumably the important parts) and discarding the rest. It is a mode of cognition.
Accuracy A measure of proximity of results to the aim-point, as opposed to precision.
Addictive technology Social media that are engineered to be addictive for massive engagement.
Advanced Persistent Threat (APT) Malware attack in which the intruder not only gains access to the network but remains active in it for a long period of time -may refer to the attack or the attacker.
Adware Software that displays advertisements, may be considered malware.
Ambient intelligence Intelligence embedded in an environment that is integrated with sensors and intelligent systems.
Analytic intelligence Intelligence as measured by a standard IQ test.
Analytics A new discipline created to discover useful metrics and patterns for novel things, such as structuring a baseball team. It consists of "a broad set of analytical methodologies that enable the creation of business value (Analytics Society, 2020)."
Anchoring Creating a reference point, often an initial opinion, with a bias toward maintaining that initial assessment.
Anti-virus tool Software to detect and delete digital viruses.
Artificial Intelligence/Machine Learning (AI/ML) Replication of some aspect of human cognition in a machine (many details and caveats; however, this is the essence)/machine learning is the ability for a computer to learn by example, as opposed to having a program and/or database to produce results. (Currently the "example" involves a very large set of data tagged with the correct answers from which the machine generates its own process for producing answers from new data.)
Associative thinking See System 1 thinking.
Attack point/surface A vulnerable point or set of points (surface).

Attention attractor Cialdini lists novelty, sexual and violent references as attention attractors for use prior to persuasion attempts.
Attention magnetizer Cialdini lists self-relevant information and unfinished tasks, presentations, etc., as attention holders for use prior to persuasion attempts.
Attention merchant Is an entity that makes money by capturing your attention and selling it to advertisers for its persuasive effects.
Augmented reality (AR) An overlaying of digital information on real-world inputs.
Authenticate session Refers to a test to ensure that the computer session is valid or continues to be valid.
Avatar A computer image or graphic that represents an online human.
Backdoor A piece of malware inserted into a system to allow access to an unauthorized user. The original programmer may create a backdoor to allow later access to the system.
Biometrics Measures of biologic (physiologic or behavioral) status or functioning.
Block redundant queries A protective action that blocks repetitive queries to a system. The queries are blocked because redundant queries are used in some computer attacks.
Bot (Web robot) is a software agent used to perform automated tasks, generate simple messages or 'conversations' on social media.
Bot attack Is a computer attack generated by bots. It can also refer to the conversion of a computer system into a bot host.
Botnet Is a system of bots that act in a coordinated manner.
Bounded reality Belief or perspective based on a restricted view of reality.
Captology The study of computers as persuasive technologies (CAPT).
Carrots and Sticks Positive and negative incentives/disincentives.
Choice architecture Thaler and Sunstein define choice architecture in terms of system design (Thaler & Sunstein, 2008). The elements include defaults, expect error, give feedback, understand mappings, structure complex choices, and incentives.
Chronotype A description of the physiologic and behavioral preference of a person for a particular part of the diurnal cycle, based on the individual's circadian rhythm (biologic clocks).
Classical computing Computing using electronic digital computers, as opposed to quantum computing.
Cognified object Object with some level of software/hardware-aided cognitive ability.
Cognition The mental actions or processes of acquiring knowledge and understanding through thought, experience, and the senses, including awareness, reasoning and judgment.
Cognitive capacity The total amount of information that can be stored, may also refer to the capability to process the information.

Cognitive capital Includes intellectual capital, emotional capital and social capital. This is the store of accumulated, processed knowledge, judgments, and experiences, sometimes used to refer to general intelligence.
Commitment and Consistency Involve using our desire for consistency to persuade us. The plan is to gain an initial commitment and then rely on this desire to cause us to become convinced the commitment must be followed through.
Competitive control A control structure that's easy and attractive for people to enter, but then locks them into a system of persuasion and coercion: a set of incentives and disincentives from which they find it extremely difficult to break out.
Complex adaptive system (CAS) Systems that comprise many interacting parts with the ability to generate a new quality of macroscopic collective behavior the manifestations of which are the spontaneous formation of distinctive temporal, spatial or functional structures.
Complex diffusion Complex diffusion of things like behavior, require reinforcement from multiple sources, which weak connections don't generally provide.
Compromised key attack A computer attack in which a decryption key has been stolen and used to decrypt transmitted data.
Computational journalism Uses analytics and AI-augmentation to discover, compose, evaluate, and distribute stories.
Computational propaganda The assemblage of social media platforms, autonomous agents, algorithms, human curation, and big data tasked with the production and distribution of misleading information to manipulate public opinion.
Corporate actor An organized group, acting as a unit.
Counter-narrative A narrative to counter another narrative.
Creative intelligence The ability to create novel and interesting ideas.
Crowdsourcing A deliberate blend of bottom-up, open, creative process with top-down organizational goals.
Cybersecurity Consists of measures to protect cyberspace from hostile action, including actions emanating from cyberspace.
Cyberweapon Is restricted to malware that is capable of and intended to do sufficient damage that the effects would be classified as the effects of a weapon in the realm of international relations.
Data broker Middlemen who buy and sell information.
Data science Encompasses a set of principles, problem definitions, algorithms, and processes for extracting non-obvious and useful patterns from large data sets.
Deductive logic We begin with a general premise and conclude that it holds for a particular instance.
Deep learning Is machine learning in artificial neural networks involving massive amounts of data and hierarchical structured AI.
Deepfake Artificial intelligence-augmented face swaps, pictures, sound and video clips putting words into the mouths of others for deception.
Default to truth bias Initial assumption of truthfulness (qualified in practice).
Deliberative thinking Slow (rule-based or System 2) thinking is expensive in terms of brain power and time. It can also be wrong, but does allow the possibility of rational consideration of multiple factors.

Denial of service attack Attacks that prevent the legitimate operation of the computer by large-scale external demands for attention.
Distance With regard to persuasion, this refers to the psychological distance between a current view and a proposed change, a barrier to persuasion.
Domain name server spoofing An attack that redirects traffic to the wrong computer.
Emergent property Behavior in a complex adaptive system (CAS) that is unexpected given what is known about the CAS itself.
Emotional capital Is the store of processed knowledge of and facility for dealing with the emotional aspects of humans.
Endowment A feeling of high valuation or comfort with the *status quo*, a barrier to persuasion.
Epigenetics The heritable, altered expression (up- or down-regulating or silencing) of genes by the environment, without changes in the DNA sequence.
Eratosthenes affiliation An Eratosthenes affiliation is a group with favored access to the expanding frontiers of science and knowledge and a system to harvest, winnow down, and make convenient that knowledge.
Ethos Credibility (as used in Aristotle's *Rhetoric*).
Exhaustive search A data search that systematically considers all alternatives.
Exposome The environment, that is, non-genetic drivers of health and disease.
Explicit knowledge Articulated or can be codified into documents. It is easy to convey.
Extended reality (xR) A term that includes virtual reality, mixed reality, augmented reality, and 360° video, all immersive realities, with or without avatars.
Fake news Fabricated information that mimics news media content in form but not in organizational process or intent or news from an accredited source that is false (either because of malice or disregard for standards of checking for truth or falsity).
Fast thinking See System 1 thinking.
Filter bubble Intellectual isolation in which searches only result in information conforming to existing beliefs or preferences.
Firewall A computer system that monitors and controls incoming and outgoing traffic based on security rules.
Flexible hierarchy Adaptive rules of hierarchy that can flatten the structure and reduce excessive rules for optimal brainstorming and collective learning.
Free press Reporting organizations unencumbered by governmental restrictions.
Frugal heuristics Simple "rules of thumb," easily "computable" algorithms.
General purpose technology (GPT) disruptor A technological invention or invention set that disrupts more than a single industry.
Generalized artificial intelligence (GAI) General, flexible human level intelligence (or better) in a computer (not yet achieved).
Generative adversarial networks (GAN) Paired neural networks, one of which is set to create something (such as malware or fake images) and the other which is set to detect (or counter) the results of the first.

Genetic engineering The deliberate modification of genetic material to change the heritable characteristics of an organism.
Genetics The source of biologically inherited characteristics.
Hacker Someone who uses computer skills to gain unauthorized access to computers.
Hactivist Someone who uses hacking to bring about political or social change.
Hard messenger A messenger with socio-economic position, competence, dominance, etc.
Heuristic search A search through options based on a function (heuristic) that is not mathematically guaranteed as optimal and which is not an exhaustive search through all options.
Honest signals Biological social signals that have evolved because they change the behavior of the receivers; the network of dialectic unconscious social signals that pass between us, providing a view of intent, goals and values. These involve facial expressions, hand and body movements (Pentland, 2008).
Honey pot A computer file or system into which misleading documents or messages are loaded to induce a break in.
Illusion of Knowledge The belief that one knows more than one actually does; the belief that one has "always" known something when, in fact, it was only recently learned.
Implicit knowledge Knowledge gained by incidental activity without full awareness of what has been learned.
Inductive logic We make observations and create rules, hypotheses and theories that provide evidence to explain the conclusion; we begin with individual facts and create a general premise.
Information security Is used to describe the control of information flows. This can be the suppression of subversive information in an autocratic state or efforts to control the exchange of child-pornography. Information security is often conflated with cybersecurity
Information Warfare Conflict in which information provides both the weapons and the targets.
Install patches The process of updating software by installing corrective software (patches).
Intellectual capital This is the store of traditional intellectually processed knowledge. It is part of cognitive capital, separate from emotional and social capital.
IA Intelligence augmentation or amplification through digital means.
Intelligence, human Intellectual ability (in humans), may be divided into analytic intelligence, creative intelligence, and practical intelligence.
Internet of things (IoT) The collection of cognified objects, objects with processing power, which are connected to the internet.
IP spoofing Attaching a source IP address that is false to a message.
Kairos Propitious timing (from the Greek god of optimal timing).
Key logger Software that records the keys struck on a keyboard.

Kill chain In military conflict, gaining understanding, deciding what to do, and taking action that creates an effect to achieve an objective; a variant of the OODA loop.
Knowledge base An ontology with the instances filled in.
Limit query types A process to restrict the types of queries (software requests for information). This can be done to prevent queries from returning so much information that it overflows the space allowed for the result or to prevent unauthorized queries.
Logic bomb A piece of code that only triggers under specified conditions, but when triggered performs some malicious, generally destructive, activity.
Logos Logic or the rational argument that is part of rhetoric (from Aristotle's Rhetoric).
Malicious insider A person with the proper credentials to access a computer system who performs malicious actions.
Malware Computer software that interferes with the correct processing of information or corrupts that information.
Man in the middle attack The attacker secretly controls the communication stream between two legitimate system users, either using this to gain information or to create problems.
Mass interpersonal persuasion (MIP) Changing attitudes and behaviors on a massive scale.
Matrix Environment.
Meme A concept, idea, behavior, or style that can spread from one person to another. The conceptual analog of a gene.
Messenger bias The influence our assessment of the messenger has on our interpretation of the message.
Meta-knowledge Knowledge about knowledge.
Metanarrative Often used to mean a larger narrative that encompasses other narratives.
Microbiomic Having to do with ecological communities of microorganisms in and on a human or other multicellular organism.
Microstate Is a temporary confluence that informs (the larger state).
Microstate cognition Within the human brain involves specifically conformal, time-limited neural circuit activation, appropriate to the need from disparate neuronal modules and locations. In an organization, microstate cognition is the collective cognition of time-limited, specifically salient conformal teams assembled for consideration of issues and decisions (e.g., team learning).
Micro-targeting Large scale persuasion attempt that is selectively aimed at a person or a particular set of people (targets) who fit a set of criteria and designed to increase the probability of successful persuasion.
Mixed reality (MR) An experience in which some parts consist of real-world inputs and some are digital or analog simulated inputs.
Model the network A method for understanding and checking on the effects of modifying the system.

Narrative warfare Warfare over the meaning of information, also called narratology.
Negative SEO attack An attack to reduce the search engine ranking of a website; it seeks to counter search engine optimization (SEO) that aims to increase the rank of a website in search engine retrievals.
Neural network In biology, a network of neurons; in a computer, an artificial neural network is a hierarchical (layered) set of computer nodes (instantiated by computer algorithms) inspired by biological neural networks, created with the goal of replicating some human cognitive function, such as pattern matching, classification, or prediction based on raw data.
Neurometrics Measurements of neural activity, such as an electroencephalogram (EEG)
Neuroplasticity The ability of the brain to change or reorganize aspects of its functions.
Neurotoxicant Substances capable of causing adverse effects in the nervous system and sense organs. The huge number and variety of potentially neurotoxic substances include metals, inorganic ions, botanical toxins, and other organic matter and their sources include solvents, pesticides, fine particle air pollution, agricultural soil contamination, and inappropriate pharmaceutical use. Entry can occur via absorption, ingestion, or injection and can be active from in-utero to current.
Non-state actor Denotes some important entity (such as a terrorist organization) that is not a country.
Noosphere The total information available to humanity.
Nootropic Pharmacological agents for cognitive enhancement.
Nudge Action to encourage, not force, a choice in a desired direction.
Ontology In information science, a structure for organizing what is known about a domain. (In philosophy, the branch of metaphysics dealing with the nature of being.)
OODA loop (Observe-orient-decide-act loop) OODA is a descriptive acronym of the process of making a decision, with the option of repeating the process as needed.
Operational narrative A narrative aimed at a middle level of operations, hierarchically between strategy and tactics.
Packet sniffer A piece of software or hardware that monitors and analyzes network traffic (made up of packets). It can be legitimate, part of network management, or illegitimate, part of an attack.
Panopticon The surveillance state, where the state sees all and knows much.
Parkerian hexad Six elements of information security—confidentiality, possession or control, integrity, authenticity, availability, and utility
Password cracker Software that recovers a password from data that are stored in or transmitted by a computer.
Pathos The emotional aspect that is part of rhetoric (from Aristotle's Rhetoric).
Pedagogy The methods and practice of teaching.
Persuasion The act of causing or attempt to cause someone to change his beliefs or actions (a form of influence).

Persuasion profile A profile of an individual's susceptibility to particular persuasion techniques.

Persuasion science The emphasis is on the "science." The investigation of the effectiveness of different means of persuasion in general, the effects of different environments during the attempted persuasion, and the differences in individual receptiveness. In practice it is combined with the art of persuasion.

Pharming Directing internet users to a false website that mimics a legitimate one, tricking the user into supplying data.

Phishing Sending an email to induce the recipient to supply information.

Port scanner Software that probes a computer to find out what ports are open.

Potemkin village Any construction whose only purpose is to provide a façade that indicates one thing, when the contrary is true.

Practical intelligence The ability to navigate the requirements of the human environment.

Precision A measure of the repeatability of the results (proximity to each other), as opposed to accuracy.

Priors In Bayesian probability, this refers to the prior probability distribution before some evidence is taken into account. In persuasion, this refers to prior beliefs and attitudes before some event.

Proactive aggression Premeditated, cold, offensive aggression, as distinguished from reactive or impulsive aggression.

Profile Description of an individual based on the data entered into a website (e.g., social media site) and the actions taken on a website. The data entries include demographic information, information about the individual's work, life, interests, etc. The actions may include purchases made and items viewed and not purchased and inferences drawn from customization choices.

Prompts Triggers of behavior (as used in Fogg's Behavioral Model).

Propaganda Communication that deliberately uses or subverts stories, speeches, ceremonies, or symbols, appealing to our emotions and prejudices and bypassing rational thought, to achieve the specific goals of the propagandist, disregarding the interests of the target.

Proteomic Having to do with the proteins.

Proxy server An intermediate server between a client and another server. The intermediate server may be authorized or duplicitous.

Psychometrics Psychological measurements.

PSYOPS Psychological operations aimed at conveying selected information to audiences to influence them.

Quantum communication Communication that takes advantage of quantum theory, produces instantaneous effects that are not subject to eavesdropping.

Quantum computing Computing using quantum theory, permits extremely rapid solutions to some problems that are practically impossible by classical computers. The term may be used more broadly to include quantum sensing and communication.

Quantum theory A branch of physics dealing with the discrete levels (quanta) of energy and space. This is a very highly successful (multiple verified tests of its diverse aspects) theory of the atomic and sub-atomic levels of physics, despite having many counter-intuitive consequences.

Ransomware Software that encrypts a computer system and demands a ransom for decrypting it.

Rational choice An economic and social theory that models behavior as a set of optimal decisions based on individual preferences.

Reactance Our innate anti-persuasion response.

Reactive aggression Hot, impulsive, defensive aggression, as distinguished from proactive aggression.

Reciprocation A mutual exchange, such as seen in requests for donations that include a "gift," such as a pen, a set of address labels, or a calendar. Reciprocity is engendered when we want or feel obligated to give in return.

Replicate data A strategy for preserving data by making and storing copies.

Rhetoric Persuasion through effective or persuasive language, classically divided into ethos, pathos, logos. and kairos, discussed in Aristotle's Rhetoric.

Rootkit Software that is installed in a normally protected area of a computer to allow external access to the computer. It often contains functions to mask its presence.

Router A piece of networking hardware that forwards data between computer networks.

Rule-based thinking See System 2 thinking.

Scareware Software that scares a user into purchasing unwanted software.

Script kiddie An unskilled person who uses programs (scripts) developed by others to attack systems and networks.

Seductive logic Appealing presuppositions, biases and irrationalities that lead astray.

Serenic Anti-aggression pharmaceutical.

Shi Shi is a principal deceptive stratagem of influencing the present for its effect in the future, often as part of a long-term zero-sum game.

Simple diffusion Simple things, like information, can diffuse through both strong connections and weak connections; however, it is the weak connections that allow for explosive contagion (going viral).

Slow thinking See System 2 thinking.

Social capital The store of interpersonal relationships, shared identity, understanding, social norms, values, trust, cooperation, and reciprocity.

Social proof Bias toward agreement with what others think or do.

Social signals Non-verbal indications to thinking and feeling. The dialectic of social signals is our universal human language.

Sociometrics Measurements of social relationships such as membership, acceptance and status.

Soft messenger A messenger with warmth, vulnerability, trustworthiness, or charisma.

Source routing attack An attacker sends a packet and uses the response to get information about the operating system of the computer to be attacked.

Spam Unsolicited and unwanted message.

Spear phishing Phishing aimed at a particular person.
Spotlight effect The belief that one is being noticed more than is actually the case; the accompanying behavior induced by being or believing that one is being noticed.
Spyware Software that resides on a computer and covertly transmits computer activities to an external recipient.
Strategic narrative A narrative aimed at the highest level of operations from which other narratives are derived.
Strong feature In classification, variables that have a high correlation to the desired class.
Surrogation Surrogation is the replacement of the actual goal with a substitute or surrogate metric goal.
Swarm A large, moving group, with collective, non-centralized control, originally referring to insects and birds; digitally, a multi-agent software platform for the simulation of complex adaptive systems or synchronous group attack.
Synthetic biology Involves redesigning biological parts, systems, or organisms, engineering them to have new abilities.
System 1 thinking Associative (intuitive) or fast thinking (or System 1 thinking) is cheap in terms of brain power and time, although it can easily be wrong (Sloman & Fernbach, 2017).
System 2 thinking Slow (rule-based or System 2) thinking is expensive in terms of brain power and time. It can also be wrong, but does allow the possibility of rational consideration of multiple factors (Sloman & Fernbach, 2017).
System of systems (SoS) A system made up of systems
Tacit knowledge Knowledge gained from human experience and embedded in human minds, expert or contextual knowledge, generally transferred from mentor to mentee.
Tactical narrative A narrative aimed at a lowest (personal or micro) level of operations, addressing the concerns of local populations, domestic audiences, and soldiers on the ground.
Technium Technology as a whole system.
Technology filter A piece of technology that selectively restricts the flow of information.
Technology readiness level (TRL) A system for describing how close a technology is to being ready for commercial or government use, by convention, ranging from 1 (low) to 9 (ready for use).
Trigger A stimulus that induces a reaction (as used in Fogg's Behavioral Model).
Trojan horse Malware that misleads users as to its true intent.
Virtual machine An emulation of a computer system running on a host computer system.
Virtual reality (VR) A simulation experience that is presented as if it were reality, generally experienced with video and audio inputs.
Virus In computers, software that replicates itself on a computer, almost always to harm the target computer; in biology, a virus is a sub-microscopic infectious agent made of DNA or RNA inside a protein shell.

Weak feature In classification, variables that have a relatively low correlation to the desired class.
Wetware Biological cognitive processing system, the brain, as opposed to hardware or software in a computer.
Whaling Spear phishing very important people.
Wisdom journalism Reporting filled with knowledge of "what is best for us as a society"—according to the journalist.
Worm In computers, software that replicates itself so it can spread to other computers, almost always cause some harm to the network, at a minimum consuming communications bandwidth.
Zero-trust networks The assumption that all networks, including internal networks, cannot be trusted.

Bibliography

Agrafiotis, I., Nurse, J. R., Goldsmith, M., Creese, S., & Upton, D. (2018). A taxonomy of cyber-harms: Defining the impacts of cyber-attacks and understanding how they propagate. *Journal of Cybersecurity, 4*(1). Retrieved October 29, 2019, from https://academic.oup.com/cybersecurity/article/4/1/tyy006/5133288.

Air Forces Cyber. (2018). *Air forces cyber home*. Retrieved December 19, 2018, from Air Forces Cyber: https://www.afcyber.af.mil/

Alter, A. (2018). *Irresistible: The rise of addictive technology and the business of keeping you hooked*. New York: Penguin Press.

Altmann, Y., McLaughlin, S., Padgett, M. J., Goyal, V. K., Hero, A. O., & Faccio, D. (2018). Quantum-inspired computational imaging. *Science, 361*, 660.

Altran, S., Axelrod, R., Davis, R., & Fischhoff, B. (2017). Challenges in researching terrorism from the field. *Science, 355*, 352–354.

Analytics Society. (2020). *Informs Analytics Society*. Retrieved from INFORMS: https://connect.informs.org/analytics/home

Ancona, D. (2020). Five rules for leading in a digital world. *MIT Sloan Management Review*, 8–10.

Anderson, E. (2019). Learning to learn. *Havard Business Review Special Issue: How to Learn Faster and Better*, pp. 15–18.

Argyris, C. (2019). Teaching smart people to learn. *Harvard Business Review Special Issue: How to Learn Better and Faster* (pp. 60–71).

Ariely, D. (2009). *Predictably irrational*. New York: HarperCollins. (revised and expanded edition).

Aristotle. (2004). *Rhetoric*. Mineola, NY: Dover Publications. (W. R. Roberts, Trans.).

Arvatu, A., & Aberdein, A. (2016). *Rhetoric: The art of persuasion*. New York: Bloomsbury USA.

Aspesi, C., & Brand, A. (2020). In pursuit of open science, open access is not enough. *Science, 368*, 574–577.

Atkinson, S. R., & Moffat, J. (2005a). *The Agile organization*. Washington: CCRP.

Atkinson, S. R., & Moffat, J. (2005b). *The Agile organization: From informal networks to complex effects and agility*. Washington: CCRP Publications.

Bahcall, S. (2019). The innovation equation. *Harvard Business Review* (pp. 74–81).

Baker, H. (2011). Personal communication with Senator Baker. (K. Jobson, Interviewer)

Baker, M. (2018). *In other words: a coursebook on translation* (3rd ed.). New York: Routledge.

Baron, E. (2018). *Stanford students boycott Google jobs over firm's military work*. Retrieved July 22, 2018, from The Mercury News: https://www.mercurynews.com/2018/06/15/stanford-students-boycott-google-jobs-over-firms-military-work/

Barrat, J. (2013). *Our final invention: Artificial intelligence and the end of the human era*. New York: St. Martin's Press.

D. S. Hartley III, K. O. Jobson, *Cognitive Superiority*,
https://doi.org/10.1007/978-3-030-60184-3

BBC. (2019). *Facebook's Libra cryptocurrency attacked at Senate hearing.* Retrieved July 17, 2019, from BBC: https://www.bbc.com/news/business-49008298

BéChard, D. E. (2019). *Deceit Gets Smarter. Can Truth Keep Up?* Retrieved October 29, 2019, from Stanford Magazine: https://stanfordmag.org/contents/deceit-gets-smarter-can-truth-keep-up

Beetham, H., & Sharpe, R. (2013). *Rethinking pedagogy for a digital age: Designiing for 21st century learning* (2nd ed.). New York: Routledge.

Berger, J. (2020). *The catalyst: How to change anyone's mind.* New York: Simon & Schuster.

Berinato, S. (2015). *There's no such thing as anonymous data.* Retrieved June 11, 2019, from Harvard Business Review: https://hbr.org/2015/02/theres-no-such-thing-as-anonymous-data

Berlin, I. (2013). *The Hedgehog and the Fox.* Princeton, Princeton University Press. (H. Hardy, Ed.).

Bernstein, E., Shore, J., & Lazer, D. (2019. Improving the rhythm of your collaboration. *MIT Sloan Management Review.*

Berwick, D. M. (2020). Choices for the "New Normal". *JAMA, 323*, 2125–2126.

Bettilyon, T. E. (2019). *Why 'anonymized data' isn't so anonymous.* Retrieved June 11, 2019, from OneZero: https://onezero.medium.com/why-anonymized-data-isn-t-so-anonymous-535d2db75a2d

Bock, P. (1993). *The emergence of artificial cognition: An introduction to collective learning.* Singapore: World Scientific.

Bombgardner, M. M. (2020). Aryballe gets funds for its digital nose. *Chemical and Engineering News, 98*(28).

Bomgardner, M. M. (2020). DNA Script, partners get $23 million grant for data storage. *Chemical & Engineering News, 98*(4).

Boon, S. (2017). *21st Century Science Overload.* Retrieved February 21, 2019, from Canadian Science Publishing: http://blog.cdnsciencepub.com/21st-century-science-overload/

Boroditsky, L. (2019). Language and the brain. Science, 366, p. 13.

Bosilkovski, I. (2018). AI everywhere. *Forbes* (p. 76).

Boussard, D., Belluck, P., & Wirz, C. D. (2019). Promises and perils of gene drives: Navigating the communication of complex, post-normal science. *Proceedings of the National Academy of Sciences (PNAS), 116*, 7692–7697.

Brabham, D. C. (2013). *Crowdsourcing*. Cambridge: MIT Press.

Brafman, O., & Brafman, R. (2008). *Sway: The irresistable pull of irrational behavior*. New York: Broadway Books.

Brainard, J. (2020). Reproducibility tool scales up. *Science* (p. 607).

Brockman, J. (Ed.). (2019). *Possible minds: 25 Ways of looking at AI.* New York: Penguin Press.

Brooks, A. W., & John, L. K. (2018). The surprising power of questions. *Harvard Business Review, 96*, 60–67.

Brose, C. (2019). The new revolution in military affairs *Foreign Affairs* (pp. 122–134).

Brose, C. (2020a). *The End of America's Era of Military Primacy.* Retrieved June 4, 2020, from The Wall Street Journal: https://www.wsj.com/articles/the-end-of-americas-era-of-military-primacy-11590155833

Brose, C. (2020b). *The kill chain: Defending America in the future of high-tech warfare*. New York: Hachette Books.

Buckley, F. H. (2019). 'Social Credit' may come to America. *The Wall Street Journal.*

Burke, C. B. (2018). *America's infxormation wars: The untold story of information systems in America's conflicts and politics from world war II to the internet age*. Lanham: Rowman & Littlefield.

Canan, M., & Warren, R. (2018). Cognitive schemas and disinformation effects on decision making in lay people. In J. S. Hurley, & J. Q. Chen (Eds.), *Proceedings of the 13th International Conference on Cyber Warfare and Security* (pp. 101–119).

Capelli, P. (2019). Your approach to hiring is all wrong. *Harvard Business Review.*

Carlson, T. (2019). *Tulsi Gabbard tells Tucker why she is suing Google.* Retrieved August 3, 2019, from The Epoch Times: https://www.youtube.com/watch?v=ZFGAAa91U3o

Carter, A. (2019). *Inside the five-sided box: Lessons from a lifetime of leadership in the pentagon*. New York: Penguin Random House.

Centola, D. (2018a). Experimental evidence for tipping points in social convention. *Science, 360*, 1116–1119.

Centola, D. (2018b). *How behavior spreads*. Princeton: The Princeton University Press.

Chairman of the Joint Chiefs of Staff. (2017). *Joint planning, Joint Publications 5-0*. Washington, DC: Chairman of the Joint Chiefs of Staff.

Chamorro-Premuzic. (2015). Persuasion depends mostly on the audience. *Harvard Business Review*.

Champer, J., Bushman, A., & Akbari, O. (2016). Cheating evolution: engineering gene drives to manipulate the fate of wild populations. (N. R. Genetics, Ed.). *Nature Biotechnology, 17*, 146–159.

Chan, S. (2001). *Complex Adaptive Systems*. Retrieved February 6, 2020, from Web.MIT.edu: http://web.mit.edu/esd.83/www/notebook/Complex%20Adaptive%20Systems.pdf

Chinese Academy of Military Science. (2018). *The science of military strategy (2013)*. Lexington: 4th Watch Publishing Co. (4. W. Co, Trans.).

Cho, A. (2019). Google claims quantum computing milestone. *Science, 365*, 1364.

Christakis, N. A., & Fowler, J. H. (2009). *Connected: The surprising power of our social networks and how they shape our lives—How your friends' friends' friends affect everything you feel, think, and do*. New York: Little, Brown and Company.

Cialdini, R. B. (2007). *Influence: The psychology of persuasion*. New York: Collins Business. (revised edition).

Cialdini, R. B. (2009). *Influence: Science and practice* (5th ed.). Boston: Pearson.

Cialdini, R. B. (2016). *Pre-suasion*. New York: Simon & Schuster Paperbacks.

Cicero, M. T. (2016). *How to win an argument: an ancient guide to the art of persuasion*. Princeton: Princeton University Press. (J. M. May, Ed., & J. M. May, Trans.).

Clarke, R. A., & Knake, R. K. (2019). *The fifth domain: Defending our country, our companies, and ourselves in the age of cyber threats*. New York: Penguin Press.

Clausewitz, C. v. (1993). *On War*. New York: Alfred A Knopf, Inc.. (M. Howard, & P. Paret, Trans.).

Cloninger, C. R., Przybeck, T. R., Svrakic, D. M., & Wetzel, R. D. (1994). *The temperament and character inventory (TCI): A guide to its development and use*. Retrieved March 13, 2020, from ResearchGate: https://www.researchgate.net/profile/Robert_Cloninger/publication/264329741_TCI-Guide_to_Its_Development_and_Use/links/53d8ec870cf2e38c6331c2ee/TCI-Guide-to-Its-Development-and-Use.pdf

Cohen, E. A. (2010). ROTC's hard road back to campus. *The Washington Post*.

Cohen, J. (2019). New 'prime' genome editor could surpass CRISPR. *Science* (p. 406).

Cohen, N., & Singer, P. W. (2018). *The US needs a cybersecurity civilian corps*. Retrieved October 26, 2018, from Defense One: https://www.defenseone.com/ideas/2018/10/us-needs-cybersecurity-civilian-corps/152311/

Conaty, B., & Charan, R. (2010). *The talent masters: Why smart leaders put people before numbers*. New York: Crown Business.

Conger, J. A. (1998). The necessary art of persuasion. *Harvard Business Review* (pp. 84–92).

Copeland, B. (2019a). Google amasses pesonal medical records. *The Wall Street Journal* (pp. A1, A2).

Copeland, R. (2019b). Google faces more political bias claims. *The Wall Street Journal* (pp. B1, B4).

Cornell University. (2019). Retrieved from arXiv.org: https://arxiv.org/

Corrigan, J. (2019). The US army is struggling to staff its cyber units: GAO. In P. Tucker (Ed.), *Cyber in the era of great power competition: November 2019*: Defense One. Retrieved from https://www.defenseone.com/assets/cyber-era-q4-2019/portal/?oref=ROS

Costa, D. L., Albrethsen, M. J., Collins, M. L., Perl, S. J., Silowash, G. J., & Spooner, D. L. (2016). *An insider threat indicator ontology, CMU/SEI-2016-TR-007*. Pittsburgh: Carmegie Mellon University.

Costa-Mattioli, M., & Walter, P. (2020). The integrated stress response: From mechanism to disease. *Science, 368*(6489), 384.

Coyle, D. (2009). *The talent code: Greatness isn't born. It's grown, here's how*. New York: Bantam Books.

Crease, R. P., & Goldhaber, A. S. (2015). *The quantum moment: How Planck, Bohr, Einstein, and Heisenberg taught us to love uncertainty*. New York: W. W. Norton & Company.

Crowdstrike. (2019). *2019 Global Threat Report*. Crowdstrike. Retrieved from http://www.crowdstrike.com

Curlee, J. (2020). *Securing US vital interests in the competition with China in space*. Washington: National Defense University.

Cutter, C., & Feintzeig, R. (2020). Smile! Your boss is tracking your happiness. *The Wall Street Journal* (pp. B1, B6).

Danby, G., Powell, J., & Jordan, J. (Eds.). (2013). *Maglev America: How maglev will transform the world economy*. USA: CreateSpace Independent Publishing Platform.

DARPA. (2019). *Artificial Social Intelligence for Successful Teams (ASIST) Proposers Day*. Retrieved May 2, 2019, from Defense Advanced Research Projects Agency: https://www.darpa.mil/news-events/artificial-social-intelligence-for-successful-teams-proposers-day

DataONE. (2020). Retrieved February 1, 2020, from DataONE: Data Observation Network for Earth: https://www.dataone.org/

Davidson, C. N. (2017). *The new education: How to revolutionize the university to prepare students for a world in flux*. New York: Basic Books.

Davis, R. (2020). It's time to consider ... 6G. *The Wall Street Journal* (p. R9).

DellaVigna, S., Pope, D., & Vivalt, E. (2019). Predict science to improve science. *Science, 366*, 428–429.

Denson, T. F., Dobson-Stone, C., Ronay, R., von Hippel, W., & Schira, M. M. (2014). A functional polymorphism of the MAOA gene is associated with response to induced anger control. *Journal of Cognitive Neuroscience, 26*(7), 1418–1427.

Department of Defense. (2015). *The DoD Cyber Strategy*. Retrieved November 15, 2019, from https://archive.defense.gov/home/features/2015/0415_cyber-strategy/final_2015_dod_cyber_strategy_for_web.pdf

Department of Defense. (2018). *Department of Defense Cyber Strategy Summary 2018*. Retrieved March 5, 2020, from https://media.defense.gov/2018/Sep/18/2002041658/-1/-1/1/CYBER_STRATEGY_SUMMARY_FINAL.PDF

Department of the Navy. (2018). *Cybersecurity*. Retrieved December 19, 2018, from Department of the Navy Chief Information Officer: https://www.doncio.navy.mil/TagResults.aspx?ID=28

Desai, A. N. (2020). Discussing the ABCs of heath security, antibiotic resistance, biothreats, and corona virus. *JAMA, 323*, 912–914.

Desmond-Hellmann, S. (2020). Preparing for the Next Pandemic. *The Wall Street Journal* (pp. C1–C2).

Diamond, J. (2020). The germs that transformed history. *The Wall Street Journal* (pp. C1, C2).

Diaz-Morales, J. F. (2007). Morning and evening-types: Exploring their personality styles. *Personality and Individual Differences, 43*(4), 769–778.

Dillard, J. P., & Pfau, M. (Eds.). (2002). *The persuasion handbook: Developments in theory and practice*. Thousand Oaks: Sage Publications.

Donovan, J. (2019). Drafted into the meme wars. *MIT Technology Review* (pp. 48–51).

Drezner, D. W. (2017). *The ideas industry: How pessimists, partisans, and plutocrats are transforming the marketplace of ideas*. New York: Oxford University Press.

Dryzek, J., Bachtiger, A., Chambers, S., Cohen, J., Druckman, J., Felicetti, A., et al. (2019). The crisis of democracy and the science of deliberation. *Science, 363*, 1144–1146.

Duarte, N. (2012). *HBR guide to persuasive presentation.* Harvard Business Review. Retrieved from https://store.hbr.org/product/hbr-guide-to-persuasive-presentations/11150?sku=11150-PBK-ENG#

Duarte, N., & Sanchez, P. (2016). *Illuminate: Ignite change through speeches, stories, ceremonies, and symbols*. New York: Penguin.

Dubois, E., & McKelvey, F. (2019). Canada: Building bot typologies. In S. C. Woolley & P. N. Howard (Eds.), *Computational propaganda: Political parties, politicians, political manipulations of social media* (pp. 64–85). New York: Oxford University Press.

Dyson, G. (2012). *Turing's cathedral: The origins of the digital universe*. New York: Vintage Books.

Edelson, M., Sharot, T., Dolan, R. J., & Dudai, Y. (2011). Following the crowd: brain substrates of long-term memory conformity. *Science, 333*(6038), 108–111.

Epstein, R., & Robertson, R. E. (2015). The search engine manipulation effect (SEME) and its possible impact on the outcomes of elections. *Proceedings of the National Academy of Sciences, 112*, E4512–E4521. Retrieved December 17, 2019, from https://www.pnas.org/content/pnas/112/33/E4512.full.pdf?with-ds=yes.

Escobar, A. (1994). Welcome to cyberia: Notes on the anthropology of cyberculture. *Current Anthropology, 35*(3), 211–231.

Eslick, A. N., Fazio, L. K., & Marsh, E. J. (2011). Ironic effects of drawing attention to story errors. *Memory, 19*(2), 184–191.

Evans, S. W., Beal, J., Berger, K., Bleijs, D. A., Cagnetti, A., & Ceroni, F. (2020). Embrace experimentation n biosecurity governance. *Science, 368*, 138–140.

Facebook. (2019). *Portal Privacy.* Retrieved March 29, 2019, from Facebook: https://portal.facebook.com/privacy

Falco, G., Eling, M., Jablanski, D., Weber, M., Miller, V., Gordon, L. A., et al. (2019). Cyber risk research impeded by disciplinary barriers. *Science, 366*, 1066–1069.

Fazio, L. K., & Marsh, E. J. (2008). Slowing presentation speed increases illusions of knowledge. *Psychonomic Bulletin & Review, 15*(1), 180–185.

Fazio, L. K., & Marsh, E. J. (2010). Correcting false memories. *Psychological Science, 21*(6), 801–803.

Fazio, L. K., Brashier, N. M., Payne, B. K., & Marsh, E. J. (2015). Knowledge does not protect against illusory truth. *Journal of Experimental Psychology, 144*(5), 993–1002.

Fedorov, A. K., Kiktenko, E. O., & Lvovsky, A. I. (2018). *Quantum computers put blockchain security at risk.* Retrieved July 4, 2020, from Nature Magazine: https://www.nature.com/articles/d41586-018-07449-z

Feiner, L. (2020). *DoD asks judge to let it reconsider decision to give Microsoft $10 billion contract over Amazon.* Retrieved May 28, 2020, from CNBC: https://www.cnbc.com/2020/03/13/pentagon-asks-judge-to-let-it-reconsider-its-jedi-cloud-contract-award.html

Fellman, P. V., Bar-Yam, Y., & Minai, A. A. (Eds.). (2015). *Conflict and complexity: Countering terrorism, insurgency, ethnic and regional violence*. New York: Springer.

Ferguson, N. (2018). *The square and the tower*. New York: Penquin Press.

Finch, B. (2019). French dummies foil Russian hackers. *The Wall Street Journal* (p. A19).

Fisher, R., Ury, W., & Patton, B. (2011). *Getting to yes: Negotiating agreement without giving in* (3rd ed.). New York: Penguin Books.

Fogg, B. J. (2003). *Persuasive technology*. Amsterdam: Morgan Kaufmann Publishers.

Fogg, B. J. (2018). *BJ Fogg's behavior model.* Retrieved December 9, 2018, from Behavior Model: https://www.behaviormodel.org/

Fogg, B. J. (n.d.). *Home.* Retrieved April 4, 2018, from Stanford Persuasive Tech Lab: http://captology.stanford.edu/

Fogg, B. J., & Eckles, D. (2014). *Mobile persuasion*. Stanford: Stanford Captology Media.

Fontaine, R., & Frederick, K. (2019). The autocrat's new tool kit. *The Wall Street Journal* (pp. C1, C2).

Forbes. (2020). The world's richest. *Forbes* (p. 32).

Forsyth, M. (2014). *The elements of eloquence: Secrets of the perfect turn of phrase*. New York: Berkely.

Fowler, G. A. (2019a). *I found your data. It's for sale.* Retrieved July 18, 2019, from The Washington Post: https://www.washingtonpost.com/technology/2019/07/18/i-found-your-data-its-sale/

Fowler, G. A. (2019b). *It's the middle of the night. Do you know who your iPhone is talking to?* Retrieved May 28, 2019, from The Washington Post: https://www.washingtonpost.com/technology/2019/05/28/Its-the-middle-of-the-night-Do-you-know-who-your-iPhone-is-talking-to

Fry, H. (2020). Big tech is testing you. *The New Yorker* (pp. 61–65).

Gaddis, J. L. (2018). *On grand strategy*. New York: Penguin Press.

Gallagher, M. (2018). *Army of 01101111: The making of a cyber battalion*. Retrieved June 14, 2018, from Wired: https://www.wired.com/story/army-cyber-troops-fort-gordon/

Ganesh, B. (2018). The ungovernability of digital hate culture. *Journal of International Affairs, 71*(2), 30–49.

Gargan, E. (2017). *Digital persuasion*. Austin, TX: Lioncrest Publishing.

Geary, J. (2005). *The world in a phrase: A brief history of the aphorism*. New York: Bloomsbury.

Gerasimov, V. (2013). The value of science in prediction. *Military-Industrial Kurier*. Retrieved March 1, 2019, from https://inmoscowsshadows.wordpress.com/2014/07/06/the-gerasimov-doctrine-and-russian-non-linear-war/

Gerrold, D. (2003). *Blood and fire*. Dallas: BenBella Books, Inc..

Gibson, W. (2003). *The Economist*. Cited in "Broadband blues" section of The Economist, June 21st, 2001 edition.

Giles, M. (2018). *The GANfather: The man who's given machines the gift of imagination*. Retrieved August 13, 2018, from MIT Technology Review: https://www.technologyreview.com/s/610253/the-ganfather-the-man-whos-given-machines-the-gift-of-imagination/

Gino, F. (2018). The business case for curiosity. *Harvard Business Review*.

Gino, F. (2019). Cracking the code of sustained collaboration. *Harvard Business Review* (pp. 73–81).

Gladwell, M. (2019). *Talking to strangers: What we should know about the people we don't know*. New York: Little, Brown and Company.

Gohd, C. (2020). *Russia tests anti-satellite missile and the US Space Force is not happy.* Retrieved May 9, 2020, from Space.com: https://www.space.com/russia-anti-satellite-missile-test-2020.html

Google Scholar. (2019). Retrieved January 8, 2019, from Google Scholar: https://scholar.google.com

Grant, A. (2017). *Originals: How non-conformists move the world*. New York: Penguin Books.

Greenberg, A. (2019). *Sandworm: A new era of cyberwar and the hunt for the Kremlin's most dangerous hackers*. New York: Doubleday.

Greene, J., & MacMillan, D. (2018). Microsoft urges facial-recognition curbs. *The Wall Street Journal* (p. B4).

Gregersen, H. (2018). Better Brainstorming. *Harvard Business Review* (pp. 64–71).

Grinberg, N., Joseph, K., Friedland, L., Swire-Thompson, B., & Lazer, D. (2019). Fake news on Twitter during the 2016 U.S. presidential election. *Science, 363*(6425), 374–378.

Groysberg, B., & Gregg, T. (2020). How tech CEOs are redefining the top job. *MIT Sloan Management Review*.

Guadagno, R. E., & Guttieri, K. (2019). Fake news and information warfare: An examination of the political and psychological processes from the digital sphere to the real world. In I. E. Chiluwa & S. A. Samoilenko (Eds.), *Handbook of research on deception, fake news, and misinformation online* (pp. 167–191). IGI Global.

Guttieri, K., Franke, V., & Civic, M. (Eds.). (2014). *Understanding complex military operations: A case study approach*. London: Routledge.

Hadfield, R. H. (2009). Single-photon detectors for optical quantum information applications. *Nature Photonics, 3*, 696–705.

Hall, C. A. (2020). Personal communication. (D. Hartley, Interviewer)

Halperin, E., Russell, A. G., Trzensniewski, K. H., Gross, J. J., & Dweck, C. S. (2011). Promoting the middle east peace process by changing beliefs about group malleability. *Science, 333*, 1767–1769.

Hao, K. (2020). Born in China taught by AI. *MIT Technology Review* (pp. 24–29).

Harari, Y. N. (2015). *Sapiens: A brief history of humankind*. New York: Harper Perennial.

Hardjono, T., Shrier, D., & Pentland, A. (Eds.). (2016). *Trust :: Data: A new framework for identity and data sharing*. Visionary Future LLC.

Harrell, E. (2019). Neuromarketing: What you need to know. *Harvard Business Review*.

Harris, M., & Tayler, B. (2019). Don't let metrics undermine your business. *Harvard Business Review* (pp. 62–69).

Hartley, D. S. (1995). A revisionist view of training and simulation validity requirements. *Phalanx*, p. 31.

Hartley, D. S. (2017). *Unconventional conflict: A modeling perspective*. New York: Springer.

Hartley, D. S. (2018). *An ontology for unconventional conflict*. New York: Springer.

Hartley, D. S. (2020). *An ontology of modern conflict: including conventional combat and unconventional conflict*. New York: Springer.

Hartley, D. S., Loebl, A., Rigdon, B., van Leeuwen, B. P., & Harrigan, R. (2004). *Costs of lack of commonality: Initial findings from the commonality pathfinder project*. Oak Ridge, TN: Oak Ridge National Laboratory. Retrieved June 8, 2016, from Hartley Consulting: http://drdeanhartley.com/HartleyConsulting/FCS/Problem.htm.

Hartley, D., & Jobson, K. (2014). Psychological profiling of world leaders. *OR/MS Today, 41*(6), 28–35.

Harvard Business Review. (2013). *HBR's 10 must reads on communication*. Boston: Harvard Business Review.

Harvard Business Review Staff. (2017). Emotional intelligence, influence and persuasion. *Harvard Business Review* (p. 13).

Harwell, D. (2019). *FBI, ICE find state driver's license photos are a gold mine for facial-recognition searches*. Retrieved July 17, 2019, from The Washington Post: https://www.washingtonpost.com/technology/2019/07/07/fbi-ice-find-state-drivers-license-photos-are-gold-mine-facial-recognition-searches/?utm_term=.fe058e1425d3

Hawkins, J., & Blakeslee, S. (2004). *On intelligence*. New York: St. Martin's Griffin.

Headquarters, Department of the Army. (2005). *Psychological Operations, FM 3-05-30*. Washington, DC: Department of the Army.

Henderson, M. T. (2019). How technology will revolutionize public trust. *The Wall Street Journal* (p. C3).

Hernandez, D., & Greenwald, T. (2018). IBM has a Watson dilemma. *The Wall Street Journal* (pp. B1–B2).

Hernandez, D., & Mack, H. (2019). Musk to unveil brain-PC advance. *The Wall Street Journal* (p. B4).

Hillson, R. (2009). The DIME/PMESII Model Suite Requirements Project. *NRL Review*, 235–239.

Hines, P. J., & Stern, P. (2019). More than a tool for communication. *Science, 366*, 48–49.

Hinshaw, D., & Pop, V. (2019). The hapless gang that hacked 2016's inauguration. *The Wall Street Journal* (pp. A1, A10).

Holland, J. H. (2012). *Signals and boundaries: Building blocks for complex adaptive systems*. MIT Press.

Homer. (1946). *The odyssey*. Baltimore: Penguin Classics. (E. V. Rieu, Trans.).

Horwitz, J., & Seetharaman, D. (2020). Facebook shut down efforts to become less polarizing. *The Wall Street Journal* (pp. A1, A10).

Hosnagar, K. (2019). *A human's guide to machine intelligence*. New York: Viking.

Humu, Inc. (2018). *Humu*. Retrieved January 5, 2019, from Humu: https://humu.com/

Hutson, M. (2018a). Hackers easily fool artificial intelligence. *Science, 361*, 215.

Hutson, M. (2018b). Has artificial intelligence become alchemy? *Science, 360*, 478.

Hvistendahl, M. (2018). Master planner. *Science, 359*, 1206–1209.

Hvistendahl, M. (2020). *How a Chinese AI giant made chatting—and surveillance—easy.* Retrieved May 21, 2020, from Wired: https://www.wired.com/story/iflytek-china-ai-giant-voice-chatting-surveillance/

Ignatius, A. (Ed.). (2019). *Harvard Business Review special issue: How to learn faster and better.*

Jackson, M. O. (2008). *Social and economic networks*. Princeton: Princeton University Press.

Jackson, M. O. (2019). *The human network: How your social position determines your power, beliefs, and behaviors*. New York: Pantheon Books.

Jinha, A. E. (2010). Article 50 million: an estimate of the number of scholarly articles in existence. *Learned Publishing, 23*(3), 258–263.

Jobson, K. O., Hartley, D., & Martin, S. (2011). First citizen of the information age. *OR/MS Today, 38*(3), 20–24.

Johansen, R. (2007). *Get there early: Sensing the future to compete in the present*. San Francisco: Berrett-Koehler Publishers.

Johnson, W. (2020). Leading remotely. *MIT Sloan Management Review* (pp. 18–20).

Johnston, P. H. (2004). *Choice words: How our language affects children's learning*. Stenhouse Publishers.

Jones, S. (2019). *Quantum supremacy milestone harnesses summit supercomputer at OR Nat'l Lab* (p. 1A). Oak Ridger: The Oak Ridger.

JSTOR. (2019). Retrieved from JSTOR: https://www.jstor.org/

Kahn, H. (2012). *On escalation: Metaphors and scenarios*. New Brunswick: Transaction Publishers.

Kahn, J. (2020). The quest for human-level A.I. *Fortune* (pp. 62–67).

Kaptein, M. (2015). *Persuasion profiling: How the internet knows what makes you tick.* Amersterdam: Business Contact Publishers.

Karp, A. (2020). *Watch CNBC's full Interview with Palantir CEO Alex Karp at Davos.* Retrieved February 24, 2020, from YouTube: https://www.youtube.com/watch?v=MeL4BWVk5-k

Kauffman, S. (1995). *At home in the universe: The search for the laws of self-organization and complexity*. Oxford: Oxford University Press.

Keegan, J. (1994). *A history of warfare*. New York: Vintage Books.

Kelleher, J. D., & Tierney, B. (2018). *Data science*. Cambridge: MIT Press.

Kello, L. (2017). *The virtual weapon and international order*. New Haven: Yale University Press.

Kelly, K. (2010). *What technology wants*. New York: Penguin Books.

Kelly, K. (2016). *The inevitable*. New York: Viking Press.

Kerbel, J. (2018). *The dead metaphors of national security.* Retrieved May 3, 2018, from Defense One: https://www.defenseone.com/ideas/2018/05/dead-metaphors-national-security/147887/

Kesling, B. (2019). Blood test could help identify troops suffering from PTSD. *The Wall Street Journal*.

Kessler, A. (2020). Don't buy into big-tech hysteria. *The Wall Street Journal* (p. A15).

Kilcullen, D. (2013). *Out of the mountains: The coming age of the urban guerrilla*. Oxford: Oxford University Press.

Klein, G. (2017). Blinded by data. In J. Brockman (Ed.), *Know this: Today's most interesting and importan scientific ideas, discoveries, and developments* (pp. 278–281). New York: HarperCollins Publishers.

Kleppner, D., & Sharp, P. A. (2009). Research data in the digital age. *Science, 325*, 368.

Koblentz, G. D. (2020). *National security in the age of pandemics*. Retrieved April 6, 2020, from Defense One: https://www.defenseone.com/ideas/2020/04/national-security-age-pandemics/164365/?oref=defense_one_breaking_nl

Koester, J. (2019). *Conference lays groundwork for successful joint warfighting assessment.* Retrieved March 4, 2020, from www.army.mil: https://www.army.mil/article/230604/conference_lays_groundwork_for_successful_joint_warfighting_assessment

Kotelnikov, V. (2019). *Accidental discoveries.* Retrieved November 6, 2019, from 1000ventures.com: http://www.1000ventures.com/business_guide/crosscuttings/discovery_accidental.html

Krishnan, K. R. (2015). *The art of learning: Learn to learn*. Lexington: Art of Learning.

Krouse, S. (2019). The new ways your boss is spying on you. *The Wall Street Journal* (pp. B1, B6).

Krum, R. (2019). *The lifespan of storage media.* Retrieved November 23, 2019, from Cool Infographics: https://coolinfographics.com/blog/2012/8/14/the-lifespan-of-storage-media.html

Kuriyama, K., Honma, M., Koyama, S., & Kim, Y. (2011). D-Cycloserine facilitates procedural learning but not declarative learning in humans: a randomized controlled trial of the effect of C-cycloserine and valproic acid on overnight properties of performance of non-emotional memory tasks. *Neurobiology of Learning and Memory, 95*(4), 505–509.

Kurzweil, R. (2005). *The singularity is near*. New York: Penguin Books.

Lang, F. (2020). *Honeywell claims to have built the "most powerful" quantum computer.* Retrieved March 13, 2020, from Interesting Engineering: https://interestingengineering.com/honeywell-claims-to-have-built-the-most-powerful-quantum-computer

Laozi. (2008). *Daodejing*. Oxford: Oxford University Press. (E. Ryden, Trans.).

Larson, C. (2014). Genome Editing. *MIT Technology Review* (pp. 26–29).

Larson, C. (2018). China's AI imperative. *Science, 359*, 628–630.

Launchbury, J. (2017). *A DARPA perspective on artificial intelligence.* Retrieved November 11, 2019, from YouTube: https://www.youtube.com/watch?v=-O01G3tSYpU

Lazer, D. M., Baum, M. A., Benkler, Y., Berinsky, A. J., Greenhill, K. M., Menczer, F., et al. (2018). The science of fake news. *Science, 359*, 1094–1096.

Lederman, O., Mohan, A., Calacci, D., & Pentland, A. S. (2018). Rhythm: A unified measurement platform for human organizations. *IEEE MultiMedia, 25*(1), 26–38.

Lee, D. J. (2017). Rise of the thought leader [Book review of The Ideas Industry]. *Science, 356*, 35.

Lee, K.-F. (2018). *AI superpowers: China, silicon valley, and the new world order*. Boston: Houghton Mifflin Harcourt.

Leenen, L., Aschman, M., Grobler, M., & van Heerden, A. (2018). Facing the culture gap in operationalising cyber within a military context. In J. S. Hurley, & J. Q. Chen (Eds.), *Proceedings of the 13th International Conference on Cyber Warfare and Security*, (pp. 387–394).

Leshner, A. J. (2019). Protect global collaboration. *Science, 366*, 1292.

Levin, M. R. (2019). *Unfreedom of the press*. New York: Threshold Editions.

Levitin, D. J. (2016). *Weaponized lies*. New York: Dutton.

Lewis, M. (2003). *Moneyball: The art of winning an unfair game*. New York: W. W. Norton & Company.

Li, S. (2020). Made-in-China censorship for sale. *The Wall Street Journal*, pp. B1, B2.

Li, S., & Wen, P. (2019a). China casts broad net to collect data. *The Wall Street Journal.*

Li, S., & Wen, P. (2019b). *This App Helps You Learn About China, While China Learns All About You.* Retrieved November 21, 2019, from The Wall Street Journal: https://www.wsj.com/articles/china-broadens-data-collection-through-propaganda-app-and-translation-service-11571058689

Lin, H., & Zegart, A. (Eds.). (2018). *Bytes, bombs, and spies: The strategic dimensions of offensive cyber operations*. Washington, DC: Brookings Institution Press.

Liu, Y., Zou, R. S., He, S., Nihongaki, Y., Li, X., Razavi, S., et al. (2020). Very fast CRISPR on demand. *Science, 368*, 1265–1269.

Loebl, A. S., & Hartley III, D. S. (2005). Commonality faults in superscaled systems: An example using the simulation domain and network-centric operations. *International Federation of Operational Research Societies & Institute for Operations Research and the Management Sciences Triennial International Conference*, July 11–15, 2005. Hawaii.

Lua, A. (2019). *21 Top social media sites to consider for your brand.* Retrieved May 22, 2020, from Buffer Marketing Library: https://buffer.com/library/social-media-sites

Lubold, G., & Volz, D. (2018). Chinese hackers breach navy data. *The Wall Street Journal*, p. A1.

Luca, M., & Bazerman, M. H. (2020). *The Power of experiments: Decision-making in a data driven world.* Boston: MIT Press.

Maan, A. (2018). *Narrative warfare*. Narrative Strategies Ink.

Machiavelli, N. (1966). *The prince*. New York: Bantam Books. (D. Donno, Trans.).

Maddux, W. W., Mullen, E. G., & Galinsky, A. D. (2008). Chameleons bake bigger pies and take bigger pieces: Strategic behavioral mimicry facilitates negotiation outcomes. *Journal of Experimental Social Psychology, 44*(2), 461–468.

Malone, T. W. (2018). How human-computer 'superminds' are redefining the future of work. *MIT Sloan Management Review* (pp. 34–41).

Margonelli, L. (2020). The warm war. *Wired Magazine* (pp. 12–16).

Martin, S., & Marks, J. (2019). *Messengers: Who we listen to, who we don't, and why*. New York: Hachette Book Group.

Mateski, M. E., Mazzuchi, T. A., & Sarkani, S. (2010). The hypergame perception model: A diagramatic approach to modeling perception, misperception, and deception. *Military Operations Research, 15*(2), 21–37.

Matsumoto, D., Frank, M. G., & Hwang, H. S. (Eds.). (2013). *Nonverbal communication: Science and applications*. London: SAGE Publications.

Mattioli, D., McMillan, R., & Herrera, S. (2019). Hacking suspect acted oddly online. *The Wall Street Journal* (pp. A1, A6).

Max, D. T. (2003). Two cheers for Darwin. *The American Scholar, 72*(2), 63–75.

McCarthy, N. (2017). The countries with the most STEM graduates. *Forbes*.

McClintock, P. K. (2020). *Indo-Pacific strategic airlift consortium: Rethinking humanitarian assistance disaster relief*. Washington: National Defense University.

McCulloch, G. (2019). *Because internet: Understanding the new rules of language*. New York: Riverhead Books.

Mcdermott, J. (2020). Navy embraces education as US advantages dwindle. *Knoxville News Sentinel* (p. 12A).

McDonald, J., Schleifer, L., Richards, J. B., & DeWitt, H. (2003). Effects of THC on behavioral measures of impulsivity in humans. *Neuropsychopharmacology, 28*(7), 1356–1365.

McFate, S. (2019). *The new rules of war: Victory in the age of disorder*. New York: William Morrow.

McGonigal, J. (2011). *Reality is broken: Why games make us better and how they can change the world*. New York: Penguin Books.

McKee, R. (1997). *Story: Substance, structure, style and the principles of screenwriting*. New York: ReganBooks.

McNamee, R. (2019). *Zucked: Waking up to the facebook catastrophe*. New York: Penguin Press.

Mercier, H. (2020). *Not born yesterday: The science of who we trust and what we believe*. Princeton: Princeton University Press.

Mervis, J. (2019). Elite advisers to help NSF navigate security concerns. *Science, 363*(6433), 1261.

Mervis, J. (2020a). *Fired Emory University neuroscientist with ties to China sentenced on tax charge*. Retrieved May 21, 2020, from ScienceMag: https://www.sciencemag.org/news/2020/05/fired-emory-university-neuroscientist-ties-china-sentenced-tax-charge

Mervis, J. (2020b). NSF rolls out huge makeover of science statistics. *Science, 367*, 352–353.

Michaels, D. (2020a). *Remote work forever? Not so fast, jobs guru says*. Retrieved June 16, 2020, from The Wall Street Journal: https://www.wsj.com/articles/remote-work-forever-not-so-fast-jobs-guru-says-11591790405

Michaels, D. (2020b). *The triumph of doubt: Dark money and the science of deception*. Oxford University Press.

Migdall, A., Polyakov, S., Fan, J., & Bienfang, J. (Eds.). (2013). *Single-photon generation and detection* (Vol. 45). Waltham, MA: Academic Press.

Milgram, S. (1974). *Obedience to authority: An experimental view*. New York: Harper & Row.

Military.com. (2020). *United States Space Force*. Retrieved February 2, 2020, from Military.com: https://www.military.com/space-force

Mims, C. (2018 On social media, a battle is brewing between bots and trolls. *The Wall Street Journal*, p. B7.

Mims, C. (2019a). Surveillance tech from a war zone. *The Wall Street Journal* (p. B5).

Mims, C. (2019b). *The day when computers can break all encryption is coming.* Retrieved July 23, 2019, from The Wall Street Journal: https://www.wsj.com/articles/the-race-to-save-encryption-11559646737

MIT Affective Computing Group. (2020). *Affective computing*. Retrieved June 16, 2020, from MIT Media Lab: https://www.media.mit.edu/groups/affective-computing/overview/

Mitchell, M. (2009). *Part IV. Network thinking; chapter 18. Evolution, complexified.* Retrieved July 7, 2018, from Complexity: A guided tour—melanie Mitchell (2009): http://publicism.info/science/complexity/19.html

Mlodinow, L. (2008). *The Drunkard's walk: How randomness rules our lives*. New York: Random House.

Moffat, J. (2003). *Complexity theory and network centric warfare*. Washington: CCRP Publication Series.

Moffett, M. W. (2018). *The human swarm: How our societies arise, thrive, and fall.* New York: Hatchett Book Group.

Moffitt, T. E. (2005). Genetic and envrionmental influences on antisocial behaviors: Evidence from behavioral-genetic research. *Advances in Genetics, 55*, 41–104.

Mohammed, A. D., & Sahakian, B. J. (2011). The ethics of elective psychopharmacology. *International Journal of Neuropsychopharmacology, 15*(4), 559–571.

Mojo Vision Inc. (2019). Retrieved January 21, 2019, from Mojo: https://www.mojovision/

Morath, E. (2020). AI threat targets higher-paying jobs. *The Wall Street Journal* (p. A2).

Muller, J. (2014). *Warren buffett shares the inside scoop: He bought a cadillac, not a subaru.* Retrieved August 17, 2018, from Forbes: https://www.forbes.com/sites/joannmuller/2014/07/15/warren-buffett-shares-the-inside-scoop-he-bought-a-cadillac-not-a-subaru/#31c2e7ec3682

Nakashima, E. (2019). U.S. ponders exposing personal information to halt interference. *The Atlanta Journal-Constitution* (p. A3).

Nakasone, P. M. (2019). *Statement of general Paul M. Nakasone, commander United States cyber command before the senate committee on armed services, 14 February 2019.* Washington: US Senate. Retrieved March 4, 2020, from http://www.armed-services.senate.gov/imo/media/doc/Nakasone_02-14-19.pdf

Narayanan, A., & Shmatikov, V. (2008). Robust de-anonymization of large sparse datasets. *Proceedings IEEE Symposium on Security and Privacy* (pp. 111–125). IEEE. Retrieved June 11, 2019, from https://www.cs.utexas.edu/~shmat/shmat_oak08netflix.pdf

NASA. (2018). *Nuclear thermal propulsion: Game changing technology for deep space exploration*. Retrieved February 2, 2020, from NASA: https://www.nasa.gov/directorates/spacetech/game_changing_development/Nuclear_Thermal_Propulsion_Deep_Space_Exploration

NASA. (2020). *Explore moon to mars*. Retrieved February 2, 2020, from NASA: https://www.nasa.gov/topics/moon-to-mars/lunar-gateway

Negroponte, N. (1995). *Being digital*. New York: Alfred A. Knopf.

Neudert, L.-M. N. (2019). Germany: A cautionary tale. In S. C. Woolley & P. N. Howard (Eds.), *Computational propaganda: Political parties, politicians, and political manipulation on social media* (pp. 153–184). New York: Oxford University Press.

Neuralink Corp. (2018). Retrieved August 17, 2018, from Neuralink: https://www.neuralink.com/

New England Complex Systems Institute. (n.d.). *Home*. Retrieved April 4, 2018, from NECSI: http://necsi.edu/

Nye, A. (2020). *Two nations, two hemispheres: One region, one treaty, and a rising China.* Washington: National Defense University.

Ockham, W. (2013). *The noosphere (part I): Teilhard de Chardin's vision.* Retrieved September 5, 2019, from Teilhard de Chardin: https://teilhard.com/2013/08/13/the-noosphere-part-i-teilhard-de-chardins-vision/

O'Connor, C., & Weatherall, J. O. (2019). *The misinformation age: How false beliefs spread.* New Haven: Yale University Press.

O'Neill, P. H. (2019). The US is under cyberattack. What happens next? *MIT Technology Review* (pp. 52–55).

O'Toole, E. (2015). *Decentralised detection of emergence in complex adaptive systems*. Dublin: University of Dublin, Trinity College.

Owen, D., & Davidson, J. (2009). Hubris syndrome: An acquired personality disorder? A study of U.S. presidents and UK prime ministers over the last 100 years. *Brain, 132*(5), 1396–1406.

Packard, N. (2020). *Partnering for a secure future: A blueprint for global leadership in the 21st century*. Washington: National Defense University.

Paganinin, P. (2018). *Malware in dark web.* Retrieved July 25, 2018, from Infosec Institute: https://resources.infosecinstitute.com/malware-dark-web/#gref

Pentland, A. (2004). *Social dynamics: Signals and behavior.* retrieved June 8, 2020, from MIT Media Lab: https://www.media.mit.edu/publications/social-dynamics-signals-and-behavior/

Pentland, A. (2008). *Honest signals: How they shape our world.* Boston: MIT Press.

Pentland, A. (2014). *Social physics*. New York: The Penguin Press.

Peplow, M. (2019). Automation for the people: Training a new generation of chemists in data-driven synthesis. *Chemical & Engineering News, 97*(42).

Peter, W. H. (2019). *Manufacturing demonstration facility*. Retrieved January 8, 2019, from Oak Ridge National Laboratory: https://www.ornl.gov/facility/mdf

Pillsbury, M. (2015). *The hundred-year marathon: China's secret strategy to replace America as the global superpower*. New York: St. Martin's Press.

Pink, D. H. (2009). *DRiVE: The surprising truth about what motivates us*. New York: Riverhead Books.

Plato. (2016). *The republic* (B. Jowett, Trans.). Digireads.com Publishing.

Poibeau, T. (2017). *Machine translation*. Boston: MIT Press.

Polanyi, M. (1958). *Personal knowledge: Towards a post-critical philosophy*. Chicago: University of Chicago Press.

Polanyi, M. (2009). *The tacit dimension*. Chicago: The University of Chicago Press.

Polson, N., & Scott, J. (2018). *AIQ: How people and machines are smarter together*. New York: St. Martin's Press.

Polya, G. (1945). *How to solve it: A new aspect of mathematical method.* Princeton: Princeton University Press.

Pons, J. (2019). Witnessing a wearable transition. *Science, 365*(6454), 636–637.

Popkin, G. (2017). *China's quantum satellite achieves 'spooky action' at record distance*. Retrieved November 21, 2019, from Science: https://www.sciencemag.org/news/2017/06/china-s-quantum-satellite-achieves-spooky-action-record-distance

Poria, S., Hussain, A., & Cambria, E. (2018). *Multimodal sentiment analysis*. Cham: Springer International.

Powell, J., & Danby, G. (2013). Chapter 2: The maglev 2000 system—How it works. In G. Danby, J. Powell, & J. Jordan (Eds.), *Maglev America: How maglev will transform the world economy* (pp. 47–68). North Charleston: CreateSpace Independent Publishing Platform.

Powell, J., Danby, G., & Coullahan, R. (2013). Chapter 9: Description of the Maglev energy storage system. In G. Danby, J. Powell, & J. Jordan (Eds.), *Maglev America: How maglev will transform the world economy* (pp. 261–290). North Charleston: CreateSpace Independent Publishing Platform.

Powell, J., Maise, G. R., & Jordan, J. (2013). Chapter 13: Maglev launch of space solar power satellites. In G. Danby, J. Powell, & J. Jordan (Eds.), *Maglev America: How maglev will transform the world economy* (pp. 353–383). North Charleston: CreateSpace Independent Publishing Platform.

Powell, J., Maise, G., & Pellegrino, C. (2013). *StarTram: The new race to space*. Shoebox Press.

Powers, B. (2018). Teaching machines to read our feelings. *The Wall Street Journal* (p. B12).

Preskill, J. (2018). *Quantum Computing in the NISQ era and beyond.* Retrieved November 20, 2019, from Quantum: the open journal for quantum science: https://quantum-journal.org/papers/q-2018-08-06-79/

Purves, D., & Lotto, R. B. (2011). *Why we see what we do redux: A wholly empirical theory of vision*. Sunderland: Sinauer Associates.

Qiao, L., & Wang, X. (1999). *Unrestricted Warfare*. Brattleboro, Vermont: Echo Point Books & Media, (unknown, Trans.).

Ramirez, S., Liu, X., Lin, P.-A., Suh, J., Pignatelli, M., Redondo, R. L., et al. (2013). Creating a false memory in the hippocampus. *Science, 341*, 387–391.

Rather, J. D. (2013). Maglev power storage—The proposed TVA project sisyphus. In G. Danby, J. Powell, & J. Jordan (Eds.), *Maglev America: How maglev will transform the world economy* (pp. 306–322). North Charleston: CreateSpace Independent Publishing Platform.

Rather, J. D., & Hartley, D. S. (2017). Retrieved January 3, 2020, from Sysiphus Energy, Inc.: Grid-level energy storage: http://sisyphusenergy.com/

Rather, J. D., & Hartley, D. S. (2018a). *The power of synergy space symposium: Advancing human space development by 2030*. Oak Ridge: Tennessee Valley Interstellar Workshop.

Rather, J. D., & Hartley, D. S. (2018b). *The power of synergy space symposium: Summary final report*. Oak Ridge: Rather Creative Innovations Group.

Redden, K. (2020). *The relationship between the "Gray Zone," conventional deterrence, and the balance of power*. Washington: National Defense University.

Restuccia, A., & Volz, D. (2020). Surveillance program gets a hard look. *The Wall Street Journal* (p. A3).

Rigby, D. K., Sutherland, J., & Noble, A. (2018). Agile at scale. *Harvard Business Review* (pp. 88–96).

Roberts, D. (2019). *Clean energy technologies threaten to overwhelm the grid. Here's how it can adapt*. Retrieved May 30, 2020, from Vox: https://www.vox.com/energy-and-environment/2018/11/30/17868620/renewable-energy-power-grid-architecture

Robson, D. (2019). *The intelligence trap: Why smart people do stupid things and how to avoid them*. New York: W. W. Norton & Company.

Rosen, R. J. (2012). The single biggest change in education since the printing press. *The Atlantic*.

Rothrock, R. A. (2018). *Digital resilience: Is your company ready for the next cyber threat?* New York: American Management Association.

Rouse, M. (2012). *Offensive security*. Retrieved August 16, 2018, from WhatIs.com: https://whatis.techtarget.com/definition/offensive-security

Rozin, P., & Royzman, E. B. (2001). Negativity bias, negativity dominance, and contagion. *Personality and Social Psychology Review, 5*(4), 296–320.

Rubin, P. (2019). Title page: NO sets. No cameras. No worries. *Wired* (pp. 82–85).

Ruths, D. (2019). The misinformation machine. *Science, 363*(6425), 348.

Ryder, B. (2018). Michel Foucault's lessons for business. *The Economist* (p. 57). Retrieved December 22, 2019, from https://www.economist.com/business/2018/06/21/michel-foucaults-lessons-for-business

Sahakian, B. (2018). Personal communication with Dr. Sahakian of Clinical Neuroscience Institute, Cambridge University. (K. Jobson, Interviewer)

Sahakian, B., & Morein-Zamir, S. (2007). Professor's little helper. *Nature, 450*, 1157–1159.

Samuelson, D. A. (2018). Wargaming cybersecurity. *OR/MS Today* (pp. 20–23).

Sanger, D. E. (2018a). Russian hackers train focus on U.S. power grid. *The New York Times* (p. A11).

Sanger, D. E. (2018b). *The perfect weapon: War, sabotage, and fear in the cyber age*. New York: Broadway Books.

Santa Fe Institute. (2016). *Home*. Retrieved April 4, 2018, from SantaFe: https://www.santafe.edu/

Sapolsky, R. (2017). *Behave: The biology of humans at our best and worst*. New York: Penguin Books.

Sawyer, R. K. (Ed.). (2014). *The Cambridge handbook of the learning sciences* (2nd ed.). New York: Cambridge University Press.

Scher, A. A., & Levin, P. L. (2020). Imported chips make America's security vulnerable. *The Wall Street Journal* (p. A17).

Schmidt, E., & Rosenberg, J. (2017). *How google works*. New York: Grand Central Publishing.

Schweitzer, G. (2019). Personal communication with Professor of Nuclear Chemistry at University of Tennessee. (K. Jobson, Interviewer)

SciFinder. (2019). Retrieved January 8, 2019, from SciFinder: https://scifinder.cas.org

Seabrook, J. (2019). The next word. *The New Yorker* (pp. 52–63).

Seffers, G. I. (2018). *Taking the cyber out of cyber command.* Retrieved March 4, 2020, from Signal: https://www.afcea.org/content/taking-cyber-out-cyber-command

Seffers, G. I. (2019). *U.S. in counter-attack mode in cyber domain.* Retrieved March 4, 2020, from Signal: https://www.afcea.org/content/us-counter-attack-mode-cyber-domain

Seffers, G. I. (2020). *Information warfare platform goes to sea.* Retrieved March 4, 2020, from Signal: https://www.afcea.org/content/information-warfare-platform-goes-sea

Seife, C. (2014). *Virtual unreality: The new era of digital deception.* New York: Viking Penguin Press.

Senate Judiciary Subcommittee on Constitution. (2016). *User clip: Robert Epstein answers Sen. Cruz questions.* Retrieved December 17, 2019, from C-Span: https://www.c-span.org/video/?c4811966/user-clip-robert-epstein-answers-sen-cruz-questions

Senge, P. M. (2006). *The fifth discipline: The art and practice of the learning organization.* New York: Doubleday.

Service, R. F. (2019). Modified CRISPR cuts and splices whole genomes. *Science, 365*(6456), 8, 19.

Servick, K. (2020). Cellphone tracking could help stem the spread of coronavirus. Is privacy the price? *Science.* Retrieved April 21, 2020, from https://www.sciencemag.org/news/2020/03/cellphone-tracking-could-help-stem-spread-coronavirus-privacy-price

Shakespeare, W. (1919). *The tragedy of Julius Caesar.* New Haven: Yale University Press, (L. Mason, Ed.).

Shannon, C. E. (1948a). A mathematical theory of communication, part 1. *Bell System Technical Journal, 27*(3), 379–423.

Shannon, C. E. (1948b). A mathematical theory of communication, part 2. *Bell System Technical Journal, 27*(4), 623–656.

Shannon, C. E., & Weaver, W. (1963). *The mathematical model of communication.* Urbana: University of Illinois Press.

Sharot, T. (2017). *The influential mind: What the brain reveals about our power to change others.* New York: Henry Holt.

Sharpe, R., Beetham, H., & De Freitas, S. (2010). *Rethinking learning for a digital age.* New York: Routledge.

Shaw, G. B. (2018). *George Bernard Shaw quotes.* Retrieved July 7, 2018, from BrainyQuote: https://www.brainyquote.com/quotes/george_bernard_shaw_385438

Shaywitz, D. A. (2018). Flirting with disaster. *The Wall Street Journal* (p. A13).

Silver, N. (2012). *The signal and the noise: Why so many predictions fail—But some don't.* New York: Penguin Press.

Simonite, T. (2019). Are you for real? *Wired* (pp. 24–25).

Singer, P. W., & Brooking, E. T. (2018). *LikeWar: The weaponization of social media.* Boston: Houghton Mifflin Harcourt.

Sloman, S., & Fernbach, P. (2017). *The knowledge illusion.* New York: Riverhead Books.

Snyder, T. (2018). *The road to unfreedom: Russia, Europe, America.* New York: Penguin Books.

South, H. (2020). *Chinese arms sales as a source of influence.* Washington: National Defense University.

Southwick, S. M., & Charney, D. S. (2018). *Resilience: The science of mastering life's greatest challenges.* New York: Cambridge University Press.

SPARC. (2019). Retrieved from SPARC: https://sparcopen.org/

Stanford Computational Journalism Lab. (n.d.). *Stanford Computational Journalism Lab.* Retrieved September 7, 2019, from Stanford Computational Journalism Lab: http://cjlab.stanford.edu/

Stanford University VHIL. (2019). Retrieved January 6, 2020, from Virtual Human Interaction Lab: https://vhil.stanford.edu/

Steiner, G. (1997). *Errata: An examined life*. New Haven: Yale University Press.

Stephens, M. (2014). *Beyond news: The future of journalism*. New York: Columbia University Press.

Stern, J. (2020). The trouble with contact-tracing apps. *The Wall Street Journal* (p. B2).

Stover, S. P. (2019). *Task force echo mission and transition is critical to American cybersecurity*. Retrieved March 4, 2020, from www.army.mil: https://www.army.mil/article/218528/task_force_echo_mission_and_transition_is_critical_to_american_cybersecurity

Stubblebine, D. (2018). *Henry Stimson*. Retrieved July 8, 2018, from World War II Database: https://ww2db.com/person_bio.php?person_id=488

Summerville, A. (2019). 'Deepfakes' trigger hunt for solutions. *The Wall Street Journal* (p. B4).

Sun-Tzu. (1963). *The art of war*. New York: Oxford University Press. (S. B. Griffith, Trans.).

Susskind, R., & Susskind, D. (2017). *The future of the professions: How technology will transform the work of human experts*. New York: Oxford University Press.

Tarafdar, M., Beath, C. M., & Ross, J. W. (2019). Using AI to enhance business operations. *MIT Sloan Management Review, 60*(4), 37–44.

Taylor, R., & Germano, S. (2018). Spy chiefs agreed to contain Huawei. *The Wall Street Journal* (p. A8).

Taylor, S. (2020). *Will cameras that measure body temp become common at businesses & events due to COVID-19?* Retrieved June 10, 2020, from WJLA.com: https://wjla.com/features/7-on-your-side/a-new-weapon-against-covid-19-that-monitors-your-body-temp

Tegmark, M. (2017). *Life 3.0: Being human in the age of artificial intelligence*. New York: Alfred A. Knopf.

Temming, M. (2018). Detecting fake news. *Science News* (pp. 22–26).

Tennyson, A. (1842). *Le Morte d'Arthur*.

Thaler, R. H., & Sunstein, C. R. (2008). *Nudge*. New York: Penguin Books.

The Cambridge Analytica Files: 'I made Steve Bannon's psychological warfare tool': meet the data war whistleblower. (2019). Retrieved March 28, 2020, from TheGuardian.com: https://www.theguardian.com/news/2018/mar/17/data-war-whistleblower-christopher-wylie-faceook-nix-bannon-trump

The United States House of Representatives. (2017). *Interview Transcript of Shawn Henry December 5*. Retrieved May 12, 2020, from Documentcloud.org: https://www.documentcloud.org/documents/6884138-Interview-Transcript-of-Shawn-Henry-December-5.html

Tierney, J., & Baumeister, R. F. (2019). *The power of bad: How the negativity effect rules us and how we can rule it*. New York: Penguin Press.

Timian, D. H. (2018). Cyber wargaming workshop. *Phalanx, 51*(2), 12–13.

Tolkien, J. R. (1965). *The lord of the rings*. Boston: Houghton Mifflin.

Tomasello, M. (2009). *Why we cooperate*. Cambridge: MIT Press.

Transportation Security Administration. (2018). *TSA cybersecurity roadmap 2018*. Washington: Transportation Security Administration.

Trinos, P. (2019). *Build a zero trust architecture with these 5 steps*. Retrieved May 4, 2020, from CDW Solutions Blog: https://blog.cdw.com/security/build-a-zero-trust-architecture-with-these-5-steps

Tucker, P. (2019a). Foreword. *Cyber in the era of great power competition: November 2019*. (P. Tucker, Ed.) Defense One. Retrieved from Defense One: https://www.defenseone.com/assets/cyber-era-q4-2019/portal/?oref=ROS

Tucker, P. (2019b). Weapons makers unveil a herd of robotanks—As the army worries about battlefield bandwidth. *Cyber in the Era of Great Power Competition: November 2019*. (P. Tucker, Ed.) Defense One. Retrieved from https://www.defenseone.com/assets/cyber-era-q4-2019/portal/?oref=ROS

Tucker, P. (2020). *Russia has new tool for massive internet shutdown attack, leaked documents claim*. Retrieved March 21, 2020, from Defense One: https://www.defenseone.com/technology/2020/03/russia-has-new-tool-massive-internet-shutdown-attack-leaked-documents-claim/163983/?oref=d-river

Tufekci, Z. (2018). The {divisive, corrosive, democracy poisoning} golden age of free speech. *Wired.*

Tufekci, Z. (2019). False promise. *Wired* (pp. 20, 22).

Tullis, P. (2019). Signal intelligence. *MIT Technology Review* (pp. 36–39).

Turner, D. C., Robbins, T. W., Clark, L., Avon, A. R., Dawson, J., & Sahakian, B. J. (2003). Cognitive enhancing effect of modafinil in healthy volunteers. *Psychopharmacology, 165*(3), 260–269.

U.S. Army Cyber Command. (2019). *About us.* Retrieved March 4, 2020, from U.S. Army Cyber Command: https://www.arcyber.army.mil/Organization/About-Army-Cyber/

U.S. Army Cyber Command. (2020). *780th Military intelligence brigade (cyber).* Retrieved March 4, 2020, from U.S. Army Cyber Command: https://www.arcyber.army.mil/Organization/780th-MI-Brigade-Cyber/

U.S. Department of Energy Infrastructure Security and Energy Restoration Office of Electricity and Energy Reliability. (2012). *Large power transformers and the U.S. electric grid.* Retrieved April 30, 2020, from Energy.gov: https://www.energy.gov/sites/prod/files/Large%20Power%20Transformer%20Study%20-%20June%202012_0.pdf

U.S. Government Accountability Office. (2014). *Nanomanufacturing: Emergence and implications for U.S. competitiveness, the environment, and human health, GAO-14-181sp.* Washington: GAO. Retrieved from https://www.gao.gov/products/gao-14-181sp.

Underwood, K. (2019a). *Army cyber to become an information warfare command.* Retrieved March 4, 2020, from Signal: https://www.afcea.org/content/army-cyber-become-information-warfare-command

Underwood, K. (2019b). *Putting a spotlight on information.* Retrieved March 4, 2020, from Signal: https://www.afcea.org/content/putting-spotlight-information

Underwood, K. (2019c). *The air force sets its scope on information warfare.* Retrieved March 4, 2020, from Signal: https://www.afcea.org/content/air-force-sets-its-scope-information-warfare

US Space Force. (2019). *Fact sheet.* Retrieved February 2, 2020, from United States Space Force: https://www.spaceforce.mil/About-Us/Fact-Sheet

Valiant, L. (2013). *Probably approximately correct: Nature's algorithms for learning and prospering in a complex world.* New York: Basic Books.

Vanatta, N. (2017). Envisioning the future to empower action. *Computer, 50*, 85.

Vermeulen, R., Schymanski, E. L., Barabasi, A.-L., & Miller, G. W. (2020). The exposome and health: Where chemistry meets biology. *Science, 367*, 392–396.

Villasenor, J. (2019). *Artificial intelligence, deepfakes and the uncertain future of truth.* Retrieved April 27, 2019, from Brookings: https://www.brookings.edu/blog/techtank/2019/02/14/artificial-intelligence-deepfakes-and-the-uncertain-future-of-truth/

Virgil. (1969). The trojan horse. In A. Dulles (Ed.), *Great spy stories from fiction* (pp. 289–293). New York: Harper & Row.

Visner, S. S. (2018). *Challenging our assumptions: Some hard questions for the operations research community.* Retrieved December 11, 2018, from MORS Emerging Techniques Forum 2018: http://www.mors.org/Events/Emerging-Techniques-Forum/2018-ETF-Presentations

Volk, T. (2017). *Quarks to culture: How we came to be*. New York: Columbia University Press.

Volz, D. (2018). President opens new era on use of cyberattacks. *The Wall Street Journal* (p. A5).

Waliden, P., & Kashefi, E. (2019). Cyber security in the quantum era. *Communications of the ACM, 62*(4), 120.

Wall Street Journal. (2019). *The Wall Street Journal* (p. C1).

Wallace, R. (2018). *Carl von Clausewitz, the fog-of-war, and the AI revolution: The real world is not a game of go*. Cham: Springer.

Walton, G. (2016). *Unique histories from the 18th and 19th centuries.* Retrieved July 7, 2018, from Geri Walton: https://www.geriwalton.com/words-said-during-french-revolution/

Wang, P. (2019). Retrieved December 6, 2019, from ThisPersonDoesNotExist: https://thispersondoesnotexist.com/

Wang, Y., Hong, S., & Tai, C. (2019). *China's efforts to lead the way in AI start in its classrooms.* Retrieved October 28, 2019, from The Wall Street Journal: https://www.wsj.com/articles/chinas-efforts-to-lead-the-way-in-ai-start-in-its-classrooms-11571958181

Weinberger, S. (2019). The everything war. *MIT Technology Review* (pp. 24–29).

Weinstein, D. (2018). America goes on the cyberoffensive. *The Wall Street Journal* (p. A17).

Wells, G., & Horowitz, J. (2019). Content factories swamp instagram, diluting its appeal. *The Wall Street Journal* (pp. A1, A9).

Wexler, N. (2020). No computer left behind. *MIT Technology Review* (pp. 19–23).

Wheeler, J. A. (1989). Information, physics, quantum: The search for links. *Proceedings of the 3rd International Symposium on Foundations of Quantum Mechanics in the Light of New Technology* (pp. 309–336).

Whittaker, Z. (2020). *The Air Fore wants you to hack its satellite in orbit. Yes, really.* Retrieved May 9, 2020, from techcrunch.com: https://techcrunch.com/2020/04/22/air-force-hack-satellite/

Wihbey, J. P. (2019). *The Social Fact: News and Knowledge in a Networked World.* Boston: MIT Press.

Wikipedia. (2018a). *Cuneiform.* Retrieved November 28, 2018, from Wikipedia: https://en.wikipedia.org/wiki/Cuneiform

Wikipedia. (2018b). *Gödel's incompleteness theorems.* Retrieved July 7, 2018, from Wikipedia: https://en.wikipedia.org/wiki/G%C3%B6del%27s_incompleteness_theorems

Wikipedia. (2018c). *Johari window.* Retrieved June 5, 2018, from Wikipedia: https://en.wikipedia.org/wiki/Johari_window

Wikipedia. (2018d). *Neolithic revolution.* Retrieved November 25, 2018, from Wikipedia: https://en.wikipedia.org/wiki/Neolithic_Revolution

Wikipedia. (2018e). *OODA loop.* Retrieved April 4, 2018, from Wikipedia: https://en.wikipedia.org/wiki/OODA_loop

Wikipedia. (2018f). *Pythia.* Retrieved November 25, 2018, from Wikipedia: https://en.wikipedia.org/wiki/Pythia

Wikipedia. (2018g). *United States cyber command.* Retrieved December 19, 2018, from Wikipedia: https://en.wikipedia.org/wiki/United_States_Cyber_Command

Wikipedia. (2019a). *Superconductivity.* Retrieved January 1, 2020, from Wikipedia.

Wikipedia. (2019b). *Technology readiness level.* Retrieved September 10, 2019, from Wikipedia: https://en.wikipedia.org/wiki/Technology_readiness_level

Wikipedia. (2019c). *Temperament and character inventory.* Retrieved April 27, 2019, from Wikipedia: https://en.wikipedia.org/wiki/Temperament_and_Character_Inventory

Wikipedia. (2019d). *Vietnam War body count controversy.* Retrieved November 6, 2019, from Wikipedia: https://en.wikipedia.org/wiki/Vietnam_War_body_count_controversy

Wikipedia. (2020). *Mark G. Frank.* Retrieved April 21, 2020, from Wikipedia: https://en.wikipedia.org/wiki/Mark_G._Frank

Wolf, M. (2018). *Reader, come home: The reading brain in a digital world.* New York: HarperCollins.

Woolley, S. C., & Howard, P. N. (Eds.). (2019a). *Computational propaganda: Political parties, politicians, political manipulations of social media.* New York: Oxford University Press.

Woolley, S. C., & Howard, P. N. (2019b). Conclusion: Political parties, politicians, political manipulations of social media. In S. C. Woolley & P. N. Howard (Eds.), *Computational Propaganda: political parties, politicians, political manipulations of social media* (pp. 241–248). New York: Oxford University Press.

Woolley, S. C., & Howard, P. N. (2019). Introduction: Computational propaganda worldwide. In S. C. Woolley & P. N. Howard (Eds.), *Computatonal propaganda: Political parties, politicians, and political manipulation on social media* (pp. 3–18). New York: Oxford University Press.

World Health Organization (WHO). (2020). *Novel Coronavirus (2019-nCoV) Situation Report - 13.* Retrieved March 19, 2020, from WHO: https://www.who.int/docs/default-source/coronaviruse/situation-reports/20200202-sitrep-13-ncov-v3.pdf

Wrangham, R. (2019). *The goodness paradox: The strange relationship between virtue and violence in human evolution*. New York: Pantheon Books.

Wu, T. (2016). *The attention merchants: The epic scramble to get inside our heads*. New York: Knopf.

Zappen, J. P. (2005). Digital rhetoric: Toward an integrated theory. *Technical Communications Quarterly, 14*(3), 319–325.

Zissis, C. (2007). *China's Anti-Satellite Test.* Retrieved May 9, 2020, from Council on Foreign Relations: https://www.cfr.org/backgrounder/chinas-anti-satellite-test

Zolli, A., & Healy, A. M. (2012). *Resilence: Why things bounce back.* New York: Simon & Schuster.

Index

D. S. Hartley III, K. O. Jobson, *Cognitive Superiority*,
https://doi.org/10.1007/978-3-030-60184-3

B

J

K

T

U

V

CPSIA information can be obtained
at www.ICGtesting.com
Printed in the USA
LVHW021551190721
693092LV00002B/247

9 783030 601836